*Information
Retrieval
Today*

Information Retrieval Today

Revised, Retitled, and Expanded Edition
(Originally Published as
Information Retrieval Systems:
Characteristics, Testing and Evaluation)

F. Wilfrid Lancaster
and Amy J. Warner

I**R**P. **INFORMATION RESOURCES PRESS**

Available from
Information Resources Press
1110 North Glebe Road
Suite 550
Arlington, Virginia 22201

Library of Congress Catalog Card Number 93-077931

ISBN 0-87815-064-1

Parts of the present work appeared in a slightly different version in *Information
Retrieval Systems: Characteristics, Testing, and Evaluation* (1st and 2nd editions).
© 1968 and 1979, respectively, by John Wiley & Sons.

To Our Families

Contents

EXHIBITS   xi

PREFACE   xvii

1 SOME BASICS OF INFORMATION RETRIEVAL   1

   The Information Transfer Cycle   1
   The Role of Information Services   4
   Types of Information Need   5
   Information Retrieval Systems   7
   The Problems of Information Retrieval   12
   The Components of Information Retrieval Systems   15
   The Library as an Information Retrieval System   16

2 THE DATABASE INDUSTRY   21

   Offline Systems   22
   Online Systems   23
   Trends in the Industry   27
   Information Products and Services   29
   Online Retrieval Systems and Online Catalogs   41

3 SUBJECT ACCESS: PROBLEMS AND
   PERFORMANCE CRITERIA   43

   Measures of Retrieval Performance   43
   Pertinence and Relevance   47

Relevance   51
Pertinence   52
The Literature on Relevance   57

4   THE USER–INTERMEDIARY INTERFACE   65

Needs Versus Demands   65
Requests for Information   69

5   SUBJECT ANALYSIS AND REPRESENTATION   79

Human Indexing   80
Partial and Full-Text Indexing   85
Summary   87

6   LANGUAGE IN RETRIEVAL   89

Characteristics of Language and the Controlled Vocabulary   89
Choice of Terminology   93
The Controlled Vocabulary   98
Improvements in Design   104
Natural Language in Information Retrieval   104

7   THE SELECTION AND EVALUATION OF DATABASES   109

Printed Sources   110
Database Indexes   111
Automatic Aids   112
Related Studies   115
Database Quality   115
The Future   125

8   SEARCHING THE DATABASE   129

Search Logic   129
Search Strategy   133
Broadening and Narrowing Search Strategies   136
Some Sample Searches   140
Searching Free Text   148
Weighted-Term Searching   151
Fractional Search   153
Screening of Output   153

Characteristics of Searchers   154
Factors Affecting the Success of a Particular Search   156

9   EVALUATION CRITERIA AND EVALUATION PROCEDURES   159

Criteria Used in the Evaluation of Information Retrieval Systems 159
Recall and Precision   162
Alternative Measures for Evaluating a Search   168
Conducting an Evaluation   171
Deriving Performance Figures   177
Interpretation of the Results   185
Cost-Effectiveness Studies   189
Cost–Benefit Analysis   196

10 FACTORS AFFECTING PERFORMANCE IN
    INFORMATION RETRIEVAL   203

System Factors in Information Retrieval   205
Trade-Offs in Information Retrieval   235
Human Factors in Indexing and Searching   238

11 AUTOMATIC METHODS OF INFORMATION RETRIEVAL   243

General Approaches in Automatic Methods of Information
    Retrieval   243
Linguistic Approaches to Information Retrieval   248
Statistical Approaches to Information Retrieval   252
Categories of Automatic Methods of Information Retrieval   258
Evaluation of Automatic Methods   278

12 TRENDS AND POSSIBLE FUTURE DEVELOPMENTS   283

Proliferation of Information Sources and Information
    Technology   284
Information Retrieval and the Paradigms of Computing   288
The Migration from Print on Paper to the Electronic Document   289
The Library and Information Center Environment   293
Other Views on the Future   297
Artificial Intelligence and Expert Systems   301

BIBLIOGRAPHY   307

INDEX   331

Exhibits

1   The information transfer cycle.   2

2   The interface role of an information service.   5

3   The major functions of many types of information services.   8

4   The essential problems of information retrieval.   13

5   The online searching situation in the United States.   17

6   Sample inverted and linear files.   24

7   Sample MARC record.   26

8   Database-use chain.   28

9   Sample bibliographic database records.   31

10   Sample record from *Harvard Business Review* (non-bibliographic/source [full text]).   32

11   Sample record from PTS U.S. Time Series (nonbibliographic/source [numeric]).   33

12   Sample record from TRADEMARKSCAN—FEDERAL (nonbibliographic/source [image]).   34

13   Sample database records revealing lack of standardization.   36–37

14   Examples of lack of standardization in information systems.   39

15   The problem of retrieving pertinent items from a database.   44

16   Factors affecting the performance of a database search.   45

17   Loss of recall at each step in the information retrieval chain.   46

18   Some relationships important in the evaluation of information
     retrieval systems.   49

19   Some relationships of importance in information retrieval.   56

20   Complexity of the "information need" situation.   68

21   The request is more general than the information need:
     Most documents retrieved are not pertinent.   70

22   The request is more specific than the information need:
     Documents of pertinence are not retrieved.   71

23   Factors affecting the quality of user–intermediary interaction.   73

24   Various possible approaches to subject representation.   80

25   Exhaustivity of indexing in a typical catalog record
     compared with exhaustivity in the ERIC database.   82

26   ERIC bibliographic record and inverted index.   86

27   Comparison of precoordinate and postcoordinate approaches
     to indexing.   94

28   Differences between precoordinate and postcoordinate
     indexing.   95

29   The structure of a typical thesaurus.   99

30   *Medical Subject Headings* displays.   101

31   Comparison of term displays in the 10th and 11th editions
     of *Library of Congress Subject Headings.*   102

32   Most highly ranked databases in terms of possible relevance
     to the topic "damage to metals by laser cutting."   112

33   Plot of the scatter of the AIDS literature, 1982–1987.   120

34   Example of distribution of "superconductor" items under
     terms in a database.   123

35   Scatter of items under index terms.   124

36   Ranking of databases by the number of times that the term
     ACID RAIN occurs as of September 14, 1983 (from DIALINDEX
     search).   126

37   Possible search approaches to the topic of "measurement
      of the width of cracks in partially prestressed concrete beams."   146

38   Criteria by which information retrieval systems can be evaluated.   161

39   2 × 2 table of results of a literature search.   163

40   Typical results of a search in a retrieval system.   165

41   Plot of recall versus precision.   166

42   Possible questions to be answered by a retrieval system
      evaluation.   172

43   Simple design of an experiment.   173

44   Some of the variables in an experiment.   175

45   A: Example of a search request form. B: Example of a
      search strategy based on the request.   178

46   MEDLARS relevance assessment form.   180

47   Estimation of recall by extrapolation of results from a
      known population X_1 to an unknown X.   183

48   Scatter diagram of search results.   186

49   Recall and precision results for three groups of searches.   187

50   Major categories of failures identified in the MEDLARS
      evaluation.   189

51   Structure of the cost-effectiveness analysis program.   192

52   Factors studied in the evaluation of information retrieval
      systems.   204

53   Some major qualitative aspects of databases.   206

54   Bradford distribution of 375 articles published in 155 journals.   210

55   Effect of specificity of vocabulary on the performance
      of a retrieval system.   213

56   Hypothetical index term assignments for services that
      do (X) and do not (Y) index by the rule of exclusively
      specific entry.   224

57   Hypothetical performance curve of exhaustivity level
      versus recall ratio.   227

58   Search request and strategy (building block approach).   230

59   Ways to increase recall (may decrease precision) and
      precision (may decrease recall) in a given search.   231

60   Trade-off comparison of two hypothetical information
      systems.   237

61   General view of automatic methods of information retrieval.   244

62   Sample requests, processing components, and matching
      documents.   245

63   Comparison of levels of processing in commercial,
      statistical, and linguistic methods of information retrieval. 250

64   Simplified architecture of an intelligent information
      retrieval system.   251

65   Upper (C) and lower (D) frequency cutoff for words.
      Middle-frequency words (E) have appropriate resolving power. 253

66   Example of statistical phrase generation: (a) Original
      sentence; (b) Word stems generated from original
      sentence; (c) Word pairs (phrases) generated assuming
      no more than three intervening words between word pairs.   254

67   Sample index phrase output from grammatical analysis.   256

68   Statistical indexing and matching of documents and queries.   257

69   A comparison of manual and automatic methods for
      thesaurus representation and construction.   260

70   Results of statistical grouping of words.   261

71   Results of a linguistic grouping of words and phrases.   262

72   A comparison of manual and automatic methods for
      indexing procedures and representations.   264

73   Automatic indexing results.   266

74   Example of results from a machine-aided indexing operation.   268

75   Example of results from a machine-aided indexing system
      at the National Library of Medicine.   269

76   A comparison of manual and automatic approaches to query
      analysis and representation.   270

77 Automatic query formulations. 272

78 A comparison of manual and automatic methods for abstracting procedures and representations. 275

79 Results from two automatic abstracting procedures. 276

80 Information technology resources and environment: Trends and issues. 284

81 The four paradigms of computing. 286

82 Comparison between traditional and hypertext documents. 292

83 Storage, transmission, and processing by libraries and information centers. 293

Preface

Much has happened in the field of information retrieval since the second edition of this book was published in 1979. Electronic databases and the telecommunications networks through which they can be accessed have both proliferated; databases in CD-ROM form can be found in libraries of all types and sizes; an increasing number of databases now include the full text of bibliographic items; and the library card catalog has very largely been replaced by online public access catalogs (OPACs).

As a result of these various developments, more interest now exists in subject access than ever before, and much research continues to be performed in this area. Many people seem to have convinced themselves that technology in itself has solved the subject access problem. This problem has not yet been solved, although certain inroads are being made by knowledge-based expert systems and other computer aids to indexing. Linguistic approaches are also showing promise. Both of these areas, as well as relational subject access, hypertext, nonsubject access, and other leading edge information topics, are examined in this edition.

This third edition of the former *Information Systems: Characteristics, Testing, and Evaluation*, first published in 1968, continues to emphasize that the problems of information retrieval are the intellectual ones of subject analysis and description and that these problems are not easily solved by technology alone.

As with earlier editions, this book is intended primarily as a text for use in courses in the area of information retrieval. The authors, however, hope that it will also be of interest and value to librarians, database producers, and all other professionals concerned with the subject access problem.

F. Wilfrid Lancaster
Amy J. Warner

1

Some Basics
of Information Retrieval

THE INFORMATION TRANSFER CYCLE

Information retrieval is the major activity engaged in by information centers. The information center, or information service, includes libraries, producers of published databases in printed or electronic form, and any other type of service that provides information resources to a population of users. The important functions performed by information centers can best be understood when viewed in the broader context of the complete cycle by which information is transferred through formal channels.

The major elements of the cycle are depicted in Exhibit 1. The "user community" is those individuals working in a particular subject area. Some are involved in "research and development activities" and some in a variety of other activities loosely referred to as "application activities." All are users of information, and some are also creators of information products; that is, some people, whose activities are presumed to be of interest to others in the community, describe their experiences, research, or opinions in some form of report. This activity is the "role of the author" in the information transfer cycle. But authorship is not in itself a form of communication. The work of an author has little or no impact on the professional community until it has been reproduced in multiple copies and formally distributed, that is, published. Publishing is the "role of the primary publisher" in the information transfer cycle. A primary publication may be a book, a journal, a technical report, a dissertation, a patent, or the like. Primary publications are distributed to the user community in two ways: (1) directly through subscription and purchase by individuals and (2) indirectly through subscription and purchase by information centers.

1

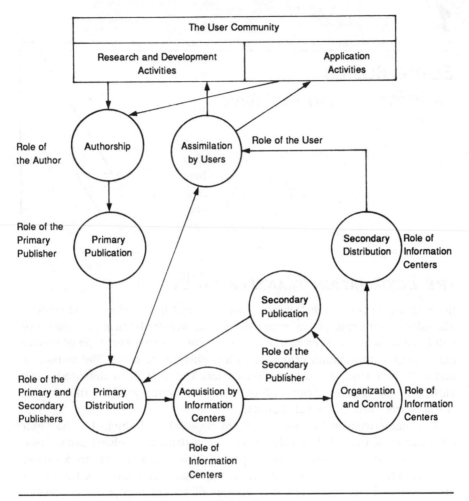

EXHIBIT 1   The information transfer cycle.

Information centers have very important roles in the information transfer cycle. Through their acquisition and storage policies, libraries provide a permanent archive of professional achievement and a guaranteed source of access to these records. In addition, libraries and other information centers organize and control the literature by cataloging, classification, indexing, and related procedures. Indexing and abstracting services and publishers of national bibliographies also organize and control literature. They are responsible for the publication and distribution of "secondary publications." Some secondary publications go directly to the user community, although the great majority go to institutional subscribers (the information centers).

Information centers also perform important presentation and dissemination functions in the cycle. These activities, which constitute a form of secondary distribution of publications and information about publications, include circulation of materials and various types of current awareness, reference, and literature searching services. Since the 1970s, machine-readable databases produced by secondary publishers have been increasingly important in providing various types of information services.

The final stage in the information transfer cycle is "assimilation." This, the least tangible, is the stage at which information is absorbed by the user community. Here a distinction is made between document transfer and information transfer. The latter occurs only if a document is studied by a user and its contents are assimilated to the point where the reader is informed by it, that is, the user's knowledge of the subject matter is altered. Assimilation of information by the professional community can occur through primary or secondary distribution. Different levels and speeds of assimilation are associated with different documents, and the contents of some may never be assimilated because they are never used.

The processes of formal communication are presented as a cycle because they are continuous and regenerative. Through the process of assimilation, readers may gain information that they can use in their own research and development activities, which, in turn, generates new writing and publication, and thus the cycle continues.

Exhibit 1 is oversimplified in one important respect. It shows the dissemination of information through formal channels but does not explicitly illustrate the processes of informal communication. The informal channels, however, do not generally disseminate information that is different from information that is disseminated through the formal channels. Both disseminate the results of the same experience or research, but the informal channels disseminate information in a different format or in the same format but at a much earlier time, as, for example, in the distribution of drafts or preprints. They are important because they disseminate information more rapidly than the formal channels, at least to those individuals who are well integrated in a professional community, and because they disseminate information to some individuals who choose not to use the formal channels.

This brief discussion of the information transfer cycle is presented to clarify the role of information centers in the complete cycle. The main concerns of this book lie in the areas of "acquisition by information centers," "organization and control," and "secondary distribution," as depicted in Exhibit 1. Because some information centers also create secondary databases, which may be used in offering various services, the activities of "secondary publication" and "primary distribution" of secondary publications also fall, at least partly, within its scope. The other activities depicted, relating to authorship, primary publication and distribution, and the assimilation of information by users, are outside the direct control of information services.

THE ROLE OF INFORMATION SERVICES

The major function of any information service is to act as an interface between a particular population of users and the universe of information resources in printed or other form (Exhibit 2).

To fulfill its interface role, an information service is engaged in three major activities (Exhibits 1 and 2): the acquisition and storage of documents; the organization and control of these documents; and the distribution of these documents, or information about them, to users by circulation, literature searches, photocopying, and other services.

The user community is usually defined by geographic area, institutional affiliation, subject interest, or some combination of these; the user population for a national information system is the community of scientists and other professionals working throughout the country. For most information centers, the most important type of information resource is in document form, using the term "document" in its widest sense. It is the function of the information service to bring together (interface) the user population and the information resources as efficiently and economically as possible. In a somewhat passive role, its function is to ensure that any document or information needed by a member of the user community will be made available, insofar as possible, at the time the user needs it. In its more active role, it is the function of the information service to bring documents or data to the attention of the user community, perhaps through searches of the literature designed to notify them, on a continuing basis, of newly published literature in their areas of interest (current awareness).

An efficient, modern information service should be able to guarantee that virtually any document in the universe of available literature, or any data contained in documents, will be accessible to any member of the user community. This implies that the universe of document resources is available to the user population at different levels of accessibility. Because no information center can own everything, it is important that the documents it does collect have the greatest chance of being of value to its users. It is also important that the information center be able to acquire quickly any other document for which there is a legitimate need in the user community, whether through purchase, photocopying, or interlibrary loan. Moreover, in the center's own collections, documents need to be organized according to expected levels of demand, with those that are most likely to be used being most accessible. Thus, the universe of document resources should be made available to the users of an information

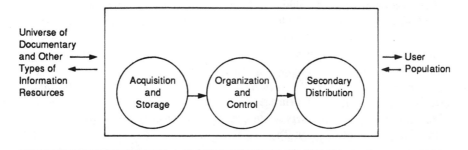

Universe of Documentary and Other Types of Information Resources

User Population

Acquisition and Storage

Organization and Control

Secondary Distribution

EXHIBIT 2   The interface role of an information service.

center according to tiers of accessibility that might, for certain institutions, be as follows:

1. Documents in the center's collections and on open shelves
2. Documents in the center's collections but in controlled-access stacks
3. Documents in off-site storage areas
4. Documents not in the center's collections.

This sequence is one of decreasing accessibility, but it is an oversimplification because a copy of a document that is not owned by the center may be more accessible than one that is but which is mislaid, at the bindery, or out on loan. Moreover, all items that are not in the center's collections are not equally accessible or inaccessible because geographic distance from the center may have some effect on their accessibility (although this is becoming less important because of the wide availability of telefacsimile and related technologies). Other factors also affect accessibility, including whether the document is in some union catalog, the reliability and speed of the delivery service, and so on.

TYPES OF INFORMATION NEED

The principal needs and demands of users of information services fall into two broad categories:

1. The need to locate and obtain a copy of a particular document for which the author or title is known
2. The need to locate documents on a particular subject or that are capable of answering a particular question.

The first of these needs may be referred to as a "known-item need" and the second as a "subject need." The ability of the information center to supply known items when needed is its "document delivery capability." The ability of the center to retrieve documents on a particular subject, or to provide the answer to a specific question, is its "information retrieval capability." These two functions—document delivery and information retrieval—are the major activities engaged in by information services. The functions are closely related in that many requests for known documents are likely to stem directly from earlier information retrieval activities.

Subject needs fall clearly into three main types:

1. The need for information to help solve a particular problem or to facilitate decision making
2. The need for background information on some subject
3. The need for information on new developments in a particular field.

The last is usually referred to as a current awareness need, but there is no single term that is generally accepted to describe the other two types. In practice, these types of need are usually satisfied through a search of the past literature by an information service in response to a specific demand from a user, usually referred to as a "retrospective search."

The retrospective search differs from the current awareness search in a number of ways. It is more purposive—the user must initiate the action whereas, in the current awareness situation, the information service may take the initiative; it tends to be more specific; it may need to cover a much greater volume of literature than a current awareness search, that is, go back many years; and its results are likely to be judged more stringently by the user than the results of the current awareness search.

Retrospective search needs may themselves be divided into several types:

1. *The need for a single item of factual data.* This is the typical "ready reference" inquiry handled by libraries. Although documents are usually involved in satisfying such a need, the requester does not necessarily have to receive the document—the answer to the question can be given by telephone.

2. *The need to have one or more documents on a particular subject, but less than the total literature or everything that is available from a particular center.* This is a typical library situation, as exemplified by a request for a few recent papers on acid rain. A special category is the type of need that is completely satisfied when the first document of a particular type is found. For example, a patent examiner may need to find only one case of a previous application in the literature to disallow a patent claim.

3. *The need for a comprehensive search—one that retrieves as much as possible of the literature published on a particular subject during a particular period.* Such a search might be needed by someone writing a book or a review article or by a scientist beginning a research project. A special category is a search to confirm that nothing exists in the literature on a particular topic; that is, the requester sets out to prove that nothing has been published on the topic—for instance, the inventor who wants to confirm the patentability of an invention.

INFORMATION RETRIEVAL SYSTEMS

The major activities of many types of information services are presented in simplified form in Exhibit 3. The input consists of documents that are acquired by the information service. This implies the existence of selection criteria and policies, which, in turn, implies a detailed and accurate knowledge of the information needs of the community to be served. The most obvious criterion governing document selection is the subject, but other criteria, such as type of document, language, or source, also may be important. For information services that deal primarily with journal articles, the selection criteria will usually focus on the journal rather than the article: Certain journals will be covered and others will not (although some may be indexed in their entirety and others selectively). To a large extent, the coverage of many services is governed by considerations of cost-effectiveness, particularly services dealing with a highly specialized field—only those journals that publish most on the subject will be included.

Subject Analysis of Documents

Once documents are acquired, they need to be organized and controlled so they can be identified and located in response to user demands. Organization and control activities include classification, cataloging, subject indexing, and abstracting. The subject indexing process involves two distinct intellectual steps: the conceptual analysis—or content analysis—of a document and the translation of the conceptual analysis into a particular vocabulary (Exhibit 3). Rarely are the two steps clearly distinguished. This is unfortunate because each step offers different constraints and brings in different factors that affect the performance of the system. For efficient conceptual analysis, the indexer needs to understand what the document is about and must have knowledge of user needs. The recognition of what the document is about and why users may be interested in it—that is, what aspects of the document are of most concern—constitutes conceptual analysis. The conceptual analysis of a document may be

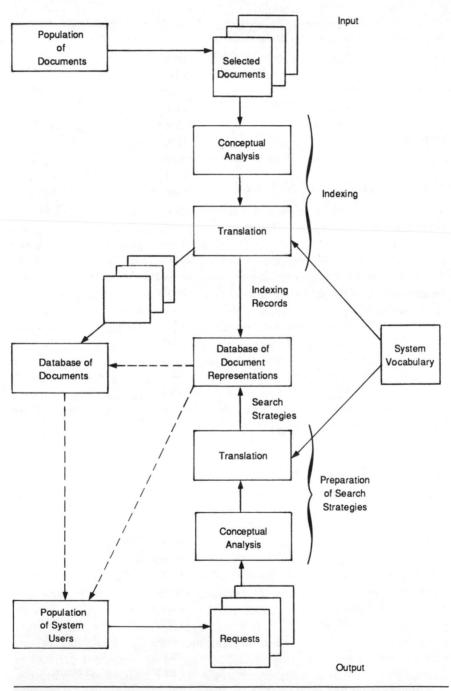

EXHIBIT 3   The major functions of many types of information services.

recorded on paper or at a terminal; however, it is more likely that it exists only in the mind of the indexer.

Next, the conceptual analysis must be translated into some vocabulary or index language. In many systems this involves a "controlled vocabulary," that is, a limited set of terms that must be used to represent the subject matter of documents. Such a vocabulary might be a list of subject headings, a classification scheme, a thesaurus, or simply a list of "approved" keywords or phrases. An "uncontrolled vocabulary," in contrast, places no restrictions on the terms the indexer may use. The uncontrolled vocabulary usually implies the use of words or phrases that occur in the document being indexed. The terms used by an indexer to represent the subject content of documents, whether from a controlled or an uncontrolled vocabulary, are referred to generically in this book as "index terms."

Once the indexing process has been completed, the documents are filed in some form of document database and the indexing records are entered into a second database where they are organized so that they can conveniently be searched in response to various requests. The database of indexing records, or "document representations," may be as simple as a card file or an index in printed form. Today, however, it is more likely to be a machine-readable file on magnetic tape or disk. This database can be considered the "index" to the document database.

The distinction between the database of documents and the database of document representations is now becoming blurred. The representation of a document that is being searched may not be a set of index terms but a piece of text—the title, an abstract, or even the complete text of the item. A database in which the complete text of a document exists in searchable form in effect serves the functions of both the document database and the database of representations.

Search Strategy

The steps involved at the output side of the system are very similar to those involved at input. The user population submits various requests to the information service, and staff prepare search strategies for the requests. The preparation of search strategies can also be considered as involving conceptual analysis and translation. The first step involves an analysis of the request to determine what the user is really looking for, and the second involves the translation of the conceptual analysis into the vocabulary of the system. The conceptual analysis of the request, translated into the language of the system, is the "search strategy," which can be regarded as a "request representation" in much the same way that an indexing record may be regarded as a document representation. The only real difference between the two is that the search strategy usually contains explicit logic—a certain set of logical relationships among the index terms is specified—whereas in the document representation, logical relationships among index terms may not be explicitly stated.

Once the search strategy has been prepared, it is "matched" against the database of document representations. This activity might involve a search of card files, printed indexes, microfilm, or magnetic tape or disk. Document representations that match the search strategy—that is, satisfy the logical requirements of the search—are retrieved from the database and delivered to the requester. The process, which may be iterative, is completed when the requester is satisfied with the results of the search, which, in some cases, might mean that the requester is satisfied that nothing in the database is exactly relevant to his or her needs.

The steps shown in Exhibit 3 illustrate a delegated search situation, that is, one in which the person with the information need delegates the responsibility for searching the database to an information specialist. In a nondelegated search, the process is simplified because the user goes directly to the database. Even in this situation, however, users must conceptually analyze their own information need and translate their analyses into the language of the system. In searching many kinds of systems, the search strategy is not constructed away from the database and separately from the searching operation itself. The strategy for searching a card catalog, a printed index, or an electronic database (in CD-ROM form or accessible through telecommunications connections) is likely to be developed interactively and heuristically; that is, the conceptual analysis and translation activities are more or less concurrent with the file searching activities. Nevertheless, it is convenient to separate conceptual analysis from translation even in this situation.

The only real difference between a retrospective search service and a current awareness service—for example, selective dissemination of information—is that the search strategies, or "user interest profiles," in the latter represent the current research interests of system users. They are matched against the representations of incoming documents on a regular basis—every time the database is updated—and the results of such matches are presented to the users at regular intervals.

Information Retrieval Distinguished from Related Activities

Some requests are for specific documents for which the author or title is known, rather than for information on a particular subject. These requests (Exhibit 3) are made directly to the document database by author or title access points in the indexes or catalogs of the collection, or by some other approach such as a report or patent number. The ability of the center to supply needed documents is its "document delivery capability."

So far, no attempt has been made to give a precise definition of "information retrieval system," although the scope of this term has been addressed. "Information retrieval," as it is most commonly used, is synonymous with "literature searching"; it is the process of searching some collection of documents (using the term document in its widest sense) to identify those that deal with a particular subject. Any system that is designed to facilitate this literature searching activity may legitimately be called an information retrieval system. The subject catalog of a library is one type; so is a printed subject index.

The output of an information retrieval system usually consists of one or more bibliographic references, sometimes with added information such as an abstract or a list of the terms under which the document has been indexed. These document representations are delivered to the person who requested the search. That person may then ask the information center, or other service, to provide the documents referred to. In some cases, an information center eliminates the intermediate step and delivers directly to the requester the actual documents or a sample of the documents that staff members judge are most likely to be relevant. Sometimes the information retrieval and document delivery functions are combined in a single system. For example, a computer-based system might include the full text of documents, and the output of the search is a printout of the documents rather than their representations. Most information retrieval systems, however, deliver document representations. Document delivery is an entirely separate activity that may or may not be provided by the organizations conducting literature searches.

Clearly, "information retrieval" is not a particularly satisfactory term to describe the type of activity to which it is usually applied. An information retrieval system does not retrieve information. Indeed, information is intangible; it is not possible to see, hear, or feel it. We are "informed" if our state of knowledge on a subject is somehow changed. Giving a requester a document or a reference to a document on lasers does not inform him or her on the subject of lasers. Information transfer can take place only if the user reads the document and understands it. Information, then, is something that changes a person's state of knowledge on a subject. This may not be a very precise definition, but it is the best that we can offer. It is at least adequate for our purposes.

The inappropriateness of the term *information retrieval* is further emphasized by a reconsideration of Exhibit 1. The activities of information retrieval systems end with the circle labeled "Secondary Distribution," the items distributed being documents or their representations. But information transfer, if it takes place at all, occurs only in the circle labeled "Assimilation by Users." The assimilation stage of the information transfer cycle is not controlled by information centers.

An information center activity sometimes referred to as "question answering" can also be regarded as a form of information retrieval. A question-answering service attempts to produce the direct answer to a particular question, for example, What is the height of. . .?   What is the melting point of. . .? What is the address of. . .?, rather than simply referring to documents that might provide an answer. Many libraries and other types of information centers provide a question-answering service. Sometimes it is referred to as a "ready reference" or a "factual reference" service. Question answering may be the second stage in a larger information retrieval activity. The first stage involves the use of some type of information retrieval system, perhaps a library subject catalog, a printed index, or even an index in the back of a book, to identify documents that are likely to provide the answer to a particular question. The second stage involves extracting the answer from the document and transmitting it to the user.

Several computer-based question-answering systems have been developed. These systems accept a question in natural language, although a prescribed syntactic structure may be required, and produce the answer in print or on a screen. Because of the complex design of such systems, those that have been developed to date are restricted to rather limited bodies of knowledge like baseball results or state highway codes. A system that stores physical, chemical, or other types of data, and answers questions from the stored data, can be referred to as a "data retrieval system." The stored data may be referred to as a "data bank." Examples are census data, thermophysical properties data, or data on interatomic potentials.

Another type of information retrieval system is one that stores the complete text of a set of documents and can retrieve those portions of it that match a search strategy representing an information need. A computer-based system may store a body of legal text such as the statutes of a particular state and allow the retrieval of those paragraphs of text in which particular word combinations occur—for example, a word indicating *child* and a word indicating *physical cruelty.*

Question-answering systems, data retrieval systems, and text retrieval systems are all legitimate forms of information retrieval systems. Although question-answering systems and data retrieval systems are sometimes referred to in this book, the major emphasis is on systems that retrieve references to documents or document texts in response to subject requests.

THE PROBLEMS OF INFORMATION RETRIEVAL

Exhibit 3 presented a rather simplistic picture of the information retrieval problem. A more sophisticated version is given in Exhibit 4. In essence, the

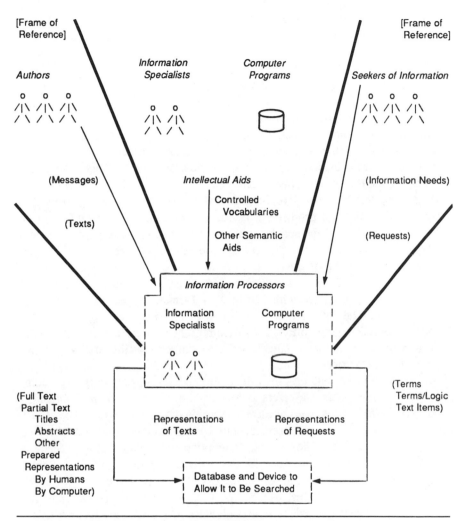

EXHIBIT 4   The essential problems of information retrieval.

problem is that of matching information needs against messages. This can only be done in an indirect way. Most messages (what authors want to convey) appear as texts (some are in pictorial, audio, or other nontextual form), whereas information needs are presented as requests made to some type of information service. The information service creates representations of the texts (which can consist of the full text—for example, an exact electronic reproduction of words printed somewhere on paper; parts of the text; or some other form that is humanly or automatically constructed), stores these in a database, and provides some device that allows these representations to be searched. The database can be stored in paper, microimage, or electronic form, and the "device" allowing it to be searched can be as simple as a card catalog or printed index or as sophisticated as a set of computer programs. The information service also creates representations of the requests (search statements of some type, consisting of terms, terms presented in logical relationships, textual statements, or "items"—for example, a system may allow a searcher to enter details of an item already known to be relevant and will then look for others that resemble it) and processes these against the database, retrieving those text representations that best match the request representations.

Texts may not be perfect representations of messages (although this is a definite communication problem, it is not usually considered an information retrieval problem), and the representations of texts (for example, by indexers or abstractors) may also be imperfect. By the same token, requests are rarely perfect representations of information needs, and search statements may not be perfect representations of requests. Moreover, the requester's frame of reference may not coincide with that of an information specialist or, indeed, of the authors. The information retrieval problem, then, can be considered essentially one of trying to match approximations of information needs with approximations of messages. Small wonder that the results are not always completely satisfactory.

As Bates (1986) points out, the information retrieval problem is more complex than it first appears; she refers to it as "indeterminate" and "probabilistic." It now seems fashionable to concentrate more on the output side of the activity (information need and request representation) than on the input side (message and text representation), the implicit assumption being that the output side is more "complex." In fact, Belkin (1980) and Belkin et al. (1982a,b) refer to matching the "anomalous state of knowledge" of a requester with the more "coherent state of knowledge" of authors. But the indexer's role—predicting the types of requests for which a particular document is likely to be a useful response—is not necessarily simpler than that of the search intermediary— understanding what types of documents might satisfy some requester at a given time.

Be that as it may, Exhibit 4 also shows that algorithmic processes can be used in various information retrieval activities as a substitute for human intellectual processing. Computers can be applied in automatic indexing and automatic abstracting, as well as in other operations involving the formation of classes of documents and terms, in developing search strategies, and in establishing networks of associations among terms. As the diagram implies, computers can aid humans or to some extent substitute for them in virtually all the component activities that make up the broad activity of information retrieval.

THE COMPONENTS OF INFORMATION RETRIEVAL SYSTEMS

The major components of an information retrieval system are evident in Exhibit 3. The system comprises six major subsystems:

1. The document selection subsystem
2. The indexing subsystem
3. The vocabulary subsystem
4. The searching subsystem
5. The subsystem of interaction between the user and the system (user–system interface)
6. The matching subsystem, that is, the subsystem that actually matches document representations against request representations.

In most operating environments, the matching subsystem is considered the least important of the six, because it has no direct influence on the effectiveness of the complete system, that is, on whether it can retrieve items that satisfy the information needs of users (although, clearly, the efficiency of the matching subsystem exerts a great influence on system economics and overall system efficiency as measured by response time). In a conventional computer-based system, the computer contributes directly only to the matching operation, acting as a giant matching device. In many systems, the computer contributes little or nothing directly to the selection of documents, the indexing of documents, the control of the vocabulary used in indexing and searching, the preparation of search strategies, or the interaction with system users—for example, for request negotiation. These are all intellectual activities, performed by humans in most existing systems, that govern the effectiveness of the system. Several experimental systems do exist, in which the activities are more fully automated. These activities are dealt with in Chapter 11.

The most important factors controlling the effectiveness of a retrieval system may be separated into two groups: database factors and factors associated with the exploitation of the database.

The major database factors, which can also be regarded as "input factors," are (1) what documents are included, (2) how completely and accurately their subject matter is recognized and represented in the indexing operation, and (3) the adequacy of the system vocabulary to represent the subject matter.

There are also three "exploitation" or output factors: (1) how well the staff of the information center is able to understand the information needs of the users (user–system interaction), (2) how well they can transform these needs into search strategies, and (3) the adequacy of the system vocabulary to represent the subject interests of system users. The intellectual components of information systems, and their influence on system performance, are the major themes of this book.

THE LIBRARY AS AN INFORMATION RETRIEVAL SYSTEM

An information retrieval service is one that responds to a user's request for information on some topic by searching printed or electronic databases to identify bibliographic items that appear to deal with this topic.

It is only during the last 20 years that information services of this kind have become fairly common in most types of libraries. Earlier, these services were available only in certain special libraries, particularly those in industry. Public, school, and academic libraries generally lacked the resources to attempt anything but the simplest bibliographic searches. Instead, they directed users to appropriate printed sources where they could perform their own searches and instructed them how to use these sources, if necessary.

This situation has changed dramatically since the early 1970s. The use of online networks to search bibliographic databases is now commonplace in academic and special libraries of all sizes, as well as in some of the larger public libraries. Databases distributed in CD-ROM (Compact Disk–Read Only Memory) form also are becoming commonplace in libraries of all kinds, and some universities are now mounting large bibliographic databases on their own computer facilities for access through terminals throughout the university community.

A complex set of interrelationships now exists among the individuals and institutions involved in online searching (Exhibit 5). The database *producer* plays key roles in the overall operation as compiler and publisher of the database. Compilation involves the acquisition of published materials within the stated scope of the database (which implies careful selection criteria) and the processing of these materials to form bibliographic representations (records) within the database. This may involve descriptive cataloging, subject indexing (perhaps using terms drawn from a controlled vocabulary such as a thesaurus), and sometimes the writing of abstracts. In some cases, however, the intellectual processing is minimized: keywords in titles and abstracts are used as access points instead of humanly assigned index terms. Most frequently today, the database is distributed in two versions: machine-readable (electronic) form and a printed index (with or without abstracts) roughly equivalent to the electronic form.

Machine-readable databases are acquired by database vendors. These vendors have developed software to convert all databases to a common processing format, to make them accessible online via various telecommunications networks, and to allow them to be interrogated by remote users. Libraries generally

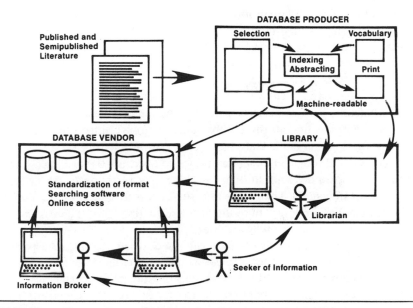

EXHIBIT 5   The online searching situation in the United States.

access these databases through one or more database vendors although, in a few cases, the database producer may also make online access possible through computers of its own. Moreover, it is becoming increasingly common for libraries to acquire databases in electronic form (CD-ROM), or for the parent institution to acquire the database and permit online access for users.

The seeker of information may ask a librarian to do the search; this usually will be done online, although it might also involve the use of databases in printed form or on CD-ROM. Alternatively, users could visit a library to perform their own searches in printed tools or to use the library's terminals to access databases directly. As terminals become increasingly available in offices and in homes, more and more individuals may perform their own online searches without the help of a librarian. Indeed, some special libraries now prefer to train users to perform their own searches instead of doing the searches for them. Finally, rather than going to a library or performing searches for themselves, some individuals or institutions may prefer to use the services of an information broker, who will conduct database searches for a fee.

In a broader sense, a library can be considered an information retrieval system. In other words, the activities depicted in Exhibit 3 are those that most libraries engage in; for example, they acquire publications of various types to form a collection—a database of documents—and also compile a database of document representations—the catalog of the library. Users of the library search this catalog to identify items dealing with a particular subject, or librarians perform such searches for them. In fact, the activities of a library are very similar to the activities of the database publisher. Exhibit 3 could apply as well to a library as to, say, Chemical Abstracts Service, or to some specialized information center within a government agency.

Unfortunately, card catalogs (or, for that matter, catalogs in printed book form) have definite limitations as subject access tools. Since online catalogs have become common in libraries, however, a resurgence of interest in subject access is evident throughout the library profession because online catalogs offer the possibility for more sophisticated searching approaches and more effective subject access in general. The factors affecting access to subject matter through the library catalog are identical to the factors affecting subject access through any other type of bibliographic database.

Regrettably, the terminology traditionally used to refer to various aspects of subject access within the library profession does not coincide exactly with the terminology used by others, such as publishers of bibliographic databases. In the literature of library and information science, a distinction is sometimes made among the three terms *subject cataloging, subject indexing,* and *classification.*

Subject cataloging usually refers to the assignment of subject headings to represent the overall contents of complete bibliographic items (books, reports, periodicals, and so on) within the catalog of a library.

Subject indexing is used more loosely; it may refer to the representation of the subject matter of parts of complete bibliographic items, as in the case of an index at the back of a book or an index to articles appearing in periodicals. Thus, a library may catalog a book under the subject heading DOGS to indicate its overall subject matter; the detailed contents of the book are only revealed in the subject index. This distinction between the terms subject cataloging and subject indexing—one referring to complete bibliographic items and the other to parts of items—is artificial, misleading, and inconsistent. The process by which the subject matter of bibliographic items is represented in published databases—printed or machine-readable—is almost invariably referred to as subject indexing, whether overall items or their parts are being discussed. Thus, the subject index to, say, *Chemical Abstracts* might refer to complete books or complete technical reports as well as to parts of bibliographic items (chapters in books, papers within conference proceedings, articles in periodicals). On the other hand, libraries may choose to represent parts of books (chapters or papers) within the catalog; this is usually referred to as analytical cataloging. When applied to subject matter, this activity would be analytical subject cataloging.

The situation is even more confusing when the term *classification* is considered. Librarians tend to use this term to refer to the assignment of class numbers (drawn from some classification scheme—Dewey Decimal [DDC],

Universal Decimal [UDC], Library of Congress [LC]) to bibliographic items, especially for the purpose of arranging these items on the shelves of libraries, in filing cabinets, and so on. But the subject catalog of a library can be either alphabetically based (an alphabetic subject catalog or a dictionary catalog) or arranged according to the sequence of some classification scheme (a classified catalog). Suppose a librarian picks up a book and decides that it is about "birds." He or she might assign the subject heading BIRDS to this item. Alternatively, he or she might assign to it the class number 598.2. Many people would refer to the first operation as subject cataloging and to the second as classification, a completely nonsensical distinction. More confusion occurs when one realizes that subject indexing may involve the use of a classification scheme or that a printed subject index might follow the sequence of some classification scheme. These terminological distinctions are meaningless and only serve to confuse. The fact is that classification, in the broadest sense, permeates all the activities associated with information storage and retrieval. Part of the terminological confusion is caused by failure to distinguish between the conceptual analysis and the translation stages in indexing.

Suppose that an information specialist picks up a bibliographic item and decides that it deals with robots. The intellectual activity involved in the decision is the same regardless of the item dealt with—book, part of book, periodical, article in a periodical, conference proceedings, conference paper, or whatever. The information specialist has classified the item—that is, put it into the conceptual class of "items discussing robots."

The process of translation involves the representation of the conceptual analysis by a term or terms drawn from some vocabulary. A term assigned to a bibliographic item is merely a label identifying a particular class of items. This label could be the English word ROBOTS, drawn from a thesaurus, a list of subject headings, or the document itself; an equivalent word in another language; or a label such as 629.892 from some classification scheme.

The process of deciding what an item is about, and of giving it a label to represent this decision, is conceptually the same whether the label assigned is from a classification scheme, a thesaurus, or a list of subject headings; whether the item is a complete bibliographic entity or a portion of it; whether the label is subsequently filed alphabetically or in some other sequence (or not filed at all); and whether the object of the exercise is to organize items on shelves or records in catalogs, printed indexes, or machine-readable databases.

In the field of information storage and retrieval, document classification refers to the formation of classes of items on the basis of their subject matter. Thesauri, subject headings, and bibliographic classification schemes are primarily lists of the labels by which these classes are identified and arranged. The process of searching for information involves deciding which classes to consult in a printed index, card catalog, or machine-readable database. A search can involve the examination of a single class (for example, everything appearing under the heading ROBOTS) or it can involve combinations of classes (for example, items appearing under ROBOTS and also under ARTIFICIAL INTELLIGENCE). How much combination is possible, or how easily various classes can be combined, is very much dependent on the format of the tool used for searching, especially on whether it is in printed or electronic form.

In short, subject indexing is conceptually identical to subject cataloging. The activity involved is that of subject classification, that is, forming classes of objects on the basis of their subject matter. In this text, the terms *subject indexing* or *indexing* refer to all activities of subject classification. The problems of information retrieval are dealt with from a broad perspective. No conceptual distinction is made between subject access through library catalogs and subject access through other forms of database—for example, a published indexing service in printed, online, or CD-ROM form—although examples are drawn from all types of tools to illustrate that they are not all equal in capabilities.

This overview has introduced the major components of the information retrieval activity and the major factors affecting the performance of information retrieval systems. These topics are dealt with in greater detail in subsequent chapters.

2

The Database Industry

The early history of information retrieval by computer has never been well documented. In fact, it is not altogether clear which system can legitimately be regarded as the first computer-based system for information retrieval. Among the earliest true computer-based systems were those established at the Naval Ordnance Laboratory in Silver Spring, Maryland in 1959 and the system put into operation by Western Reserve University for the American Society for Metals, circa 1960.

It is probably safe to say, however, that the first major information retrieval systems in the United States emerged in the Federal Government in the early 1960s. Perhaps the most important were those initiated by the Armed Services Technical Information Agency (later the Defense Documentation Center and now the Defense Technical Information Center); the National Aeronautics and Space Administration during 1962; and the National Library of Medicine, whose MEDLARS service was launched in 1963. These agencies must be regarded as the pioneers of large-scale bibliographic processing by computer, although many other organizations have followed in their footsteps.

In the 1960s, it was difficult to justify economically the dedication of a computerized system solely for retrospective searching of bibliographic records. Most of the very large bibliographic systems were justified by their virtuosity. They tended to be—and still are in many cases—multipurpose, generating a range of products or services from a single input operation. Many of these systems were developed as an outgrowth of the automated publishing process and the need to manipulate citations in machine-readable form for error checking, sorting, formatting, and computer typesetting. The machine-readable tapes produced from this activity could then be used to generate additional publications and to offer further services. The major service that was made possible by the machine-readable database was a retrospective search service on demand (demand search service), although the database was also used in current awareness activities (selective dissemination of information [SDI]).

OFFLINE SYSTEMS

The characteristics of the operational computer-based retrieval systems of the 1960s were very similar. They were offline batch-processing systems that used magnetic tape as the storage medium and that, by and large, were searched serially. Search strategies were matched sequentially against document representations, and a printed bibliography was produced. Retrospective searches of the entire database were intended to be performed once, and the result consisted of all documents in the system that matched the search request. For SDI, stored search profiles were periodically processed against recent updates of the database, and results were mailed to subscribers.

Computer retrieval systems of the 1960s offered many advantages over their predecessors, including the following:

1. Through batch processing, many searches could be conducted at the same time.

2. Many access points to a document could be provided very economically.

3. Complex searches involving large numbers of terms in complex relationships could be handled.

4. Output could be generated in the form of a bibliography, and a high-quality publication could be produced by interfacing the retrieval system with a photocomposition device. Output could also be made directly to microfilm (computer output microfilm [COM]).

5. Management data on how and how much the system was used could be collected, on a regular basis and as a by-product of normal system operations.

6. Many outputs and services could be produced from a single input— a general printed index, specialized indexes, retrospective searches, and SDI searches.

7. The database, once captured in machine-readable form, could be duplicated simply and cheaply; it was easily shipped and thus could be used to provide information services by different information centers.

Despite their many advantages, the offline batch-processing systems also had disadvantages. They were essentially "one-chance" searching systems in which the searcher had to think of all the possible search approaches in advance and construct a search strategy that, when matched with the database, was likely to retrieve all the relevant literature. In other words, they were noninteractive and nonheuristic, and they did not provide any real browsing capability.

Another major disadvantage of the offline systems was that the search results were substantially delayed—it was not possible to get an immediate response. At best, it took hours; at worst, as in the case of searches processed by a large national information center, it might take several days or weeks.

The search in an offline system was generally "delegated"; that is, the individual who needed the information had to delegate the responsibility for preparing the search strategy to an information specialist, with no opportunity to conduct his or her own search. Nondelegated searching is not invariably better that delegated searching, but the process of delegation is tricky. It is obvious that a search will produce very poor results if, in the process of delegation, the requester is unable to explain clearly what he or she is seeking or if the information specialist misinterprets the real needs of the user.

ONLINE SYSTEMS

The batch-processing systems of the 1960s were followed by the online interactive retrieval systems of the 1970s and beyond. These were made possible by advances in hardware, software, and telecommunications.

In online systems, data are stored on magnetic disk. Generally the system consists of both a linear file (containing each full record in the system) and one or more inverted indexes (often called index files) created from the linear file. Exhibit 6 shows a simplified example of a few records from a linear file with accompanying inverted index entries. Each element in the inverted index consists of a value or element from a database record in the linear file (for example, an author name or a keyword) along with a unique key element (usually an accession number) that is used to retrieve the records in which that value can be found. The linear and inverted files are stored on magnetic disks, where information can be accessed randomly—hence, the ability to perform interactive searches in real time.

Innovations in telecommunications also had a major impact on the online industry. Even though online systems were available in the late 1960s and early 1970s, their use was not widespread, particularly in libraries, because of the necessary expense of accessing them over long-distance telephone lines. Packet-switching networks such as TELENET and TYMNET lowered communications costs substantially, since the network was activated for a particular user only when a message was ready to be sent, rather than maintaining a permanent connection during the entire course of a communication. It was after the introduction of these networks that online retrieval found a widespread market.

Chan, Lois Mai
Pollard, Richard C.
Thesauri used in online databases
Greenwood Press:us
1988
United States   LINEAR
Language: English   FILE
Subject heading: Thesauri/Bibliography
Subject heading: Information systems/Directory
BLIB88009087
Monograph

Instructional materials used in teaching cataloging
and classification
Chan, Lois Mai
Cataloging & Classification Quarterly 7:131-44 Summ '87
Language: English
Subject heading: Cataloging/Teaching
Subject heading: Surveys/Library science literature
Subject heading: Textbooks
BLIB87009368
Article

Author	Chan, Lois Mai	88009087
		87009368
	Pollard, Richard C.	88009087

INVERTED

INDEXES

	Bibliography	88009087
	Cataloging/Teaching	87009368
	Directory	88009087
	Information systems	88009087
Subject	Information systems/Directory	88009087
	Library science literature	87009368
	Surveys	87009368
	Surveys/Library science literature	87009368
	Teaching	88009087
	Textbooks	87009368
	Thesauri	88009087
	Thesauri/Bibliography	88009087

EXHIBIT 6   Sample inverted and linear files. SOURCE: *Library Literature* database. Reprinted with permission of The H. W. Wilson Company.

Online retrieval systems have all the advantages that apply to batch-processing systems but avoid all the major disadvantages. They are heuristic and interactive, permit browsing, provide rapid response, and can be used in a nondelegated search mode.

Virtually all of the early online retrieval systems operated as depicted in Exhibit 5. Primary documents were acquired by an organization (a database producer) where document representations were generated, consisting of an appropriate citation and often index terms and an abstract. These representations were entered into machine-readable form and stored on magnetic tape. The information on tape was processed in various ways to produce printed indexes and sometimes also was maintained by the producer to do offline batch processing of search requests. The information on magnetic tape was also loaded onto magnetic disk, and the representations were processed to create the inverted indexes that were necessary for online, interactive searching. This was done either by leasing the tape to another organization (the database vendor) or locally by the database producer. In either case, the organization that processed the database for online searching also had to provide appropriate interactive search software.

The systems that provide bibliographic data for library catalogs underwent a similar evolution; however, rather than having producers that lease databases to vendors, member libraries input records to a centralized database that is owned and operated by an organization known as a bibliographic utility. Such an organization—for example, the Online Computer Library Center (OCLC)—then provides the appropriate services and technical support for libraries to receive, from the centralized database, copies of records that correspond to items in their own collections. These records, in either paper or machine-readable form, can then be added to an existing catalog.

Operating from the beginning with the Machine Readable Cataloging (MARC) standard for storing and manipulating cataloging records (Exhibit 7), the bibliographic utilities first were used exclusively in batch mode for the production of catalog cards for member libraries. Later, in the 1970s, the databases thus compiled were also offered online so that libraries could search and modify records interactively.

Although the technological evolution of bibliographic utilities and database producers and vendors was quite similar, there are also some substantial differences between them. Bibliographic utilities exist because all member libraries that produce and enter records into the centralized database use the same standards—the second edition of the *Anglo American Cataloging Rules*, or *AACR2*—for deciding the content of document representations and the MARC standard for structuring, maintaining, and manipulating these records in machine-readable form. With few exceptions, online catalogs in libraries accept and work with MARC records. Most of the database industry, on the other hand,

►NO HOLDINGS IN OCL - FOR HOLDINGS ENTER dh DEPRESS DISPLAY RECD SEND
OCLC: 3349989   Rec stat: n Entrd: 771108   Used: 790312 ¶
►Type: a Bib lvl: m   Govt pub: Lang: eng Source: Illus: a
Repr: Enc lvl: Conf pub: 0 Ctry: nyu Dat tp: s M/F/B: 10
Indx: 1 Mod rec: Festschr: 0 Cont: b
Desc: i Int lvl: Dates: 1977.   ¶
► 1   010   77-77941 ¶
► 2   040   DLC ‡c DLC ¶
► 3   020   0525171940 : ‡c S17.95 ¶
► 4   050 0   GN31.2 ‡b .L43 1977 ¶
► 5   082   573.2 ¶
► 6   090   ‡b ¶
► 7   049   OCLC ¶
► 8   100 10   Leakey, Richard E. ¶
► 9   245 10   Origins : ‡b what new discoveries reveal about the
emergence of our species and its possible future / ‡c Richard E. Leakey
and Roger Lewin. ¶
►10   260 0   New York : ‡b Dutton, ‡c c1977. ¶
►11   300   264 p. : ‡b ill. (some col.) ; ‡c 25 cm. ¶
►12   504   Bibliography: p. 257. ¶
►13   500   Includes index. ¶
►14   650 0   Anthropology. ¶
►15   650 0   Human evolution. ¶
►16   700 10   Lewin, Roger, ‡e joint author. ¶

EXHIBIT 7   Sample MARC record. SOURCE: Adapted from OCLC Online Union Catalog. Reprinted with permission of the OCLC Online Computer Library Center, Incorporated.

has never been standardized, and the content and structure of records varies considerably among databases. Furthermore, although the types of documents on all these systems are becoming increasingly diverse, the entries contained in bibliographic utilities and online catalogs typically tend to be bibliographic citations relating to items in the collections of libraries. The database industry, however, provides not only bibliographic data but also other types of records, including numeric data and even the full text of documents.

The scenario drawn in this section is greatly simplified, and it is, in fact, evolving in several key ways. Boundaries are no longer clear regarding the roles various organizations can play and the kind of information they provide access to, and there are many other kinds of databases and organizations involved in this arena. Much of the remainder of this chapter provides a sense of the richness and diversity of this continually changing environment.

TRENDS IN THE INDUSTRY

By every indicator, the online industry is growing continuously. A good idea of its current size and diversity can be gained by browsing through a current directory of databases, including *Computer-Readable Databases* (Marcaccio, Adams, and Williams, 1990) and the *Directory of Online Databases* (Cuadra Associates, 1992). Although this is a dynamic market—databases and vendors sometimes do not survive for long—the overall trend has been toward a net increase.

Several factors have contributed to this growth. Williams (1988, 1992) states that the number of databases offered in online and batch modes doubled from 300 to 600 between 1975 and 1981 and quintupled from 600 to 3,000 between 1981 and 1985. One million searches were performed in 1975 and 15 million in 1985. And the number of database records increased from 52 million in 1975 to 1.68 billion in 1985 (Williams, 1980a, 1988). Williams (1992) also states that by 1991, 34.5 million searches were performed in 7,637 databases containing 4 billion records.

The July 1992 *Directory of Online Databases* (Cuadra Associates, 1992), which includes only online sources, lists more than 5,300 online databases developed by 2,158 producers and made searchable by 731 vendors. These databases and online services are offered all over the world. In fact, the internationalization of the online industry has been a growing trend that is likely to continue (Landau, 1988), with companies developing overseas and foreign investments being made in many areas, including the United States.

Bibliographic utilities and online catalogs show a similar evolution. In 1976, there were only 2 million cataloging records in the machine-readable database maintained by OCLC, the largest bibliographic utility. In 1991, there were more than 23 million records (OCLC, Inc., 1991). In the 1970s, there were only a handful of academic institutions with an economic and technical infrastructure rich enough to develop and support online catalogs. Today, technological developments, particularly the introduction of affordable online catalog software and hardware, have made it possible for all sizes and types of libraries to create and maintain an online catalog. There are undoubtedly thousands now in existence.

The online industry is not only large, it is also very complex. Compare Exhibit 5 in Chapter 1, which shows database producers and vendors and their roles, with Exhibit 8, which considers these organizations along with others involved in the database-use chain (Williams, 1986). The roles of the producer (to create databases) and vendor (to process these databases and make them searchable online) have already been mentioned. Gateway services came into being more recently (around the mid-1980s) and were introduced specifically because of the proliferation of databases and online services. They allow users

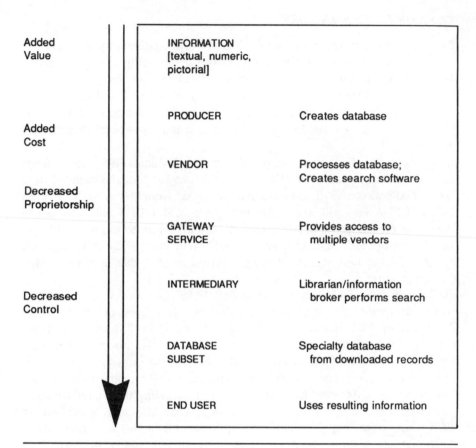

Added
Value

INFORMATION
[textual, numeric,
pictorial]

PRODUCER   Creates database

Added
Cost

VENDOR   Processes database;
                        Creates search software

Decreased
Proprietorship

GATEWAY   Provides access to
SERVICE   multiple vendors

INTERMEDIARY   Librarian/information
                           broker performs search

Decreased
Control

DATABASE   Specialty database
SUBSET   from downloaded records

END USER   Uses resulting information

EXHIBIT 8   Database-use chain. SOURCE: **Adapted from Williams (1986) by permission of John Wiley & Sons, Inc.**

to access a variety of remote online services through a single "gateway" computer and often provide a common interface to these services as well, a very useful feature that eliminates the need to learn the different commands needed to access each system. Databases can be searched by intermediaries (information professionals in libraries or information brokerage firms). Results are sometimes used to create a new database subset, often referred to as an "in-house" database, which can then be searched locally in the library or information center. Finally, the end user interprets and uses the resulting information.

Although all these players currently exist in today's information industry, they are not always operating every time a search is performed. Furthermore, the same organization or individual can occupy more than one role in this chain. The National Library of Medicine (NLM), for example, both produces and sells access to its MEDLINE database.

As one moves down the database-use chain, value is added by the processing or screening of data. This often results in an added cost, which is usually passed on to the user. Each step along the chain increases the potential for access to the stored information, but this is achieved at the expense of less control. Moreover, adding value increases the danger of distorting the original message—something important might be left out, changed, or added.

Furthermore, as the distance between the published information and the customer increases, and more and more organizations provide access to this information, it becomes increasingly difficult to decide not only who should assess the user's needs and meet them, but which user's needs are more usefully and appropriately met by a given information product or service—those of the intermediary user or the end user. It also complicates the choice for the user who is assessing options for gaining access to information sources.

The database-use chain also can describe the roles played by bibliographic utilities, libraries, and online catalogs. The utilities can be considered both the producers and vendors of cataloging records in the MARC format. Intermediaries in this case are librarians who search, modify, and request copies of MARC records from the database. The online catalog then effectively becomes a database subset, processed, indexed, and made searchable in ways deemed appropriate for that library's end users.

INFORMATION PRODUCTS AND SERVICES

The most important information product is the machine-readable database, which can be described by its scope or subject matter, the physical form of its contents, or its various uses.

Because no database contains all the world's information, all databases are somehow restricted in their scope. One very common restriction is subject area. The first databases were restricted to the scientific and technical information required by their sponsoring governmental agencies. When the commercial sector began to develop databases in the 1970s, abstracting and indexing services extended the offerings to other domains: first to engineering and the applied sciences, then to the social sciences (including business and economics), and finally to the arts and humanities. Virtually all these databases contain information that is primarily of interest to the scholar, businessman, or engineer. Later, however, databases were developed that focus on material of interest to the ordinary citizen—from consumer information for a wide variety of products to practical information on child care, drugs, and similar everday concerns (Williams, 1985).

Databases can also be grouped by the form of the data they contain and the uses to which they can be put. A number of dichotomies are presented in the literature:

1. *Word-oriented versus number- or picture-oriented.* Databases are viewed in terms of whether the data they contain are primarily textual or in some other format, such as numeric or graphic (Williams, 1985).

2. *Bibliographic versus nonbibliographic.* Databases containing citations to the literature are placed in one group and all other databases are placed in another group that includes directory, full-text, and numeric databases (Borgman, Moghdam, and Corbett, 1984).

3. *Reference versus source.* Reference databases are bibliographic as well as databases containing entries from sources such as directories of establishments, individuals, and software. Source databases are all other databases containing primary data, such as numeric information and the full text of documents (Harter, 1986).

Databases in machine-readable form can thus be placed in one of five different categories reflecting their content, purpose, and scope:

1. *Bibliographic/reference/word-oriented databases* contain citations to the primary literature. They are used to perform retrospective and SDI searches, usually in support of research and scholarly activities. They are sometimes restricted by the subject or the form of documents they provide access to (for example, technical reports, monographs, periodical articles). Exhibit 9A shows a sample record from *America: History and Life,* which contains citations dating from 1964 to the full range of U.S. and Canadian history, area studies, and current affairs literature.

2. *Bibliographic/referral/word-oriented databases* contain information about people, companies, research projects, and media such as software and audiovisual materials. They are not used to point to literature sources but to answer questions about nonprint sources; they are often used to answer ready-reference queries. Exhibit 9B shows a sample record from a typical referral database (*American Men and Women of Science*) that contains biographical data on 130,000 American and Canadian scientists in the physical and biological sciences.

3. *Nonbibliographic/source/word-oriented* databases are full-text databases that contain the texts of original documents in machine-readable form. These documents can be journal articles, newspapers, newsletters, encyclopedias, dictionaries, and other types of reference books. Full-text databases are used to answer factual questions and to retrieve citations to the literature. In the

A: *America: History and Life (Bibliographic/Reference)*

950008   26-8
AMERICAN HOMESTEADERS AND THE CANADIAN PRAIRIES, 1899 AND 1909.
  Percy, Michael B ; Woroby, Tamara
  Explorations in Economic History 1987 24(1): 77-100.
  NOTE: Based on published census records and other public documents; 2
  fig., 3 tables, 12 notes, ref., appendix.
DOCUMENT TYPE: ARTICLE
ABSTRACT: The out-migration of American homesteaders to the Canadian
  prairies is best explained by human-capital investments in wheat farming
  in 1899 and 1909 and by the techniques of dry farming in 1899. Canadian
  promotional expenditures also contributed to higher rates of
  out-migration. High tenancy rate and low agricultural wages in the
  United States were not important contributors to out-migration. (P. J.
  Coleman)
DESCRIPTORS: Prairie Provinces ; USA ; Homesteading and Homesteaders ;
  Agriculture ; 1894-1913 ; Migration
HISTORICAL PERIOD: 1890D 1900D 1910D 1800H 1900H
  HISTORICAL PERIOD (Starting): 1894
  HISTORICAL PERIOD (Ending): 1913

B: *American Men and Women of Science (Bibliographic/Referral)*

0010037
Brown, Donald D
  DISCIPLINE: BIOLOGY, GENERAL (00200207)
  SUBJECT SPECIALTY: DEVELOPMENTAL BIOLOGY
  BORN: Cincinnati, Ohio, Dec 30, 31 MARRIED: 57 NO. OF CHILDREN: 3
  EDUCATION: Univ Chicago MS & MD 56
  HONORARY DEGREES: DSci Univ Chicago 76 Univ Maryland 83
  PROFESSIONAL EXPERIENCE: Intern Charity Hosp New Orleans La 56-57; res
    assoc biochem NIMH 57-59; spec fel Pasteur Inst Paris 59-60; spec fel
    60-61 MEM STAFF BIOCHEM CARNEGIE INST DEPT EMBRYOL 61 to present, DIR
    DEPT EMBRYOL 76 to present
  CONCURRENT POSITIONS: Prof Johns Hopkins Univ 69 to present
  MEMBERSHIPS: Nat Acad Sci; Am Soc Biol Chem; Soc Develop Biol; Am Acad
    Arts & Sci; Am Soc Cell Biol (pres 92); Am Philos Soc
  HONORS AND AWARDS: US Steel Found Award Molecular Biol Nat Acad Sci 73; V
    D Mattia Lectr Roche Inst Molecular Biol 75; Boris Pregel Award NY Acad
    Sci 77; Ross G Harrison Prize Int Soc Develop Biologists 81; Feodor
    Lynen Medal 87
  RESEARCH: Control of genes during development; isolation of genes
  ADDRESS: Dept Embryol, Carnegie Inst Washington 115 W University Pkwy
    Baltimore , MD 21210

**EXHIBIT 9 Sample bibliographic database records. SOURCES: Exhibit 9A
reprinted from DIALOG File 38 by permission of ABC-CLIO; Exhibit 9B reprinted
from *American Men & Women of Science 1992–1993*, 18th Edition, © 1992,
by Reed Publishing (USA) Inc., p. 795, with permission of R. R. Bowker, a
Reed Reference Publishing Company.**

118565   825040   **COMPLETE TEXT AVAILABLE**
How Global Companies Win Out
Hout, Thomas - Boston Consulting Group ; Porter, Michael E. - Harvard
Univ. Graduate School of Business Administration ; Rudden, Eileen - Boston
Consulting Group
HARVARD BUSINESS REVIEW, Sep/Oct 1982, p. 98
TEXT:
Hold that obituary on American manufacturers. Some not only refuse to die but even dominate
their businesses worldwide. At the same time Ford struggles to keep up with Toyota, Caterpillar
thrives in competition with another Japanese powerhouse, Komatsu. Though Zenith has been hurt
in consumer electronics, Hewlett-Packard and Tektronix together profitably control 50% of the world's
industrial test and measurement instrument market. American forklift truck producers may retreat under
Japanese pressure, but two U.S. chemical companies--Du Pont and Dow--dramatically outperform their
competitors.

How do these American producers hold and even increase profitability against international competitors? By forging integrated, global strategies to exploit their potential; and by having a long-term
outlook, investing aggressively, and managing factories carefully.

The main reason is that today's international competition in many industries is very different from
what it has been. To succeed, an international company may need to change from a multidomestic
competitor, which allows individual subsidiaries to compete independently in different domestic markets,
to a global organization, which pits its entire worldwide system of product and market position against
the competition. (For a more complete discussion of this distinction, see the ruled insert.)

The global company--whatever its nationality--tries to control leverage points, from cross-national
production scale economies to the foreign competitors' sources of cash flow. By taking unconventional
action, such as lowering prices of an important product or in key markets, the company makes the
competitor's response more expensive and difficult. Its main objective is to improve its own effectiveness
while eroding that of its competitors.

Not all companies can or should forge a global strategy. While the rewards of competing globally are
great, so are the risks. Major policy and operating changes are required. Competing globally demands
a number of unconventional approaches to managing a multinational business to sometimes allow:

Major investment projects with zero or even negative ROI. Financial performance targets that vary
widely among foreign subsidiaries. Product lines deliberately overdesigned or underpriced in some
markets. A view of country-by-country market positions as interdependent and not as independent
elements of a worldwide portfolio to be increased or decreased depending on profitability. Construction
of production facilities in both high and low labor-cost countries.

Not all international businesses lend themselves to global competition. Many are multidomestic in
nature and are likely to remain so, competing on a domestic-market-by-domestic-market basis. Typically
these businesses have products that differ greatly among country markets and have high transportation
costs, or their industries lack sufficient scale economies to yield the global competitors a significant
competitive edge.

Before entering the global arena, you must first decide whether your company's industry has the right
characteristics to favor a global competitor. A careful examination of the economies of the business will
highlight its ripeness for global competition. Simply put, the potential for global competition is greatest
when significant benefits are gained from worldwide volume--in terms of either reduced unit costs or
superior reputation or service--and are greater than the additional costs of serving that volume.

SEE RECORD 118564 FOR A CONTINUATION OF THIS TEXT.

**EXHIBIT 10 Sample record from *Harvard Business Review* (nonbiblio-
graphic/source [full text]). SOURCE: Adapted from machine-readable Dialog
file 122. Reprinted with permission of *Harvard Business Review*.**

```
0126913      USDA RS   92/04/00   P32     United States
rice. land use. yr begin 8/1.
```

YEAR	MIL acres
1979	2.89
1980	3.38
1981	3.83
1982	3.29
1983	2.19
1984	2.83
1985	2.51
1986	2.38
1987	2.36
1988	2.93
1989	2.73
1990	2.90
1991	2.86

```
GROWTH RATE= -1.8%
CC=1USA     PC=0112000     EC=411
```

EXHIBIT 11 Sample record from PTS U.S. Time Series (nonbibliographic/ source [numeric]). SOURCE: Adapted from DIALOG File 82. Reprinted with permission of Predicasts.

latter case, they serve the same function as a bibliographic database. A full-text record from *Harvard Business Review* is shown in Exhibit 10; that file contains the complete text equivalent and bibliographic database of the full-length journal articles from 1976 onward.

4. *Nonbibliographic/source/number-oriented databases* are numeric databases, found particularly in the sciences, business, and economics. These are not used to perform complex subject searches but to retrieve factual, numeric data in a manner that is usually straightforward and uncomplicated. The real power of numeric databases, however, lies in their analysis and display capabilities. For example, they can be used to perform sophisticated statistical analyses, do forecasting, and identify chemical compounds, and they can display raw numbers or format these data into charts or graphs (Berger and Wanger, 1982). Exhibit 11 shows a sample of time series data from the "PTS U.S. Time Series," which contains statistical data for a period of more than 20 years, as well as a calculated growth rate for data covering all aspects of national economics, demographics, industry, finance, and other business activities.

04183916 DIALOG File 226: TRADEMARKSCAN(r)-Federal
DESIGN ONLY
    INTL CLASS: 5   (Pharmaceuticals)
                    42   (Miscellaneous Service Marks)
    U.S. CLASS: 44   (Dental, Medical & Surgical Appliances)
                   100   (Miscellaneous Service Marks)
    T&T U.S. CLASS: 18 (Medicines & Pharmaceutical Preparations)
    STATUS: Pending; Non-Final Action - Mailed
    GOODS/SERVICES: (INT. CL. 5) VETERINARY PRODUCTS (INT. CL. 42)
        SERVICES, MEDICAL INFORMATION, AND INFORMATION SERVICES
        TO PET OWNERS AND VETERINARIANS
    SERIAL NO.: 74-183,916
    FIRST USE: June 14, 1991 (Intl Class 5)
               June 14, 1991 (Intl Class 42)
    FIRST COMMERCE: June 14, 1991 (Intl Class 5)
                    June 14, 1991 (Intl Class 42)
    FILED: July 11, 1991
    ORIGINAL APPLICANT: PROFESSIONAL COMMUNICATIONS GROUP,
        INC. (New York Corporation), 40 SANDRINGHAM RD., P.O. BOX 10515,
        ROCHESTER, NY (New York), 16410, USA (United States of America)
    FILING CORRESPONDENT: PROFESSIONAL COMMUNICATIONS
        GROUP, INC., 40 SANDRINGHAM RD., P.O. BOX 10515, ROCHESTER,
        NY 14610
    DESIGN CODES:
        03   (ANIMALS)
        0301   (CATS, DOGS, WOLVES, FOXES, BEARS)
        030104   (DOMESTIC CATS)
        030108   (OTHER DOMESTIC DOGS)
        030124   (STYLIZED ANIMALS IN THIS DIVISION (0301))
        030126   (COSTUMED ANIMALS IN THIS DIVISION (0301) & THOSE
                    WITH HUMAN ATTRIBUTES)
        02   (HUMAN BEINGS)
        0207   (HUMAN DRESS, ATTIRE OR APPEARANCE)
        020792   (OTHER MALE ANIMAL ATTIRE)
        10   (TOBACCO, SMOKERS' MATERIALS, FANS, TOILET
                    ARTICLES, MEDICAL DEVICES & APPARATUS, & TABLETS,
                    CAPSULES OR POWDERS)
        1007   (MEDICAL DEVICES & APPARATUS)
        100704   (BANDAGES, CASTS, SLINGS)

EXHIBIT 12 Sample record from TRADEMARKSCAN—FEDERAL (nonbiblio-graphic/source [image]). SOURCE: DIALOG File 226. Reprinted with permission of Thomson & Thomson.

5. *Nonbibliographic/source/picture-oriented databases* consist of actual images, usually in addition to text or numbers. Pictorial information retrieval is a relatively unexplored area, although attention has been given to the important differences between indexing and retrieving texts and images. Exhibit 12 shows a sample from TRADEMARKSCAN—FEDERAL. This file provides access to all active registered and pending trademarks on file in the U.S. Patent and Trademark Office. Much of its retrieval capability comes from its textual fields, although, in the future, it is intended that actual design elements will be directly searchable—for example, all active trademarks that have an eagle as part of the design (Thompson, 1989).

Whereas virtually all machine-readable databases initially had print counterparts, the information industry has evolved to the point where now many databases exist only in machine-readable form. This may be associated with the evolution from primarily paper-based to electronic information systems (Lancaster, 1978). It is particularly true of numeric databases, where part of the retrieval process involves manipulating and analyzing data—obviously not possible with a print product. But many full-text and bibliographic files can be found only in electronic form because their producers do not anticipate a large market for their highly specialized subject content.

In the 1980s, databases began to be produced on optical disk. It is now possible to find many databases on CD ROM, including that of the Educational Resources Information Center (ERIC) and MEDLINE (bibliographic); the *American Library Directory* (referral); Grolier's Electronic Encyclopedia (the *Academic American Encyclopedia*) (full text); and AmericanProfile (numeric). Nicholls and Van Den Elshout (1990), however, note that it has become difficult to neatly categorize CD-ROM products because an increasing number of types of product or content are found on a single disk. Consider OncoDisk, a complete reference source containing bibliographic references from the CancerLit index, PDQ (Physician's Data Query) treatment protocols, directories of physicians and medical organizations, and the full text of certain basic textbooks. By 1992, more than 1,300 CD-ROM products were commercially available, and this continues to be a rapidly growing segment of the industry.

Database Vendors

Vendors are those organizations that process databases and make them searchable through interactive software. There has been a steady rise in the number of vendors, from 59 in 1979 to more than 700 in 1992. Some provide only the technical infrastructure necessary to search the databases supplied to them; others produce databases as well. Major vendors include BRS Information Technologies and ORBIT Search Service (both subsidiaries of InfoPro Technologies);

A. PSYCINFO

Document I

00700633   76-37259

Light therapy for seasonal affective disorder: A review of efficacy.

Terman, Michael; Terman, Jiuan S.; Quitkin, Frederic M.; McGrath, Patrick J. et al

Columbia U, New York State Psychiatric Inst, US

Neuropsychopharmacology

1989 Mar Vol 2(1) 1-22

Coden; NEROEW   ISSN; 0893133X

Journal Announcement; 7611

Language; English

Document Type; JOURNAL ARTICLE

Composite Age; ADULT

Major Descriptors; *ILLUMINATION; *TREATMENT; *SEASONAL VARIATIONS; *AFFECTIVE DISTURBANCES

Minor Descriptors; ADULTHOOD

Descriptor Codes; 24420; 54190; 46030; 01260; 01150

Identifiers; light therapy efficacy, patients with seasonal affective disorder

Section Headings; 3300 -TREATMENT AND PREVENTION

Document II

00569589   74-00475

A circadian pacemaker for visual sensitivity?

Terman, Michael; Terman, Jiuan

Columbia U, New York State Psychiatric Inst

Annals of the New York Academy of Sciences

1985 Mar Vol 453 147-161

Coden; ANYAA9   ISSN; 00778923

Journal Announcement; 7401

Language; English

Document Type; JOURNAL ARTICLE

Major Descriptors; *VISUAL PERCEPTION; *BIOLOGICAL RHYTHMS; *PROFESSIONAL MEETINGS AND SYMPOSIA

Minor Descriptors; RATS

Descriptor Codes; 55980; 05980; 40740; 42930

Identifiers; interactions between visual sensory & circadian functions, male rats, conference presentation

Section Headings; 2520 -NEUROLOGY & ELECTROPHYSIOLOGY

B. MEDLINE

07119743 90026743

Light therapy for seasonal affective disorder. A review of efficacy.

Terman M; Terman JS; Quitkin FM; McGrath PJ; Stewart JW; Rafferty B

Department of Psychiatry, Columbia University, New York, NY.

Neuropsychopharmacology   Mar 1989, 2 (1) p1-22, ISSN 0893-133X

Journal Code; ADQ

Contract/Grant No.; KO2 MH00461; RO1 MH42931; MHCRC 30906

Languages; ENGLISH

Document type; CLINICAL TRIAL; JOURNAL ARTICLE; MULTICENTER STUDY

JOURNAL ANNOUNCEMENT; 9002

Subfile; INDEX MEDICUS

Tags; Female; Human; Male; Support, U.S. Gov't, P.H.S.

Descriptors; *Affective Disorders--Therapy--TH; *Phototherapy; Circadian Rhythm; Multicenter Studies; Seasons

C. *EMBASE*

7560871 EMBASE No; 89126194

Light therapy for Seasonal Affective Disorder; A review of efficacy

Terman M.; Terman J.S.; Quitkin F.M.; McGrath P.J.; Stewart J.W.; Rafferty B.

Department of Psychiatry, Columbia University, Columbia, NY USA

NEUROPSYCHOPHARMACOLOGY (USA) , 1989, 2/1 (1-22) CODEN: NEROE ISSN: 0893-133X

LANGUAGES: English

SUBFILES: 032

EMTAGS:

Psychological aspects 0138; Therapy 0160; Short survey 0002; Human 0888

MEDICAL DESCRIPTORS:

*affective neurosis--therapy--th; *phototherapy

circadian rhythm; seasonal variation; statistics

EXHIBIT 13 Sample database records revealing lack of standardization. SOURCES: A - reprinted with permission of the American Psychological Association, publisher of *Psychological Abstracts* and the PSYCINFO Database (© 1967–1992); B - reprinted with permission of the National Library of Medicine; C - reprinted with permission of Elsevier Science Publishers B.V.

CompuServe Information Service; Data-Star; Dialog Information Services; Dow Jones News/Retrieval; I. P. Sharp Associates; Mead Data Central; the National Library of Medicine; OCLC; Questel; STN International; and VU/TEXT.

Some vendors provide access to a wide variety of databases (for example, DIALOG and BRS) and others specialize, whether by subject matter (NLM has databases related to biomedicine), the type of databases they provide access to (Mead has mainly full-text databases, and OCLC specializes in bibliographic information), and their intended users (CompuServe targets users with personal computers in their homes). In many cases, however, a vendor may provide access to only one database, the one it produces.

Vendors process the databases, indexing them in various ways. The examples in Exhibits 9 to 12 show entries for a selection of different types of databases offered by DIALOG. In addition to allowing users to access the data in each record by fields such as title, author (Exhibits 9A and 10), name of biographee (Exhibit 9B), and product code (Exhibit 11), vendors also often process the contents of each field—for example, individual words may be extracted and added to the indexes for bibliographic and full-text databases.

Given that individual databases and search services have evolved relatively independently of one another, it is not surprising that there is tremendous variety in how information products are developed, processed, and accessed. Williams (1980b) summarizes the problems associated with the lack of standardization in the database industry. Access to information is highly nonstandardized in the following ways:

1. Database producers have their own formats for determining the structure and content of records. Records in the different databases may vary in the way they refer to the same concept or a person's name (this is referred to as a lack of vocabulary control or authority control). In addition, records within the same database may differ in how they represent an individual's name.

2. Database vendors process databases in different ways.

3. Protocols (command names and syntax) for searching databases differ from vendor to vendor.

These points are illustrated in Exhibits 13 and 14. Exhibit 13 shows sample records for two different documents. Column 1 shows three separate representations for a single document produced by different organizations (the American Psychological Association, the National Library of Medicine, and Excerpta Medica). Column 2 displays a record for a different document in the PsycINFO database. Data elements extracted from these records and displayed in Exhibit 14A clearly show the lack of standardization among subject and author representations. The concept "seasonal affective disorders," which is

A. Subject and author field elements

	DOCUMENT I		DOCUMENT II
Database	*Subject*	*Author*	*Author*
PSYCINFO (a)	Affective disturbances Seasonal variations	Terman, Jiuan S.	Terman, Jiuan
MEDLINE (b)	Affective disorders Seasons	Terman JS	
EMBASE (c)	Affective neurosis Seasonal variation	Terman J.S.	

B. Processing and search protocols of vendors

Vendor	*Processing*	*Search statement*
DIALOG	Descriptors entered into index as phrases	Select affective disorders
BRS	Descriptors hyphenated and entered into index	Search affective-disorders

EXHIBIT 14   Examples of lack of standardization in information systems.

needed to describe a concept in the same primary document, is represented by three different combinations of index terms. Further, one of the authors (Jiuan Terman) is not represented consistently among the different producers' records or even by the same producer describing two different documents by the same individual. (The producers of databases, however, frequently accept the form of author name that appears in the source they are indexing/abstracting, so some of the inconsistency is due to the primary publisher or, occasionally, even to the author.)

Exhibit 14B illustrates the lack of standardization introduced by the vendors. The most obvious way they differ is in their command names; however, there are also differences in processing that must be considered, such as descriptors that are hyphenated in BRS but not in DIALOG.

Users must allow for this lack of standardization when interacting with information systems, but it certainly adds to the complexities of searching. The problem was not unmanageable when search intermediaries (such as librarians) were frequent users of a small number of systems and databases, because they could learn to search them all effectively. The growing number of vendors and producers, however, makes it harder, if not impossible, for the intermediary to know about all the databases and vendors in even one subject area. Furthermore, end users now form a growing market sector, and they often use the systems infrequently, which gives them little opportunity to acquire much technical knowledge.

There are basically two ways to address the variety problem: (1) eliminate it at the source or (2) make it transparent to the user. Eliminating it at the source would involve an agreement by all producers to standardize the content and structure of different categories of databases (for example, bibliographic). This is essentially what has happened with the content of library catalog data through adherence to cataloging codes and the MARC record structure; however, these MARC records are processed and made searchable in a variety of ways by different online catalog software. Requiring commercial vendors to standardize their processing and searching protocols has also met with limited success, although a subcommittee of the National Information Standards Organization (NISO) has been charged with creating a common command language to standardize the protocols needed to search various online systems (Morrison, 1989).

Making the variety problem transparent involves creating common interfaces so that the user does not need to remember and manipulate the variety in log on procedures, command syntax, searchable fields, and representation of data such as names and subjects. There are several options here (Tenopir, 1986):

1. *End user systems.* These are developed and maintained by vendors and provide either menu-driven or simplified versions of commands to search families of databases on their systems. Examples are BRS/Afterdark (BRS) and Knowledge Index (DIALOG).

2. *Front-end software.* These are microcomputer software packages that help users formulate search strategies, usually offline, and then connect automatically to a host to upload and run the search. Examples are PRO-SEARCH and WILSEARCH.

3. *Gateways.* These connect a user through another host mainframe computer (a gateway service) to one or more vendors. Many gateways also provide automatic search assistance features that help with search strategy development and vendor database selection. A well-known example of such a gateway is EASYNET.

A variety of front-end systems also exist for library catalogs, where end users have always been the major clientele.

An important advantage of these systems—the ability to easily conduct a search—also turns out to be a major disadvantage and a major issue in their ongoing development. Because it is relatively easy to construct a search, users may think that their searches are more successful than they really are (Smith, 1986). The situation remains because these user-friendly systems continue to automate only the relatively easy aspects of database selection and individual search strategy development. More difficult problems, such as automatically modifying the terminology in a search strategy on the basis of previous results (Ide and Salton, 1971) and switching terminology from that of one database to another (Niehoff and Mack, 1985), continue to be explored in information retrieval systems research.

ONLINE RETRIEVAL SYSTEMS AND ONLINE CATALOGS

One goal of this book is to clarify and broaden the established definition of an information storage and retrieval system. Historically, the field of library and information science dealt with the library catalog as a retrieval environment completely different and isolated from the database industry. This was unfortunate because it resulted in separate and isolated literatures, a situation that to some extent continues even today. Perhaps this is understandable, given the typical scenario depicted by Potter (1989):

Today most catalogs provide access only to the books and the set titles of serials. Readers interested in the other types of materials are compelled to consult indexes that are separate from the catalog such as printed indexes, CD-ROM databases, or commercial online services. (p. 99)

The literature, then, may have reflected the separateness of the library catalog from other information products. It is becoming clear, however, that the differences set out in the scenario between the "catalog" and the "index" and the technical infrastructure that surrounds them are becoming less and less pronounced. Several trends documented in the literature continue to be increasingly prevalent and serve to explain how this situation is developing.

Historically, there was a difference between vendors like DIALOG, which provided searchable databases, and bibliographic utilities like OCLC, which provided databases of records for producing catalog entries. Today, bibliographic utilities are taking on more roles associated with commercial online vendors and gateways. For example, OCLC's searching functions used to be strictly related to the display of MARC records for producing catalog records, but the database of MARC records can now be searched via a very powerful retrieval language (EPIC), with all the retrieval capabilities of other major vendors (Whitcomb, 1990). Furthermore, OCLC has produced CD-ROM products

(MARC records and the ERIC database) since the mid-1980s and is now beginning to load databases (for example, ERIC and GPO *Monthly Catalog*) onto its mainframe computer. In 1991, OCLC introduced a new product, First Search™, designed primarily for end users. It provides access to the OCLC Online Union Catalog and also to a wide range of other bibliographic databases and reference tools produced by governmental and commercial agencies.

The domains for accessing MARC cataloging records and records supplied by the commercial producers were quite clear, but this also is changing. Many commercial vendors provide access to MARC databases (including those provided by the Library of Congress and the British Library). And online catalogs are increasingly loading and making available machine-readable indexes to journal articles, special collections, and the full text of certain materials like encyclopedias (Potter, 1989). Furthermore, it is now possible to retrieve information from a wide variety of heterogeneous information resources that are now accessible via the Internet, a worldwide network of computer networks (Krol, 1992). From a given node or "host" on the Internet, a user can access a wide variety of information products at other hosts, including traditional bibliographic databases, online library catalogs, full texts of journals and books, images, and so forth. Search and retrieval software, such as GOPHER, WAIS (Wide Area Information Server), and WWW (World Wide Web), is also available in many cases, making it possible to access this information from a common interface no matter what the database type or structure.

Possibly the most important point is that the same questions that have been asked about commercial and experimental retrieval systems providing access primarily to journal articles can be asked of library catalogs. These involve the issue of retrieval performance and what affects it—index language, indexing policy, number of records in the database, and related factors.

3

Subject Access: Problems and Performance Criteria

A user searching a database for items on a particular subject wants to find some or all of the items that deal with the subject and avoid retrieving items that do not. This is true for a database of books in a library or group of libraries, as well as for databases that provide access to journal articles and other bibliographic items from a wide variety of sources.

The subject access problem is more complicated than it initially appears. It is depicted graphically in Exhibit 15. The entire rectangle represents a database and the items it contains. Items denoted by "+" are those that a hypothetical requester would find useful in satisfying an information need. Items that would not be judged useful are denoted by "−". For any particular information need, there will be many more "−" than "+" items. Indeed, if the diagram was drawn "to scale," one would expect that the 11 useful items might be accompanied by a wall of useless ones. The problem is to retrieve as many as possible of the useful items and as few as possible of the useless ones.

MEASURES OF RETRIEVAL PERFORMANCE

The smaller of the two interior rectangles in Exhibit 15 represents the results of a search performed in the database. It retrieved 57 items, of which 6 were useful and 51 were not useful. The ratio of useful items to total items retrieved (6/57, or approximately 0.1) is usually referred to as a precision ratio. The ratio commonly used to express the extent to which all useful items are found is the recall ratio. In this case the recall ratio is 6/11, or approximately 0.54.

To improve recall in this situation, one would probably need to search more broadly. This is depicted in the larger of the two interior rectangles, where recall has been raised to 8/11 (0.73) but precision has declined further to

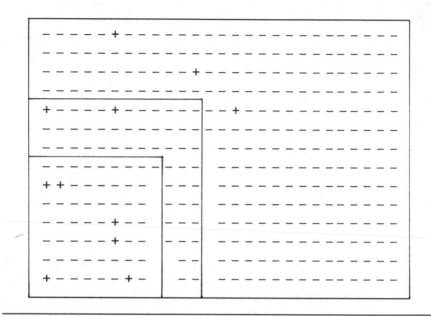

EXHIBIT 15   The problem of retrieving pertinent items from a database.

8/112, or approximately 0.07. An unfortunate characteristic of the information retrieval situation is that an improvement in recall will usually cause a deterioration in precision and vice versa.

Exhibit 15 suggests another phenomenon. It might be possible to search broadly enough to find all the useful items (achieve 100 percent recall), but precision would probably be intolerable. Furthermore, the larger the database the less tolerable will be a low precision. Although a user might be willing to look at abstracts of, say, 57 items to find 6 useful ones, he or she may be much less willing to examine 570 abstracts for 60 useful ones. With very large databases, then, it becomes increasingly difficult to achieve an acceptable level of recall at a tolerable level of precision. This phenomenon is readily apparent today in the online catalogs of very large libraries, in which a search on a subject heading or a keyword in a title may well retrieve several hundred records.

In this book, the term *recall* will be used to refer to the ability to retrieve useful items, and *precision* will be used to refer to the ability to avoid useless ones. These and other measures of performance of database searches are discussed in more detail in Chapter 9.

Factors Affecting the Performance of Retrieval Systems

Many factors determine whether or not a database search is successful. These are illustrated at the macrolevel in Exhibit 16. The diagram depicts a situation in which the user of a library or information center approaches an information specialist to request that a particular database be searched. Various steps occur before the results of the search are delivered to the user, and recall or precision failures can occur at each step.

First, the information specialist must gain a clear understanding of what the user is really seeking. The user's information need must be transmitted to the searcher as some form of request. Such requests are rarely exact representations of the underlying information needs. The request is then transformed into a search strategy appropriate to the database to be consulted. This strategy may be less than perfect, especially if the information specialist does not

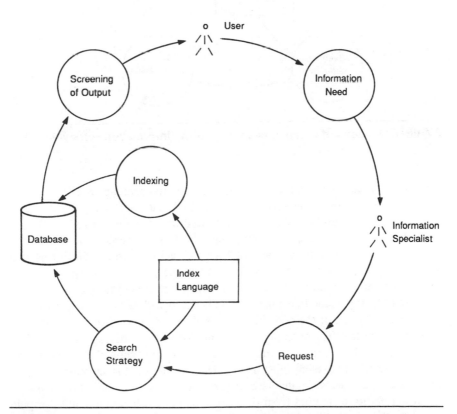

EXHIBIT 16   Factors affecting the performance of a database search.

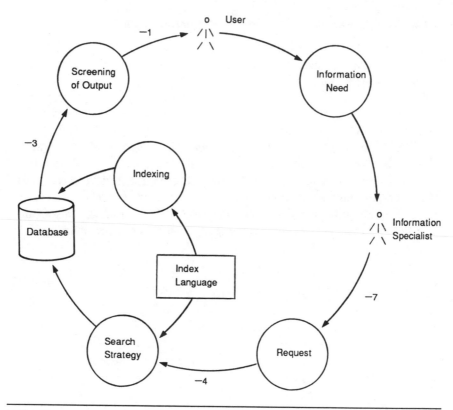

EXHIBIT 17   Loss of recall at each step in the information retrieval chain.

clearly understand what the user wants; perhaps the searcher overlooks some important terms, or some terms that are used may not really be relevant. Moreover, if the searcher uses terms that are drawn from a controlled vocabulary, these may not adequately represent the desired subject matter or the structure of the vocabulary may not lead the searcher to all the terms that are needed for a comprehensive search. When the search strategy is matched against the database, all the database characteristics come into play: errors can occur in indexing, some items may not be indexed with enough terms (a matter of indexing policy), or the controlled vocabulary may not adequately represent the subject matter (for example, it may not be sufficiently specific). Before the results are delivered to the user, the searcher may "screen" them and send only those items that seem most useful. The success of this screening process depends on the searcher's understanding of the user's information need and on his or her ability to predict from the search output (for example, bibliographic references or references and abstracts) whether or not items are likely to be relevant.

Exhibit 16 shows why it is difficult to perform a search that will give high recall at an acceptable level of precision, especially in large databases. This difficulty can be demonstrated further through an example (Exhibit 17). Suppose in the database to be searched, there are 30 items that the user would judge useful in satisfying his or her information need. Unfortunately, because the user's request is imperfect, 7 of the 30 items will not be retrieved. The search strategy is not complete, since the searcher overlooks a few relevant terms, and this causes four more useful items to be missed. Inadequacies in the indexing of the database are responsible for further failures, and three more items are lost. Finally, the searcher fails to send to the user one of the retrieved items that the user would actually judge useful, perhaps because the bibliographic record does not clearly indicate its relevance. Obviously, the user will not receive all the items that would be useful, but rather only 15 of them (30 −7 −4 −3 −1). The recall ratio for the search is only 0.5 (15/30) because some items have been lost at each step in the chain. By the same token, precision failures also may occur at each step (for example, due to lack of specificity in the vocabulary or to further indexing errors), so the search may only achieve, say, a recall of 0.5 and a precision of 0.4.

As this discussion indicates, the major factors that affect the performance of a subject search in a database are intellectual rather than technological. These factors are discussed in detail in later chapters.

PERTINENCE AND RELEVANCE

The term *relevance* is frequently used to express the appropriateness of a document for a particular user. But it is not a precise term. The remainder of this chapter attempts to draw a meaningful distinction between *pertinence* and *relevance,* two terms that have been used in the literature of information science to express a relationship between a document and a request for information, a need for information, or an individual who requests or needs information. Thus, it might be said that a particular document is relevant, or pertinent, to a particular request, information need, or individual who requests information on a particular subject. The relationship implied by these terms is extremely important to the evaluation of information services. Unfortunately, the two terms have been used rather loosely in the literature, and much controversy exists on what the two terms actually mean and whether or not relevance is in fact germane to the evaluation of information services. Rees and Saracevic (1966), for example, raise the following questions:

1. Is relevance an adequate criterion for measures; is it the only criterion?

2. If relevance is an adequate criterion, what does it represent?

3. Can relevance be used at all in practice; is it measurable? If so, under what conditions (restrictions, constraints) can it be employed? (p. 227)

The concept of relevance needs to be viewed in the broader context of a person needing information and coming to an information retrieval system to seek it. In this connection, it is important to distinguish among information needs, their recognition, and their expression. Information retrieval systems cannot respond to the information needs of individuals as such but only to expressions of the needs; an individual who needs information must recognize the need and be sufficiently aroused to take steps to satisfy it. Only after the individual recognizes the need and is sufficiently motivated can the need be expressed as a request to an information center. The degree to which the exact nature of the information need is recognized and the degree to which the need is accurately expressed determine, to a great extent, how successful the information service is in satisfying the user. The information service can operate only on the basis of the stated request (expressed need) and, clearly, cannot respond to unrecognized needs or even to recognized needs that are unexpressed. As pointed out in more detail in Chapter 4, one of the major challenges faced by any information service that operates in a delegated search mode is to ensure that expressed needs accurately reflect recognized needs. It is not always easy for the person who needs information to express that need clearly and unequivocally to the person who is to search for the information.

Let us assume, then, that a person who needs information comes to an information center to seek it. Let us also assume that this person does not need factual data but needs to see documents that describe or discuss a particular subject area—for example, the treatment of disease X with drug Y. The user tries to make this need known to the staff by a request statement. An information specialist converts the request into a search strategy that is then matched against one or more databases. Assume that the search is conducted in a computer-based system and that the output of the search is a printout of representations—for example, bibliographic references—of documents that match the search strategy, that is, documents that are so indexed that they satisfy the logical and terminological requirements of the strategy. There is now a whole set of possible relationships to contend with, as depicted in Exhibit 18.

It is fairly certain that the document representations match the search strategy or they would not have been retrieved. It is less certain that the documents themselves match the search strategy. Some may have been indexed incorrectly. In other cases, the terms that caused the document to be retrieved

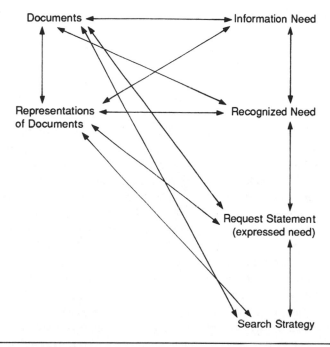

EXHIBIT 18 Some relationships important in the evaluation of information retrieval systems.

may be essentially unrelated in the document (a false coordination) or related in a different way from that wanted by the searcher (an incorrect term relationship). Some of the retrieved documents may match the search strategy but not the request statement (expressed need of the requester). This would occur, for example, if the search strategy included some terms that were inappropriate to the request or if the search was conducted at a higher generic level than that specified in the request. Some retrieved documents may match the request statement but not the recognized need of the user. This would occur when the request statement did not completely and accurately represent the recognized need of the requester. Finally, it is conceivable that some of the documents may match neither the request statement nor the recognized need but, completely fortuitously, match the actual information need. This would imply that the system has retrieved some items that the requester recognizes as helpful in satisfying the information requirement. These documents are outside the scope of the request statement because the user was unaware that documents of this type exist. Consequently, the recognized need could not be formulated with sufficient clarity to allow this type of document to be encompassed by the request statement.

Clearly, complex relationships exist among the information need, recognized need, expressed need, searching strategy, documents, and document representations. The entire situation is further complicated because some of the relationships are not constant over time. Both recognized needs and actual needs are likely to change. Thus, a document may match the recognized need of a requester one day but not the next; the user's perception of his or her need has changed.

Note that the innocuous word *match* has been used in this discussion to refer to various relationships among requests, information needs, documents, and document representations. It is now necessary to examine the types of matches that are involved, who can decide whether or not a match of a particular type has occurred, and what these matches might be called. The information specialist who conducts the search, or some other information specialist associated with the system, is probably best qualified to determine whether the document representation matches the search strategy. *Match* is really a very appropriate term for this relationship: A document representation matches if it contains a certain term, or combination of terms, included in the strategy. Anyone, in fact, who can read and understand the logic of the strategy can decide whether or not a match has occurred.

Whether or not a particular document matches a search strategy is also best determined by the person constructing the strategy, although it could possibly be decided by another information specialist. This situation is more complicated than the other in two respects: (1) We are concerned with more than a simple term or word match. We are now concerned with relationships among terms or words, that is, syntactic and semantic relationships. (2) The match we are concerned with is, in a sense, between a document and an *intended* strategy. Therefore, the person formulating the search strategy is in the best position to judge whether or not the intended match has occurred.

This situation is best illustrated by a simple example. Consider the case in which the searcher uses the strategy READING *and* EPILEPSY; that is, the searcher asks for documents that contain both words or that have been indexed under both terms. Several document representations containing the terms or words are retrieved—they all match the strategy. The system has retrieved what it was asked to retrieve, and the search programs have behaved perfectly. But the searcher, when looking at the set of documents corresponding to the retrieved representations, discovers that they are of two types: (1) a large group of documents discussing epilepsy caused by reading, that is, a kind of photic epilepsy, and (2) a small group of documents discussing the reading abilities of epileptic children. It is the first group only that the searcher intended to retrieve. The second group was not wanted and, perhaps, not expected.

In this case, all the representations retrieved match the search strategy, but some do not match the intended strategy. The fault lies not with the search programs or with the searcher's interpretation of the requester's needs, but with the indexing procedures and the index language of the system. If the indexing procedures were such that relationships among terms could be specified precisely—for instance, by the use of role indicators (for example, READING (4) and EPILEPSY (2), where 4 represents cause and 2 represents effect)—or if the vocabulary was more specific—for instance, if the term READING EPILEPSY existed in the thesaurus—these unwanted items would have been avoided. Another situation can be hypothesized, in which a document representation contains the index term READING and the index term EPILEPSY— that is, it correctly matches the search strategy—but refers to a document that deals not with reading epilepsy but with some other form of the disease. The indexer misinterpreted the document and indexed it incorrectly. In this case the representation, as it stands, matches the strategy, but the representation is incorrect because of an indexing error.

These relationships between a document representation and a search strategy are, in a sense, internal to the information system, and decisions as to whether appropriate matches have occurred need not involve either system users (requesters) or other subject specialists. In fact, in some cases, individuals who are not directly involved with the system may not understand why a particular failure occurred or even why a particular item was retrieved. It is probably best if we use neither *relevance* nor *pertinence* for these relationships but simply refer to document representations "matching a search strategy" and documents "matching an intended strategy."

RELEVANCE

Information retrieval concerns more than matches between documents or their representations and searching strategies. It concerns relationships between documents and request statements and between documents and the information needs of users. After an information retrieval system has retrieved a set of document representations in response to a particular request, the documents themselves can be retrieved and it can be decided which match the request and which do not. Who is qualified to make this decision? It might be the information specialists associated with the system, the requester, or independent subject specialists. Clearly, the person making the decision must know enough about the subject matter to be able to ascertain that certain documents are "legitimate responses" to the request and others are not.

The term *legitimate response* is admittedly vague. The person making the assessment presumably judges a document to be a legitimate response if he or she thinks that the subject matter of the document is sufficiently close to the subject matter requested that the system was "correct" in retrieving it. Unfortunately, these relationships are not very exact. How close is sufficiently close? Closeness of a document to a request cannot be measured precisely; the relationship is subjective and equivocal rather than objective and unequivocal; different judges may make different decisions on the degree of association between a document and a request. It is also possible that the same judge may make different decisions on a particular request–document pair at different times. Be that as it may, it seems reasonable to refer to this relationship as *relevance*. In other words, if a judge decides that a certain document is sufficiently close in subject matter to a particular request that the system was correct in retrieving it, it is justifiable to say that he or she has judged the document to be relevant to the request.

Although other terminology could be used, the term *relevance* is appropriate to indicate that a relationship exists between a document and a request statement in the eyes of a judge. It would be wrong to assume that relevance represents a precise, invariant relationship; it does not. In fact, rather than saying that a document is relevant to a request, it would be better to say that the document *has been judged* relevant to the request.

Since relevance decisions are subjective and likely to be inconsistent, it may be dangerous to use a single set of relevance decisions by one individual as the basis for evaluating the performance of a retrieval system. Rather, to evaluate the performance of a retrieval system solely on the basis of the request–document statement relationship, a group of judges should be involved, who try to arrive at a consensus as to which documents are relevant to which requests. Several judges, working independently in making relevance decisions, would at least allow one to rank documents in terms of "relevance consensus." The results of a particular search could then be expressed in the following form:

1. Thirty-five percent of the documents retrieved were judged relevant by all five judges.

2. Forty-three percent were judged relevant by at least four of the five judges.

3. Sixty-two percent were judged relevant by at least three of the judges, and so on.

PERTINENCE

Relevance decisions based on the relationship between documents and request statements have only limited use in the evaluation of operating information services. They tell nothing about the degree of success that is achieved in meeting the information needs of users, yet, presumably, the service exists to meet such needs. It is possible for a document to be judged relevant to a particular request statement by all members of a panel of judges but for the requester to decide that the document is of no value in satisfying the information need that prompted the request to the system. If all the documents retrieved by a search are judged of no value by the requester, he or she will consider the search a failure no matter how many judges agree that the documents are relevant to the request statement.

Significant differences between request–document relevance judgments made by a panel of judges and document–information need value judgments made by the requester would indicate that the request statement (expressed need) on which the system operated was an imperfect representation of the actual information need. It should not be surprising, in fact, if these two sets of judgments differed widely, because it is frequently difficult for even a sophisticated requester to make actual information needs known to an information center. For example, Lancaster (1968a) reported in his evaluation of MEDLARS that a search conducted on the basis of the request statement "cancer in the fetus or newborn infant" retrieved 1,167 journal articles, most of which would be judged relevant to the request statement by any panel of medical practitioners. But the requester made an inexcusably bad request to the system, one much more general than the actual information need. The requester was really interested in the relationship between teratogenesis and oncogenesis at the cellular level—a highly specific topic—and judged only one of the 1,167 documents retrieved to be of value in satisfying his information need.

It has been argued in the literature that a system should be judged only on the basis of the request–document relationship and that it can be expected to do only what it is asked to do. If a system is asked to retrieve documents on cancer in the fetus or newborn infant and does so, in the estimation of a panel of judges, it has behaved properly despite what the requester may think of the result. This is a very narrow philosophy, one that completely ignores the fact that it is the responsibility of the system to ensure, insofar as possible, that the requests received accurately reflect the information needs of users. A system that accepts all requests at face value and judges its own performance in terms of how well it responds to them is almost certainly doomed to fail.

To evaluate a "real" information service, one with real users making real requests based on real information needs, it is imperative that the criterion be how well the service satisfies the information needs of its users. Clearly, only the requester can decide whether or not a particular document contributes to the satisfaction of his or her information need, because only the requester knows what that need is. These decisions also can be referred to as relevance decisions. They are "relevance to an information need" decisions rather than "relevance to a request" decisions. It is more appropriate, however, to use the term *pertinence* in this case—that is, to use *relevance* to refer to a relationship between a document and a request, based on the subjective decision of one or more individuals, and *pertinence* to refer to a relationship between a document and an information need, based on the decision of only the person with the information need.

Frankly, what terms are used is unimportant. What is important is that we recognize the distinction between the two relationships (request–document and information need–document), that we recognize who is qualified to make the decisions in each case, and that we consistently use whatever terminology we choose. To achieve this consistency in this book, the term *pertinence* is used to refer to a relationship between a document and an information need, and the term *relevance* is used to refer to a relationship between a document and a request statement. This is an arbitrary decision made purely for the sake of convenience. (It might actually be preferable to think of these relationships as relevance to a request and relevance to an information need, discarding the term *pertinence* completely.)

As just defined, pertinence decisions are value judgments made by requesters. The decision reflects the value of a document to a particular person, at a particular time, in contributing to the satisfaction of a particular information need. A set of such value judgments is "true" only at a certain point in time—the time at which the decision is made—because information needs change. Thus, a user may come to an information service and make a request based on a recognized information need. Suppose that the system is able to respond virtually immediately and retrieves 25 documents. The moment the requester sees the first document, his or her perception of need may change, and this inevitably will influence the remainder of his or her pertinence decisions. This first document may be exactly what the requester needs; it satisfies the information requirement completely. He or she may judge the sixth document of no value because it essentially duplicates the first. But had the sixth document been seen first, the requester might well have judged it pertinent and the first document, coming later in the sequence, of no value. If, instead of receiving the search results on the day of the request, they are delivered some days later, the requester's perception of need will have been influenced by all that he or she has learned during the intervening period. The value judgments made on the 25 documents on day 10 will not necessarily be the same as those that would have been made on day 1, and both of these may differ from the judgments that would have been made on day 5.[1]

---

[1] One recent study that looked at the effect of order of document presentation on relevance judgments is reported by Eisenberg and Berry (1988). Parker and Johnson (1990), however, have produced data to suggest that sequence of presentation only affects relevance judgments when the

Pertinence decisions, then, are very transient, much more so than relevance decisions. They are influenced by both time and the sequence in which the decisions are made. This does not make the operation of information services any easier, but it is a fact that designers, managers, operators, and evaluators must recognize and be able to adapt to.

The various relationships that have been discussed are shown in Exhibit 19, along with statements on who is qualified to judge whether or not a relationship holds and reasons for wanting to determine whether or not it holds. The four relationships are listed in increasing order of complexity. In terms of their value in system evaluation, the data reflecting the relationships may be considered cumulative. This statement can be explained as follows:

1. If it is known which document representations retrieved by a particular search actually match the search strategy used, problems can be identified in the search programs. This is actually a trivial case: no failures of this type are expected in any but a grossly inefficient system. Nothing is learned at this level of evaluation about the quality of the indexing, index language, or search strategies.

2. If it is known which documents, corresponding to the representations retrieved by the search, satisfy the intended strategy of the searcher, possible problems in the search programs can be identified, as well as certain indexing, index language, or search strategy problems, as identified in Exhibit 19. Nothing is learned, however, about the quality of the search strategy as a representation of the request statement.

3. If it is known which documents, corresponding to the representations retrieved by the search, are judged relevant to the request statement by, say, a jury of subject specialists, problems can be identified in the search programs, indexing, index language, and search strategies. Cases can also be identified in which the search strategy does not completely or accurately reflect the content of the request statement. Still, nothing is known about how well the retrieved documents satisfy the information needs of the user, and thus it is not possible to identify inadequate or misleading request statements due to imperfect user–system interaction.

4. If it is known which of the retrieved documents are judged by the requester to contribute to the satisfaction of the information need—pertinent documents—and if it is also known why other documents are judged nonpertinent, then the relevance of the search results can be distinguished from their

---

number of items to be evaluated exceeds some threshold. They hypothesize that items presented earlier are more likely to be judged relevant than later items, but only when the total number of items involved exceeds 15.

Relationship	Question to Be Asked	Terminology	Person Qualified to Answer Question	Reasons for Wanting Answer to Question
1. Between search strategy and document representation.	Do the terms included in the representation satisfy the logic of the strategy?	Match between strategy and document representation.	Any information specialist who understands the system in use.	To determine if the search programs or procedures are working correctly.
2. Between document and search strategy.	Is this the type of document, in terms of subject matter, that the searcher wanted to retrieve?	Match between document and intended strategy.	The person preparing the search strategy; other individuals knowledgeable on the subject matter and the system.	To identify the problems listed in number 1; to identify cases of misindexing; to identify syntactic (relational) problems in the system and other problems relating to its vocabulary; to identify errors in the search strategy.
3. Between document and request statement.	Is this document a correct response to the request made to the system? (Is its subject matter the subject matter requested?)	Relevance of the document to the request.	Someone knowledgeable on the subject matter or a jury of people knowledgeable on the subject.	To identify the problems listed in number 2 and to identify problems of misinterpretation of the request by the searcher.
4. Between document and information need.	Does the document contribute to satisfying the information need of the requester?	Pertinence of the document to the information need.	Only the requester.	To identify the problems listed in number 3 and to identify problems of user–system interaction leading to discrepancies between the recognized information need and the expressed need (request statement).

EXHIBIT 19   Some relationships of importance in information retrieval.

pertinence. In this situation, through appropriate analysis techniques, all types of problems that might occur in the retrieval system can be identified, whether in search programs, indexing, index language, search strategy, interpretation of the request by the searcher, or user–system interaction. The use of this type of diagnostic analysis is exemplified in the evaluation of MEDLARS (Lancaster, 1968a).

Note, however, that the levels of evaluation mentioned in Exhibit 19 are based only on the documents that the system retrieves and not on those it does not retrieve; that is, not identified are

1. Documents whose representations match the search strategy but that have not been retrieved (as previously stated, one would not expect this to happen in a properly designed system)

2. Documents that match the intended strategy but that have not been retrieved

3. Documents that are relevant to the request statement but that have not been retrieved

4. Documents that are pertinent to the information need but that have not been retrieved.

To make these determinations requires some method of estimating how many matching, relevant, or pertinent documents the system failed to retrieve. And there must be some means to identify at least some of them. Some possible procedures for doing this are described in Chapter 9.

THE LITERATURE ON RELEVANCE

Other literature addresses the problems of pertinence and relevance. A complete survey is not provided in this section but, rather, the reader is referred to sources that may help to clarify some of the distinctions made earlier and which give a more complete picture of the factors that influence relevance or pertinence decisions.

Kemp (1974) and Foskett (1970, 1972) both adopt the distinction between relevance and pertinence that has been used in this chapter. Kemp points out that for some purposes of evaluation, relevance decisions suffice; for other purposes, however, pertinence decisions are needed. Kemp refers to relevance decisions as being public and objective and pertinence decisions as being private and subjective. We do not fully agree with this. Relevance is not objective. If it were, there should be perfect agreement among a group of judges on the relevance of various documents to various requests. Such complete agreement is highly unlikely to occur. Kemp also draws analogies between the relationship of pertinence and relevance, on the one hand, and those relationships that are implied in alternative pairs of terms derived from other fields: denotation and connotation, semantics and pragmatics, formal and informal communication, and public and private knowledge.

Foskett (1972) makes the same distinction between relevance and pertinence that has been made in this chapter. He defines a relevant document as one "belonging to the field/subject/universe of discourse delimited by the terms of the request, as established by the consensus of workers in that field" (p. 77) and a pertinent document as one "adding new information to the store already in the mind of the user, which is useful to him in the work that prompted the request" (p. 77). Foskett notes that frequently, but not always, pertinent documents are also relevant, and vice versa.

Cooper (1971) discusses the subject of relevance at considerable length. Essentially, he draws the same distinctions that have been drawn here; however, he uses the term *logical relevance* (or *topicality*) rather than *relevance* and the term *utility* for *pertinence*. Elsewhere, Cooper (1973) has argued that information retrieval systems must be evaluated on the basis of the utility of their results: "It is really documents of high utility, and not merely relevant documents, that the user wants to see" (p. 92). We fully agree with Cooper on this point.

Goffman (1964) fails to distinguish between relevance and pertinence. He defines relevance as "a measure of information conveyed by a document relative to a query" (p. 201), which is comparable to the position taken by Foskett, Kemp, and ourselves and equivalent to Cooper's "logical relevance." Goffman, however, goes on to say that "any measure of information must depend on what is already known: a fact which must be recognized in any assessment of the relevance of a document with respect to a query" (p. 201). This statement is somewhat confusing because the expression "what is already known" suggests the pertinence relationship rather than the relevance relationship. Goffman's point is that relevance cannot be determined for every request–document pair independently but that a decision on the relevance of one document, with respect to a request, must be made in relation to decisions on other documents with respect to the same request. We agree with the assumption that appears to underly this—that relevance is relative and capable of being judged on some type of scale. In other words, it should be possible to ask relevance judges to divide a set of documents into at least three sets: (1) clearly relevant to a particular request statement, (2) relevant to the request statement but less relevant than the documents in the first set, and (3) not relevant. In this sense, the relevance decisions are relative, because they group or separate documents on the basis of extent of relevance. But if Goffman's statement implies that the sequence with which documents are presented to the judges influences relevance decisions and that a judge might decide that a particular document is irrelevant because it duplicates one seen earlier, then it does not agree with the definitions in this chapter. This type of decision would not be a relevance decision but a pertinence decision—a value judgment made on a document in relation to an information need. Unfortunately, it is not clear what Goffman really means because he fails to distinguish between relevance and pertinence and between actual information needs and expressed needs.

Wilson (1973) has introduced the term *situational relevance,* which he defines as "relevance to a particular individual's situation—but to the situation as he sees it, not as others see it or as it 'really is'" (p. 460). He further states that situational relevance is related to concern and not merely to interest. A person might be interested in a particular object or activity without being concerned about it, that is, without caring about its condition. Wilson views items of information as situationally relevant if they "answer, or help answer, questions of concern" (p. 463). The notion of situational relevance is compatible with the set of relationships identified earlier in this chapter. Although Wilson places many more restrictions on the definition of the term, *situational relevance* refers to the relationship between information and perceived information need rather than to that between information and actual need or expressed need.

Belzer (1973) uses "relevance" where we have used "pertinence": "Upon completion of reading the document the user would know, precisely, whether it was relevant to him or not. This is irrespective of the query posed to the system" (p. 301). Belzer clearly recognizes the distinction between relevance to request and pertinence to information need, but he chooses to ignore the former.

O'Connor (1967) has discussed the subject of relevance in a series of articles. In one he analyzes in detail the request–document relationship and the effect of the clarity of the request on relevance judgments. Elsewhere, he has reported on an empirical study of agreements and disagreements in deciding whether a particular document "answers" a particular question (O'Connor, 1969). Although he never explicitly says so, he implies that relevance decisions are acceptable bases for system evaluation but that pertinence decisions are not. At least, he is critical of those who claim that a system must be evaluated in terms of user needs, mainly on the grounds that "satisfaction of a user's need" is rarely defined precisely. Although one might agree with O'Connor on the last point, the idea that satisfaction of a user's need is in any way obscure or that it is not susceptible to definition is not acceptable. These points have been argued in the literature by O'Connor (1968a,b) and Lancaster (1968b) to neither's satisfaction.

Swanson (1977) distinguishes between relevance to a topic and the relevance of an item to an individual because it provides new knowledge. It is difficult to see how this differs from the relevance/pertinence distinction or indeed the distinction he makes in a later article between "objective" and "subjective" relevance (Swanson, 1986).

Various investigators have explored the effect that different forms of document surrogates have on relevance decisions. Typically, these studies compare relevance or pertinence decisions made by the same judges when given various levels of information about a particular group of documents. For example, the judges may first be asked to make relevance predictions on the basis of titles, then on titles plus abstracts, or titles plus selected paragraphs of text. Finally, they are asked to judge the relevance of the documents themselves. The results are then compared to determine how much agreement there is between the relevance predictions made on the basis of the various forms of surrogates and the actual relevance decisions based on the documents.

Studies of this type have been reported by Rath et al. (1961), Resnick (1961), Dym (1967), Kent et al. (1967), Shirey and Kurfeerst (1967), Saracevic (1969), Marcus, Benenfeld, and Kugel (1971), and Belzer (1973), among others. As might be expected, relevance predictions generally improve, in the sense that the surrogate-based predictions agree with the document-based decisions, as more information is made available to the judges. Marcus, Benenfeld, and Kugel (1971) refer to the quality of a surrogate, in terms of its value in making correct relevance predictions, as its *indicativity*. They point out that, in general, the indicativity of a record increases directly with its length in number of words. In a more recent study, Janes (1991) found that abstracts were by far the most useful representation in relevance prediction, followed by titles, bibliographic information, and index terms. The rather poor performance of the index terms is surprising. Clearly, the value of a list of index terms, as an indicator of content, depends very much on the type of indexing used and the number of terms assigned. One could visualize a situation in which long lists of index terms would give a more complete picture of a document's content than brief indicative abstracts. As Marcus, Benenfeld, and Kugel (1971) found, all other things being equal, it is the length of the representation that is the major factor governing indicativity (Lancaster, 1991).

Two major series of studies have investigated the factors that influence relevance decisions. One of these, conducted by the System Development Corporation (SDC), has been reported by Cuadra and Katter (1967a,b) and by Cuadra, Katter, Holmes and Wallace (1967). The second, conducted by Western Reserve University, has been reported by Rees (1966) and Rees and Schultz (1967).

Many variables influencing relevance judgments were identified and investigated in the SDC studies; pertinence to information needs, however, was really not considered. Cuadra and Katter (1967b) summarize as follows:

> The studies offer clear evidence that relevance judgments can be influenced by the skills and attitudes of the particular judges, the documents and document sets used, the particular information requirement statements, the instructions and setting in which the judgments take place, the concepts and definitions of relevance employed in the judgments, and the type of rating scale or other medium used to express the judgments. These findings cast serious doubt on the wisdom of treating relevance scores, as usually obtained, as fully adequate criteria for system or subsystem evaluation. (p. 98)

The Western Reserve studies took into account four major variables influencing relevance decisions: (1) stage of research, (2) documents, (3) document representations, and (4) relevance judges. Again, relevance rather than pertinence was investigated. As in the SDC studies, the Western Reserve investigators were able to show that many variables affect the decision on whether a particular document is relevant to a particular request. For example, the degree of the judge's subject knowledge influences the relevance decisions and the consistency with which such decisions are made by a group of judges. Likewise, somewhat different relevance judgments may be made for a particular set of documents in relation to a particular request statement at different stages of a research project; that is, the documents that are judged most relevant by an investigator at the beginning of a research project may not be judged most relevant toward the end of the project when the research results are analyzed.

The most complete discussion of the relevance question is in a doctoral dissertation by Saracevic (1970a). He has also prepared a very useful, concise summary of the major findings of various investigators working in relevance experimentation over a 10-year period (Saracevic, 1970b).

Because so many factors influencing relevance judgments have been identified, particularly in the SDC and Western Reserve investigations, it is hardly surprising that serious doubts have been voiced on the wisdom of basing system evaluations on relevance decisions. It must be recognized, however, that although some of the work on relevance decisions applies equally to pertinence decisions (for example, the influence of the research stage and the indicativity of a surrogate), much of it is not directly related. In particular, many of the variables investigated relate to interjudge consistency and do not necessarily affect pertinence decisions, which are highly individualistic. In pertinence decisions, which are essential to the evaluation of operating information services, the concern is with factors influencing intrajudge consistency but not directly with those influencing interjudge consistency. Stated in more concrete terms, when conducting a search in a database for a particular user, the primary concern should be the user's evaluation of the retrieved items in terms of their pertinence to the user's information need. The searcher should also be concerned with the factors influencing the user's pertinence decisions. But one need not be directly concerned when a group of subject specialists, presented with the documents retrieved and the user's request statement, do not agree among themselves as to which documents are relevant to the request. One should be even less concerned with the factors influencing their decisions. Such a study may have academic interest, but it is not directly related to the evaluation of this particular information service. Much interesting and valuable work that has been done on the relevance problem has little direct application to the pertinence problem. Indeed, most of the investigations could not contribute directly to an understanding of the pertinence problem because they were conducted in controlled, experimental settings. Studies of pertinence can be done only in the context of a particular information system serving real users who have real information needs. This situation cannot be simulated successfully in a laboratory setting.

This does not mean that the relevance problem is not worth investigating or that the studies of factors influencing relevance decisions have no value. In fact, for some purposes of evaluation, relevance decisions rather than pertinence decisions may be wanted. A danger exists, however, in assuming that research on relevance has direct applicability to pertinence and, more important, that the large number of variables affecting the consistency with which relevance judgments are made are directly related to the factors influencing pertinence decisions—they are not, or, at least, not necessarily. Clearly, many factors influence the user's decision as to whether a particular item is pertinent to his or her information need. These may not be the same factors that would influence the user's decision were he or she asked, somewhat artificially, to judge if the same item was relevant to his or her request statement. The fact is that although much work has been done on relevance, the more important problem of pertinence has largely been ignored by investigators, perhaps for the very reason that it is not amenable to controlled, experimental study.

Another point worth emphasizing is that although one may get disagreement among a group of judges as to which documents are relevant to a particular request statement, the variations in relevance judgment do not necessarily invalidate certain types of evaluation. Lesk and Salton (1968), for example, have shown clearly that inconsistency among relevance judges may have no effect on certain internal aspects of system evaluation. For example, if one wants to compare three different ways of conducting searches in a particular system, one may arrive at the same relative ranking of the performance of these alternatives (in terms of recall/precision), whichever of, say, five judges makes the relevance decisions; that is, there could be inconsistency among the judges but the relative rankings of the search techniques would not change. In fact, the Lesk and Salton study revealed that even "large scale differences in the relevance assessments" did not produce "significant variations in average recall and precision" for various searching options (p. 343).

Interest in the relevance/pertinence issue is increasing as more librarians become concerned with the evaluation of online public access catalogs. The importance of relevance in this context has been discussed by O'Brien (1990).

A rather comprehensive review of the relevance issue has recently been published by Schamber, Eisenberg, and Nilan (1990), who point out that

1. Relevance is a multidimensional cognitive concept whose meaning is largely dependent on users' perceptions of information and their own information need situations.

2. Relevance is a dynamic concept that depends on users' judgments of the quality of the relationship between information and information need at a certain point in time.

3. Relevance is a complex but systematic and measurable concept if approached conceptually and operationally from the user's perspective. (p. 774).

Although Schamber, Eisenberg, and Nilan make a useful contribution to the literature on the subject (even though they use the term *relevance* where this book would use *pertinence*), they do tend to exaggerate the importance of arriving at a well-accepted definition for relevance, going so far as to claim that "We consider the pursuit of a definition of relevance to be among the most exciting and central challenges of information science, one whose solution will carry us into the 21st century" (p. 774).

In conclusion, remember that for certain evaluation purposes, relevance decisions are needed and for others pertinence decisions are essential. Much work has been done on factors influencing relevance but very little on those influencing pertinence. Factors affecting pertinence are subjective and transient. This does not make them any less important in the evaluation of information retrieval activities.

In Chapters 4 through 8, the various factors affecting the performance of information retrieval systems, as depicted in Exhibit 16, will be discussed, namely, the user–intermediary interface, database factors (subject analysis/representation and language components), the selection of databases, and the search process.

4

The User–Intermediary Interface

Chapter 3 introduced some criteria by which information retrieval services can be evaluated and mentioned the most important factors affecting the performance of such systems. Chapters 4 through 8 deal in more detail with these performance factors. One problem faced by the authors was the order in which to place these chapters. If one followed the chronological sequence of Exhibit 16, one would deal first with user–intermediary interaction, move on to database selection, discuss search strategy, and end with a treatment of the database factors (indexing and other aspects of subject analysis and vocabulary-related matters). Although this is a logical chronological sequence, it is not necessarily a logical order of presentation, because a discussion of database selection and of search strategy should build on an earlier discussion of the database factors affecting performance. The sequence finally chosen then— user–intermediary interaction, subject analysis and representation, vocabulary matters, database selection and evaluation, search strategy—was to us more logical than the chronological sequence.

NEEDS VERSUS DEMANDS

The first steps in the information retrieval operation (see Exhibit 16) are those where an individual in the community to be served by an information center recognizes a need for information and visits the center to try to satisfy this need. Users can perform their own searches or delegate the responsibility to an intermediary (information specialist). This chapter deals with the delegated search.

When considering the evaluation of information services, it is important to distinguish between the information needs of the community to be served and

65

the demands actually made on the service. The needs can be assumed to be more numerous than the demands (expressed needs), because not all information needs are converted into demands. The managers of information services must be concerned with identifying the information needs of the population to be served and with recognizing discrepancies between needs and demands. An important aspect of evaluation should be the identification of differences between needs and demands in terms of quantitative considerations (how many needs are not converted into demands) and qualitative considerations (what types of needs are not converted into demands, what factors determine whether a need is converted into a demand, and how well the demands of users accurately reflect their real information needs). Most evaluations of information services, unfortunately, concentrate almost exclusively on measuring the degree to which the demands of users are satisfied by the service. This is a somewhat superficial approach to evaluation in that it ignores the unexpressed needs of users and assumes that the demands made by users are identical with their needs, a dangerous assumption.

Concentrating exclusively on the demands actually made and accepting them at face value is like focusing on the tip of a large iceberg and assuming that the tip fully represents the much greater mass below. Line (1973) has pointed out the dangers of this approach. Obviously, demands can be recognized much more easily than needs. But an important facet of evaluation cannot be ignored simply because it is difficult to grasp.

Kochen (1979) has attempted to distinguish among needs, problems, and expressions of needs and problems. In a very simplified form, the situation may be represented as follows:

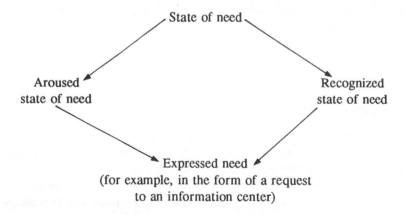

Kochen distinguishes between the state of need and its recognition or arousal. Certain states of need may be aroused without being recognized; in other cases, the need may be recognized without being aroused. In the context of information services, it is quite important to distinguish among information needs, their recognition, and their expression. Information systems cannot respond to the information needs of individuals as such but only to expressions of their needs; that is, an individual who needs information must recognize that need and must be sufficiently aroused to take steps to satisfy it. Only after the need is recognized and the individual is sufficiently aroused (motivated) is the need expressed in the form of a request to an information center. The degree to which the individual is able to recognize the exact nature of an information need and the degree to which the need is accurately reflected in its "expression"—the request statement—largely determine how successful the information service will be in satisfying that need; the information service can operate only on the basis of the stated request (expressed need) and cannot respond to unrecognized needs or even to recognized ones that are unexpressed. One of the major challenges faced by any information service operated in a delegated search mode is to ensure that expressed needs accurately reflect recognized needs. It is not always easy for the person who needs information to express that need clearly and unequivocally to the person who will be searching for the information.

The distinction between needs for information services and demands for them is important: Managers should be as much concerned with the evaluation of services in terms of the extent to which they match the needs of potential users as with their evaluation in relation to the demands made by actual users. Restricting evaluation considerations to the demands presently made on an information service ignores the needs of present users that are not converted into demands for information service and the needs of people within the community to be served who presently make no demands on the service.

In many situations, the nonusers of a service greatly outnumber the actual users. Moreover, not all the information needs of actual users are converted into demands. A further problem is that not all demands made on a service are perfect representations of the information need underlying the demand. Users sometimes demand less than they need. There is, in fact, some tendency for users of information services to ask for what they think the system can provide rather than what they really want (Lancaster, 1968a). Frequently, this means a demand that is much more general than the information need behind it.

The major categories of information need—by context, purpose, type of questions, and amount of information needed—and the most important factors influencing the probabilities that (1) an information need might arise in someone's mind, (2) that the person should decide to seek the needed information, and (3) that a particular information source is selected, are identified in Exhibit 20. The exhibit is generalized; it deals with all types of information need, including needs of the general public. It would require modification to apply more clearly to a particular environment or individual (such as information

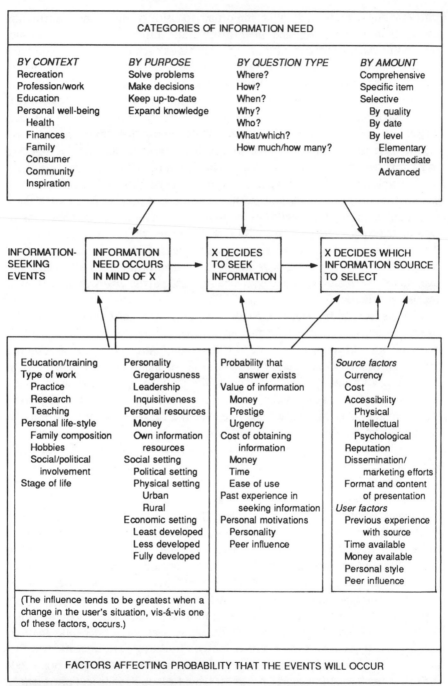

EXHIBIT 20   Complexity of the "information need" situation.

needs within a pharmaceutical company or the information needs of a research chemist), although many of the influences would still be relevant.

Most of the influences identified in the exhibit are self-explanatory, but a few may require clarification. Whether a particular information need is converted to a demand for information service is largely dependent on the value of the solution to the information problem—a solution valued at $100,000 to a particular company is more likely to be converted to a demand for information than one valued at $500 or one perceived to have no monetary value—and the greater the probability that a solution exists in the literature. The value of the information should not be considered solely in monetary terms. In some cases, for example, information may be needed to prove a point or to gain prestige. Clearly, many of the influences listed are closely related and trade off against one another. The cost of the information service is likely to be a negligible consideration if the perceived value of the solution to a problem is great.

Of course, factors relating to the probability that an information need will arise or the probability that a solution will be sought are not under the direct control of managers of information services. Nevertheless, it is important to recognize that these factors exist and that they have a significant effect on the need or the demand for information services. The system (source) factors are more directly under the control of the managers of the service, but even these are strongly affected by outside influences—for example, technological improvements and external costs—that are not directly controllable by the information service.

It is not likely that an information center can directly influence the need for information within the community served. But it can certainly influence the demand for information service through recognition of the system factors that influence demand; through continuous evaluation of the extent to which the services provided match existing needs within the community; and through evaluation of the extent to which demands are satisfied promptly, accurately, and completely.

Requests made to a formal information service are likely to relate to information needs that the requester has been unable to satisfy elsewhere. More than likely, the requester will first have tried to obtain the information from a more accessible source—a personal literature collection or another individual. The requests that come to the information service, then, are likely to be harder rather than easier to satisfy.

REQUESTS FOR INFORMATION

So far, this chapter has covered some of the factors that determine whether or not an individual is likely to have a need for information and whether or

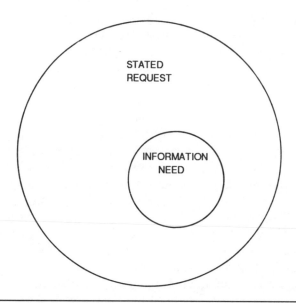

EXHIBIT 21   The request is more general than the information need: Most documents retrieved are not pertinent.

not he or she is likely to try to satisfy it. Another important matter also must be considered: the factors that influence whether or not the demand actually made on the information service (the expressed need) accurately reflects the real information need of the requester.

Assume that a person needing information must convey this need to a staff member of the information center by telephone, letter, or personal visit. This user–intermediary interaction is clearly of the greatest importance to the whole information retrieval process. The vocabulary of the system can be adequate to represent the concepts occurring in the request; the search strategy can be a complete and accurate representation of the request; and the indexing of the database can be complete, accurate, and consistent. But all these things are of little value to a particular user if the request (expressed need) is an inadequate representation of the user's real need.

If a search in a retrieval system is to be successful, the stated request must be a reasonable approximation of the information need. The greater the disparity between the stated request and the information need, the less success-ful the search is likely to be. Unfortunately, it is usually not easy for a user to completely and accurately describe his or her information need to another person. In Lancaster's (1968a) evaluation of MEDLARS, a large percentage of the failures in 300 searches was attributed to inadequate user–intermediary interaction, which resulted in verbal requests that inadequately represented the true information needs of requesters.

The usual tendency is to make requests more general than the actual information need, presumably because the requester suspects that the system can operate at the broader level but not at the more specific level (Exhibit 21). In other words, the requester is conditioned by his or her expectations of the system and what it can provide. This surely is the only explanation for the nationally known cancer research scientist who asked for a search on cancer in the fetus or newborn infant, a subject on which much literature exists and which was retrieved by the system, almost all completely unrelated to the scientist's precise information need (Lancaster, 1968a). What he was really looking for was information on a very precise topic for which very little literature exists, namely, the relationship between teratogenesis and oncogenesis at the cellular level. The documents retrieved matched his stated request exactly, but certainly they were not pertinent to his information need.

Less frequently, a request is more specific than the information need (Exhibit 22). Take the requester who asked for information on the crossing of fatty acids through the placental barrier and on normal fatty acid levels in the placenta or fetus. In retrospect, it was discovered that this researcher was really interested

EXHIBIT 22 The request is more specific than the information need: Documents of pertinence are not retrieved.

in a somewhat broader topic, namely, crossing of lipids (that is, fatty substances in general) across the placental barrier and normal lipid levels in the placenta, fetus, or newborn infant. The result of a request that is more specific than the actual information need is a failure to retrieve some documents that would be of value to the requester. This situation is more complex than the reverse, because the expansion of the request is likely to come about only as a result of a browsing, heuristic search and is unlikely to occur at all when the person with the information need delegates the responsibility for the search to someone else. In the previous example, the stated request represented what the scientist thought he wanted when he first approached the system. It was only when he saw some documents peripheral to his stated request, namely, on maternal-fetal exchange of lipids and on lipid levels in the newborn, that he realized his request was too restrictive and that these documents, outside the scope of his stated request, were in fact also useful.

Quality of User Requests

In any delegated search information system, a major source of failure occurs at the user–system interface, where one human being must communicate his or her information needs completely and accurately to another. Several investigators have tried to identify the processes that are involved in transforming a latent need for information into a request made to an information service. Taylor (1967) recognized four levels of need: (1) visceral, (2) conscious, (3) formalized, and (4) compromised. At the visceral level, the need is vague or even subconscious—a problem must be solved or a decision made, but the individual is not yet able to define what information would be helpful. At the conscious level, a description of the need exists in the mind of the individual, although it may still be ill-defined. At the formalized level, the need is recognized with sufficient clarity that it can be articulated. The compromised need is the request that is actually made to the information service. It is compromised because it may be expressed in a form that the requester considers understandable by the information service but does not accurately reflect the true need.

Belkin (1980) and Belkin et al. (1982a,b) view the information retrieval problem as one of matching an anomalous state of knowledge (what a requester does not know) with a coherent state of knowledge (what authors do know as embodied in their publications). They claim that information needs are not precisely specifiable but that one should be able to obtain from users "problem statements" from which representations of the anomalous state of knowledge (ASK) underlying the need can be derived.

Allen (1988) claims that the way users understand and express their needs will be affected by the cognitive structures (*schemata*) by which they have

1. The ability of the user to define the information need in his or her own mind

2. The user's ability to express himself or herself

3. The intermediary's skill as a communicator

4. The degree to which the personal schemata (frame of reference) of the intermediary agrees with that of the user

5. The user's expectations about the system's capabilities

6. The complexity of the subject matter dealt with (for example, abstract versus concrete) and the degree to which it can be verbalized precisely

7. The aids to interaction provided by the system (for example, search request form)

EXHIBIT 23   Factors affecting the quality of user–intermediary interaction.

organized their knowledge of the topic and by the schemata introduced in the questions that intermediaries ask. Differences in personal schemata may mean that the same problem could lead to completely different questions in the minds of different individuals. Indeed, one major problem in user–intermediary interaction is that the personal schemata (frame of reference) of the user and that of the information specialist may be far apart. Moreover, various "external schemata" (such as the vocabulary used in indexing a database) may also exert strong influence on the interactions between user and intermediary.

Taylor (1967) views the user–intermediary interaction as involving the processing of a question through a series of filters, each one improving the intermediary's understanding of what the user really wants. Taylor's filters can be identified as (1) the user's statement of need, (2) the intermediary's understanding of the objective and motivation of the user, (3) the personal characteristics of the user, (4) the intermediary's knowledge of the contents and structure of the database to be searched, and (5) the intermediary's understanding of the type of response required (for example, a single fact, a few pertinent references, a comprehensive search).

A large body of literature now exists on the interview between user and information specialist (for example, Crum, 1969; Ingwersen, 1982; Katz, 1987; King, 1972; Knapp, 1978; Lynch, 1978; Markey, 1981; Roloff, 1979; Somerville, 1977; White, 1981, 1983, 1985). A distinction is frequently made between the characteristics and quality of "open" versus "closed" questions in the interview. Closed questions are those that can be answered yes or no, whereas open questions require longer responses. The open questions tend to reveal much more about the requester's context, whereas the closed questions are more constrained by the original request.

It should be clear that many factors are significant in determining the quality of the user–intermediary interaction (Exhibit 23). Several of these have already been alluded to; others are self-evident.

Modes of User–Intermediary Interaction

Some modes of user–intermediary interaction are likely to be more effective than others. One could hypothesize that when a user visits an information center in person and discusses an information need with a staff member, the resulting request statement probably will be a better representation of the actual information need than a request that comes to the information center by mail, without benefit of direct face-to-face interaction between user and information specialist.

Surprisingly, the evidence from the MEDLARS study (Lancaster, 1968a) does not support this hypothesis; quite the reverse, in fact. If one takes the 300 searches on which the MEDLARS evaluation was based and divides them into two groups, the first consisting of searches based on requests made by personal visit to an information center and the second of searches based on requests submitted by mail, the performance on the second group is clearly superior; that is, the searches based on mailed requests were able to retrieve, on the average, more of the documents judged pertinent by requesters and fewer of the documents judged not pertinent.

This discovery was unexpected by most people. It suggested that users were able to communicate their needs for information more effectively in writing than orally. Subsequent analyses of these results began to reveal some reasons for this situation. Apparently, users who write their requests on a request form or in a letter in the privacy of their home or office generally have two advantages over users who make a personal visit to an information center. First, the need to write down a request imposes discipline on requesters. They are forced to think about what they are really looking for and must attempt to express it clearly in writing. Second, they are generally not influenced by system constraints. Because they are physically remote from the system, they tend not to consider that the system may have limitations in its vocabulary and its search capabilities. Under these conditions, users tend to describe their information needs in their own language and ask for what they really want rather than what they think the system can supply. Requests made to an information center in writing tend to be reasonably accurate descriptions of the information actually sought.

In contrast, consider those users who personally visit an information center. In all probability, they have not gone through the mental discipline of writing out a statement of need. Consequently, it is likely that they have not completely formed a notion of what they really want. When they come to an information center and attempt to describe their needs, there is a very strong tendency to be influenced, probably unconsciously, by system constraints. Under these conditions, they are much more likely to ask for what they think the system is able to give them rather than for the precise information they are really seeking. This phenomenon is well known to librarians. It is exemplified by the user who comes to the library needing the address of a particular hotel in Copenhagen. But, instead of asking for this, the user asks to see books on travel in Scandinavia.

However well intentioned the information specialist is, there is some tendency for him or her to influence the requester in the way the latter describes a need. This influence may be deleterious when a requester has not clearly thought out an information need and has not stated it in writing. The likelihood of distortion is greatest when the user and the information specialist discuss the request in terms of the controlled vocabulary of the system. This immediately places an undesirable and artificial constraint on the requester. Under these conditions, the information need is "forced," probably unconsciously, into the language of the system, and the user may settle for something less precise or less complete than what is really wanted.

This phenomenon can be illustrated by a very simple example. A user comes to an information center and indicates an interest in the fabrication of tubes of stainless steel by welding processes. The user and the information specialist examine the system vocabulary together, specifically the metals terms, the welding terms, and the fabricated products terms. Because the user sees the term STAINLESS STEEL (not subdivided further) in the vocabulary, he accepts this, along with the term TUBES. In reviewing the welding terms, he sees that the specific term SHIELDED ARC WELDING exists as a subdivision of welding. Again, the specific term is accepted. The request left with the information center, then, is for a search on the fabrication of stainless steel tubes by shielded arc welding processes. Unfortunately, this search will not be completely satisfactory. The user is really interested in something more specific—information on a stainless steel of a particular composition (chromium–nickel–vanadium) and the specific welding process called helium arc welding. The system can in fact search this specifically by incorporating the alloy terms for chromium, nickel, and vanadium and by adding the gas term HELIUM, but the user does not realize this. Thus, a search more general than need be commences. The user has been adversely influenced by his own interpretation of the system's capabilities.

It should be a cardinal rule that users of information centers be required to write a statement of their information need in their own language, and that they should not attempt, initially at least, to express their need in system terms. This is important for a reason other than the matter of clarity of request. If users are asked to express their needs in terms selected from the controlled vocabulary of the system, it will never be possible to identify areas in which the vocabulary is insufficiently specific. For example, if users are constrained to ask for shielded arc welding when they really want to search more specifically for helium arc welding or argon arc welding, the need to add these more specific terms to the vocabulary will never be recognized. Eventually, the information center will lose many of its customers because its vocabulary has not been made sufficiently specific to keep pace with new developments in the fields covered and, consequently, searches cannot be conducted with enough precision to satisfy users.

This discussion may give the impression that any form of interaction between a requester and an information specialist for the purpose of improving or clarifying a statement of need is likely to degrade this statement, making it further removed from the actual requirement. This is not so. It appears, however, that there is an optimum stage at which this interaction process should take place.

As a result of his findings in the MEDLARS evaluation, Lancaster (1968a) stressed the importance of a well-designed search request form. He hypothesized that the sequence of interactions—user visits center, user is asked to complete form, intermediary interviews user to clarify and refine what is recorded on form—would generally give much better results than the sequence: user visits center, user is interviewed by intermediary, request form is completed by intermediary while interview is taking place.

This hypothesis remained untested until Fitzgerald (1981) compared the two sequences of interaction in a medical library. Using a single intermediary who both interviewed the user and performed the search, Fitzgerald had one group of requests handled one way and a second group handled the other way. A randomization procedure was used to assign the requests to one or the other mode. The results of the searches were then compared in terms of recall, precision, search cost, and unit cost per relevant item retrieved. The hypothesis was not supported by these data; for most of the evaluation criteria, the results achieved in one interaction mode were not significantly different from those achieved in the other. As it happens, however, an important event took place in this medical library that the researcher was unaware of at the time the study was designed: In every case, the requester and searcher sat together at a terminal while the search was conducted. Thus, the search was truly heuristic, involving interactions among user, searcher, and database. This is likely to be so much more effective than other forms of interaction that it virtually wipes out any differences that might occur in presearch interaction.

The situation in which user and intermediary sit together at a terminal while the search proceeds is highly desirable. If this is not possible, some form of simultaneous remote search might be feasible (Graham, 1980). In this case, the requester and the searcher are separated geographically but telephones enable the two to communicate, and network connections make it possible for the requester to observe on his or her terminal what the searcher is doing and what is being retrieved. If no form of user–intermediary interaction is possible while the search is in process, it then is likely that the preferred presearch interaction would be one in which a search request form is completed by the user before any user–intermediary discussion takes place.

Search Request Forms

An important function of an information service is to help its users formulate adequate requests. Assistance can take a number of forms, from general instruction on the characteristics and capabilities of the system—by means of a user manual, for example—to the preparation of a search request form designed to help the user precisely state his or her need. The search request form, if well designed, can be valuable in collecting data that are useful to the information staff in interpreting the needs of requesters. Besides a complete natural-language request statement, such a form would record details on the purpose of the search and the type of search required (comprehensive or selective). It also might present the user with a series of check-off boxes by which the scope of the search can usefully be restricted. For example, in the field of medicine, check-off boxes can be used to determine whether the requester is interested only in human studies, only in animal studies, or both; whether the user is interested only in a certain gender or age group; and whether case studies, in vivo studies, or in vitro studies are desired. A well-designed form can help a user state a request explicitly and completely. In particular, it should help the user exclude various areas or aspects—for example, animal studies—that are not of interest. Probably the user would not think of such exclusions without the help of the form. The form should also include space to allow the requester to record, if available, bibliographic references for items that are already known to be relevant. These can be used for various purposes: as a check on whether the search statement appears to be at the correct level of specificity, as a check on the completeness of the search (are the known relevant items retrieved, assuming they exist in the database?), or as the basis of a search strategy (retrieve records for the items known to be relevant and create a strategy to find others like them). As a result of the MEDLARS evaluation, a search request form containing all the elements discussed was designed for the National Library of Medicine (Lancaster, 1971). This form influenced many that followed it. A typical search request form is illustrated in Exhibit 45 later in this book (p. 178).

5

Subject Analysis
and Representation

The methods and forms of document subject representation are central concerns in the design of information retrieval systems (Exhibits 3 and 16). Decisions about subject analysis and description are extremely important because they affect the searches that can be performed on the system. Although the provision of topical information has been the primary focus of the information retrieval industry, subject access in library catalogs has not always been given the attention it deserves. Fortunately, the library profession has devoted much more attention to the subject access problem since card catalogs have been replaced by online public access catalogs (OPACs).

The possibilities for subject representations are given in Exhibit 24. In every case, subject analysis and representation begin with a primary document; however, the exhibit shows that the various treatments of subject matter are fundamentally different. These differences can be summarized as follows:

1. Subject analysis may be performed by human intellectual effort or by some computer algorithm.

2. The subject description may use the language of the primary document or some other vocabulary.

3. The subject description may result from the selection of (virtually) all the words that are found in the full or partial text of the document or from some principled selection among the words or concepts that are found in the document.

Thus, the term "indexing" can refer to

1. An analytic process consisting of the human identification, selection, and representation of document concepts (Pao, 1989). This may involve the

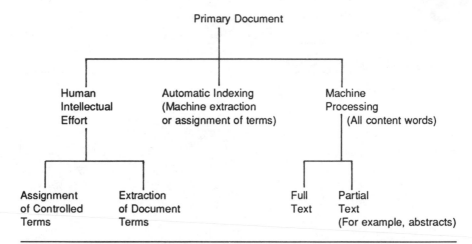

EXHIBIT 24   Various possible approaches to subject representation.

translation of identified concepts into controlled vocabulary terms or the extraction of terms from the primary document.

2. An automated process in which a subset of terms considered representative of the subject matter of the document is extracted.

3. An automated process in which all content words in all the subject-related fields (index terms, title, abstract, full text) are placed in an inverted file for online searching.

This chapter covers the issues, definitions, policies, and problems that are associated with the first and third types of indexing; the second type is the focus of Chapter 11.

HUMAN INDEXING

Indexing may consist of drawing words and phrases directly from the document (derivative indexing) or of representing the subject matter with terms drawn from a controlled vocabulary (assignment indexing) (Exhibit 24). In assignment indexing, subject analysis and description consist of several steps carried out by a human analyst (indexer or cataloger). The document is analyzed for indexable concepts (conceptual analysis) that are then converted to a suitable indexing vocabulary (translation). The result is a set of terms that is intended to describe the document and that will result in its retrieval when matched with the same terms in a query. Behind these steps are several policies that guide the indexing process and its final outcome and that often affect retrieval system performance.

One policy establishes the indexable material of the document. The indexable domain for the documents found in most bibliographic databases is usually the text of the entire document. The analyst must therefore base indexing decisions on the entire document rather than just portions of it, such as title and abstract. Furthermore, analysts are often instructed to also index the form of the material, that is, what it *is* (in contrast to what it *is about*). For example, if the item under consideration is a bibliography of sources on the topic of illiteracy, it would be assigned terms both for its form (BIBLIOGRAPHY) and for its topic (ILLITERACY).

There are several intellectual aspects of documents that may be considered indexable. For example, indexing policies often specify that elements such as genre (a literature database), time period (a history database), or educational target group (an education database) should always be identified and assigned appropriate index terms. The major effort in subject description, however, consists of identifying and representing the topics discussed in the document, that is, what the document is about. In this important area, policies emphasize that the subject content of the document is what should be analyzed and described in a set of index terms. Hutchins (1978) calls this the summarization approach to subject analysis.

Another policy concerns indexing exhaustivity. *Exhaustivity* is the extent to which all the distinct subjects discussed in a particular document are recognized in the indexing operation and translated into the language of the system. The effects of this policy on retrieval system performance are dealt with in more detail in Chapter 10. In general, highly exhaustive indexing tends to promote high recall but causes low precision, whereas highly selective indexing yields high precision but does not allow high recall. In exhaustive indexing, more index terms are assigned per document because indexers are directed to assign terms for both major and minor document topics, that is, topics central to the document (major) and topics treated only briefly (minor). Thus, searchers generally will retrieve larger sets of documents containing items that deal with the topic as a central issue, as well as those that treat it briefly (higher recall). With less exhaustive (more selective) indexing, on the other hand, searchers will tend to retrieve smaller sets of documents containing only the items that deal with the topic as a central concern (high precision).

Degree of exhaustivity is one of the two key differences between what is generally thought of as "subject cataloging" and "subject indexing," the other being the degree of coordination that exists in the indexing language (see Chapter 6). Exhibit 25 shows a bibliographic record from a library catalog

Meadow, Charles T.
  Basics of online searching / Charles T. Meadow, Pauline (Atherton) Cochrane.
  -- New York : Wiley, 1981.
  xiv, 245 p. : ill. ; 26 cm. -- (Information sciences series)
  "A Wiley-Interscience publication."
  Includes bibliographical references and index.
  ISBN 0-471-05283-3
SUBJECT HEADINGS (Library of Congress; use s=):
  On-line bibliographic searching

MIRLYN Online Catalog, University of Michigan

ED205181# IR009484
  Basics of Online Searching.
  Meadow, Charles T.; Cochrane, Pauline (Atherton)
  Wiley (John) & Sons, New York, N.Y.
  1981
  255p.; A Wiley-InterScience Publication.
  Report No.: ISBN-0-471-05283-3
  Available from: Wiley-InterScience, 605 Third Ave., New York, NY 10158.
  Document Not Available from EDRS.
  Language: English
  Document Type: BOOK (010); CLASSROOM MATERIAL (050)
  Geographic Source: U.S.; New York
  Journal Announcement: RIEDEC81
  Intended to teach the principles of interactive bibliographic searching to those with little
or no prior experience, this textbook explains the basic elements of online information
retrieval and compares the major database search systems. Its chapters address (1)
relevant definitions and vocabulary; (2) the conceptual facets of database searching, search
formulation, and online costs; (3) the presearch interview; (4) terminals and networks;
(5) search languages; (6) database organization and record structures; (7) basic system
commands; (8) text searching; (9) beginning and ending a search; (10) storing searches and
selective dissemination of information (SDI); (11) search aids; and (12) search strategies.
Appendices provide a summary of search languages, a list of available online databases,
and examples of database descriptions and search aids. Examples are based on the BRS,
DIALOG, and ORBIT search systems. (FM)
  Descriptors: Databases; *Information Retrieval; Information Systems; *Online Systems;
*Search Strategies
  Identifiers: Command Language; Search Keys; Search Negotiation (Computer Science)

ERIC database (*Current Index to Journals in Education*)

EXHIBIT 25 **Exhaustivity of indexing in a typical catalog record com-**
pared with exhaustivity in the ERIC **database.** SOURCES: MIRLYN **Online Catalog,**
reprinted with permission of the University Library, University of Michigan;
Current Index to Journals in Education, **reprinted with permission of the**
Educational Resources Information Center.

and one from the ERIC database. It is immediately apparent that exhaustivity is higher in the latter than in the former. Catalogs tend to provide very general subject access to complete items (for example, complete books, journals, or conference proceedings), whereas indexes may refer to complete items or to parts of items (for example, individual articles, papers, or chapters) that have been more exhaustively analyzed (approximately 11 descriptors per item in ERIC) than is normal for library catalogs (where 1–3 subject headings per record is typical).

In the ERIC record, the indexer has used eight index terms ("descriptors" and "identifiers") and marked those of greater importance with an asterisk. If the document with both major and minor descriptors is taken to be the analysis of maximum exhaustivity, three levels of exhaustivity can be established in Exhibit 25: (1) overall document content only, and therefore the least exhaustive (the MIRLYN catalog record); (2) major descriptors only (the asterisked items in the ERIC record); and (3) both major and minor descriptors, and therefore the most exhaustive (the full ERIC record). Thus, the analyst who indexes for a database producer tends to represent an item in much more detail than an analyst ("cataloger") who performs the equivalent function for the library catalog. In the past, the low level of exhaustivity has been considered entirely appropriate for catalogs, which for many years existed exclusively in the inflexible, highly precoordinate paper format; that is, users were not given the capability of combining subject headings when searching for subject matter that was more specific than that covered by a single subject heading.

Although the combination of major and minor descriptors represents the maximum exhaustivity of indexing for this document, it is useful to distinguish major and minor topics. Not all concepts in a document are covered in equal detail and therefore not all deserve the same treatment. The explicit marking of major descriptors in some databases allows searchers to either select documents that are related in a major way to a request (high precision) or in both major and minor ways (high recall). Making a distinction between major and minor descriptors is a rather crude attempt at "weighted indexing."

A term that is common in the literature, but is deliberately avoided in this book, is "depth." As used in the literature, depth indexing merely implies the use of more terms than in nondepth indexing. Whether the additional terms are used to cover further topics (increasing the exhaustivity) or to index a limited number of topics more exactly (increasing specificity) is rarely stated. In other words, deep indexing, or depth indexing, has been used by some authors to describe preciseness of class definition, and other authors have applied the same terminology to describe the extent to which all topics discussed in a document are recognized in its indexing.

Another indexing policy concerns specificity. The indexer or cataloger must, for any indexable concept, assign a term or terms at the same level of *specificity* as that concept. Thus, if a document is about online catalogs, the term ONLINE CATALOGS should be assigned rather than the term CATALOGS. This policy facilitates precise searches at various levels of specificity, that is, it is assumed that users who want information about online catalogs will use that term, and that if they want to broaden a search (increase recall), they will add to their strategy further terms from the same facet in the controlled vocabulary (broader, narrower, or at the same level in the hierarchy).

An issue related to indexing policy concerns the nature of the vocabulary that is used to describe the documents. This vocabulary may be controlled, semicontrolled, or uncontrolled. Indexing that uses a controlled vocabulary (such as a thesaurus or a list of subject headings) is called *assignment indexing*. Assignment indexing is performed by many indexing and abstracting services as well as by the library community. The indexing for some bibliographic databases does not use a controlled vocabulary; rather, it involves the selection of terms that are found in the document itself. This is called *indexing by extraction* or *derivative indexing*.

A total lack of vocabulary control in human indexing is rare, because indexers are generally instructed to use at least particular morphological variants (usually nouns) of the terms they select. More control can be exercised by instituting more elaborate rules for coining terms within different categories—for example, proper names of individuals and organizations. A crucial difference exists between the controlled and semicontrolled or uncontrolled indexing environments, however, in that the controlled vocabulary consists of a finite, published list, whereas the semicontrolled or uncontrolled vocabulary can admit new terms as they appear and that are useful within the indexable matter. The ERIC record in Exhibit 25 shows a semicontrolled (identifier) field containing typical terms of this type. In this file, documents are indexed with both a controlled and a semicontrolled vocabulary.

Because indexing by human intellectual effort is costly and time-consuming, considerable research has been devoted to determining whether it is effective. A number of important issues have been identified and discussed in the literature. Some authors have questioned the major assumption behind indexing, which is that documents are "about" some topic or topics and that it is the task of the indexer to summarize these in a set of suitable terms. Many researchers, however, including Maron (1977), Swift, Winn, and Bramer (1978), and Hutchins (1978), have noted the problems associated with this assumption, claiming that the characteristics of users and their search behavior are more important criteria than what the document is about in establishing which documents will satisfy a particular information need. Their proposals suggest that one should index *for* the intended individual users rather than *about* the document. Database producers have attempted this on a small scale, but, in general, the summarization of documents remains the central principle in indexing.

PARTIAL AND FULL-TEXT INDEXING

At the other end of the indexing spectrum is the fully automatic procedure in which all content words in all subject-related fields are placed in an inverted file for online searching. In this case, the database vendor uses what is known as a parsing algorithm to process each bibliographic surrogate or full text. Although this algorithm differs in its specifics from vendor to vendor, it always has the following characteristics:

1. It selects only meaningful terms from the record by using a stop list (consisting mainly of function words such as articles, prepositions, and conjunctions) to exclude unwanted terms.

2. It processes subject-related fields, including titles; descriptors; and, if present, identifiers, abstracts, and full texts.

3. It places these content terms into an inverted index, along with information about the fields they were taken from and their exact positions within those fields.

The example in Exhibit 26 shows how this process works by providing an ERIC bibliographic record and its associated inverted index entries in the DIALOG system. Single terms in the inverted index come from titles, abstracts, identifiers, and descriptors. The phrases in this index are entire descriptors or identifiers. Searchers may select single words or phrases from any field or fields in the database record; the matching of any term or phrase in any of these fields is referred to as *free-text searching*. This contrasts with searches where an exact match of an entire descriptor or identifier is desired; this is often called *controlled vocabulary searching*.

In effect, then, the document may be said to deal with those topics represented by the totality of meaningful words and phrases found in all these fields. The advantages and disadvantages of this approach can be summarized by contrasting this machine process with the human intellectual process already described. One of the results of human indexing is often that a given concept may be represented with only one term that may or may not be the one used by the searcher. The parsing of the database fields in this way may aid in the retrieval of relevant documents since, for example, the searcher might use a term that matches a word or phrase in the abstract rather than the indexer-assigned descriptor. This supports the view that the processing, storage, and retrieval of bibliographic records are based on the assumption that linguistic redundancy is a desirable feature in information retrieval—that a given concept represented by different linguistic types in different fields will facilitate the retrieval of relevant documents. Closely related to this view is the fact that the language used in fields such as titles, abstracts, and full texts is sometimes

Bibliographic Record (from CIJE, 1979)

EJ206829 IR507016

Title: Status of   Stasis: Academic Librarians 10   Years Later.
         TI1   TI2   TI3   TI4   TI5   TI6   TI7 TI8

Author: Galloway, R. Dean
Source: American Libraries, v10 n6 p349-352 Jun 1979
Available from: Reprint, UMI
Language: English
Document Type: JOURNAL ARTICLE (080); HISTORICAL MATERIAL (060);
POSITION PAPER (120)
Journal Announcement: CIJDEC79

Abstract: Despite higher qualifications, academic librarians still
            AB1   AB2   AB3   AB4   AB5   AB6
lack equality with faculty.
AB7   AB8   AB9 AB10

Descriptors: *Academic libraries; Attitude change; Historical
               DE1   DE2   DE3   DE4   DE5

reviews; Librarians; Professional continuing education;
DE6   DE7   DE8   DE9   DE10

Professional recognition; *Qualifications; Research; *Status
   DE11   DE12   DE13   DE14   DE15

Additions to inverted index:

10	EJ206829	TI6
academic	EJ206829	TI4
	EJ206829	AB4
	EJ206829	DE1
academic libraries	EJ206829	DE1DE2
attitude	EJ206829	DE3
attitude change	EJ206829	DE3DE4
change	EJ206829	DE4
continuing	EJ206829	DE9
despite	EJ206829	AB1
education	EJ206829	DE10
equality	EJ206829	AB8
faculty	EJ206829	AB10
higher	EJ206829	AB2
historical	EJ206829	DE5
historical review	EJ206829	DE5DE6
lack	EJ206829	AB7
later	EJ206829	TI8
librarians	EJ206829	TI5
	EJ206829	AB5
	EJ206829	DE7
libraries	EJ206829	DE2
professional	EJ206829	DE8
	EJ206829	DE11
professional continuing education	EJ206829	DE8DE9DE10
professional recognition	EJ206829	DE11DE12
qualifications	EJ206829	AB3
	EJ206829	DE13
recognition	EJ206829	DE12
research	EJ206829	DE14
reviews	EJ206829	DE6
stasis	EJ206829	TI3
status	EJ206829	TI1
	EJ206829	DE15
still	EJ206829	AB6
with	EJ206829	AB9
years	EJ206829	TI7

EXHIBIT 26   ERIC **bibliographic record and inverted index.** SOURCE: *Current Index to Journals in Education.* **Reprinted with permission of the Educational Resources Information Center.**

highly specific and will therefore be more useful for searchers who have requests for very specific information.

This approach may also be contrasted with human indexing in terms of time and money. The existence of a human indexing component adds considerably to the producer's cost for the database because it requires the use of personnel and physical resources to maintain a controlled vocabulary and to apply it in the analysis of incoming documents. For producers who create databases without human-indexed records, the absence of that resource-intensive component results in substantial cost savings. There are also trade-offs for the searcher. In general, more time and effort will have to be expended in searching databases that do not use controlled terms because the searcher will have to think of and incorporate all synonyms of a given concept—that is, synonym control occurs at the search stage. On the other hand, the searcher does not need to think of synonyms in searching controlled terms that are assigned by indexers, since synonym control should have occurred at the indexing stage.

SUMMARY

It is useful to sum up this chapter by reviewing some of the major indexing policies and issues and by making a general comparison between what are generally referred to as subject indexing and subject cataloging.

In terms of exhaustivity, subject cataloging, with its intent to assign one or a few terms that sum up the entire focus of the document, is the least exhaustive. Although exhaustivity is usually discussed in terms of human selection of terms, partial and full-text indexing would generally be more exhaustive since both make no selection among terms.

Human processing carries greater monetary burdens for the database producer because it requires an additional component of personnel and physical resources. Partial and full-text indexing, although not as costly to the database producer, place additional time and effort burdens on the user in the formulation of successful search strategies.

Relating this to vocabulary, the *assignment* of terms to an item is based on the notion of concept indexing with a controlled vocabulary. Human indexing by *extraction* uses the author's terminology and therefore might be termed "symbol" rather than "concept" oriented (Anderson, 1983); however, it is usually semicontrolled (with some attention paid to morphological consistency), whereas partial and full-text indexing are totally symbol oriented and uncontrolled.

Opportunities are provided by the complementary relationship between the (primarily) controlled selective descriptor fields and the uncontrolled, non-selective textual fields. In fact, the uncontrolled textual fields, often including the abstract, are taken as given by the authors of the primary document.

The abstract, if written by a professional, could be deliberately worded to ensure that the bibliographic records that result would be rich in synonyms. Fidel (1986), however, has noted that few database producers have exploited this opportunity by requiring their abstractors to deliberately use synonymous terms.

It is not clear at what point there is too much subject information and when its impact on the system is just more noise (unwanted items) rather than additional useful information (Blair, 1986). This is obviously an issue in full-text retrieval, where it is clear that subject representation as every word from the entire document results in systems that are difficult to search effectively. In fact, many full-text articles are also provided with index terms and abstracts; a major component of information retrieval research now focuses on how to automatically index full-text documents. This effort will be further discussed in Chapter 11.

6

Language in Retrieval

The overview of retrieval system components in Chapter 3 highlighted the centrality of language in the retrieval process. Users articulate their information needs to intermediaries in linguistic terms, and intermediaries (both human and machine) translate the information request into the language of the system. Clearly, language is very important, because it affects two components of the retrieval situation depicted in Exhibit 3: the producers' activities in constructing databases and the users' activities in exploiting them.

To provide subject retrieval capabilities, modern information retrieval systems process documents and queries in ways that allow words and phrases in document representations to be matched with those in queries. Document representations and queries can reflect either terms that are extracted from a limited vocabulary of terminology that is intended to represent a given subject area (descriptors from a thesaurus or subject headings from a subject heading list) or unrestricted natural-language representations (terms from the user's own vocabulary or terms that are found in textual fields such as the title, abstract, and full text of the document). This chapter focuses on both controlled and natural-language vocabularies for subject representation and retrieval, the characteristics of each, and the effects of each on the search process.

CHARACTERISTICS OF LANGUAGE AND THE CONTROLLED VOCABULARY

To best understand the objectives and characteristics of vocabulary control, it is first necessary to understand the retrieval problems posed by systems in which no vocabulary control is imposed.

A number of problems are likely to occur in a retrieval system in which indexers use natural-language terms to describe subject matter or, in the case of a computer-based system, in which the complete text of a document or an abstract is stored in machine-readable form (the searcher in such a system, of course, uses natural language).

Synonymy

One problem is inconsistency in the representation of identical subject matter. In other words, a particular topic may be represented in many different ways in different documents or by different indexers. This situation, referred to in linguistics as *synonymy,* means that more than one term exists to refer to a given object or concept. This is depicted as follows:

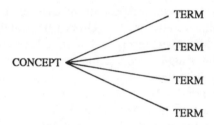

For example, the same pathological condition may be represented by one indexer as PULMONARY TUBERCULOSIS and by another as TUBERCULOSIS OF THE LUNG. Or the drug metharbital may be represented as METHARBITAL or by any of its synonyms—METHYLPHENOBARBITAL, GEMONIL, or ENDIEMAL (trade names). Clearly, then, in an uncontrolled vocabulary situation, the searcher must think of all synonymous words or expressions so as to find all relevant literature on a particular topic. The burden on the searcher is probably not so great for single words, but can become overwhelming when dealing with synonymous phrases. For example, the concept of level (of a chemical substance) in the blood might be variously represented in text as

> blood levels
> serum levels
> blood concentration
> serum concentration
> level of . . . in the blood
> level of . . . in the serum
> concentration of . . . in the blood
> levels in the blood, and so on.

It is highly unlikely that the searcher would be able to come up with all synonyms.

One of the major functions of the controlled vocabulary is to control synonyms—to specify which of several synonymous expressions is to be used by indexers and searchers and thus avoid the separation of identical subject matter under different terms in the system. Such control is achieved in two ways. One consists of choosing a standard part of speech for terms—they are normally coined in the nominal (noun) form—thus avoiding dispersion of a subject under different morphological variants (EDUCATION rather than EDUCATE or EDUCATED). When completely different linguistic tokens are involved (for example, ONLINE PUBLIC ACCESS CATALOGS/OPACS), control is achieved by choosing one of the possible alternatives—the "preferred term"—and referring—by *see* or *use*—to the preferred term from synonyms that users may select when they approach the system.

Synonym control, the expression most commonly used for this process, results in an "equivalence relationship." True synonyms are certainly candidates for this relationship but, apart from abbreviations, there are comparatively few English words that are exactly synonymous (Ullmann, 1963). Terms considered equivalent include near synonyms (LIBRARY BUILDINGS/LIBRARY ARCHITECTURE), antonyms (such as ROUGHNESS/SMOOTHNESS), and other terms that have considerable semantic overlap (such as DIET/NUTRITION). These combinations are certainly not synonymous in the linguistic sense, but each pair is composed of terms that may be considered equivalent for search purposes. For example, Mandersloot, Douglas, and Spicer (1970) maintain that antonyms that represent different viewpoints on the same property continuum may be considered mutually substitutable for the purpose of retrieval. Clearly, roughness may be regarded as merely the absence of smoothness and vice versa, and an article discussing the effects of roughness on the aerodynamic properties of metal plates also deals with the aerodynamic effects of smoothness.

Homography

Homography is another problem resulting from a lack of vocabulary control and is caused by words with identical spelling but different meanings. Homography is a special case of the situation referred to in linguistics as *ambiguity.* It is depicted as follows:

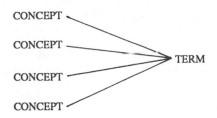

Thus, MERCURY can refer to a mythological character, a planet, a metal, or a car. The controlled vocabulary usually distinguishes among homographs by a parenthetical qualifier or scope note. Thus, MERCURY (MYTHOLOGY) indicates that this term is to be used exclusively for a mythological character and not for any other entity.

The retrieval problem of ambiguity caused by homographs is often more theoretical than actual. Words that may be ambiguous on their own are no longer ambiguous when used in association with other words. PLANT may be ambiguous, but when used with STEEL in searching a retrieval system, the ambiguity disappears and the searcher knows that the term PLANT relates to an industrial plant and not some other variety.

Comprehensive Search

A third problem resulting from a lack of vocabulary control is that searchers must think of all semantically related terms that are necessary to conduct a comprehensive search. To conduct a search on cereal production in the Middle East, a searcher needs to come up with all the terms that might indicate cereals and all those that might indicate Middle East. A controlled vocabulary groups such related terms together. If the vocabulary is well constructed, it brings together terms that are hierarchically related, in a formal genus–species relationship, and also reveals semantic relationships across hierarchies. Gardin (1965) has referred to these two types of relationship as paradigmatic and syntagmatic. A paradigmatic relationship is invariable, one that always exists— as exemplified by the terms ALUMINUM, MAGNESIUM, and LIGHT METALS. A syntagmatic relationship is transient, one that is true in certain situations only—ALUMINUM may be related to BEER BARRELS, but it is not always related to beer barrels and beer barrels are not always related to aluminum.

Controlled Vocabulary Functions

The major functions of the controlled vocabulary are:

1. To provide for consistent representation of subject matter, thereby avoiding subject dispersion, at input (indexing) and output (searching) by control of synonyms, near synonyms, and quasi synonyms and by differentiation of homographs.

2. To facilitate the conduct of broad (generic) searches by bringing together in some way terms that are semantically related, including both paradigmatic and syntagmatic relationships.

The purposes of a controlled vocabulary, then, are to achieve a one-to-one relationship between linguistic terms and the entities or concepts they refer to and to specify the paradigmatic and syntagmatic relationships among terms or the concepts they refer to.

CHOICE OF TERMINOLOGY

The first step in constructing a controlled vocabulary is to choose the terms to be included. Lancaster (1986) outlines the major ways of gathering terms, including literary warrant (where terms are derived from the type of literature to be indexed) and user warrant (where terms come from the potential users of the information service). Two issues that have an impact on indexing and searching prove particularly problematic in choosing terms: (1) the appropriate level of specificity of the vocabulary and (2) the extent to which words are combined to form more complex and specific indexing terms.

User warrant is particularly crucial in deciding the level of specificity of the chosen terminology. One could probably develop a list of several hundred species of dogs, whose names would all be warranted bibliographically, but if the users of a particular system never need anything more specific than DOGS, there is no valid reason to develop this part of the vocabulary in such great detail. The implication of this is that the compiler of a controlled vocabulary must have considerable information about the potential users of the system and about the types of requests they are likely to make, a point that is strongly emphasized by Soergel (1974) and Lancaster (1972, 1986).

Once a vocabulary compiler has decided to include a concept because it is bibliographically or user warranted, he or she must decide whether the concept is best represented by a complex phrase or by breaking the phrase into two or more components. Consider a hypothetical document on learning disorders in preschool children, which is to be indexed at a very low level of exhaustivity (see Chapter 5).

Depending on the type of vocabulary used, this document could be indexed using one, two, or four terms, as shown in Exhibit 27. And, depending on how the concepts were grouped at the vocabulary design stage, it could be considered to belong to one or many possible classes of documents, as represented in the accompanying Venn diagrams.[1] This example shows the difference between precoordination and postcoordination in information retrieval. Both documents and queries are made up of component concepts or facets— "language," "disorders," "preschool," and "children." In a precoordinate environment, these concepts are combined in some way and represented as one

---

[1] Venn diagrams will be dealt with in more detail in Chapter 8.

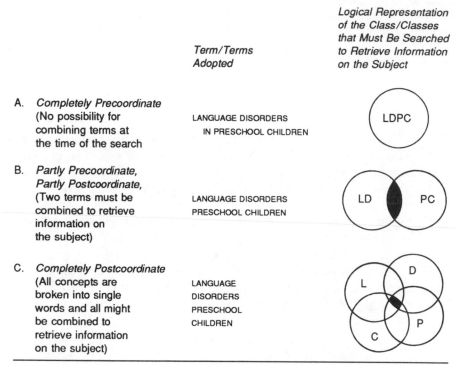

	Term/Terms Adopted	Logical Representation of the Class/Classes that Must Be Searched to Retrieve Information on the Subject
A. *Completely Precoordinate* (No possibility for combining terms at the time of the search	LANGUAGE DISORDERS IN PRESCHOOL CHILDREN	LDPC
B. *Partly Precoordinate, Partly Postcoordinate,* (Two terms must be combined to retrieve information on the subject)	LANGUAGE DISORDERS PRESCHOOL CHILDREN	LD PC
C. *Completely Postcoordinate* (All concepts are broken into single words and all might be combined to retrieve information on the subject)	LANGUAGE DISORDERS PRESCHOOL CHILDREN	L D C P

EXHIBIT 27   Comparison of precoordinate and postcoordinate approaches to indexing.

or more complex statements (for example, a main heading followed by a subheading). Concepts that are thus precombined do not have to be combined explicitly at the searching stage. In a postcoordinate situation, conceptually simple terms are assigned to the document that then must be explicitly combined using Boolean operators at the searching stage to make the semantically complex connections. Thus, precoordination and postcoordination are activities that apply to the language used in the indexing of the documents and to the operations that must be used to search the database.

Lancaster (1972) distinguishes between enumerative and synthetic vocabularies. A totally enumerative vocabulary simply provides a list of terms without the ability to combine them to express something more complex. Synthetic vocabularies, on the other hand, allow some combination of terms to form other more complex terms, either at the indexing or the searching stages. The enumerative/synthetic distinction is not completely clear. The *Library of Congress Subject Headings*, which enumerates many very complex terms, also provides some facility for building new terms by adding subheadings to

	Precoordinate	Postcoordinate
Number of terms in indexing/ query	fewer	more
Number of terms in vocabulary	more	fewer
Conceptual redundancy	more	less
Specificity of terminology	more	less
Flexibility of conceptual associations	less	more
Type of file	paper	electronic (earlier versions involved paper or microform)
Dimensionality	unidimensional	multidimensional
Spurious relationships	fewer	more

EXHIBIT 28   Differences between precoordinate and postcoordinate indexing.

main headings. And thesauri, although intended to be used for postcoordinate applications, contain many phrases representing the precoordination of topics.

Exhibit 27A is totally enumerative and precoordinate, whereas Exhibit 27C is totally synthetic and postcoordinate. Exhibit 27B shows some degree of enumeration and precoordination in its use of phrases and also allows for some synthesis or postcoordination by allowing these phrases to be combined at the searching stage.

Exhibit 28 summarizes the principal differences between precoordination and postcoordination. It would seem that as the language becomes increasingly postcoordinate, more discrete terms are needed to cover a given topic, in indexing as well as in searching. This is actually misleading and illustrates the dangers associated with generalizing from a single example. In fact, the single words used as index terms in Exhibit 27C can be components in the formation of many different phrases. Numerous phrases can be built from a few component words in the same way that many words can be constructed from a small alphabet. Therefore, for a given subject area, a highly precoordinate vocabulary will contain many more terms than a postcoordinate vocabulary and, as such, precoordinate vocabularies contain more conceptual redundancy than postcoordinate vocabularies (Milstead, 1984). This is illustrated by the following example:

Entity	*Process*
apples	drying
pears	canning
etc.	etc.

A precoordinate vocabulary might contain each separate term (APPLES, PEARS, DRYING, CANNING) as well as all the terms combining both the fruit and the process (DRYING OF APPLES, CANNING OF APPLES, DRYING OF PEARS, CANNING OF PEARS). This is redundant and makes the precoordinate vocabulary much larger than the corresponding postcoordinate vocabulary, where only the single terms are listed and the more complex relationships are created at the searching stage.

Precoordinate vocabularies appear more specific because they contain more detailed, lengthier terms than postcoordinate vocabularies. Although precoordinate and postcoordinate vocabularies both allow for searches on specific subjects, these subjects are built into the vocabulary at the outset for precoordinate systems and derived during the search process for postcoordinate systems. In the long run, postcoordinate systems tend to allow greater specificity than precoordinate ones because they allow new relationships among concepts to be generated flexibly and easily.

Retrieval systems based on print-on-paper files, such as card catalogs and printed indexes, are almost exclusively precoordinate. Users of these systems often need to think of only one access point, but it must be the one that is determined by the indexer, and the file must be accessed correctly through the first word in the string. This rigidity may be alleviated somewhat by listing citations under various permutations of the same component terms, as in the PRECIS system (Austin 1984), but this adds significantly to the size of the file and thus to its cost. Postcoordination, in contrast, results in many potential combinations of terms, but only the computer provides sufficient power and accuracy to flexibly unite and intersect them during complex searches. The two file types just described are referred to by Lancaster (1986) as unidimensional (paper) and multidimensional (electronic) and by Bernier (1956) as non-manipulative (paper) and manipulative (electronic). Soergel (1974) prefers the terms "precombination" and "postcombination."

Despite the many advantages of postcoordinate systems, problems do occur. Particularly in single-word systems, syntactic and semantic ambiguities can cause completely irrelevant items to be retrieved. Consider the following group of terms, which have all been assigned in the indexing of a single report:

ALUMINUM
COPPER
WELDING
CLEANING
ULTRASONIC

The report discusses the manufacture of electronic components. One of the operations involves the welding of aluminum, another the cleaning of copper by ultrasonics. Unfortunately, the report would be retrieved in response to requests for information on the welding of copper, the cleaning of aluminum, and ultrasonic welding, although it is not relevant to any of them: False associations or false coordinations between terms are occurring: A document is retrieved because it has been indexed under, or contains, two or more terms specified by the searcher, although they are essentially unrelated in the document or its representation.

There is another possible ambiguity, which can be referred to as an incorrect term relationship. Consider a request for literature on separation anxiety, that is, the anxiety of a child who has been separated from his or her mother. A search on this subject might retrieve a report that has been indexed as follows:

> MOTHER
> CHILD
> ANXIETY
> ILLNESS
> HOSPITAL

But this report does not deal with separation anxiety. Rather, it is about the anxiety of a mother toward a child who is ill and must be hospitalized. This is not a false coordination because the terms ANXIETY, CHILD, and MOTHER are all directly related in the items retrieved. Instead, it is a good example of an incorrect term relationship, a situation that occurs when the terms that caused a document to be retrieved are related in a way other than that desired by the requester—in this report, it is the mother who is anxious and not the child.

These are very simple examples of the types of ambiguous and spurious relationships that can occur in an information retrieval system. This type of communication problem causes the retrieval of irrelevant documents—"noise" in the system, in the communications sense of the word. It is clear that the more terms that are used to index a document, the greater the probability of false coordinations and incorrect term relationships. Since many computer-based systems routinely index at a level of 10–30 terms per document, these problems can be quite severe.

There are ways to avoid false coordinations and incorrect term relationships. One is to use more precoordinate index terms (as shown in Exhibit 27)—for example, separation anxiety and maternal anxiety—or, related to this, to provide for the use of some form of subheading, using one term as a subdivision of another, as in the example ALUMINUM/WELDING. Another way of resolving such ambiguities, characteristic of systems during the 1960s and early 1970s, is the use of links and roles. Links can reduce the number of false coordinations in a retrieval system by tying together (linking) terms that are related in the document and separating (leaving unlinked) terms that are not related, as in this example (Lancaster, 1972):

ALUMINUM (A)
CLEANING (B)
COPPER (B)
ULTRASONIC (B)
WELDING (A)

Because of the assigned links, this document would be retrieved for requests about the welding of aluminum or cleaning of copper by ultrasonics, but not for requests on welding of copper or cleaning of aluminum by ultrasonics.

Roles, more complex devices, explicate the actual semantic relationship between the index terms (Lancaster, 1972):

DESIGN
AIRCRAFT (4)
COMPUTERS (2)

where 4 = object of action, patient, recipient, and 2 = tool, agent, means of accomplishment. This document would be retrieved by a request for the design of aircraft by computers, but not by a request for the design of computers.

Many relationships that are theoretically ambiguous are not ambiguous in practice. The terms ENGLAND, LAMB, NEW ZEALAND, and EXPORT might indicate the export of lamb from England to New Zealand, but the reverse situation is more likely to be true. The ambiguity problem, and means of avoiding it, will be discussed further in Chapter 10.

The decision on how much precoordination should be built into a controlled vocabulary has not been clearly resolved in the literature. A solution for a given subject area (rubber technology) has been proposed by Jones (1971). He puts forward syntactic and semantic rules to guide the decision on when to split a compound and when to retain it. The issue is also covered in standards and guidelines for thesaurus construction, most notably the *Guidelines for the Establishment and Development of Monolingual Thesauri* (British Standards Institution, 1979), later critiqued by Jones (1981), and the *Unesco Guidelines for the Establishment and Development of Monolingual Thesauri* (Unesco, 1981), which is substantially identical to ISO 2788 (International Organization for Standardization, 1986) and to B.S. 5723 (British Standards Institution, 1987).

THE CONTROLLED VOCABULARY

Modern information retrieval systems generally use a controlled vocabulary to index journal articles, technical reports, and other documents that are found in online bibliographic databases, some printed index counterparts, and some full-text databases. The controlled vocabulary can take several forms, including a thesaurus, subject heading lists, and classification schemes. The thesaurus is used most frequently, but the information retrieval thesaurus bears little resemblance to a conventional thesaurus of the *Roget* type.

The Thesaurus

A thesaurus is usually an alphabetic list of terms in a given subject area that can be used in indexing and searching. It provides control over synonyms, distinguishes homographs, and brings related terms together. Consider the simple example of selected thesaurus entries in Exhibit 29. Words considered close enough in meaning to be synonymous are "controlled," in that one is selected and referred to under the others by the *use* instruction. An indexer may not use the term CEREALS but instead must use the term GRAIN, thereby avoiding separation of like subject matter. Homographs (words with the same spelling

Barley

    Broader term: *Grain*

Cereals

    Use: *Grain*

Corn

    Broader term: *Grain*

Factories

    Used for: *Plants (industry)*

Grain

    Used for: *Cereals*

    Broader term: *Crops*

Narrower terms:	*Barley*	Related terms:	*Flour*
	Corn		*Flour mills*
	Maize		*Harvesting*
	Oats		*Milling*
	Rye		*Threshing*
	Wheat		

Plants (botany)

Plants (industry)

    Use: *Factories*

EXHIBIT 29 The structure of a typical thesaurus.

but different meanings) are distinguished and separated by parenthetical scope notes—PLANTS (BOTANY) and PLANTS (INDUSTRY). Semantically related terms are linked in two ways: Words that are related formally as genus–species are indicated by *broader term* and *narrower term*. The term GRAIN has listed beneath it both a broader term—its genus, CROPS—and narrower terms—its species, namely the individual grains. Terms semantically related to GRAIN in ways other than a formal genus–species relationship—for example, agricultural or industrial operations related to grain—are displayed as *related terms*. Note also that each reference is reciprocated: CORN shows GRAIN as a broader term, so GRAIN must list CORN as a narrower term. And because CEREALS is referred to GRAIN (that is, CEREALS *use* GRAIN), GRAIN must show a reference from CEREALS (that is, *used for* CEREALS).

Thus, the searcher, as well as the indexer, is given a complete picture of all terms in the vocabulary that are considered to be related to grain. The thesaurus is able to prevent the separation of related material under synonymous terms, distinguish among homographs, and assist the searcher in comprehensively searching a particular subject area. A searcher who wishes to expand a query with terms specifying kinds of crops may do so by simply including all those terms listed as narrower terms. The searcher may also elect to expand the search in other semantic directions by including related terms, and the well-designed thesaurus will explicitly distinguish these terms from the true genus–species relationship. This helps both the indexer and searcher select the terms that are most appropriate for a particular situation.

Subject Headings

Another controlled vocabulary is the list of subject headings, which is the type of vocabulary that has traditionally been used to provide subject access to monographic and other literature in library catalogs. Two excerpts from subject heading lists are shown in Exhibits 30 and 31.

Subject heading lists maintain the basic controlled vocabulary principles: synonym control, ambiguity resolution, and a syndetic structure reflecting semantic relationships among terms. Synonym control and ambiguity resolution are achieved in subject heading lists just as they are in thesauri: A preferred term is designated in a set of equivalent terms (synonym control) and parenthetical qualifiers are used (ambiguity resolution). A subject heading list may also distinguish between genus–species and other semantic relationships in its syndetic structure, as in Exhibit 30 from *Medical Subject Headings (MeSH)*. Or this distinction may be blurred, as in Exhibit 31 from the *Library of Congress Subject Headings (LCSH)*.

In *MeSH*, the alphabetic arrangement of terms explicitly displays the relationships that are not genus–species relationships (CHILD PSYCHOLOGY is shown

A. Tree Structure

MEDICINE

ADOLESCENT MEDICINE	G2.403.28
BEHAVIORAL MEDICINE	G2.403.90
COMMUNITY MEDICINE	G2.403.220
EPIDEMIOLOGY	G2.403.290
GENETICS, MEDICAL	G2.403.388
GERIATRICS	G2.403.398
MILITARY MEDICINE	G2.403.458
NAVAL MEDICINE	G2.403.478
SUBMARINE MEDICINE	G2.403.478.508
PSYCHIATRY	G2.403.642
ADOLESCENT PSYCHIATRY	G2.403.642.80
BIOLOGICAL PSYCHIATRY	G2.403.642.100
CHILD PSYCHIATRY	G2.403.642.130
COMMUNITY PSYCHIATRY	G2.403.642.150
PREVENTIVE PSYCHIATRY	G2.403.642.150.580
FORENSIC PSYCHIATRY	G2.403.642.208
GERIATRIC PSYCHIATRY	G2.403.642.260
MILITARY PSYCHIATRY	G2.403.642.508
SOCIAL MEDICINE	G2.403.720
SPECIALTIES, MEDICAL	G2.403.776
ALLERGY AND IMMUNOLOGY	G2.403.776.30
DERMATOLOGY	G2.403.776.185
FAMILY PRACTICE	G2.403.776.230
INTERNAL MEDICINE	G2.403.776.409
CARDIOLOGY	G2.403.776.409.163
ENDOCRINOLOGY	G2.403.776.409.323
GASTROENTEROLOGY	G2.403.776.409.440
HEMATOLOGY	G2.403.776.409.543
MEDICAL ONCOLOGY	G2.403.776.409.708
NEPHROLOGY	G2.403.776.409.752
RHEUMATOLOGY	G2.403.776.409.808
PEDIATRICS	G2.403.776.671

B. Alphabetic Display

CHILD, PRESCHOOL
   M1.471.392.448
   age 2-5 yr; IM only as psychol & sociol or social entity: Manual 18.5.11, 34.10; NIM as check tag: Manual 18.5+; no qualif for IM but psychol of the preschool child = CHILD PSYCHOLOGY (IM) & check the tag CHILD, PRESCHOOL: Manual 34.12
   66

CHILD PSYCHIATRY
   F4.96.544.193   G2.403.642.130
   G2.403.790.600.258
   SPEC: SPEC qualif; not for mental disord in children (= MENTAL DISORDERS (IM) + CHILD or other child check tag (NIM)): Manual 27.9

CHILD PSYCHOLOGY
   F4.96.628.193
   SPEC but also the way a normal child thinks & acts; GEN only: consider also /psychol with specific child terms (e.g., CHILD, ABANDONED/psychol, ONLY CHILD/ psychol); SPEC qualif; Manual 27.11, 27.12, 34.12; check also tag CHILD or specific
   X INFANT PSYCHOLOGY
   XR CHILD DEVELOPMENT

EXHIBIT 30 *Medical Subject Headings* displays. SOURCE: *Medical Subject Headings.* Reprinted with permission of the National Library of Medicine.

10th Edition

Child psychiatry   (Indirect) (RJ499)
Here are entered works on the clinical
and therapeutic aspects of mental disorders in children. Descriptive works
on mental disorders of children are entered under Child psychopathology.
Works on mentally ill children themselves are entered under Mentally ill
children.
  sa Adolescent psychiatry
    Autism
    Child development deviations
    Child guidance clinics
    Child mental health
    Child psychology
    Child psychopathology
    Child psychotherapy
    Children of the mentally ill
    Cognition disorders in children
    Hysteria in children
    Infant psychiatry
    Mentally handicapped children
    Mentally ill children
    Psychomotor disorders in children
    Psychoses in children
    Schizophrenia in children
    School phobia
    Sleep disorders in children
  x Children—Mental disorders
    Pediatric psychiatry
    Psychiatry, Child
  xx Child mental health
    Child mental health services
    Child psychology
    Child psychopathology
    Pediatric neurology
    Psychiatry

11th Edition

Child psychiatry   (May Subd Geog)
  [RJ499]
Here are entered works on the clinical
and therapeutic aspects of mental dis-
orders in children. Descriptive works
on mental disorders of children are en-
tered under Child psychopathology.
Works on mentally ill children them-
selves are entered under Mentally ill
children.
UF Children—Mental disorders
    Pediatric psychiatry
    Psychiatry, Child
BT Child mental health services
    Pediatric neurology
    Psychiatry
RT Child mental health
    Child psychology
    Child psychopathology
NT Adolescent psychiatry
    Child development deviations
    Child psychotherapy
    Children of the mentally ill
    Cognition disorders in children
    Hysteria in children
    Infant psychiatry
    Interviewing in child psychiatry
    Mentally handicapped children
    Mentally ill children
    Psychomotor disorders in children
    Psychoses in children
    Schizophrenia in children
    Sleep disorders in children

**EXHIBIT 31   Comparison of term displays in the 10th and 11th editions
of *Library of Congress Subject Headings*. Copyright by The Library of
Congress outside the United States. Reprinted with permission of The
Library of Congress, Cataloging Distribution Service.**

as related—XR—to CHILD DEVELOPMENT). It also indicates for each term the number or numbers of the hierarchical trees in which it appears, thus leading to the *Tree Structures*. In this vocabulary, then, the hierarchical (tree) display takes care of the genus–species relationship, while the alphabetic display deals with the problem of synonymy (CHILD PSYCHOLOGY is referred to from—X— INFANT PSYCHOLOGY) and with nongeneric relationships.

In older editions of the *Library of Congress Subject Headings*, the notations used to reflect the syndetic structure differed from those found in a thesaurus (see the left-hand panel of Exhibit 31). *See*, rather than *use*, referred the user from an entry element to the preferred term (for example, an entry—not shown in Exhibit 31—will refer from "Children—Mental disorders" to "Child psychiatry"); *x* ("see from"), rather than *used for*, was the reciprocal used under the preferred term to indicate the equivalent entry terms. The notations *sa* ("see also") and *xx* ("see also from") were used in combination to reflect both genus–species (broader–narrower) and nongeneric (associative) relationships. Dykstra (1988b) claims that the 11th edition of *LCSH* has been made to look like a thesaurus by adopting the broader term (BT), narrower term (NT), and related term (RT) conventions but that the relations depicted are still very imprecise. For example, in the righthand panel of Exhibit 31, the "children" terms listed as NTs under "Child psychiatry" are not legitimate narrower terms since children are not kinds (species) of child psychiatry. Furthermore, Dykstra points out that *LCSH* is not a thesaurus, even though it looks like one, and that it is unlikely to be useful for searching online catalogs.

Thesauri are largely postcoordinate, whereas subject headings are primarily precoordinate. This can be seen in both the *LCSH* and *MeSH* examples, which contain many phrases and also allow documents to be indexed with more complex terms through main/subheading combinations. This complexity, when applied in catalogs in printed or card form, creates the need for extensive cross-referencing to provide multiple access points. Thus, a term such as INTERVIEWING IN CHILD PSYCHIATRY requires a reference CHILD PSYCHIATRY, INTERVIEWING IN *see* INTERVIEWING IN CHILD PSYCHIATRY to bring this term to the attention of someone who is interested in a complete search on child psychiatry.

Classification Schemes

Classification schemes can also be considered a vocabulary control device. Structurally, they resemble thesauri; indeed the BT/NT relationships displayed in the alphabetic arrangement of the thesaurus should be based on a perfect genus–species classification. In fact, a number of thesaurus standards and guidelines, including the *Unesco Guidelines* (Unesco, 1981), call for such an underlying structure. The *MeSH* trees shown in Exhibit 30 (panel A) are good examples of the classified organization of terms. From such a classification the BT/NT structure of a thesaurus can be derived, perhaps automatically by computer program. Of course, in most classification schemes, the terms will be represented by an alphanumeric notation (as in the example G2.403.28 in Exhibit 30) and this notation (the *class numbers*) can be used in place of the terms in retrieval operations. Lancaster (1972) provides an in-depth description of the role of classification in vocabulary control and information retrieval.

IMPROVEMENTS IN DESIGN

Although the basic principles of good vocabulary design have been relatively constant for years (and in some respects can be traced back to Cutter [1876]), a few suggestions have been made for improvements and refinements. One of these, suggested by the work of Wang, Vandendorpe, and Evens (1985), involves the incorporation of many more semantic distinctions among terms than the current BT–NT, RT, and USE–UF relationships provide. In addition to the genus–species (BT–NT) and synonymy (USE–UF) relationships, they propose breaking the RT relationships into a number of more specific categories, such as part–whole (for example, HORN–COW).[2] Experimentation with term groups formed by these relationships suggests that they may improve retrieval performance in some cases.

More wide-ranging suggestions have been proposed for the improvement of subject headings, particularly *LCSH*. These include restructuring *LCSH* as a thesaurus (Dykstra, 1988a,b) and changing the term form to be uninverted (direct) and more postcoordinate (Cochrane, 1986). It is widely acknowledged that changes of this type are crucial if *LCSH* is to function adequately in the online environment.

NATURAL LANGUAGE IN INFORMATION RETRIEVAL

There are four possible approaches to handling the vocabulary that is used to represent documents and conduct searches in a retrieval system:

1. *Control of vocabulary at input and output.* This approach uses a precontrolled vocabulary such as a conventional thesaurus.

---

[2]The international standards for thesaurus construction—those of Unesco and the International Organization for Standardization (ISO)—do permit a distinction to be made between the generic and the partitive relationship.

2. *No control of any kind at input or output.* This approach is characteristic of a pure natural-language retrieval system.

3. *Control of vocabulary at input but no control at output.* Searchers can use any terms they choose, and these are "mapped" by computer through table lookup, or some other procedure, to the controlled terms of the system.

4. *No control at input but loose control at output.* This approach is implemented through the use of a "search-only" thesaurus and can be referred to as a postcontrolled vocabulary.

The first of these options was covered in detail in the preceding section; however, a number of events have prompted some researchers to suggest that controlled vocabularies be abandoned (Cleverdon, 1984) in favor of natural-language systems. This opinion has emerged for a variety of reasons, including

1. The increase in the number of documents that need to be indexed

2. The increasing volume of natural-language text that can be searched, particularly the full texts of documents

3. The expense associated with the development, maintenance, and application of a controlled vocabulary

4. The delay in the appearance of documents in bibliographic sources due to the time needed to index them

5. The artificiality of the controlled vocabulary and the undesirability of its imposition on the searcher, particularly the naive end user.

Pure natural-language retrieval systems generally use elements that are already present in a bibliographic record (that is, terms do not need to be intellectually assigned by the database producer); these include the title, abstract (produced by the author), and sometimes the full text. These bibliographic records are processed by the online vendor in the same way that records indexed by humans are, but the only means of subject access is through words that are actually used in the title, abstract, or text.

The problems of searching in such an environment were discussed earlier in this chapter on justifying the use of controlled vocabularies. In natural-language retrieval, the searcher must work harder to develop a search strategy, relying largely on his or her knowledge of the subject area or on terminology gleaned from the individual for whom the search is being conducted. For the naive end user, who may not understand that all synonyms and semantically related terms must be included, the search will not be truly comprehensive. But natural language does have several clear advantages over controlled vocabulary besides the primarily economic ones. A major advantage is its open-endedness. Whereas a controlled vocabulary is a finite list from which relevant terms must be chosen, natural-language document representations and queries allow possibilities in the choice of words and phrase combinations that are restricted only by the limits of the language itself. Natural language is also more specific than a controlled vocabulary. The compilers of a controlled vocabulary should determine appropriate levels of specificity by examining requests made to the system. This process must be ongoing because a term that is specific enough at one point may later be too general. This is particularly true in rapidly developing subject areas: Where an all-encompassing term may at first be adequate (for example, COMPUTERS), the literature may later become so large and subspecialized that more specific terminology is necessary (for example, MINICOMPUTERS, MICROCOMPUTERS). Natural language is always current and sufficiently specific, whereas controlled vocabularies are often outdated and too general.

A compromise between pure controlled vocabulary and pure natural-language systems is the use of control at either the indexing or the search stage, with no control at the opposite end. Control at input without complete control at output has existed for some time in a few systems, where it is possible for the searcher to use certain *entry vocabulary* terms that are converted by table lookup to the controlled terms of the system. But, clearly, an extremely large entry vocabulary would be needed to ensure that a searcher's natural-language terms would be recognized by the system. Rada, Mill, Letourneau, and Johnston (1988) have proposed a means for systematically creating and evaluating *MeSH* entry terms.

The other compromise, the postcontrolled vocabulary, seems to have much to commend it for computer-based information retrieval. If implemented properly, this approach combines the advantages of natural language with many of those of the conventional controlled vocabulary. Thus, a search can be conducted at a highly specific level on text words—for example, on Hussein or Varig— or it can be conducted more generically with the word groups of the search thesaurus—for example, on the "Jordan" group or the "airline" group. With this approach, the specificity exists if the searcher needs to use it, but the capability for various levels of generic search also exists. In the conventional approach to vocabulary control, however, the search is entirely limited by the specificity of the terms of the controlled vocabulary, and this may mean that a search for references to King Hussein must retrieve everything indexed under JORDAN, much of which may not be relevant. One approach to the postcontrolled vocabulary has been described by Lefever, Freedman and Schultz (1972). The "hedges" (groups of words and phrases on frequently searched subjects) provided for several databases available on commercial information retrieval services are representative of this concept (Sievert and Boyce, 1983).

In general, current thinking seems to be that bibliographic information retrieval systems should allow both natural-language and controlled vocabulary searching. Those investigating subject-searching capabilities in online catalogs emphasize system designs that allow for keyword searching (Markey 1984b) and enhancement of catalog records with natural-language representations, such as indexes and tables of contents (Cochrane, 1986). The provision of both approaches is justified by the different nature of these languages and further supported by research studies demonstrating the complementary nature of natural-language and controlled vocabulary in retrieval. Studies by Katzer et al. (1982), Tenopir (1984), and others have shown that each approach can retrieve relevant documents that were not found by the others. A recent study by Fidel (1992) suggests which factors will favor the controlled vocabulary search and which the text search. From a study of 281 real searches performed by 47 trained searchers, Fidel identified various factors affecting searcher choice of controlled terms versus text words. She found that there is more reliance on text in some subject areas than others (although this may be less related to the characteristics of the subject or its language than to the quality of the controlled vocabularies used in various databases—especially their specificity—and to the quality of the controlled vocabulary indexing).

7

The Selection and Evaluation of Databases

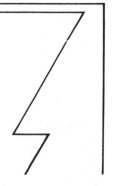

Once the information specialist understands the requester's information need, he or she must decide which databases to search. Thirty years ago this decision was relatively simple, at least in the small library or information center: The candidates were the relatively few printed indexing and abstracting services immediately at hand. The situation today is very different, because even the smallest libraries can have access to hundreds of databases. This enhances the information retrieval capabilities of the library, but it also presents the librarian with great challenges. The danger is that he or she will concentrate on a handful of sources that are more comprehensive or familiar even though these will not always be the ones that are most appropriate to a particular information need. Special problems are posed by interdisciplinary topics, which might be approached through a wide variety of databases.

It is not always true that a search should be performed in an electronic source. A search in a printed tool will be cheaper and quicker than accessing an online database if one needs only a few recent references on some simple topic. Even in this situation, however, a database that is readily accessible on CD-ROM may be preferable to the printed index, since it will yield a convenient printout of references or abstracts.

In dealing with certain types of "ready-reference" questions, the librarian also may have to decide whether to use a printed or an electronic source. Havener (1990) has described a study in which print sources were compared with online sources for answering ready-reference questions. He reports that "simple factual" questions (for instance, finding an address) were answered faster using print sources but that the online sources gave better results for conceptual questions. Because the conceptual questions involved requests for references to periodical articles—that is, a true literature search, albeit not comprehensive—it is doubtful that they are really ready reference. Anderson

(1989) has dealt with true ready reference; he presents compelling evidence that online searching is cost-effective for many types of questions that are commonly received by a public library.

This chapter covers the various tools that are available to the information specialist in the selection of databases and discusses several studies that have looked at the database selection process in detail. It also deals with the evaluation of databases.

PRINTED SOURCES

Most online vendors produce catalogs of their databases, as well as separate data sheets on each. Such sources give general information on subject scope, time span of the data, search capabilities, costs, and related matters. Subject indexes are usually included in these catalogs, but they tend to be at a very general level. These sources are useful, of course, but more for general background on the databases that are available or for specific details on a database that one has already decided to search. They are of limited value in database selection: For any particular topic, they may draw a searcher's attention to the most obvious database, but the searcher would probably go to that database anyway.

Printed directories of databases also exist (for example, the Cuadra/Elsevier *Directory of Online Databases* [Cuadra Associates, 1992]). These have the advantage of not being limited to the databases offered by a single vendor and may provide more information than the vendor catalogs and data sheets. Nevertheless, they do not provide detailed indexes to the contents of databases, so they are of limited value in helping a searcher determine which databases to use for a specific topic. For example, they might lead a searcher for information on fracture mechanics of tool steels to the METADEX database, which is the one that is most obviously relevant to any metals search, and may even point the searcher to COMPENDEX, but they are unlikely to indicate that CA Search, INSPEC, and NTIS (National Technical Information Service) may also be important sources.

Some libraries have constructed their own guides to the databases they make accessible online. For example, a subject index to more than 250 databases has been compiled at the State University of New York, at Albany (Atkinson and Knee, 1986) that provides several hundred access points. Although a few specific terms are included, the index still deals more with generalities (almost 20 databases are listed under MEDICINE, 10 under ENERGY, and 6 under SUICIDE).

The *BSO Referral Index* (1985) is fairly specific. It is a printed index to the contents of 36 databases that are available on DIALOG. It is a relative index— for instance, the term AGRICULTURE is shown in many different contexts, such as economics, engineering, management, marketing, and statistics—and the access points are those provided by Unesco's Broad System of Ordering.

The thesauri that are used in the indexing of databases are very useful in indicating the precise scope of any given database, but one would not want to consult multiple thesauri, even assuming they were readily accessible, to select the best database for every search. Moreover, not all databases use controlled vocabularies. A tool that combines the vocabularies of many different databases would be much more useful; such a tool is described in the next section.

DATABASE INDEXES

Some vendors have compiled databases that are, in effect, indexes to the databases they make available. These include DIALINDEX (Dialog Information Services), CROS (BRS Information Technologies), and DBI (Orbit Search Service).[1] These tools (which have also been referred to as "cross-file indexes," "term frequency indexes," or, simply, "online indexes") are essentially searchable files containing all access points provided in all the databases the vendor supplies (such as index terms plus keywords occurring in titles, abstracts, or full text). They can be searched in much the same way as other databases—on logical combinations of terms.

The potential value of these types or tools is illustrated in Exhibit 32, which shows the most highly ranked databases for a search in DIALINDEX on the topic of damage to metals caused by laser cutting. To perform this search, an experienced academic librarian chose the METADEX database, which, since it deals exclusively with metals, was the obvious choice. The DIALINDEX results, however, suggest that METADEX might have actually been a poor choice: The INSPEC database contains many more potentially relevant items than METADEX, and six other databases (some rather surprisingly) look more useful for this topic than METADEX. The exhibit also illustrates the value of a tool such as DIALINDEX in reminding the searcher not to overlook databases that emphasize particular documentary forms: technical reports (NTIS), conference papers (EI Engineering Meetings), and full text (Kirk-Othmer Encyclopedia of Chemical Technology).

The data presented in Exhibit 32 suggest that using this kind of index is much easier than it really is. In the first place, different databases use different terminology, so it frequently will be necessary for the searcher to think of all possible synonyms for a term—not a trivial task, as explained in Chapter 6. Moreover, a superficial search may give different results from a more sophisticated approach. For example, the idea of "damage" may be implicit in an article rather than explicit; the knowledgeable searcher will want to use additional terms, such as "vaporization," that are likely to relate to damage from

---

[1] BRS and Orbit are subsidiaries of InfoPro Technologies (formerly Maxwell Online).

Rank	Database	Number of Items Matching Strategy
1	INSPEC	57
2	COMPENDEX	35
3	AEROSPACE	34
4	NTIS	23
5	WELDASEARCH	19
6	DOE ENERGY	17
7	SPIN	13
8	METADEX	12
9	EI Engineering Meetings	7
10	Kirk-Othmer Encyclopedia of Chemical Technology [others]	7

EXHIBIT 32   Most highly ranked databases in terms of possible relevance to the topic "damage to metals by laser cutting." SOURCE: Hu (1987). Reprinted with permission of the author.

lasers. Finally, the indexes group the databases that they cover into categories, and the user must select the categories to be searched. A single category will frequently be the one that is most obviously relevant to a particular topic, but some topics may cross several categories (DIALINDEX now has more than 100 categories). And some databases that may be highly relevant to a certain subject category are not necessarily members of the category. For example, the environment/pollution categories in DIALINDEX do not include the Department of Energy's ENERGY database, even though for some pollution topics, such as acid rain, it may actually contain more relevant items than any other database. Nor do they include NTIS, also important for environmental topics, although this database does appear in DIALINDEX's energy category.

Despite their drawbacks, these indexes are potentially very valuable in optimizing the selection of databases and can be powerful tools in the hands of sophisticated searchers. They are useful in the selection of the most productive sources for a particular topic and also in the identification of sources that are most relevant to the scope of a particular library or information center (Byler and Ravenhall, 1988).

AUTOMATIC AIDS

In an ideal situation, a searcher would be able to enter a narrative description of an information need into some form of database selector that would then rank all available databases according to probable relevance to the need described and provide a facility to connect the searcher to any database selected. The desirability of such a tool was recognized nearly 20 years ago (Lancaster, 1974a), and work toward interfaces that would include a device of this kind has gone on for some time (see, for example, Marcus and Reintjes [1977]) and Williams [1977]).

This ideal has not yet been reached, but tools that approach it have been developed. For example, Trautman and von Flittner (1989) have described an "expert system" for use on a microcomputer. The prototype they discuss will give all databases that are included a composite numerical score earned on nine different attributes, including type of material covered, subject area, time span, language, and target audience. This seeming sophistication, however, is somewhat misleading. For almost all searches, the overriding factor in the selection of databases will be the match between the subject matter of the request and the subject coverage of the database (rather than type of document, language, or other attribute). In the prototype described, database coverage is represented only in general terms (derived, in fact, from categorizations in the published directories), not at the specific term level provided by the database indexes, so it will draw one's attention to the obvious databases rather than to those that are less obvious. As the authors point out, this tool may help the novice but is unlikely to be of much use to the expert searcher.

At least one multiple-vendor gateway that will lead a user of online facilities to the selection of an appropriate database is commercially available. EASYNET, developed by Telebase Systems, Inc., provides access to several hundred databases made available by DIALOG, InfoPro Technologies, and other vendors (Hu, 1987, 1988; McCarthy, 1986; O'Leary, 1988; van Brakel, 1988a). EASYNET exists in various versions, each intended for a particular audience, including one called INFOMASTER that is offered by the Western Union Telegraph Company. EASYNET offers several capabilities to the user of online information services, including access to a multitude of online sources through one log-on operation, a single billing procedure, and a common query language, as well as database selection. It uses a menu approach to help the user narrow the scope of a search and to select an appropriate database.

Use of the EASYNET/INFOMASTER menu, which incorporates the type of materials covered by the databases as well as the subject area, can be illustrated by a simple example from Hu (1987), who wanted to find periodical articles on artificial intelligence. The first subject screen gave her a choice of six broad subject categories, from which she selected the category Computer, Science, Technology. The next screen presented seven subdivisions of this broad area, from which Computer, Engineering, Technology was selected. This subdivision also had seven subdivisions, from which Computer was selected. The next screen offered three categories of computer information: (1) home, business, or educational use, (2) research and technical information, and (3) telecommunications. Hu selected the first of these, and the next screen offered a choice among the types of materials covered: research and popular magazines, the full text of magazines, books on computers, encyclopedias, and a list of related databases. She chose the first of these and was then asked to enter the specific topic of the search. The terms ARTIFICIAL INTELLIGENCE *or* AI, when entered by Hu, led to the selection of the MICROCOMPUTER INDEX database, which was then searched, informing Hu that there were 461 items satisfying the search requirement.

The implication of this particular menu approach is that the terms input by the searcher, once the subject scope has been narrowed and the type of material selected, will lead the user to the most appropriate database within that category. Hu's study, however, suggests that this is not true—that, for example, once a searcher has used the menu to narrow down to "databases of periodical articles on home, business, or educational use of computers," the same database (in this case MICROCOMPUTER INDEX) may be selected, whatever terms are input by the searcher. In fact, Hu showed that a completely nonsensical string of characters, when entered in place of subject terms, led to the selection of the same database. It was not clear to her on what basis the final selection of database was made; she suggests that commercial interests may play a part.

EASYNET offers another feature—EASYNET SCAN. Once the searcher has narrowed the search as far as the menus will allow, he or she can enter search terms and get a display of the databases within the category, showing the number of times the term or combination of terms occurs in each, as well as the level of information offered by the database (bibliographic reference, abstract, or full text). Most displays thus generated will also include a "recommended database indicator (RDI)," which is a symbol indicating the database that Telebase Systems, Inc. recommends most strongly within a particular category, presumably because it is the obvious primary database for that category (ERIC for education, PAIS International for public and international affairs, and so on). In a series of four articles, Meyer and Ruiz (1990a,b,c) and Ruiz and Meyer (1990) have studied the databases selected by EASYNET users through the SCAN feature. They concluded that the presence of an RDI in a display exerted more influence than any other factor, including cost, on user selection of a database. Users were influenced more by the RDI than even the number of times the search terms occurred in the database.

The analysis by Meyer and Ruiz casts further light on the results achieved by Hu. Almost without exception, the database selected in Hu's study was one bearing an RDI. It seems, then, that EASYNET always selects the RDI database within a category or subcategory that was arrived at by the searcher whenever an RDI has been assigned to databases in that category/subcategory.

Dialog Information Services has developed its own interface approach to selected databases: DIALOG Business Connection provides access to DIALOG business databases and DIALOG Medical Connection to DIALOG sources on medicine. These are similar to EASYNET in that they operate through the use of menus, but differ from it because they do not lead the user to a particular database; instead, they guide the user to a search approach that is then applied to the group of databases. As O'Leary (1986) points out, "the user never does know which database is actually being searched" (p. 15).

RELATED STUDIES

Many articles compare the coverage and quality of databases in various subject fields. Some authors also offer guidelines on the selection of databases in broad subject areas. Snow (1985) deals with the life sciences. El-Shooky et al. (1988) present guidelines on the selection of databases to answer industrial information requests, with special reference to the needs of developing countries. Wanger (1977) has discussed criteria for database selection, and Chamis (1988) describes the use of Battelle's Vocabulary Switching System in database selection, although this tool is not widely accessible.

Hu (1987, 1988) has undertaken a major investigation of the database selection process. She compared actual database selections made by experienced searchers with selections made by graduate students in library science, aided by INFOMASTER, for the same group of 50 queries. She concluded that the results using INFOMASTER depend heavily on the human decision concerning the broad subject area into which a query falls (the menu selection process) and that when the gateway user selects the best subject category for a query, INFOMASTER can do database selection as well as the experienced searcher. In 29 of the 50 searches, the database selected by INFOMASTER was the same as that selected by the experienced searcher; in 13 cases the searcher was judged to have made a better selection, and in 8 cases the INFOMASTER selection was judged better. The standard by which the selection process was judged was the number of "possibly relevant" items that were contained in the database as revealed by a search in DIALINDEX. A more limited evaluation of EASYNET was undertaken by van Brakel (1988b), who also compiled a detailed list of criteria by which gateways should be evaluated. His experiences with the database selection features were similar to those reported by Hu.

DATABASE QUALITY

So far in this chapter the value of databases has been discussed only in relation to their coverage of the literature on specific topics. At this point, it seems appropriate to look at the quality of databases from a broader perspective.

A bibliographic database cannot be evaluated in isolation but only in terms of its value in responding to various information needs. In relation to a particular information need, it can be evaluated according to four principal criteria:

1. *Coverage*. How much of the literature on the topic, published within a particular time period, is included?

2. *Retrievability*. How much of the literature on the topic, included in the database, can be found using reasonable search strategies?

3. *Predictability*. Using information in the database, how well can a user judge which items will and which will not be useful?

4. *Timeliness*. Are recently published items retrievable or do indexing/ abstracting delays lead to a situation in which items retrieved represent old rather than new research results?

Coverage

Evaluating the coverage of a database is similar to evaluating the completeness of a library collection. One way to evaluate the coverage of a library's collection on some subject is to find reliable bibliographies on the topic and to check these against the collection. This technique also can be used to evaluate the coverage of indexing/abstracting services. Martyn (1967) and Martyn and Slater (1964) have illustrated the use of this method. Suppose, for example, that you want to evaluate the coverage of MEDLARS/MEDLINE on the subject of psychosomatic diseases and that you can find a bibliography that looks or claims to be comprehensive on this subject for some period. In this case, the task is easy: Entries in the bibliography are checked against the database by author to determine which are included and which are not. As a result, one might conclude that the database covers, say, 84 percent of this literature. Of course, one needs to know something about the policies of the database being evaluated—for example, that MEDLINE is devoted almost exclusively to periodical articles and includes no monographs.

This technique is not without flaws. Comprehensive bibliographies are not easy to find. Moreover, one may know nothing about how a bibliography was compiled. If a bibliography was compiled primarily from the use of MEDLINE or *Index Medicus* (roughly MEDLINE's printed equivalent), it would be of very little use in evaluating this database, although it would be useful in evaluating some other database. But a comprehensive bibliography is not really needed to estimate coverage on some subject; all that is needed is a representative sample of items. One way of obtaining a sample is to use one database as a source of items through which to evaluate the coverage of another. For example, suppose one wanted to know how complete the coverage of COMPENDEX is on the subject of superconductors. One might go to INSPEC to identify, say, 200 items that this service has indexed under SUPERCONDUCTORS or SUPERCONDUCTIVITY and use this set to estimate the coverage of COMPENDEX. After checking these items by author, one might find that 142 of the 200 are included in COMPENDEX, giving it a coverage estimate of 71 percent. The fact that the 200 items are not all the items published on superconductors is not important; they form, in some sense, a representative set of items on superconductors and are therefore a legitimate sample to use in estimating coverage.

One could just as easily use items drawn from COMPENDEX to assess the coverage of INSPEC. In this way, one could also determine overlap and uniqueness in two or more databases, as in the following example:

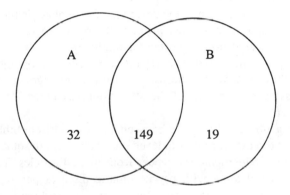

These results might be achieved by drawing a random sample of items on superconductors from database A and checking it against database B and drawing a random sample of superconductor items from B and checking it against A. Such samples would allow an estimate of A's coverage (181 [32 + 149] of 200, or approximately 90 percent in this example), B's coverage (168 [149 + 19] of 200, or approximately 84 percent), the overlap between the services (149/200, or approximately 75 percent), and the uniqueness (approximately 16 percent of the items included by A—that is, 32/200—appear only in that service, whereas the comparable figure for B is a little below 10 percent [19/200]). The same kinds of results could be achieved, and in some ways more easily, if a sample was drawn from a third source, C, to estimate the coverage, overlap, and uniqueness of A and B.

It is tedious, of course, to enter hundreds of author names to determine the coverage of some database in CD-ROM or online form. The solution is to first perform a broad subject search and then supplementary searches by author. Using the same example, after drawing a sample of superconductor items from INSPEC, one would search COMPENDEX on the superconductor terms to see how many of the sample items were retrieved. Then author searches would be performed to discover whether or not the other sample items appear in COMPENDEX and, if so, how they are indexed.

In drawing samples from one database to evaluate another, one must take into account publication dates. For instance, one might draw a sample of items included in INSPEC in the year 1987. In using this to evaluate the coverage of COMPENDEX, one would presumably check by author indexes for 1987 first. Any items not found there should be checked against 1988 (and, perhaps, even later) or, depending on publication date, 1986 or even earlier to account for the fact that one database producer will not necessarily have indexed things in the same time frame as another.

Another source for assessing the coverage of a database is the bibliographic references that appear in journal articles. To return to an earlier example, suppose that one can identify a substantial number of recently published journal articles that deal with psychosomatic diseases. The bibliographic references included in these articles can be used to form a bibliography that could be applied to assess the coverage of the MEDLINE or *Excerpta Medica* databases on this subject.

There is one obvious difference between using items from bibliographies on psychosomatic diseases (or items indexed under this term in some bibliographic tool) and using bibliographic references from journal articles: The former are presumably items dealing with psychosomatic diseases per se, whereas the latter are the sources that are needed by researchers working in this area. The latter can be expected to extend well beyond the specific subject and, indeed, may encompass a broad area of the biological and behavioral sciences and perhaps even other fields. The evaluator may choose to exclude any items that seem peripheral to the topic of the evaluation or may include them on the grounds that a bibliographic tool that is useful to the investigator on the topic of his search should provide access to all related materials that are needed to support research in this area.

In the evaluation of a database that restricts itself almost completely to journal articles (as is the case with MEDLINE), one could take a shortcut to obtain an estimate of coverage. Having drawn a sample from other sources, one could identify the journal articles and then check to see if the journals themselves are routinely covered by the database. In all probability, this would give an acceptable estimate of coverage. If one wants to be more precise, however, the sample items (or at least a subset picked at random) should be checked by author, because some journals may be indexed only selectively and some articles (and perhaps even complete issues of some journals) that should have been indexed were not indexed for some reason.[2] The journal title is less useful in evaluating the coverage of a database that includes published items of all types and of no use in the case of a highly specialized database that attempts to include everything on some topic, from whatever source, and does not restrict itself to a particular set of journals.

There are several possible reasons why coverage might be evaluated. For example, an information center may want to know if a particular database deals comprehensively with some area or if the center needs to draw on several databases for more complete coverage. The producer of a database, too, may be interested in knowing how well it covers a particular subject. In this case, it would be important to determine which types of publications are covered well and which less well. To do this, one would need to categorize the items that are covered and those that are not covered by such characteristics as document type, language, place of publication, and journal title. From these data, one could determine how the coverage might be improved in the most cost-effective manner.

In considering the coverage of databases, it is important to be aware of the phenomenon of scatter. Scatter works against the highly specialized database and the highly specialized library or information center and favors the more general database, library, or center. Consider, for example, a specialized information center on AIDS (acquired immunodeficiency syndrome) that wants to collect all the literature on this subject to create a comprehensive database. The dimensions of this problem are illustrated by the fact that only 24 journal articles had been published on AIDS through the end of 1982, but that by 1987 the literature had grown to 8,510 items (Self, Filardo, and Lancaster, 1989). In 1982, all the AIDS literature was embraced by three languages, but by 1987 there were 25 languages involved and 54 countries contributing to the literature. Most telling is the fact that the entire AIDS literature could be found in only 14 journals in 1982, but that by 1987 almost 1,200 journals had contributed! This example clearly demonstrates scatter. As the literature on some subject grows, it becomes increasingly scattered (more countries, languages, journals, and document types are involved) and thus more difficult to identify, collect, and organize.

The most dramatic aspect of scatter relates to the dispersion of journal articles over journal titles. Bradford first observed this phenomenon in 1934, now referred to as Bradford's Law of Scattering. It is demonstrated clearly in Exhibit 33, which plots the percentage of AIDS articles published in 1982–1987

---

[2] For example, Thorpe (1974), studying the rheumatology literature, got a somewhat different coverage estimate for *Index Medicus* on the basis of journal titles than he did on the basis of journal articles. Brittain and Roberts (1980) also present evidence on the need to study coverage and overlap at the article level.

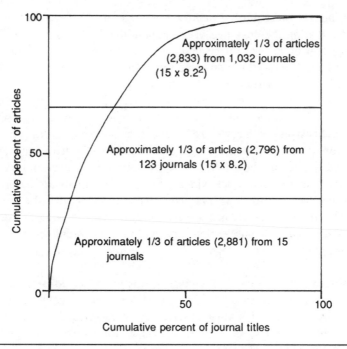

EXHIBIT 33   Plot of the scatter of the AIDS literature, 1982–1987.

against the percentage of journals contributing. Note that as one moves up the curve, the scatter of articles over titles increases at an approximately geometric rate: The first third of the articles comes from 15 journals, the second third from 123 journals (15 × 8.2), and the final third from 1,032 journals (15 × 8.2^2). Such a distribution is typically Bradfordian. In fact, the top journal in the ranking published 550 papers on AIDS during the six-year period, the second contributed 351, and the third 307. These three alone were responsible for almost one-seventh of the AIDS articles published during this period.

An information center establishing a database on the subject of AIDS clearly could not form such a resource by subscribing to all contributing journals. The ranked list of contributing journals, however, can identify a core of journals that should be worth purchasing and scanning on a regular basis. How far down the ranked list the information center can afford to go will depend partly on its financial resources. But even with unlimited resources, a center could not acquire all the journals that publish on some subject. As one goes down the ranked list, the predictability of the journal titles diminishes. Thus, the top 10 titles for some subject for 1986–1990 may well be the top 10 for the next five years, although a new journal devoted to the subject could appear and be ranked in the top 10 from 1991 onward. It is quite likely, then, that the journals at the top of the ranking for some subject will continue to be among the most productive journals on that topic for some time to come. The journals in the middle of the ranking are much less predictable—they may continue to publish articles on the subject or they may not. Those titles at the bottom are quite unpredictable—a journal that has contributed only one paper on some subject in five or six years may never contribute another. Although Bradford discovered the scatter phenomenon in the sciences, and most other studies of scatter have involved scientific and technical topics, Walker and Atkinson (1988) have shown that the phenomenon also exists in the humanities. In trying to build a specialized database, then, an information center must cover some of the literature by direct subscription and identify other pertinent items by regular searches in databases of broader scope.

Martyn (1967) and Martyn and Slater (1964) have performed classic studies of the coverage of indexing/abstracting services, and many other studies of coverage or overlap also exist in the literature. *Index Medicus* seems to have been looked at more often than any other tool, but the *Bibliography of Agriculture* has been the subject of the most intensive coverage study. In two related reports, Bourne (1969a,b) compared the coverage of this tool with that of 15 other services and estimated its coverage on specific topics using bibliographies accompanying chapters in annual reviews.

Retrievability

For someone seeking information on a particular subject, the coverage of a database will be important, especially if a comprehensive search is required. Also important is retrievability: Given that a database includes *n* items on a subject (which can be established through a study of coverage), how many of these is it possible to retrieve when searching the database?

Retrievability can be tested by a study that is supplementary to an investigation of coverage. Suppose one wants to study coverage and retrievability in a variety of subject areas falling within the scope of the AGRICOLA database. For each of 10 topics, a set of bibliographic items has been found by one of the methods described earlier and, for each set, it is known which items are included in AGRICOLA and which are not. A search could be performed for each topic by an information specialist familiar with AGRICOLA, and retrievability could be judged on the basis of the proportion of known items that the searcher is able to retrieve. For example, in the first search, on insects hazardous to soybeans, it is known that 80 items on this topic are included in AGRICOLA. The searcher, however, was able to find only 60 of these, a *recall ratio* of 75 percent.

This type of study tests more than the database and its indexing; it also tests the ability of a particular searcher. The effect of this variable can be reduced by having the same search performed independently by several information specialists to determine what results can be expected in a search on this subject *on the average*. The results can be considered as probabilities as well as recall ratios: for example, 50 of the 80 items were found by all three searchers (therefore, the probability of retrieving these 50 items is 1.00), 6 of the 80 were found by two of the three searchers (so the probability of retrieval is 0.66), 4 of the 80 were found by only one of the three searchers (the probability of retrieval is 0.33), and 20 of the 80 were found by none of them (the probability of retrieval is zero).

Note that retrievability (recall) is judged only on the basis of the items known *in advance* to be relevant to the search topic and to be included in the database. The search on insect pests affecting soybeans may retrieve a total of 250 items, of which, say, 150 seem relevant. If only 60 of the 80 "known relevant" items are retrieved, the recall estimate is 0.75, implying that the 150 items retrieved represent roughly 75 percent of the total relevant items in the database.

The recall ratio relates to only one dimension of the search. To establish a precision ratio, one would need to have all items retrieved judged for relevance in some way (for example, by a group of subject specialists). To measure cost-effectiveness, one would need to determine the cost per relevant item retrieved. For example, the total cost of an online search (including the searcher's time) might be $75. If 150 relevant items are retrieved, the cost per relevant item is $0.50.

An alternative way of studying the retrievability of items from a database involves a type of simulation. If one knows of 80 items relevant to topic X that are included in a database and can retrieve and print out records to show how these were indexed, one can simulate a search by recording the number of items that are retrievable under various terms or term combinations. An example of this is shown in Exhibit 34. In this case, 38 of 80 items known to be relevant to the subject of superconductors appear under the term SUPERCONDUCTORS, and 12 more can be found under the term SUPERCONDUCTIVITY. Additional items cannot be found under these two terms but only under terms A, B, C, . . . J. One might conclude from an analysis of this type that 50 of the 80 items are easily retrievable and that 62 of the 80 should be found by an intelligent searcher, because terms A and B are either closely related to superconductors or are explicitly linked to the term SUPERCONDUCTORS by cross-references in the database. One might further conclude that 18 of the 80 would probably not be retrieved because they appear only under terms that are not directly related to superconductors (perhaps they represent applications of the principle of superconductivity).

Term	Number of Items Retrievable
SUPERCONDUCTORS	38
SUPERCONDUCTIVITY	12
A	7
B	5
C	3
D	3
E	3
F	2
G	2
H	2
I	2
J	1
TOTAL	80

EXHIBIT 34   Example of distribution of "superconductor" items under terms in a database.

Albright (1979) undertook a detailed study of this type using *Index Medicus*. Simulated searches, performed for 10 different topics, revealed that, on the average, 44 different terms would have to be consulted to retrieve all items that are known to be relevant to a particular topic. Although some of these were linked through the hierarchical or cross-reference structure of the database vocabulary, many were not so linked and it would be unlikely that even a persistent and ingenious searcher would consult them.

Just as journal articles are scattered over journal titles, items on a topic included in a database may be scattered over many different terms. This is represented diagrammatically in Exhibit 35. It may be that for any particular topic, a relatively high percentage, say, 60 percent, of the relevant items can be found under a small number of obvious terms, like SUPERCONDUCTORS or SUPERCONDUCTIVITY for a search on superconductors. By adding other closely related terms, perhaps linked to these terms in the structure of the vocabulary of the database, recall might be pushed up to, say, 80 percent. There remains, in this case, an elusive 20 percent of the covered items that the searcher would not be likely to find.

This discussion on simulations has been deliberately simplified in that it assumes a search will have only a single facet, whereas many database searches will be multifaceted. Thus, in a search on insect pests affecting soybeans, one would have to assume that an item would be retrieved only if it had been indexed under an "insect" term as well as under a term indicating soybeans.

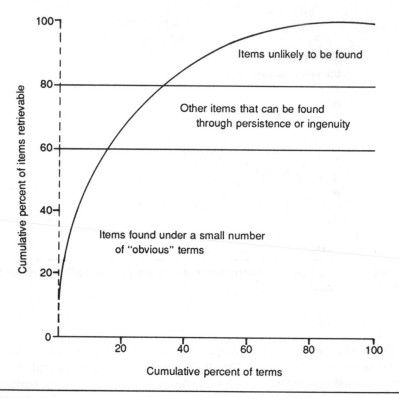

EXHIBIT 35   Scatter of items under index terms.

Predictability

The discussion on evaluation of retrievability made a major assumption: that it is possible to recognize a "relevant" item from the information on that item that is contained in a database. This information may include the title of the item, the title and a list of index terms, the title and an abstract, or the title and terms and an abstract. In general, the longer the representation the more clues it provides as to whether or not an item will be of interest to a user. The least information provided by a database would be the title of the item. How well the title reflects the subject matter is very largely dependent on the type of publication involved. In general, articles in scholarly journals tend to have descriptive titles, whereas newspaper articles may have eye-catching titles that are not very descriptive of their contents.

Titles are not provided in isolation. In a printed index, the title may be considered within the context of the index term under which the title appears. The title "A Rare Complication of Tuberculosis" tells little about the contents of an article, even if it appears under the heading TUBERCULOSIS, PULMONARY. If the title appears under the subject heading AMYLOIDOSIS, however, one gains a much better idea of what the article deals with. In some cases, a clue to the subject matter may be provided by the title of the journal or book in which an article appears. An article entitled "Effects on the Presentation of Information" has little meaning on its own. But within a book entitled *Electronic Publishing*, the title is much more predictive of the article's content.

It is rare for a printed index to include a complete list of the index terms that are associated with an item, but it is usually possible to generate such a list in a printout from an online database in which human indexing has been used. The combination of title and index terms may be quite powerful in indicating what a publication is about. Abstracts, of course, should be the best indicators of content. How well they perform as predictors is the major criterion by which their quality can be judged. Janes (1991) has produced data suggesting that abstracts are the most useful representations for judging relevance, followed by titles, bibliographic information, and, finally, index terms. Methods by which one can assess the value of various forms of document surrogates as indicators of content have been described by Lancaster (1991).

Timeliness

Timeliness, or "currency," is a measure of the speed with which new publications are included in a database. The study of timeliness, not a trivial task, usually involves the following three steps:

1. Drawing of a sample of items, usually about 200–300, from the printed or electronic file being evaluated

2. Measurement of the amount of time between the publication of the original, primary document and the publication of its representation in the secondary file

3. Expression of average publication lag for the file.

Further details about this process can be found in Martyn and Lancaster (1981).

THE FUTURE

The database industry has not yet reached the saturation point. New databases will continue to become accessible online, particularly in specialized subject areas. Obviously, the more databases there are, the more difficult it becomes to know them and to select from among them. Moreover, there is another type of scatter phenomenon in addition to those already addressed. As discussed earlier,

Rank	Database	Number of Occurrences
1	DOE ENERGY	1,175
2	ENVIROLINE	729
3	BIOSIS	432
4	CHEMICAL ABSTRACTS	361
5	NTIS	313
6	NATIONAL NEWSPAPER INDEX	216
7	AGRICOLA	207
8	SCISEARCH	206
9	CONGRESSIONAL INFORMATION SERVICE	187
10	MAGAZINE INDEX	186
11	ENVIRONMENTAL BIBLIOGRAPHY	148
12	CAB ABSTRACTS	144
13	TRADE AND INDUSTRY INDEX	133
14	POLLUTION ABSTRACTS	117
15	LIFE SCIENCES COLLECTION	116
16	COMPENDEX	89
17	EI ENGINEERING MEETINGS	89
18	UPI NEWS	88
19	CHEMICAL INDUSTRY NEWS	86
20	EXCERPTA MEDICA	84
21	NEWSEARCH	66
22	INSPEC	66
23	AQUATIC SCIENCE AND FISHERIES ABSTRACTS	61
24	CONFERENCE PAPERS INDEX	58
25	CRIS	54
26	AQUALINE	48
27	PAIS INTERNATIONAL	48
28	APTIC	41
29	GPO MONTHLY CATALOG	38
30	AMERICAN STATISTICS INDEX	27
31	BHRA FLUID ENGINEERING ABSTRACTS	6
32	FEDERAL REGISTER	6
33	GPO PUBLICATIONS REFERENCE	6
34	ZOOLOGICAL RECORD	4
35	ISMEC	4
36	COMPREHENSIVE DISSERTATION ABSTRACTS	4
37	IRIS	4
38	OCEANIC ABSTRACTS	3
39	METADEX	3
40	TELEGEN	1
41	STANDARD & POORS DAILY NEWS	1
42	WORLD AFFAIRS REPORT	1

EXHIBIT 36   Ranking of databases by the number of times that the term ACID RAIN occurs as of September 14, 1983 (from DIALINDEX search).

as the literature on a subject grows, it becomes increasingly scattered over documentary types, languages, and journal titles. It also becomes increasingly scattered throughout databases, a phenomenon alluded to by Bar (1988) and El-Shooky et al. (1988). This form of scatter was demonstrated clearly by Lancaster and Lee (1985) using the example of acid rain. In 1971, the entire literature on acid rain (one item!) appeared in a single database. Two other databases were involved in 1972, and by 1974 the literature on acid rain had spread to at least six databases. Exhibit 36 shows how the literature, as reflected in the number of databases in which the term "acid rain" appeared, had spread by 1983. At that time, 42 databases were involved. Note the many different contexts in which acid rain had been discussed by 1983: the energy industry (the culprits!), environmental concerns in general, biological and medical effects, chemistry (including, presumably, atmospheric chemistry), agricultural and aquatic effects, engineering solutions, materials effects, and so on. Presumably, if the search was done today, many more databases would be involved because the effects of acid rain have been noted in other contexts, such as the effects on historically important buildings and sites of archaeological significance. Exhibit 36 also illustrates how a topic of concern can diffuse through databases representing different document types: scholarly journals, technical reports, newspapers, popular magazines, conference papers, dissertations, government publications, congressional testimony, and the like.

It is clear from the exhibit that the database selection problem is complicated (a truly comprehensive search on acid rain would involve many sources, and the best one for a search on some specific aspect of the topic may not be the source that first comes to mind), and it is likely to get worse in the future. If so, more sophisticated selection aids will probably have to be developed. Various authors have mentioned the need for tools that incorporate artificial intelligence or expert system features, and El-Shooky et al. (1988), Hu (1987), and Morris, Tseng, and Newham (1988), have discussed what some of these features should be. The tool described by Trautman and von Flittner (1989) already has some expert system features, and INFOMASTER can be considered to have some rudimentary characteristics of this kind, but no database selection aid yet developed can be considered to incorporate true artificial intelligence, despite the fact that Hu (1987) attributes such sophistication to the simple branching menu approach of INFOMASTER.

8

Searching the Database

Creating a strategy for searching a database is similar in many ways to the indexing of documents. The process of indexing can be divided into two steps: *conceptual analysis* (deciding what a document is about and why users of a particular service are likely to be interested in it) and *translation* of this conceptual analysis into a particular set of terms. Likewise, construction of the search strategy involves conceptual analysis and translation. The searcher first tries to understand what the user is really looking for and what types of items in the database are likely to be useful in satisfying the information need. The searcher then translates this conceptual analysis into terms that are appropriate to the database selected. This task may merely mean deciding which subject headings to consult in a printed index or library catalog or it may mean deciding which terms, in which combinations, to use in searching an electronic database. The parallel between indexing and searching can be carried one step further. In indexing, conceptual analysis should not be constrained by the vocabulary to be used. These constraints come later, when the indexer attempts to translate the conceptual analysis into system terms (for example, from a thesaurus). In searching, too, the limitations come at the translation stage. The searcher may be constrained not only to a particular set of terms but also may face limitations on how these terms can be combined.

SEARCH LOGIC

In the broadest sense, information retrieval involves classification. The process of indexing essentially involves the assignment of documents to certain classes, a class being the set of all items to which a particular index term has been assigned (most items will belong to several classes). Index terms can be thought of as labels that identify the various classes. A search in a database involves a decision on which classes to consult so as to satisfy an information need, and a search strategy can thus be considered as a statement of the classes that a bibliographic item must belong to if it is likely to be relevant to the information need.

A very simple search strategy may involve the consultation of only one class; for example, all items dealing with the Middle East. Or it could involve two classes, either of which would be acceptable, as in MIDDLE EAST *or* WESTERN EUROPE, which can be represented diagrammatically as

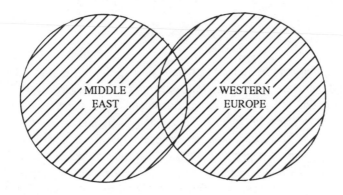

The *or* relationship has several possible names. Frequently, it is referred to as the *sum* or *logical sum* of the two classes; it can also be called *joint membership, alternation, logical alternation, disjunction,* or the *join* or *union* of the two classes. Note that the *or* relationship includes the *and* relationship; for example, MIDDLE EAST *or* WESTERN EUROPE means MIDDLE EAST *or* WESTERN EUROPE *or both*. Items that belong to both classes are just as acceptable as items belonging to either one.

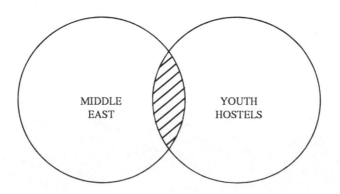

The other major relationship involved in searching is the *and* relationship, as in the example MIDDLE EAST *and* YOUTH HOSTELS. This can be shown as where the shaded area represents the logical set that is wanted. The searcher is looking for items that belong both to the class MIDDLE EAST *and* to the class YOUTH HOSTELS. The *and* relationship also has various names: the *common membership, conjunction, meet, intersection, product,* or *logical product* of the two classes.

Of course, information needs do not always fall neatly into the simple binary relationships just diagrammed. Consider the statement "Youth hostels in the Middle East or Western Europe." As an equation, this can be represented as

YOUTH HOSTELS *and* (MIDDLE EAST *or* WESTERN EUROPE)

and in diagrammatic form as

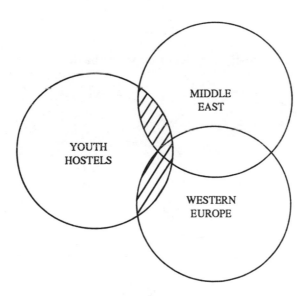

where, again, the shaded area represents the set that satisfies the logic of the search requirement.

A third important relationship is the *not* relationship. For example, the user of an information service could express an interest in any literature on youth hostels in Middle East countries, other than Israel. This relationship usually is represented as

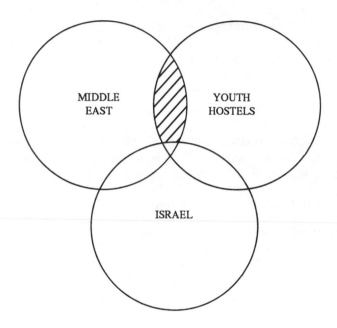

A more accurate representation, however, would be

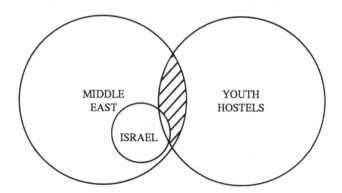

because, clearly, Israel is part of the Middle East.

The logical *not* relationship is frequently referred to as *negation* (in this example, the negation of the class ISRAEL); it implies logical *complementation* (the logical *complement* of the class ISRAEL). Although negation can be useful in searching databases, it can also be misused. Whenever possible, a positive approach to searching is better than a negative one. For example, items that discuss youth hostels in several Middle East countries, including Israel, could well be of interest to a requester. Such items would not be retrieved in a search that specified *not* ISRAEL because the *not* relationship usually takes logical precedence over all others in the programs used to search databases, and the items would be indexed under ISRAEL as well as terms for other Middle East countries. Thus, one would probably get better results by combining YOUTH HOSTELS with terms indicating "Arab countries of the Middle East," which would not exclude items dealing both with Israel and with the Arab countries.

The formal logical relationships (*and, or, not*) among classes and operations on these classes are governed by lattice algebra, particularly Boolean algebra, in many important applications. The diagrams used to represent these relationships are usually referred to as Venn diagrams. Students and, unfortunately, some textbooks frequently misuse Venn diagrams. Venn diagrams should be used to represent search strategies at the conceptual level only, *not at the term level*. Thus, the *class* Middle East is not necessarily the same as the *term* MIDDLE EAST. For example, the term may retrieve only items that deal with the region in general and not those that deal with individual countries. To represent the class Middle East, one might need a whole group of terms in an *or* relationship:

MIDDLE EAST *or* JORDAN *or* ISRAEL *or* LEBANON (and so on)

Another error involves the drawing of Venn diagrams in which not all circles intersect. In a Venn diagram each circle must intersect with every other circle. The following diagram is not acceptable because it implies that no logical relationship could possibly exist between the Middle East and Western Europe:

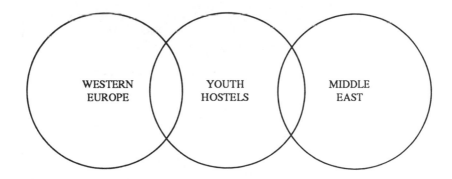

SEARCH STRATEGY

Search strategy involves the conceptual analysis of an information need and the translation of the conceptual analysis into a set of terms. In conceptual analysis, an information need is broken down into its component facets. Consider, for example, a request for a search on education of the handicapped. This request has two facets, "education" and "handicapped," and both are needed to satisfy the logic of the requirement. This relationship can be represented as follows (logical diagrams must show intersecting areas but they do not necessarily have to be circles):

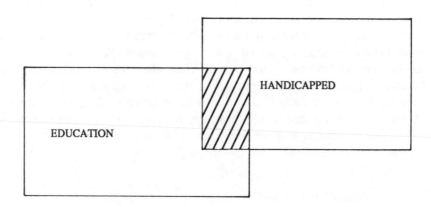

When the conceptual analysis is translated into the vocabulary of a particular database, several terms might be needed to cover each facet:

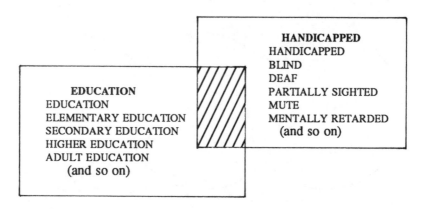

The searcher would need to use a group of terms (in an *or* relationship) to cover education and another group of terms (in an *or* relationship) to cover handicapped and then combine these two sets by the logical *and*. For searches in electronic databases, the task will probably involve entering first one set of terms and then the other, and then asking the search program to combine both sets, as

1. EDUCATION *or* ELEMENTARY EDUCATION *or* SECONDARY EDUCATION *or* HIGHER EDUCATION *or* ADULT EDUCATION
    (2,095)

2. HANDICAPPED *or* BLIND *or* DEAF *or* PARTIALLY SIGHTED *or* MUTE *or* MENTALLY RETARDED
    (828)

3. 1 *and* 2
    (71)

The numbers in parentheses at the end of each search statement indicate that the database contains 2,095 items indexed under one or another of the education terms, 828 items indexed under one or another of the handicapped terms, and 71 items indexed under at least one term from each group.

Not all requests will be so simple. Some will involve three facets or, occasionally, more than three. But, however complex the information need, it can always be dissected into its component facets. The process of searching a database online, then, involves

1. Conceptual analysis
2. Translating the conceptual analysis into acceptable terms
3. Entering the terms to build document sets (classes)
4. Combining the classes in a way that satisfies the logical requirements of the information need.

There will not always be a one-to-one relationship between a conceptual analysis and the vocabulary used in a particular database. Consider a request for information on the effect on fish of elevated water temperatures caused by industrial discharges. The searcher could factor this request into three facets: fish, water pollution, and heat. But the thesaurus used by the database may include the term THERMAL POLLUTION, which implies heat, pollution, and (usually) water. Therefore, THERMAL POLLUTION combined with fish terms would be the preferred first approach to this topic, and it would be redundant to also require the term WATER POLLUTION.

Sometimes a particular search may logically require that different numbers of terms be combined in substrategies. Consider a request for information on expenditures for military-related research. This topic might be searched on the term EXPENDITURES, the term RESEARCH, and whatever terms are needed to cover the military facet. Now suppose that the term WEAPONS RESEARCH exists in the database's thesaurus. This term implies military, so it would be redundant to combine it with other military terms. A logically acceptable strategy might then be

WEAPONS RESEARCH *and* (EXPENDITURES *or* FUNDING)

or

RESEARCH *and* (EXPENDITURES *or* FUNDING) *and* (ARMED FORCES
or NAVY *or* AIR FORCE *or* ARMY *or* DEFENSE)

In translating a conceptual analysis into the vocabulary of a particular database, the searcher must look for the terms that are most logically appropriate to the request. In many cases, a request statement will not translate precisely into the controlled terms. For example, if the term WATER POLLUTION is in the database, the topic "lake pollution" must be searched by using WATER POLLUTION *and* LAKES, rather than POLLUTION *and* LAKES.

The searcher should always be aware of possible redundancy in a strategy.[1] This has already been illustrated at the term level in the weapons research example. Because the term implies "military," there is no reason to combine it with any other general military term (although a specific term—for example, NAVY—may be needed if the search is to be restricted to a particular branch of the military). There is also the phenomenon of "database redundancy." Terms used in a database exist in a particular context. In a database devoted to education, one might assume that the term BLIND has something to do either with education of the blind or with education of people to help the blind. But, in a database dealing with library science, it is most likely to relate to library services for the blind.

BROADENING AND NARROWING SEARCH STRATEGIES

It is possible to express the results of a search in terms of recall and precision ratios (see Chapter 3). Within certain system constraints, a searcher can design a strategy to seek high recall, high precision, or some compromise between the two. Clearly, combining two terms in an *or* relationship will retrieve more items than either term alone and, if the combination is sensible, should improve recall. Combining terms by using *and* or *and not* will retrieve fewer items, thus tending to improve precision. Broadening a search to improve recall will usually reduce precision, and narrowing a search to improve precision will usually reduce recall.

There are many models that show how to broaden or narrow the scope of a search. One approach is to think of the search strategy as having two dimensions: exhaustivity and specificity. Consider a request for information

---

[1] This point has also been made by Harter (1988).

on "lung diseases of spider monkeys in Brazil," which can be represented as follows:

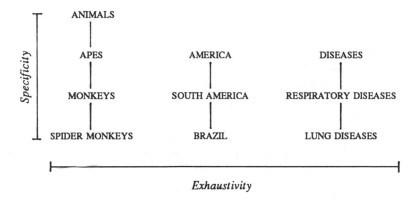

Exhaustivity is the extent to which all facets implicit in the request are required in the search strategy (this is also referred to as the *coordination level*), whereas *specificity* is the level of detail in which a particular facet is represented. The specificity of the strategy is governed by the specificity of the vocabulary that is used in the database. If the term SPIDER MONKEYS does not exist in the database, one cannot search this facet precisely but must settle for something more general, probably MONKEYS. The request is represented specifically and exhaustively by requiring the combination

SPIDER MONKEYS *and* BRAZIL *and* LUNG DISEASES

This exact strategy may not retrieve many items, but any that it does retrieve are likely to be highly relevant. One can broaden the search to retrieve more items—and hope that recall is improved—by reducing exhaustivity or specificity or both.

For example, one could argue that any item discussing lung diseases of Brazilian monkeys in general might have some relevance, so the search could be broadened to

MONKEYS *and* BRAZIL *and* LUNG DISEASES

Note that "moving up" a hierarchy of terms in this way (that is, going from very specific to less specific terms) involves more than the substitution of one term for another. It involves a *generic search*—substituting for the specific term all the terms that are needed to bring in the entire genus. In this case, the term MONKEYS and all terms in the database that refer to specific types of monkeys (including spider monkeys) will have to be used. (Of course, the specificity of any facet or facets can be reduced—for instance, the searcher might choose to move up the hierarchy from BRAZIL to SOUTH AMERICA instead of from SPIDER MONKEYS to MONKEYS or reduce it in more than one of them.) Assuming that the database makes use of a well-structured vocabulary, such as a thesaurus, efficient searching programs should make it possible to bring into a strategy all terms that are needed to perform a generic search of this kind (that is, the term MONKEY and all the terms below it in the hierarchy) with a single command. This capability is referred to as an *explode* capability in MEDLINE.

The alternative approach to broadening a search is to reduce exhaustivity in the strategy—that is, drop one of the facets. For example, one could argue that any articles on lung diseases in spider monkeys, whether in Brazil or not, may well be of use to the requester, so the geographic facet may be dropped completely. Presumably, this will retrieve more items and perhaps improve recall. Clearly, both specificity and exhaustivity in a strategy can be reduced at the same time.

Consider the following strategies and their effect on retrieval:

	Number of Items Retrieved	
Strategy	Relevant	Not Relevant
SPIDER MONKEYS *and* BRAZIL *and* LUNG DISEASES	2	0
MONKEYS *and* BRAZIL *and* LUNG DISEASES	5	1
MONKEYS *and* LUNG DISEASES	8	12

Note the effects of reducing specificity and exhaustivity on recall and precision. The most precise strategy achieved perfect precision but retrieved only one fourth of the relevant items (2 of 8), whereas the most general strategy retrieved many more of the relevant items (perhaps all in the database) but with a precision of only 40 percent (8 of 20).

A popular categorization, described by Markey and Cochrane (1981), among others, identifies four major approaches to the construction of search strategies:

1. Building block approach
2. Successive fractions approach
3. Specific facet first approach
4. "Citation pearl growing" approach.

The building block approach has been used throughout this chapter: Identify the component facets, identify the terms needed to fully represent each, and then combine these terms in the appropriate logical relationships, as in this example:

1. BRAZIL
2. SPIDER MONKEYS
3. LUNG DISEASES
4. 1 *and* 2 *and* 3

In the successive fractions approach, a set is first retrieved that represents one of the facets and then it is narrowed by bringing in the other necessary facets that were identified in the conceptual analysis, as in the example

1. BRAZIL
2. 1 *and* SPIDER MONKEYS
3. 2 *and* LUNG DISEASES

This is merely a minor variation of the building block approach. The results of the two approaches are the same; only the sequencing of the strategy differs.

The specific facet first approach makes much more sense than either the building block or successive fractions approach. Markey and Cochrane (1981) distinguish between this approach and one they refer to as the "lowest postings facet first" (that is, the facet that is likely to retrieve the fewest items is tried first). Although there might be some examples of searches in which the most specific facet is not also the facet that will retrieve the fewest items, this situation is unlikely to occur in practice, so there is little point in making the distinction. For all intents and purposes, the "specific facet first" and the "lowest postings facet first" approaches are identical in principle to the approach referred to in earlier editions of this book as the "least common factor" approach. For many searches, there will be a facet that likely will retrieve many fewer items than the others; which facet it is will be related to the scope of the database. In the example used here, it seems logical to expect that in many databases the facet SPIDER MONKEYS would retrieve fewer items than the other facets (BRAZIL and LUNG DISEASES). The sensible approach to this search would therefore be to try SPIDER MONKEYS first. Perhaps this approach would retrieve so few items that one would want to examine them all, without restricting the search in any other way.

The approach referred to as "citation pearl growing" by Markey and Cochrane (1981) is quite different from the others. It is an iterative method in which the searcher uses the most direct approach possible to locate one or more useful items. The bibliographic records for these items are then examined to see what terms are associated with them (from a controlled vocabulary or words in titles or abstracts). Appropriate terms are then incorporated into the strategy.[2] The revised strategy may then retrieve items that suggest further terms, and so on, until the searcher is satisfied with the results. This approach is really complementary to the others. For example, the lowest postings approach could be used to find the first few items. Alternatively, of course, the first item or items could be retrieved by "known item" characteristics because they are relevant items previously known to the requester.

In discussing the search process, Bates (1979b, 1987) distinguishes between search strategy and search tactics. The former relates to the overall plan for performing a search, whereas the latter relates to the specific moves made in the conduct of the search (for example, selecting the terms to use, broadening or narrowing the scope of the search, and generally keeping on track). Bates (1979a) also identifies "idea tactics," which are really approaches to the conceptual analysis of search requirements.

SOME SAMPLE SEARCHES

It is always wise to factor a request for information into its component facets before proceeding with a search. A request for information on the prevention of odors in the paper industry can be recognized to have two facets: odor prevention and paper industry. Documents are sought on the logical product of these two facets:

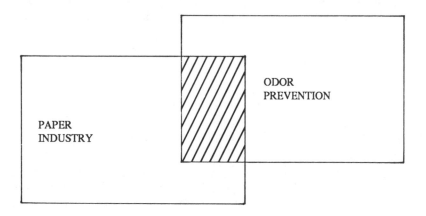

---

[2]The value of this approach has recently been highlighted by Lancaster et al. (1993) in comparing the search methods used by library users and by librarians experienced in searching databases.

The conceptual analysis has to be translated into the terms that are used to represent these concepts in the particular database to be searched. The term expansion can be represented diagrammatically:

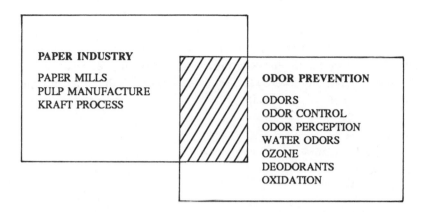

Some interesting points emerge from this example. The searcher has, perhaps, entered the vocabulary of the database under the term ODOR PREVENTION. This term is not present, but the alphabetic display leads to ODORS, ODOR CONTROL, and ODOR PERCEPTION, which are all potentially useful search terms. Using the cross-reference structure of the thesaurus, the searcher is led from ODORS to WATER ODORS and from ODOR CONTROL to DEODORANTS. The term DEODORANTS, in turn, leads to OXIDATION and OZONE, which can be presumed to have something to do with the deodorizing process. A similar expansion of the paper industry facet leads the searcher to PAPER MILLS, PULP MANUFACTURE, and KRAFT PROCESS, which appear to be the only terms in this database that are relevant to the manufacture of paper. If the cross-reference structure of the thesaurus is complete, this set of terms is also complete. If the thesaurus structure is incomplete, it is quite possible that additional search terms will be suggested (by the records retrieved) as the search proceeds. By the same token, an imperfect thesaurus structure may lead the searcher to use some inappropriate terms; for example, OXIDATION and OZONE may not be good choices for this particular topic.

The diagram, with index terms included, may be considered to represent a reasonable search strategy for the request. If a document has been indexed by at least one of the paper industry terms and at least one of the odor prevention terms, it is likely to have something to do with odor prevention in the paper industry.

Of course, not all the terms carry equal weight in relation to the request. Although the terms on the left of the diagram are equally useful indicators of the paper industry, those on the right are not all equally relevant to odor prevention. The term ODOR CONTROL seems most relevant with, perhaps, the terms that might represent particular approaches to odor control—OXIDATION, DEODORANTS, OZONE—at the next level. The terms ODORS, WATER ODORS, and ODOR PERCEPTION are lower in the ranking because they do not directly imply the element of prevention. Nevertheless, a document indexed under one of these terms and also under a paper industry term may reasonably be expected to have some degree of relevance to the subject of odor prevention in the paper industry. The fact that the list of terms can be ranked in a sequence of probable relevance is important because this sequence represents the order in which the search should logically proceed:

1. A
2. A *and* B
3. A *and* C
4. A *and* D

where A represents the paper industry terms and B, C, and D the odor terms in a sequence of probable relevance. For the user who wants to locate only the most relevant documents, the search may be terminated at the second search statement, assuming that some relevant items are found. But the user who needs a comprehensive bibliography will want to carry the search further to ensure that nothing is missed.

Any information need, however complex it may seem, can be converted into a logical search strategy so long as it is reduced in the way illustrated. Some examples at the conceptual level follow.

Weldability of chemical vapor deposited tungsten

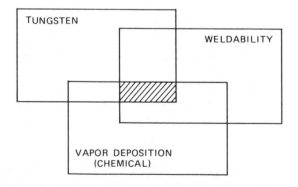

Deflection of square frames under distributed impulsive loads

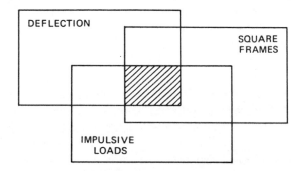

Measurement of the width of cracks in partially prestressed concrete beams

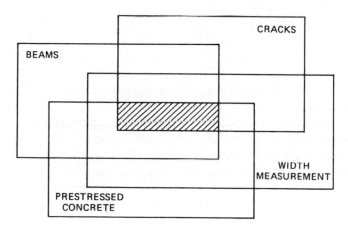

Use of gauzes other than rhodium-platinum gauzes in ammonia oxidation

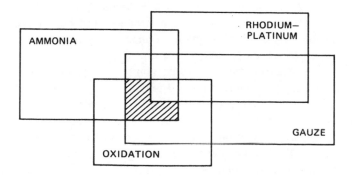

Each of these conceptual representations of an information need must now be expanded into the vocabulary of the database to be searched. As already noted, it is not always possible to represent a concept in the precise language of the database. For example, it may not be possible to specify *chemical vapor deposition*, to distinguish square frames from other types or to express *measurement* of width. In fact, one of the facets of the information need may be completely absent from the vocabulary of the database, forcing the user to search more broadly. If there is no term representing loads, one can search only on the deflection of square frames. If there is a specific load term but no deflection term, one can search only on impulsive loads on square frames, and so on.

It has also been noted that there may not always be a direct one-to-one relationship between the concepts identified and the vocabulary of the database. Sometimes a single term in the vocabulary may represent two or more facets of the search. An example would be the term AMMONIA OXIDATION or the term PRESTRESSED CONCRETE BEAMS. Moreover, the vocabulary of the database may divide subject areas in a way that is different from the searcher's conceptual analysis. It is possible, although unlikely, that the vocabulary includes the term CRACK WIDTH and also the term MEASUREMENT. One must be careful to recognize these possibilities when translating a search strategy from the level of concepts to the level of terms.

A search strategy need not be mapped out diagrammatically exactly as illustrated, although it is certainly worthwhile to adopt some systematic approach to the analysis of an information need before the search is conducted. Nevertheless, the use of diagrams of the type shown here, which can be sketched out in a few seconds, does help to clarify what is wanted in a search. The technique has been proved valuable for an information specialist to use when discussing an information need with a client (see, for example, Smith, 1976).

One has considerable flexibility in constructing a strategy for searching a database online. If only a few relevant references on a subject are needed, the most specific and obvious approach should be used. But if a really comprehensive search is required, the scope of the strategy must be enlarged to avoid missing valuable items. Indeed, being too precise in a search can be dangerous. Take the search on the measurement of the width of cracks. If the four terms BEAMS, CRACKS, PRESTRESSED CONCRETE, and MEASUREMENT are combined by the logical *and*, any documents retrieved will almost certainly be relevant. But, with such a precise strategy, it is very likely that not everything of potential relevance will be retrieved. In fact, nothing at all may be retrieved. The searcher is assuming that all relevant documents have been indexed exactly the way he or she visualized them to be, and this is a dangerous assumption.

The combination BEAMS *and* CRACKS *and* PRESTRESSED CONCRETE, omitting the term MEASUREMENT, may well produce something of relevance. It might retrieve articles on the measurement of cracks in which the term MEASUREMENT has been omitted in indexing. It may also retrieve more general reports on the cracking of prestressed concrete beams, in which the measurement of the cracks is discussed even though this aspect has not been covered specifically in the indexing. In fact, any of the term combinations illustrated in Exhibit 37 might reasonably be expected to produce some references relevant to the specific topic of concern.

It is very easy to test the various combinations presented in Exhibit 37 in an online search. The user can try the most precise approaches first and, if they are not successful, generalize the search in a logical manner. Even if the precise approach is successful—that is, it retrieves some relevant items—the searcher will want to generalize to other possibilities if really comprehensive results are needed.

There are penalties associated with generalization, too. The more general a search, the more irrelevant documents will likely be retrieved. The highly precise strategy BEAMS *and* PRESTRESSED CONCRETE *and* MEASUREMENT *and* CRACKS is unlikely to retrieve any documents that are not relevant to the current information need, but it also might not retrieve any documents. The more that one generalizes from this point, the more documents one is likely to retrieve and the greater the probability that one will find some that are relevant. At the same time, however, the possibility of retrieving irrelevant items is increasing. The combination PRESTRESSED CONCRETE *and* CRACKS may retrieve many items that have nothing specifically to do with the measurement of cracks, much less the measurement of cracks in beams. Nevertheless, this general combination may be the only one that will retrieve documents having any relevance to the subject of interest.

What all this adds up to is that users must "play it by ear" when searching an information retrieval system. Fortunately, an online system makes this very easy to do. For this reason, an online search is likely to be most effective, in terms of finding relevant documents, and most efficient, in terms of saving time, if it proceeds according to the following sequence:

1. Translate the conceptual analysis of an information need into its component facets, mentally at least, but also diagrammatically if this is helpful.

2. Use online or printed vocabulary displays to identify the relevant terms for each facet in the language of the database to be searched.

3. Try the term combinations in a logical sequence according to their probable relevance to the request.

4. Display some of the retrieved references to see if these records suggest additional search terms or search approaches.

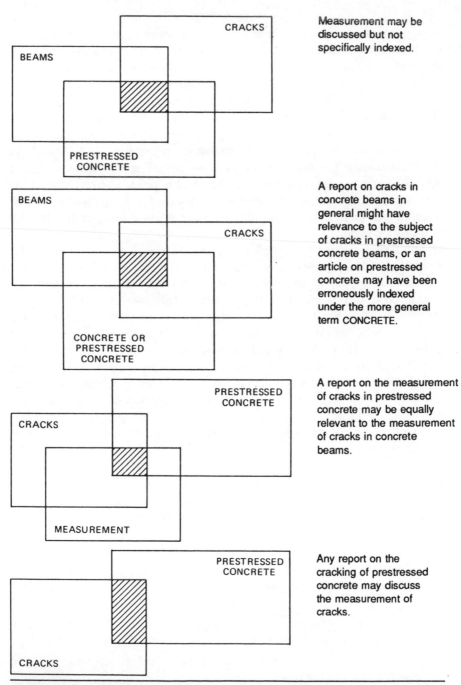

Measurement may be discussed but not specifically indexed.

A report on cracks in concrete beams in general might have relevance to the subject of cracks in prestressed concrete beams, or an article on prestressed concrete may have been erroneously indexed under the more general term CONCRETE.

A report on the measurement of cracks in prestressed concrete may be equally relevant to the measurement of cracks in concrete beams.

Any report on the cracking of prestressed concrete may discuss the measurement of cracks.

EXHIBIT 37   Possible search approaches to the topic of "measurement of the width of cracks in partially prestressed concrete beams."

5. Print the search results when this iterative procedure is no longer productive, that is, when no new search terms or search approaches are suggested.

There are ways to minimize the searching effort or search time in many online systems. A truncation feature, if used carefully, can greatly reduce the amount of typing that would otherwise be needed. For example, if a long list of paper industry terms exists in a database, it may be possible to bring most of them into a search strategy with the simple truncation PAPER:.

It is also advisable to arrange a search strategy so that the aspect on which the fewest documents can be expected to exist is handled first. Consider a search for information on the welding of chromium-nickel-vanadium steels. There may be 20 terms in the vocabulary that represent the concept of welding but only one that covers the particular steel that is of interest. It is much more sensible to try the steel term first, because there may be only a handful of documents under this term in the database. If so, it would be simpler and faster to have all these displayed online and then to select the items that deal with welding. The worst approach to this requirement would be to search on all the welding terms, which might retrieve several hundred items, and then to modify this by the specific steel of interest. It is not always possible to recognize the least common factor in a search, but frequently it is.

It may be possible to limit a search by using words that occur in titles or abstracts after the search has been narrowed by searching the controlled terms of the database. This feature permits a more specific search than the controlled vocabulary of the database allows. For example, the controlled terms may get the searcher to a set of documents that deal with cracking of prestressed concrete, but this set might contain many items. There is no controlled term for beams, nor is there one for measurement. It may nevertheless be possible to further narrow the search by searching the titles or abstracts of the documents in the set to see if the word "beam" or some word indicating measurement is present.

Some databases may have special characteristics that can be used to improve the relevance of the search output by narrowing a search that would otherwise retrieve many documents. In particular, the index terms that are assigned to a document may be weighted to reflect their relative importance in relation to the subject discussed. The weighting may simply be on a scale of two: more important and less important terms. The weighted terms carry some special symbol, perhaps an asterisk (*), in the files. Thus, THERMAL POLLUTION* might retrieve only documents in which the subject of thermal pollution is discussed in detail and avoid documents in which the subject is treated in a minor way. A weighted term can be combined with other terms to form a search strategy in the normal manner.

SEARCHING FREE TEXT

Many of the databases that are now accessible online or in CD-ROM form permit the user to search on free text (that is, natural language—words and phrases occurring in all textual fields, including titles, abstracts, and the full text of documents). Some databases provide access only through this text, whereas others allow access by both free text and controlled terms.

A free-text search benefits as much as any other type of search from the logical approach to conceptual analysis. A major difference is that the conceptual analysis is not translated into a particular set of controlled terms. Instead, the searcher must decide which words or phrases are likely to distinguish the documents of probable relevance from those unlikely to be relevant. Another major difference is that a natural-language search is likely to be based on flexible combinations of individual words and phrases, completely under the control of the searcher. The word is the major unit of search. In some respects, the searching of natural language is more difficult than the searching of a database using a controlled vocabulary. In other ways, however, natural-language searching offers a number of benefits.

The most obvious advantage of natural language is that it permits the conduct of searches of unlimited specificity. Thus, it is possible to look for documents in which individual companies, products, processes, or even persons are named. The use of Berger equations in vibration analysis, the NASA–Langley solar energy project, grinding machines produced by Schneider Maschinenbau GMBH, and the design and construction of the Bosporus Bridge are all good examples of information needs that might be satisfied very rapidly in a free-text search. It is possible to conduct these searches in a controlled vocabulary system, too, but it probably will be more difficult.

The principle of seeking the least common factor in a search is especially important in the use of natural language. A request for material on the use of Berger equations in vibration analysis, for example, could probably be handled very effectively simply by searching on the single word BERGER. It is likely that the use of the word would narrow the search to a handful of references that could be displayed to determine if any dealt with Berger equations applied in vibration analysis. It is not even necessary to think of compound names in their complete form. The word GRINDING combined with the word SCHNEIDER, for example, would probably be adequate for handling a request for grinding machines produced by Schneider Maschinenbau GMBH.

Even when searching on other than names, a natural-language search can frequently be reduced to a few "key" words (the least common factors). Some examples follow. The subject of an information need is stated and, alongside it, a possible reduction of the need to some word combination that might be sufficiently discriminating to handle the search online:

1. Floating concrete terminal
   for use in the Arctic   FLOATING *and* ARCTIC
2. The hot isostatic pressing
   process   ISOSTATIC
3. Machining metals with a
   neodymium laser   NEODYMIUM
4. Effect of antioxidants on
   refined palm oil   PALM *and* ANTIOXIDANT

The point is that it is frequently possible to zero in on a search through the choice of only one or two keywords. The searcher should always be looking for the simplest and most direct approach to retrieving relevant references. This usually means selecting the essential word that is likely to apply to the fewest items in the file. HOT or PRESSING may apply to many items, but ISOSTATIC probably applies to only a few. Therefore, it is the clear choice for a first approach to retrieving references on hot isostatic pressing.

Not all searches are as easy to handle as those used in these examples. The less specific the subject of a search, the harder it is to deal with using natural language, because of the difficulty in identifying all the words that might represent some general facet of the request. The approach illustrated earlier, of analyzing an information need into its component facets and then selecting the terms that best represent each facet, is as important in natural-language searching as it is in controlled-vocabulary searching. The only real difference is that in a natural-language search, it is unlikely that there will be a thesaurus, with cross-reference structure, to help the searcher select all the appropriate terms. In the natural-language situation, more depends on the ingenuity of the individual searcher.

Suppose one is looking for information on mercury levels in water. The mercury facet reduces to the words MERCURY and MERCURIC, but it will be completely inadequate to search on the single term WATER. There are many ways in which the water facet might be represented in documents: WATER, SEA, OCEAN, STREAM, LAKE, RIVER, and so on. For a comprehensive search on this subject, one must think of all the terms that might represent the water facet in the database to be used. This is not an insuperable task, but it will probably be much harder than in a controlled-vocabulary system, in which one might reasonably expect all the terms representing bodies of water to be linked by some form of cross-reference.

In some ways, however, natural-language searching may be easier than searching in a controlled vocabulary. Because one is often dealing at the word level, it is usually possible to reduce a search to a smaller number of elements than in the controlled-vocabulary search. The request for information on odor control in the paper industry, used in an earlier example, could probably be reduced to

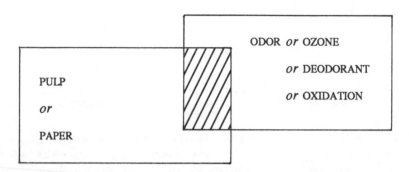

It is important to recognize that although a word may be ambiguous or imprecise on its own, this ambiguity or imprecision is likely to nearly disappear when the word is combined with other words. The word *beam* in electronics means something quite different from the word *beam* in structural engineering. But the combination BEAM *and* (CRACK *or* CRACKING) is more likely to retrieve documents discussing structural beams than electron beams. Likewise, the word *grain* and the word *migration* both have several possible contexts. But when the words are combined in an *and* relationship, they are very likely to retrieve items on grain migration in metals.

It is an oversimplification to speak of the word as the basic unit in the searching of natural-language databases. It is probably better to think of a search strategy in terms of both words and word fragments. Most online and CD-ROM systems will allow a user to search on parts of words through the use of truncation, of which four types can be recognized:

1. *Right truncation*—ignoring the ending of a word. The truncation CRACK: will, for example, retrieve documents containing CRACK, CRACKS, CRACKING, and CRACKED.

2. *Left truncation*—ignoring the beginning of a word. The truncation :MYCIN, for example, is likely to retrieve documents discussing a large group of antibiotics.

3. *Simultaneous left and right truncation.*

4. *Infix truncation*—specifying the beginning and end of a word but leaving the middle unspecified (for example, TRI. . .COBALTATE).

Right truncation is the most useful in many applications, and it is a powerful device for searching on large groups of related words. Truncation is a useful timesaver, because it avoids the need to enter separately a list of terms that all have the same stem. It must be recognized, however, that truncation may also bring in some words that have no relevance to a particular request. DOG: may cause retrieval of items on doggerel or Dogwood Bank, as well as on dogs (although it is perhaps unlikely that all these subjects would appear in the same database). The truncation CAT: is also ambiguous (CATS, CAT, CATERPILLAR, CATALYSIS, CATASTROPHE, CATAMARAN). So is the truncation CRACK:. But CAT: *and* CRACK: may prove quite precise in the retrieval of documents on catalytic cracking.

WEIGHTED-TERM SEARCHING

Before online systems became widely used, searches of databases in electronic form were performed by the sequential scanning of bibliographic records on magnetic tape, with several searches being performed at the same time (batch processing). Many information centers used a "weighted-term" approach in place of the more conventional Boolean approach to searching, particularly for searches performed for the purposes of selective dissemination of information (SDI).

The logic of the weighted-term search is no different from that of Boolean algebra. Term weighting is used to simulate a Boolean strategy, and any search approach that can be achieved through the latter can also be achieved through the former. In weighted-term searching, as in other types of searching, the first step is the conceptual analysis of the request into its component facets and the expansion of each facet through the selection of appropriate terms from the database vocabulary. Each facet is then given a numeric weight, arbitrarily assigned by the searcher, and a "threshold" is established. The threshold fixes the logical requirements of the search; it is the minimum weight that a document record must earn before it is retrieved. Consider, as an example, the following strategy:

> EVALUATION facet 5
> SEMINAR, COURSE facet 5   Threshold = 15
> INFORMATION SCIENCE facet 5

The searcher is looking for documents discussing the evaluation of courses and seminars in the field of information science. Each facet is arbitrarily given a weight of 5, and a threshold of 15 is established. This means that all three facets must be represented in a document record before it will be retrieved. This is equivalent to the Boolean strategy A *and* B *and* C, where each letter represents a facet of the strategy. Note that the same weight is given to all terms in a facet and that a document can only earn the weight of a particular facet once: The document in this example can only earn five points for having the

EVALUATION facet present, no matter how many evaluation terms were assigned to it in indexing. Logical negations (*not*) can be handled by assigning negative weights to facets of a strategy.

Weighted-term searching has one obvious advantage over the more conventional Boolean approach: It makes it easier to produce a search output that is "ranked" in a sequence of probable interest to the requester. Take the following request:

I am interested in amyloidosis as a complication of tuberculosis. I am especially interested in renal amyloidosis, and I am most interested in the use of prednisone in the treatment of this condition.

This request factors into four facets: (1) AMYLOIDOSIS, (2) TUBERCULOSIS, (3) KIDNEY, and (4) PREDNISONE. If these facets are weighted as follows:

AMYLOIDOSIS	5
TUBERCULOSIS	5
KIDNEY	2
PREDNISONE	1

and the threshold is set at 10, a four-level ranked output can be generated:

1. Documents scoring 13 (which, it is hoped, deal with the use of prednisone in the treatment of renal amyloidosis complicating tuberculosis)

2. Documents scoring 12 (renal amyloidosis as a complication of tuberculosis)

3. Documents scoring 11 (prednisone in the treatment of amyloidosis complicating tuberculosis)

4. Documents scoring 10 (amyloidosis complicating tuberculosis)

The document records are printed out in this sequence, which should be of decreasing relevance to the requester. Even the documents in the fourth group, however, are within the scope of the request and therefore likely to be of some relevance.

It is also possible to combine the Boolean and the weighted-term approaches in some batch processing systems. For example, the strategy

$$A \; and \; B_1 \; (15)$$
$$B_2 \; (14)$$
$$B_3 \; (14)$$
$$B_4 \; (13)$$
$$B_5 \; (12)$$

where the numbers in parentheses represent weights, specifies that a document must have both an A term and a B term to be retrieved. Some of the B terms, however, are of greater interest than others, so that a document indexed under A and B_1 is ranked higher than one indexed under A and B_2, and so on. A good account of weighted-term searching can be found in Sommar and Dennis (1969).

FRACTIONAL SEARCH

It is also possible to search a retrieval system by inputting a string of terms that represents some information need (from a controlled vocabulary or free-text words) without connecting logic. The system then looks for pieces of text that best match the input string. Thus, if the original string consists of five words, and some document in the database contains all five, the document gets the maximum possible weight and is ranked at the top of the list of items retrieved.

This technique has been variously referred to as coordination level search, fractional search (Heaps and Sorenson, 1968), quorum function search (Cleverdon, 1984), and best match retrieval (Al-Hawamdeh et al., 1988). It is rarely used in practice, although it has generally been shown to give good results.

SCREENING OF OUTPUT

In some information centers, an information specialist carefully examines the search output before submitting the results to the user, discarding items that seem clearly irrelevant and thus improving the precision ratio of the final product. Clearly, the success of this screening operation is directly related to the quality of the request statement, since it is on this basis that the relevance predictions are made. If the request statement is an imperfect representation of the user's information need, the searcher may well discard items that the user would judge relevant.

The quality of the request statement and the searcher's interpretation of the user's needs, then, are the most important factors influencing the success or failure of the screening operation. Other factors include the amount of time that is spent in screening and the type of document representation that is delivered by the system. The more complete the representation, the easier it is for the searcher to make fairly accurate relevance predictions: Titles plus index terms may be more informative than titles alone, and titles plus abstracts may be more informative than titles plus index terms. The utility of a document record in predicting the document's relevance to a request statement is, in fact, likely to be directly related to the record length.

CHARACTERISTICS OF SEARCHERS

Looking at the effect of experience on online searching, Fenichel (1980a,b; 1981) found surprisingly little difference in behavior: Novice searchers performed fairly well compared to searchers with much more experience. Even experienced searchers used simple approaches. Fenichel also noted great variability in searching behavior, even among individuals with similar levels of experience. Harter (1984), using a questionnaire approach, also found wide differences among searchers, both in attitude and behavior. It was the experienced searchers, however, who were more likely to exploit the full interactive capabilities of an online system by adopting a heuristic approach.

Wanger, McDonald, and Berger (1980) studied 535 MEDLINE searches performed by 191 information specialists. They found that very few of the searchers exploited the interactive capabilities of the online system and that their performance (as judged by recall and precision) seemed to be related neither to the type of training they had received nor to their degree of experience in searching this database. On the average, the search results were very disappointing.

A comprehensive study of factors affecting the effectiveness of online searches was undertaken over a period of several years at the now defunct Matthew A. Baxter School of Library and Information Science at Case Western Reserve University. The methodology and results for the final phase of this project are presented by Saracevic and Kantor (1988a,b) and Saracevic et al. (1988). The study involved 40 users, each providing one question, and 39 searchers (3 members of the project team and 36 individuals from outside). Interviews with the users were tape recorded. For each question, 9 searches were performed, 4 by project staff and 5 by outside searchers, for a total of 360 different searches. A related experiment was also undertaken, involving the classification of user questions by 21 judges. The results of the searches were evaluated by the users in terms of relevance and utility. The bewildering variety of data collected during the project makes effective summarization virtually impossible. Perhaps the most significant finding was that different searchers had different interpretations of a question and, thus, used different search approaches and retrieved different items. Moreover, each searcher tended to find some relevant items that were not found by the others, although the chance that an item would be judged relevant increased with the number of searchers retrieving it. The investigators suggest that these results provide evidence of the need for multiple searches by different searchers for the same question, but an alternative conclusion may be that a team approach to the analysis of a question and a consensus approach to an initial search strategy might be the preferred mode of operation.[3] Earlier, Fidel (1985) had discovered that experienced searchers show little agreement in the selection of terms, and even earlier studies (for example, Bates, 1977; Lilley, 1954) consistently revealed that users of card catalogs tend not to agree on what terms to use in searching for items on a particular topic.

Blackshaw and Fischhoff (1988) view online searching as a decision-making process. Volunteer searchers were observed while performing author, title, or subject searches in an online catalog in a public library. The authors report that searcher performance resembles that revealed in studies of decision making in other contexts. Bellardo (1985) has also looked at variables that might affect the performance of online searchers, using two test searches with students from six different library schools. Findings suggest that differences in performance can be attributed to general verbal and quantitative aptitude, artistic creativity, and an inclination toward critical and analytical creative thinking, but the associations are all very weak. High intelligence and other factors often cited as important attributes may not be necessary for high performance. Bellardo claims that searching performance may not be predictable on the basis of cognitive and personality traits.

Fidel (1984) distinguishes between "operationalist searchers" and "conceptualist searchers." The former tend to select and combine only the most relevant terms, thus moving in the direction of high precision, whereas the latter tend to assemble exhaustive lists of terms for each facet of a search and thus move in the direction of high recall.

Over the past 25 years, a number of attempts have been made to measure unobtrusively the quality of reference services offered by libraries. Such studies have focused on the ability of libraries to answer factual questions. McCue (1988) has now pioneered the unobtrusive evaluation of online searching in libraries. Twenty-one public libraries throughout the United States were each asked to perform the same search in two different databases; the searchers did not know that they were being tested. Two "outside expert database searchers" evaluated the results. Using a point system, each search was scored on strategy, general techniques, and results. General techniques covered such aspects as searcher mistakes in entering terms or the use of incorrect procedures. Results were also given numeric scores: A worthless citation earned no points, an excellent one earned eight points. The library scores ranged from 155 to 419. McCue concludes from her statistical analysis that the only variable that

---

[3]Lancaster et al. (1993), however, have recently shown that even a team of experienced searchers produces rather disappointing results.

correlated positively with high search scores was the number of items retrieved. This is hardly surprising. In effect, the scoring method takes recall into account because it gives positive scores to "useful" items, but it does not consider precision, since it gives zeros rather than negative values to worthless items. The entire method of scoring, however, is dubious. In the long run, it is the results that matter, so it seems pointless to devise a scoring method that takes not only results but search strategy and search techniques into account.

Hansen (1986) compares the results of a group of inexperienced subjects who performed manual searches followed by online searches with the results achieved by a matched group of subjects who performed online searches followed by manual ones. The differences in the results were not statistically significant. Nevertheless, she concludes that inexperienced searchers may get the best results when performing a manual search after an online search, at least in the case of "a large and complex topic with an expanding literature," a conclusion that is supported only very weakly by her data.

Fidel (1991) discusses how analysis of the search behavior of human intermediaries can be used to identify rules by which experts select "search keys"—descriptors from a controlled vocabulary or free-text terms. She claims that when more research has been performed on expert search behavior, it will be possible to build a knowledge base for use in an intermediary expert system for online searching. Hawkins (1988) presents a useful review of progress to date in artificial intelligence/expert system approaches to online searching.

Despite the fact that the online search process has been studied intensively over the past 20 years, Logan (1990) concludes that we have not yet learned enough to explain individual differences in the behavior of searchers.

FACTORS AFFECTING THE SUCCESS OF A PARTICULAR SEARCH

Various factors affecting the success of a search have been covered in this chapter. Those most directly related to the search process are discussed further in Chapter 10. They can be summarized as follows:

1. *The searcher's interpretation of the needs of the user.* The prime factor affecting a search outcome is the quality of the interaction between the requester and the system. Given a request statement that inadequately represents the information requirement, there is nothing that a searcher can do, except purely by chance, to produce a good search result.

2. *The complexity of the request.* The "simpler" the request, that is, the fewer facets involved, the better the result of a search is likely to be. A search that requests virtually everything on the disease of syringomyelia is single-

faceted and probably involves only one index term. With such a broad request, assuming that an appropriate term exists, it should be possible to obtain high recall and high precision. Since the requester has general needs, he or she tends to accept as relevant any article that bears in some significant way on the subject of syringomyelia. Consider, instead, a request on roentgenologic joint changes in syringomyelia. This is a more complex request, involving three facets. Many more index terms are involved, and the relationship among them becomes important. Moreover, the requester's relevance standards are likely to be much more stringent: He or she will probably reject any article that does not discuss the precise topic of roentgenologic changes in syringomyelia. Take a third request: spontaneous dislocation of the atlas simulating syringomyelia. This is more complex still, involving exact relationships among index terms, and the requester is likely to be very strict in his or her relevance standards. With this type of request, ambiguous and spurious relationships among terms are also likely. It is possible to get high recall on any of these three searches, but it will be achieved at a precision level that is likely to decrease substantially with the complexity of the request.

3. *The ability of the index language to express precisely the concepts involved.* The vocabulary of the system must be capable of expressing the subject matter of the request at a reasonable level of specificity. In addition, the vocabulary should be structured in such a way, by hierarchical and associative relationships, that it helps the searcher construct a strategy. In particular, it should assist in the conduct of generic searches by drawing attention to all the terms needed for comprehensive coverage.

4. *The precise subject field of the request.* In any particular information system, there may be certain subject areas in which searcher performance, on the average, is likely to be worse than in other subject fields. For these subjects, the language may be imprecise, the database vocabulary may be weak, or ambiguous or spurious term relationships may be more liable to occur than in other fields.

5. *Indexing policies and practices.* Consider a request for articles on testicular biopsy in cases of infertility. One can obtain high recall on this request, at least at an acceptable precision ratio, only if the indexing policy has been to use the term BIOPSY whenever an article mentions that a biopsy was done. Likewise, one cannot conduct a comprehensive search on all applications of the Pohlhausen technique if, as a matter of policy, the database producer does not index mathematical techniques when their use is mentioned in an article.

6. *The capabilities of the searching software.* This aspect governs just what the search is and is not able to do—for example, can one truncate terms and, if so, where?

7. *Adequacy and accuracy of strategy.* The quality of the strategy depends on

   a. The searcher's ability to select the correct terms to represent the subject matter sought
   b. The searcher's ability to put together terms in a way that is logically sound
   c. The searcher's ability to think of all reasonable approaches to retrieval
   d. The searcher's ability to construct a strategy, by varying exhaustivity or specificity, that matches the recall and precision requirements or tolerances of the user.

9

Evaluation Criteria and
Evaluation Procedures

The users of services of any kind usually evaluate them, consciously or unconsciously, on the basis of cost, time, and quality. A tourist planning to fly from Miami to Buenos Aires will probably first ask if one airline on this route is cheaper than others. If not, or if the differences are insignificant, the time factor may become paramount, with the traveler looking for the fastest flight or the one that leaves at the most convenient time. If several flights leave at equally convenient times, the traveler's perception of the quality of the airline, based on personal experience or that of friends, will then influence his or her decision.

CRITERIA USED IN THE EVALUATION OF
INFORMATION RETRIEVAL SYSTEMS

Users of information retrieval systems also tend to judge them on cost, time, and quality criteria. Cost is as important in evaluating information retrieval systems as it is in evaluating other services and products. The service must be provided at a cost that the user feels is reasonable in relation to its benefits. Cost to the user involves more than direct charges. It includes the cost of the user's time, that is, how much effort is involved in using the system, either on the part of the user or in delegating the search to an intermediary. Studies of the information-seeking behavior of scientists and other professionals have consistently shown that accessibility and ease of use are the prime factors influencing the choice of an information source (Allen and Gerstberger, 1966; Rosenberg, 1966). Generally, the most convenient source of information is chosen, whether or not it is perceived by the user to be the most comprehensive, the most authoritative, or the "best." Ease-of-use factors include ease of interrogating the system, that is, making one's needs known, and ease of using the output, especially for predicting the relevance of the documents referred to. A very important aspect of this latter criterion is the availability of efficient and convenient document delivery. A service that delivers just bibliographic references goes only part of the way toward satisfying an individual's information needs and causes considerable frustration if the user is unable to obtain the documents cited or can do so only through procedures that he or she views as inconvenient and time-consuming.

Users of information services have various kinds of information needs, including

1. A particular document whose identity is known

2. Specific factual information that might come from some type of reference book or from a machine-readable data bank—for example, thermophysical property data on a particular substance

3. A few "good" articles, or references to them, on a specific topic

4. A comprehensive literature search in a particular subject area

5. A current alerting service that keeps users informed of new literature relevant to their current professional interests.

These needs have different response-time requirements. For instance, a current alerting service should deliver regularly and frequently, and the information that is supplied should be as up-to-date as possible. The user needing a comprehensive literature search is usually engaged in a long-term research project. Speed of response may not be critical, unless there is some date beyond which the search results will have little or no value. The user is often willing to wait a while for a thorough search; completeness is more important than speed. For other types of information needs, however, the user generally wants a rapid response.

The cost and time criteria relevant to the evaluation of information retrieval systems are fairly straightforward and are relatively constant from one activity to another. The quality criteria are perhaps less straightforward and vary considerably with the particular system being evaluated and with the user's need.

There are two major qualitative measures of success for information retrieval systems: (1) Does the user get what he or she is seeking? (2) How completely and accurately does he or she get it? The first of these measures, which can apply to the search for a particular item or the answer to a particular factual question, is simple and unequivocal. The second is much more difficult to apply in practice because it implies both a human value judgment and the use of some graduated scale to reflect degree of success. Nevertheless, it is necessary in the evaluation of most types of information retrieval activity. Recall and precision, introduced in Chapter 3, are two criteria that are frequently used to judge the performance of a search in an information retrieval system.

Evaluation Levels

There are three possible levels at which the evaluation of an information service can be carried out (Exhibit 38): (1) evaluation of effectiveness, (2) evaluation

---

Level I. *Evaluation of effectiveness* (consideration of user satisfaction)

    A. Cost criteria

        1. Monetary cost to user (per search, per subscription, per document)
        2. Other, less tangible, cost considerations

            a. Effort involved in learning how to use the system
            b. Effort involved in actual use
            c. Effort involved in retrieving documents (through backup document delivery systems)
            d. Form of output provided by the system

    B. Time criteria

        1. Time from submission of request to retrieval of references
        2. Time from submission of request to retrieval of documents
        3. Other time considerations—for example, waiting time to use online system

    C. Quality considerations

        1. Coverage of database
        2. Completeness of output (recall)
        3. Relevance of output (precision)
        4. Novelty of output
        5. Completeness and accuracy of data

Level II. *Evaluation of cost-effectiveness* (user satisfaction related to internal system efficiency and cost considerations)

    A. Unit cost per relevant citation retrieved
    B. Unit cost per new, that is, previously unknown, relevant citation retrieved
    C. Unit cost per relevant document retrieved

Level III. *Cost–benefit evaluation* (value of system balanced against costs of operating it or of using it)

EXHIBIT 38   Criteria by which information retrieval systems can be evaluated.

of cost-effectiveness, and (3) evaluation of the cost–benefit relationship. Ideally, an evaluation of the effectiveness of an information service is a study of the extent to which the service satisfies the information needs of its users. In fact, it is more likely to be a study of the extent to which the service meets the demands—that is, the expressed needs—of its users, with the unexpressed or latent needs of present users and the needs of nonusers being largely ignored. The major criteria by which effectiveness can be evaluated include cost, time, and quality. Quality criteria include the coverage, completeness (recall) and relevance (precision) of the output, novelty, and completeness and accuracy of the data.

The evaluation of cost-effectiveness relates measures of effectiveness to measures of cost. For example, it may be possible to identify various methods by which the document delivery capability of a library can be raised from 72 percent to 80 percent. An analysis that determines which of these methods is least expensive is a cost-effectiveness analysis.

A cost–benefit study relates the costs of providing some service to the benefits of having the service available. In the information processing environment, cost–benefit analysis is unusually difficult because of the problems involved in trying to assign an actual monetary value to information.

RECALL AND PRECISION

Recall is a measure of whether or not a particular item is retrieved or the extent to which the retrieval of wanted items occurs. In the case of a user seeking a particular document, the document is either retrieved from the collection—that is, recalled—at the time it is needed, or it is not. In the case of a user wanting a comprehensive search of a database, the success of the search can be expressed in terms of the extent to which all the relevant documents, or references to them, are retrieved. The measure of the completeness of a search in a database is frequently referred to as a recall ratio, and the statement "80 percent recall" implies that four-fifths of the relevant documents in the database were found.

Precision refers to a measure of the signal-to-noise ratio in certain kinds of information systems. A literature search that retrieves 50 documents, of which 10 are judged relevant by the person requesting the search, can be said to have operated at a precision ratio of 10/50, or 20 percent.

Recall and precision ratios can be described further by a 2×2 table presenting the results achieved in a particular literature search (Exhibit 39). When a search is conducted in most information retrieval systems, the system divides the collection into two parts. The documents that match the search strategy used to interrogate the system are retrieved $(a + b)$, and the documents that fail to match the strategy are not retrieved $(c + d)$. This dichotomous

		User Relevance Decisions		
		Relevant	Not Relevant	Total
System Relevance Prediction	Retrieved	*a* (Hits)	*b* (Noise)	*a* + *b*
	Not Retrieved	*c* (Misses)	*d* (Correctly rejected)	*c* + *d*
	Total	*a* + *c*	*b* + *d*	*a* + *b* + *c* + *d* (Total collection)

EXHIBIT 39   **2 × 2 table of results of a literature search.**

partitioning of the document collection may be regarded as a form of system relevance prediction. The system, in a sense, predicts that certain documents are likely to be relevant and others are likely not to be, retrieving the former and holding back the latter.

In almost all situations, the number of documents retrieved by a search is very small in relation to the total collection size. In other words, (*a* + *b*) is small, but (*c* + *d*), the number of items not retrieved, is very large. A search might retrieve 80 document references from a total file of 500,000 references. In this case *a* + *b* = 80 and *c* + *d* = 499,920.

The other dimension of the 2 × 2 table relates to the relevance decisions of the person requesting that the search be conducted.[1] A perfect search retrieves all the documents in the database that the user judges to be relevant (*a* + *c*) and none that are judged irrelevant (*b* + *d*). There is perfect coincidence between the user relevance decisions and the system relevance predictions; that is, *b* = 0 and *c* = 0. This search has achieved 100 percent recall. It has also achieved 100 percent precision.

Recall, then, relates to the ability of the system to retrieve relevant documents, and precision relates to its ability not to retrieve irrelevant documents. The degrees of recall and precision achieved in a search may both be expressed as ratios. The recall ratio is defined as

---

[1]Here, and throughout this chapter, "relevance" refers to "relevance to an information need" (referred to as "pertinence" in Chapter 3).

$$\frac{\text{Number of relevant documents retrieved}}{\text{Total number of relevant documents in the collection}} \times 100$$

In terms of Exhibit 39, the recall ratio is $(a/[a + c])$. The precision ratio is defined as

$$\frac{\text{Number of relevant documents retrieved}}{\text{Total number of documents retrieved}} \times 100$$

In terms of Exhibit 39, the precision ratio is $(a/[a + b])$.

The recall and precision ratios together express the filtering capacity of the system—its ability to let through what is wanted and to hold back what is not. Neither one on its own gives a complete picture of the effectiveness of a search. It is always possible to get 100 percent recall: If the entire collection $(a + b + c + d)$ is retrieved, recall is 100 percent. Unfortunately, precision would be extremely low because, for any typical request, the great majority of items in the collection are not relevant.

The precision ratio can be viewed as a type of cost factor in user time—the time required to identify the relevant citations in the output of a search. Consider a search request for which there are 20 relevant documents in a particular database. Suppose that three different search strategies are used to interrogate the system and that each retrieves 15 of the 20 relevant items, a recall of 75 percent. In the first search, 30 items are retrieved, in the second 60, and in the third 150. The precision ratios in these three searches are 50 percent, 25 percent, and 10 percent, respectively. In the first search, the user has to examine only 30 citations to find the 15 that are relevant; in the second, 60; and in the third, 150. All else being equal, it takes the user longer to identify the relevant items in the second search than in the first, and considerably longer in the third search than in either the first or second. It is in this sense that the precision ratio can be regarded as a measure of user effort or cost. A search that achieves 75 percent recall at 50 percent precision is more efficient than one that achieves 75 percent recall at 25 percent precision, which is more efficient than one that achieves 75 percent recall at 10 percent precision.

These ratios measure the degree of coincidence between the user relevance decisions and the system relevance predictions. In a perfect search these coincide exactly. Perfect searches are, of course, extremely rare. Far more likely is the situation in which there is partial coincidence between the set $(a + c)$ and the set $(a + b)$ (Exhibit 40). This hypothetical, but very typical, search has retrieved most, but not all, of the relevant documents and avoided most, but not all, of the irrelevant ones.

Recall and precision tend to be related inversely. When a search is broadened to achieve better recall, precision tends to go down. Conversely, when the scope

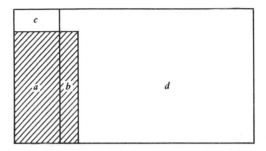

EXHIBIT 40 Typical results of a search in a retrieval system. The shaded area is all retrieved documents. The unshaded area is all unretrieved documents. The search has retrieved most of the relevant documents (*a*), missed a few relevant documents (*c*), and retrieved some irrelevant documents (*b*). Most of the collection (*a* + *b* + *c* + *d*) falls in the category of correctly rejected (*d*).

of a search is restricted to improve precision, recall tends to deteriorate. For a particular group of requests, searches could be conducted for each at a number of different levels, from an extremely broad search designed to get high recall to an extremely narrow one designed to get high precision. If recall and precision ratios were derived for each of these approaches and plotted against each other, the plot would look something like that in Exhibit 41. The plot represents the average of the recall and precision ratios for all the searches, with each search being conducted at four different levels. When the searches are conducted very generally (point *A*), a very high recall of around 90 percent is achieved; the precision, however, is very low. When the searches are made very specific, a high-precision, low-recall result (point *D*) is achieved. Points *B* and *C* represent compromise strategies between these two extremes.

Not everyone always needs high recall. Different users have different requirements for recall and precision, and a particular individual has different requirements at different times. The precision tolerance is likely to be directly related to the user's recall requirements. At one end of the spectrum is the individual who is writing a book, preparing a review article, or beginning a long-term research project. This person is likely to want a comprehensive (high recall) search and may therefore tolerate fairly low precision to ensure that nothing of importance is missed. At the other end is the typical user of, say, an industrial information retrieval system who needs a few recent articles on a subject right away. High recall is not needed, but high precision is. Other individuals may prefer a compromise—a "reasonable" level of recall at an "acceptable" level of precision.

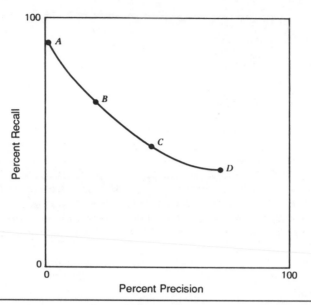

EXHIBIT 41　Plot of recall versus precision.

It is pointless to use the recall ratio in measuring the success of a search when high recall is unimportant. This fact has led some people to suggest using a measure of proportional, or relative, recall in which the success of the search is expressed in terms of the number of relevant documents retrieved over the number of relevant documents wanted by the requester. For example, a requester specifies that five relevant documents are needed, but the search retrieves only three. The proportional recall ratio is, therefore, 3/5 or 60 percent. This measure, although attractive at first glance, is artificial in that very few requesters are able to specify in advance just how many documents they want from the system.

Another limitation of the recall ratio is that it more or less assumes that all relevant documents have approximately equal value. This is not always true. A search may retrieve 5 relevant documents and miss 10 (recall ratio = 33 percent), but the 5 documents that are retrieved may be much better than the 10 that are missed. They might be more up-to-date and might, in fact, make the other 10 items almost redundant. The recall ratio, although important, must therefore be used with caution in the evaluation of information retrieval systems.

The precision ratio also has limitations. It is actually an indirect measure of user time and effort spent at the output stage of the information retrieval process; that is, the higher the precision ratio, the less effort the user needs to expend in identifying relevant items. In a search of very low precision ratio in which, say, only 10 items among 80 retrieved are relevant, considerable user time and effort might be required to identify the relevant items in a printed list, especially if it contains only bibliographic citations and the user must retrieve copies of many of the documents before deciding which are relevant and which are not. This measure of effort is used in the evaluation of a delegated search—one that is conducted on behalf of a requester by an information specialist. In this situation, the system is viewed more or less as a "black box" into which a request is placed and out of which comes a group of documents or references to documents. The precision ratio is a valid measure of the performance of any type of delegated search in which the information seeker submits a request to a system and waits for the results, whether the search is manual or electronic.

The precision ratio is less meaningful when applied to the nondelegated search. Here, the user conducts his or her own search and makes relevance decisions continuously as he or she proceeds; that is, when the user consults entries under an index term in a printed index or an online system, he or she rejects irrelevant ones and records only those that seem relevant. A precision ratio for this type of search can be derived by counting the total number of citations the user consulted and the number that were judged relevant and dividing the latter by the former. But user effort in the nondelegated search can be expressed more directly in terms of the time required to conduct the search, from which a unit cost (in time) per relevant item found can be determined. Presumably, the higher the precision of a nondelegated search, the less time the search takes, all other things being equal.

Aside from direct costs, four performance criteria have been discussed thus far by which any type of literature search, manual or electronic, can be evaluated from the viewpoint of user satisfaction: recall, precision, response time, and user effort. The salient points of these performance measures are as follows:

1. *Recall.* Important to users of information retrieval systems who are seeking bibliographic materials on a particular subject. Typically, only a minimum level of recall is required—for example, one book or a few articles on a particular subject. In some cases, however, maximum recall is sought. Consider, for example, the user who wants a comprehensive search conducted in *Chemical Abstracts.*

2. *Precision.* An indirect measure of user time and effort; less useful in the evaluation of nondelegated searches in a database.

3. *User effort.* In a nondelegated search, effort is measured by the amount of time the user spends conducting the search. In a delegated search, it is measured by the amount of time the user spends negotiating the inquiry with the system and the amount of time that is needed, when the search results are

delivered, to identify the relevant items. User effort is directly related to the precision ratio.

4. *Response time.* In a delegated search, this is the time that elapses between the submission of a request by the user and the receipt of the search results. In a nondelegated situation, it is the time involved in the actual conduct of the search; in this case, it also is a measure of user effort.

All these criteria are closely related, and there are trade-offs among them. The user who wants high recall usually tolerates a lower precision, is willing to expend more personal effort in searching, and perhaps is resigned to some searching delays. The user who requires a minimum level of recall is likely to expect high precision and fast response time and probably is not willing to put significant personal effort into the search. It is important to recognize that response time is always secondary to recall and precision. Even when rapid response is essential—for example, a poison information center—the first requirement is that information be supplied and that it be absolutely accurate, that is, there must be some recall and 100 percent precision; response time, although extremely important, is secondary. Indeed, it makes no sense to ever rank response time first among performance criteria, because this would imply that requesters would value immediate access to irrelevant information sources more than delayed access to relevant ones.

ALTERNATIVE MEASURES FOR EVALUATING A SEARCH

The 2 × 2 table (see Exhibit 39) contains all the data that are needed to evaluate a search in a retrieval system. One way to express this information is to calculate the recall and precision ratios. But several other measures of performance can be derived from the table and can be presented in various ways.

Using Exhibit 39, the following measures can be derived:

$a/(a + c)$ *The recall ratio,* also known as the "hit rate." The measure was first suggested by Kent et al. (1955), who referred to it as the "recall factor." Swets (1963) called it the "conditional probability of a hit." Goffman and Newill (1964) called it "sensitivity."

$c/(a + c)$ *The complement of recall.* Fairthorne (1965) called it the "snobbery ratio." Swets (1963) terms it "conditional probability of a miss."

$a/(a + b)$ *The precision ratio,* sometimes referred to as the "relevance ratio." Kent et al. (1955) first introduced the measure, calling it the "pertinency factor." Others have referred to it as an "acceptance rate."

$b/(a + b)$ *The complement of the precision ratio,* sometimes referred to as the "noise factor" (Kent et al., 1955).

$b/(b + d)$ Apparently first suggested by Swets (1963), who referred to it as the "conditional probability of a false drop." Cleverdon, Mills, and Keen (1966) later named it the "fallout ratio." It also has been referred to as "discard."

$d/(b + d)$ *The complement of fallout.* Goffman and Newill (1964) called it "specificity." Swets (1963) named it the "conditional probability of a correct rejection."

Each of these measures reflects a single aspect of the results of a search. When two measures are used together, as in a plot of recall versus precision or recall versus fallout, it is referred to as a "twin variable measure." When two of these separate measures are combined into a single measure—for example, one reflecting both recall and precision—the result is a "composite measure" or a "single figure of merit."

These measures are appropriate for a retrieval system that merely divides a collection into two parts, those items that are retrieved by a particular search and those items that are not retrieved. But certain systems do more than that. They generate a ranked output of documents in order of probable relevance to a request. Ranking systems should be evaluated differently than simpler systems because an indication of the success of the ranking procedure is needed. Various measures have been applied to ranking systems, including "rank recall," "log precision," "normalized recall," and "normalized precision." These measures, introduced by Salton (1971), essentially compare the actual ranking achieved by the system with an ideal ranking.

Keen (1966, 1971) and Robertson (1969) have thoroughly discussed evaluation measures, methods of averaging results, and methods of presenting results of retrieval tests. Recall and precision ratios are the measures that are most used in evaluations of information retrieval systems. They were popularized by Cleverdon (1962) and Cleverdon, Mills, and Keen (1966) in the Aslib Cranfield Project. Many writers, however, have given reasons why other measures may be regarded as more accurate or more informative. Robertson provides a useful analysis of the pros and cons of the various measures that have been proposed or used.

Another useful parameter in the evaluation of information retrieval systems is the "generality number," which relates the number of documents that are relevant to a particular request to the total number of documents in the collection; generally speaking, the higher the generality number (the greater the density of relevant items in the database), the easier the search tends to be.

Still other performance criteria can be used to evaluate information retrieval systems, including "coverage" and "novelty." Coverage is actually an extension of recall; it is expressed in terms of how much coverage of the literature on a specific subject is provided by a particular database. Suppose that a scientist wishes to find all possible references to the use of lasers in eye surgery. An obvious source would be the printed *Index Medicus* or, better, the computer-based MEDLINE service of the National Library of Medicine (NLM). Suppose also that the search in the MEDLINE database retrieves everything of relevance, that is, it achieves 100 percent recall. Even if the search is complete, so far as the database is concerned, the user who needs a really comprehensive search will also want to know the exact coverage of the database—that is, what proportion of all the literature on the use of lasers in eye surgery is contained in the database? Searching a particular database may result in 100 percent recall but give a low overall coverage of the literature.

Coverage, like recall and precision, can be expressed as a percentage. If the results of a search conducted in *Chemical Abstracts* were being evaluated, it could be estimated, with some difficulty, that the recall ratio is, say, 75 percent; it could also be estimated, with even more difficulty, that the coverage of *Chemical Abstracts* on the subject area of the search is 40 percent. With an estimated coverage of 40 percent and a recall of 75 percent, the overall estimate of the comprehensiveness of the search is 30 percent ($0.40 \times 0.75 \times 100$ percent).

The novelty ratio—the proportion of relevant items retrieved in a search that are new to the requester (that is, brought to the individual's attention for the first time by the search)—is particularly appropriate in the evaluation of literature searches conducted for current awareness purposes, since a good current awareness service brings documents to the attention of users before they learn about them by other means.

When cost criteria are related to quality criteria, cost-effectiveness criteria emerge. Some possible cost-effectiveness criteria that are applicable to information retrieval systems include the unit cost per relevant item (document or document reference) retrieved and the unit cost per new relevant item retrieved. Cost can be measured directly in monetary units or in time and effort expended.

Another evaluation criterion is accuracy of data. This criterion substitutes for recall and precision in the evaluation of information retrieval systems that are designed to answer questions that have unequivocal factual answers. The answer to a question like "What is the melting point of. . .?" is either supplied completely and correctly or it is not. Question-answering services must therefore be evaluated in terms of the completeness and accuracy of the data supplied.

CONDUCTING AN EVALUATION

From time to time, it is necessary to evaluate an information retrieval system or service to learn more about its capabilities and weaknesses, either by itself or in relation to the people involved in creating and operating it. The major steps involved in such an evaluation are as follows:

1. Defining the scope of the evaluation
2. Designing the evaluation program
3. Executing the evaluation
4. Analyzing and interpreting the results.
5. Modifying the system or service on the basis of the evaluation results.

The first step, defining the scope, entails the preparation of a precise set of questions that the evaluation must be designed to answer (Exhibit 42). Although the questions in the exhibit are divided into retrieval system components (for example, indexing and searching), there are really two general categories of questions, depending on whether system factors or human factors are being explored. Where system factors are explored, items such as search strategies and index term assignments are gathered and studied, but only as components of the system that affect retrieval performance. The evaluator, however, may want to study the effectiveness of searches or indexing decisions and relate these to one or more characteristics, such as task experience or subject knowledge, of the people who generated them. The definition of scope, therefore, is really a statement of what precisely is to be learned through the study.

In discussing evaluation scope, it is important to first distinguish whether the purpose of the evaluation is to be purely descriptive or whether the results should also be analytical and diagnostic—a distinction between a macroevaluation and a microevaluation, as detailed by King and Bryant (1971). For example, summary recall and precision percentages could be generated for a given set of searches over a given time period (macroevaluation). Alternatively, individual searches and their retrieved documents could be studied to determine the specific reasons for retrieval of irrelevant items and nonretrieval of relevant ones (microevaluation). Perhaps it would be determined that several irrelevant documents were retrieved for a given query because they were indexed incorrectly. This information could then be used to justify the clarification of one or more indexing policies or the implementation of more rigorous training procedures for indexers. If the searchers themselves were the focus of the study, it might determine whether novice searchers tend to experience problems with the system as a whole or just with certain types of searches; this information could be used to produce more effective training materials or online aids.

Overall Performance

1. What is the overall performance level of the system in relation to user requirements? Are there significant differences for various types of requests and in various broad subject areas?

Coverage and Processing

1. How sound are present policies regarding indexing coverage?
2. Is the delay between receipt of a journal and its processing in the indexing section significantly affecting performance?

Indexing

1. Is there significant variation in the performance level of different indexers?
2. If so, to what extent is this related to experience?
3. To what extent is it related to knowledge of the subject domain?
4. To what extent is it related to the degree of revising?
5. Do the indexers recognize the specific concepts that are of interest to various user groups?
6. What is the effect on search results of present policies relating to exhaustivity of indexing?

Retrieval Language

1. Are the terms sufficiently specific?
2. Do variations in specificity of terms in different areas significantly affect performance?
3. Is the need for additional precision devices, such as weighting, role indicators, or synthesized subject headings, indicated?
4. Is the quality of term association of the thesaurus adequate?
5. Is the entry vocabulary adequate?

Searching

1. What are the requirements of the users regarding recall and precision?
2. Can search strategies be devised to meet requirements for high recall or high precision?
3. How effectively can searchers screen output? What effect does screening have on recall and precision figures?
4. What are the most promising modes of user–system interaction?

    a. Having more liaison at the request stage?
    b. Having more liaison at the search formulation stage?
    c. Having the user present when the search is performed?

5. What is the effect on response time of these various modes of interaction?
6. How effective is searching by end users/intermediaries:

    a. In command mode?
    b. In menu-driven systems?

7. How do various identifiable searcher characteristics affect retrieval performance?

EXHIBIT 42 Possible questions to be answered by a retrieval system evaluation.

	Value of dependent variable before treatment	Value of dependent variable after treatment
Control group		
Experimental group		

EXHIBIT 43   Simple design of an experiment. SOURCE: Adapted from Busha and Harter (1980). Reprinted with permission of Academic Press, Inc. and Stephen P. Harter.

The second step of the evaluation—design—involves preparing a plan of action that allows the gathering of data that are needed to answer the questions posed in the definition of scope. The designer of the study must identify what data are needed to answer each question and what procedures could be used to gather the data in the most efficient and expedient way. For each question, the evaluator must decide whether it can be answered simply by collecting data from the system as it presently exists or whether some changes in the normal functioning of the system must be made to collect the necessary data. To answer a question such as "What is the present response time of the system, expressed in ranges, means, medians, and modes?" it is necessary only to collect data from the normal operation of the existing system. But to answer a question such as "What is the effect of indexing at a higher level of exhaustivity?" the performance of the system must be observed and documented, both before and after a deliberate change in indexing exhaustivity. Thus, the operation of an existing system may be surveyed, or an actual controlled experiment may be needed.

A common approach to experimental design is illustrated in Exhibit 43. The experiment proceeds by randomly assigning the objects of study to two groups: an experimental group and a control group. Two variables are measured, the independent variable, or treatment, and one or more dependent variables, characteristics of subjects that it is believed will be altered after treatment. Both the experimental and control groups are given a pretest to measure the dependent variables. The pretest is followed by the treatment (independent variable), which is administered only to the experimental group. Finally, there is a posttest, where dependent variables are again measured for both groups. If the posttest measurement shows a significant difference between the control and experimental group dependent variables that was not present in the pretest, then it can be claimed that the independent variable has been a major determining factor in the experimental group's performance.

In addition to the true experimental design just described, there is also a quasi-experimental ex post facto design. This type of study is carried out when it is not possible to have two equivalent groups of randomly assigned subjects, as is often the case in real life situations (Campbell and Stanley, 1963, p. 47). The important difference between this kind of study and the true experimental design is that in the latter, the evaluator has control over all dependent variables, whereas in the former, some or all of the dependent variables are not within the evaluator's control.[2] Thus, the predictive power—the reasonable assertion that the independent variable has had an effect on the subjects' performance—is significantly weakened in the ex post facto study.

Examples of variables identified in information retrieval evaluations are given in Exhibit 44. System variables and outcome variables have already been discussed. In addition, there are many process variables and human characteristics variables that can be studied. Process variables usually consist of components of a retrieval session, such as the number of separate commands used in a session. These data are normally collected in a transaction log, which captures in electronic form all the interactions the user has with the system. This electronic transcript can then be analyzed and categorized by the researcher. In studying human characteristics, the researcher identifies aspects such as task experience or subject knowledge that are believed to be significantly correlated with retrieval system performance. These data are usually collected by questionnaire.

Many information retrieval system variables have been studied. In general, the researcher identifies a particular variable that might have an impact on retrieval performance, say a term-weighting scheme. One (or preferably more than one) information retrieval test collection is used for the experiment. The effectiveness of test searches, measured by recall and precision, is determined for the collections before and after the introduction of the term-weighting device. This design is quasi-experimental, because the collections are not truly equivalent. Thus, any claims about the impact of the term-weighting scheme must be accompanied by the acknowledgment of other possible contributing

---

[2]This, in fact, represents the ideal case where all dependent variables can be identified and controlled. In reality, however, it is often the case—in both true and quasi-experiments—that there may be other dependent variables, unknown to the researcher and therefore not controlled by either approach. These variables are often distinguished as "confounding" or "intervening" variables.

System Variables

Indexing exhaustivity
Coordination level of retrieval language
Specificity of search

Human Characteristics Variables

Experience (in searching or indexing)
Subject knowledge (of retrieval system domain)

Outcome Variables

Recall
Precision
Novelty
Size of retrieved set
Perceived value of retrieval

Process Variables

Learning variables
    Training time
    Error rate during training

Interactiveness variables
    Number and type of
        commands used

EXHIBIT 44   Some of the variables in an experiment.

variables. Indeed, there are many, including the size of the databases, their subject matter, and the indexing policies for each.

True experimental design might be used to determine the effect of a training program on the retrieval performance of searchers. Searchers would be assigned randomly to either of two groups: (1) an experimental group, to which the training module would be administered, and (2) a control group, which would receive no training. Data would then be gathered on the effectiveness of their searches, as measured by recall and precision. If the searches in the experimental group were significantly better than those in the control group, it might be concluded that the training program had a positive effect.

These scenarios illustrate the use of very simple experimental and quasi-experimental design. For a more complete treatment of experimental methods, the reader is referred to Campbell and Stanley (1963), and for discussions related specifically to library and information science, to Goldhor (1972), Busha and Harter (1980), and Powell (1985).

The third step—execution of the evaluation—is the stage at which the data are gathered. This stage is likely to take the longest to complete. It may also be the stage in which the evaluator is least directly involved and perhaps the stage over which he or she has the least direct control.

The fourth step—analysis and interpretation—should begin well before the execution stage is concluded. The evaluator must ensure that data are received continuously from the beginning of the execution stage, so that they can be reduced to a form suitable for analysis and interpretation. During the analysis and interpretation stage of an evaluation project, the evaluator manipulates the data in such a way that the data can help answer the questions posed in the work statement.

In terms of an experimental study, the analysis stage of the project is mainly concerned with explaining the differences in performance results—for example, recall and precision ratios—by the presence of one or more characteristics, such as searcher experience or the introduction of some retrieval language device like term weighting. In a survey of the components of an operating retrieval system, performance results also are derived, followed by an analysis of recall and precision failures. The failure analysis entails an examination of each document involved, the indexing records for the documents, the requests that caused the searches to be conducted, the search strategies, the system vocabulary, and the relevance assessments of the users. By examining each of these, it should be possible to determine which component of the system was largely responsible for the failures that occurred. The evaluator can also use recall and precision ratios, or alternative measures of search performance, as indicators of conditions under which the system seems to perform well or badly. For example, searches can be grouped by broad subject category, and average performance figures can be derived for each group. Subject areas in which unusually low scores occur could then be identified.

Through the joint use of performance figures and either statistical tests for significance or analyses of failures in particular searches, the evaluator can learn a lot about the characteristics of a system and its users—their weaknesses and limitations as well as their strong points. The joint use of performance figures and failure analyses should answer most of the questions identified in the work statement for the evaluation.

The final element in the analysis and interpretation phase is that in which the evaluator presents the findings, including recommendations on what might be done to improve system performance. This task is followed by the fifth and final step of the evaluation program, in which some or all of the recommendations are implemented (and the evaluation results are thereby applied to the improvement of the system and its users).

One last word on evaluation. Before a complete evaluation is carried out, it is important to go through all the proposed procedures on a small sample of transactions to ensure that the procedures are, in fact, viable and that they are capable of gathering the data that are needed to complete the study.

DERIVING PERFORMANCE FIGURES

Remember that there are three levels at which an information retrieval service can be evaluated: effectiveness, cost-effectiveness, and cost–benefit relationship (Exhibit 38). To find out how well some of the effectiveness criteria—namely, response time, level of user effort, and monetary cost—are actually met by an information retrieval system, one has only to observe the system in operation. Qualitative criteria are more complex, and it is necessary to take specific steps to gather performance data.

The major emphasis in designing an evaluation of an information retrieval system or service is likely to be the measurement of the recall and precision that is achieved in a representative sample of the searches conducted. Recall and precision ratios (or some other methods of presenting the results in the 2 × 2 table) are the most important measures of the quality of a delegated search in any type of system. Together, they indicate how successful the system has been in filtering the database to retrieve the items that are relevant and to avoid those that are not.

The way in which these performance figures can be derived is perhaps best illustrated by an example. Suppose that the performance of a particular retrieval system is to be evaluated and that the evaluation is carried out on a random sample of, say, 100 searches conducted during a particular period. The system operates in a delegated search mode: Requests for searches are made to the information center, and the results, in the form of lists of document references retrieved, are delivered to the requesters.

Let us follow one of these searches to identify the data that must be collected and the procedures that must be adopted to evaluate the performance of the service for this particular search. The first thing that is needed is a complete written record of the user's request for information. The request should preferably be recorded, in the user's own words, on a specially prepared form. Forms vary in their layout and content, but they typically request that a user state an information need in his or her own words; provide, if possible, keywords and phrases for the topic area; provide any relevant articles that are already known; and give any other information that will be useful for limiting the search, such as language, publication date, or document form. Exhibit 45A shows a typical request form as used in an evaluation study carried out at the University of Michigan (Janes, 1991). A search strategy is prepared for the hypothetical request by a member of the staff of the information service (Exhibit 45B), and the search retrieves 25 document references from the database. A copy of the search strategy is needed for evaluation purposes.

To derive a precision ratio for the search, the requester must be asked to judge which of the retrieved items are relevant and which are not. These

A

School of Information & Library Studies
Relevance Study
Search Request Form

Please give a brief narrative description of your topic (use back if necessary):

I'm interested in the influence of weather variables on mood. More specifically, the topic of seasonal depression or winter depression is believed to be due to decreased sunlight (a weather variable) during winter. I would like information on studies that have explored the link between weather and mood. Many, but not all, of these will probably fall under the topic of seasonal or winter depression.

Do you know of any index terms, vocabulary terms, or search terms that would be useful in searching for documents on this topic? Please list them here, or underline them in the above description.

mood		seasonal
emotion	AND	winter
affect		weather
depression		sunlight

Do you know of any authors or documents relevant to this topic? Please specify them here.

N. E. Rosenthal	M. E. Thase
T. A. Wehr	C. S. Pittendrigh
B. Ainswirth	

Types of materials of interest to you (circle):

Journal Articles	(Y)	N	Conference Papers	(Y)	N
Reports	(Y)	N	Dissertations	(Y)	N

Other (specify): book chapters

Years to be covered: past 30

Languages of interest (list): English only

Please give any other information you think might be helpful in formulating a search strategy on the back.

EXHIBIT 45 A: Example of a search request form. SOURCE: Joseph W. Janes, 1991 (unpublished). Reprinted with permission of the author. B: Example of a search strategy based on the request.

EXHIBIT 45 *(Continued)*

B

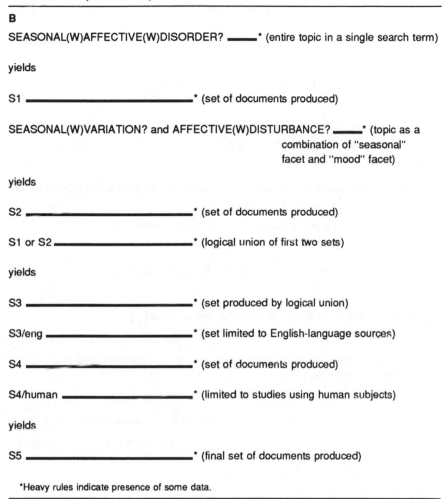

SEASONAL(W)AFFECTIVE(W)DISORDER? ━━━* (entire topic in a single search term)

yields

S1 ━━━━━━━━━━━━━━* (set of documents produced)

SEASONAL(W)VARIATION? and AFFECTIVE(W)DISTURBANCE? ━━━* (topic as a combination of "seasonal" facet and "mood" facet)

yields

S2 ━━━━━━━━━━━━━* (set of documents produced)

S1 or S2 ━━━━━━━━━━* (logical union of first two sets)

yields

S3 ━━━━━━━━━━━━* (set produced by logical union)

S3/eng ━━━━━━━━━━* (set limited to English-language sources)

S4 ━━━━━━━━━━━━* (set of documents produced)

S4/human ━━━━━━━━* (limited to studies using human subjects)

yields

S5 ━━━━━━━━━━━* (final set of documents produced)

*Heavy rules indicate presence of some data.

---

relevance[3] assessments preferably are made on the basis of the complete documents or, at least, complete document representations such as abstracts. A relevance assessment form should be completed for each document assessed. Exhibit 46 shows one example of such a form (as used by Lancaster [1968a] in the evaluation of MEDLARS), which essentially solicits responses about the novelty of each item (question 1) and its degree of relevance (question 2).

---

[3]"Relevance" here means relevance to the information need (that is, pertinence) rather than relevance to a request statement (see Chapter 3).

NATIONAL LIBRARY OF MEDICINE
Bethesda, Maryland

Request No. _____
Document No. _____

MEDLARS EVALUATION PROJECT
Form For Document Evaluation

1. Were you previously aware of the existence of this article?
    Yes [   ] *How did you learn of its existence?*
    No [   ]

2. By checking the appropriate box, please evaluate this article in relation to the information need that prompted your request to MEDLARS.

    (a) Of major value to me in relation to my information need [   ]
         Please explain why:

    (b) Of minor value to me in relation to my information need [   ]
         Please explain why:

    (c) Of no value to me in relation to my information need [   ]
         Please explain why:

         Were you glad to learn of its existence because of some other need or project?
         Yes [   ] *Please explain why:*
         No [   ]

    (d) Unable to make an assessment because of language of the document [   ]

         Do you intend to take any steps to determine the contents of this foreign language document?
         Yes [   ] *Please specify what steps:*
         No [   ] *Please explain why:*

___

EXHIBIT 46 MEDLARS **relevance assessment form.**

It is important that the requester be asked to make judgments on a scale that recognizes various degrees of relevance, since this more accurately reflects user judgment than a simple relevant/nonrelevant option. The reasons that certain documents are judged relevant and others are not also should be recorded. If the search retrieves many documents, it is sufficient for purposes of evaluation to ask the requester to assess the relevance of a random sample only.

Returning to the hypothetical search that retrieved 25 documents, suppose that the requester judges 15 to be relevant and 10 not relevant. Also suppose that the total database comprises 500,000 items. Certain values can be placed into the 2 × 2 table of search results, as follows:

	Relevant	Not relevant	Total
Retrieved	15	10	25
Not retrieved			499,975
Total			500,000

The precision ratio of the search is 15/25 or 60 percent.

The major problem remaining is the estimation of recall. The term *estimation* is used deliberately because it is not possible to establish absolute recall for the search unless the requester is willing to look at all 499,975 items that were not retrieved and to state, using the same criteria as before, which are considered relevant and which are not. Nor is it possible to arrive at the recall estimate by conventional random sampling among the items that were not retrieved, because the set of items that are not relevant to any particular request is usually significantly larger than the set of items that are relevant. Consequently, an impossibly large random sample would need to be drawn—in this example, from the 499,975 items that were not retrieved—to have any probability of finding even one relevant document in the sample. (Nevertheless, Blair [1990] has developed a method for estimating recall by using "sampling frames," as described later.)

One possible method of estimating recall involves the use of additional searches conducted by other members of the information staff. The recall of the original search, conducted by staff member A, is expressed as

$$\frac{\text{Number of relevant items found by A}}{\text{Number of relevant items found by A + number of additional}}$$
$$\text{relevant items found in the database by B, C, } \ldots$$

The implication is that any additional items found by staff members B, C, and others, but not found in the original search, must be submitted to the requester for relevance assessment.

For certain evaluation purposes, a "comparative recall" may be satisfactory. If, for example, one wanted to determine how successful chemists are in searching an online chemical database to satisfy their own information needs, as compared with having information specialists conduct the searches, it could be possible to express the recall of a chemist's search as

$$\frac{\text{Number of relevant items found by a chemist}}{\text{Number of relevant items found by chemist + number of additional relevant items found by information specialist}}$$

Note that for diagnostic microevaluation, however, estimation of the recall ratio by further searches in the same database has one obvious disadvantage: It is limited in the type of recall failure that it is likely to disclose. The technique may identify recall failures due to poor searching strategies, vocabulary deficiencies, or inadequacies in user–system interaction, but it probably will not disclose indexing failures. If a document has something to do with topic X but topic X has not been indexed, it is unlikely that searcher A will retrieve the document in a search on X. It is equally unlikely that other searchers will find it. Clearly, this method allows one to estimate only an *upper bound* for the recall of the original search, since all searchers combined may still miss some useful items. Since two searchers are unlikely to find everything of relevance in the database (indeed, Saracevic and Kantor [1988b] found that even six or more searchers do not find everything), the estimate of the chemist's recall can only be an upper bound estimate. Thus, if the chemist finds 10 relevant items and the information specialist finds 5 more, the former's recall cannot be better than 10/15, and may be much worse.

A better technique for estimating recall in an operating system is to conduct a parallel search in one or more other databases, which may be printed indexes, as was done by Lancaster (1968a) in the evaluation of MEDLARS. Suppose one wants to estimate the recall ratio for a literature search in a particular database on the subject of thermal pollution of water. The same search is performed in other databases; any database can be used so long as it is completely independent of the one in which the original search was performed. Suppose that the search, which does not necessarily have to be comprehensive, discloses 14 papers that appear to be relevant to the subject of thermal pollution of water. These papers are submitted to the requester of the original search, who judges 12 to be relevant. These 12 papers are then checked against the database of the system being evaluated, and 10 are found to be included. These 10 are checked against the printout of the original search in the system, and 7 had been retrieved. Our recall estimate is therefore 7/10, or 70 percent.

This technique is one of extrapolating from a known population of relevant documents to an unknown population of relevant documents (Exhibit 47). For any particular request to the system, the database, represented by the entire rectangle in the exhibit, contains a subset of documents X that the requester would judge relevant if he or she saw them; however, the complete identity of set X is not known. The extrapolation technique identified a subset of X, namely, X_1, and the recall ratio for X_1 was found to be 7/10. It is reasonable

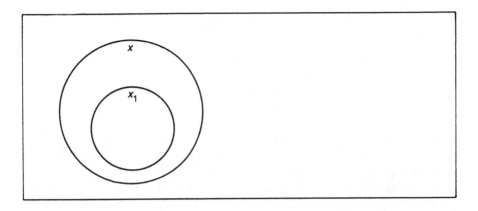

EXHIBIT 47   Estimation of recall by extrapolation of results from a known population X_1 to an unknown X.

to suppose, then, that if X_1 is fully representative of X, the recall ratio for X (unknown) should approximate that for X_1 (known). The technique gives a recall estimate for X rather than absolute recall, but this is the best that is possible under most circumstances. The estimate can also lead to the other values of the 2×2 table of search results. The recall estimate in the example indicates that the 15 relevant documents retrieved make up approximately 70 percent of the total relevant documents in the database. Therefore, 100 percent would be approximately 21. The complete values for the table of search results thus become

	Relevant	Not relevant	Total
Retrieved	15	10	25
Not retrieved	6*	499,969*	499,975
Total	21*	499,979*	500,000

The values marked with an asterisk are estimates; the other values in the table are absolutes.

Another way of estimating recall in a large operational system relies on unconventional sampling techniques. Instead of randomly sampling from the entire document collection, methods have been developed for random sampling from "sample frames"—subsets of the database that are anticipated to be rich in relevant documents (Blair, 1990). An estimation of recall is then made on the basis of a random sample from these subsets.

There are basically two methods for deriving these frames. One relies on a logical modification of the original search strategy: If the query was for "A *and* B *and* C *and* D," for instance, the following more general searches would be performed and the resulting sets would be used to draw the sample:

A *and* B *and* C *and not* D
A *and* B *and* D *and not* C
A *and* C *and* D *and not* B
B *and* C *and* D *and not* A

The other way to produce these frames is to use additional synonyms in the original search strategy to perform a more exhaustive search, thereby producing a larger pool of documents, some of which might be relevant. Blair (1990) admits that these sampling techniques give an indication of the maximum possible recall of the original search, rather than an estimate of true recall.

Using the procedures just described, it is possible to derive performance figures for a representative sample of the searches performed in an online system in a delegated mode. The evaluation of an online search conducted in a nondelegated mode is a different situation. It is still necessary to estimate recall using one of the techniques described earlier, but the precision ratio is a less useful measure than a more direct measure of unit cost per relevant item retrieved. Probably the cost of the search, in dollars or in user time, rather than the precision ratio, should be balanced against the recall ratio.

If relevance assessment forms of the type shown in Exhibit 46 are used, a novelty ratio and a precision ratio can be calculated for each search. The novelty ratio can be expressed in one of two ways:

$$\frac{\text{Number of new relevant documents retrieved}}{\text{Number of relevant documents retrieved}}$$

or

$$\frac{\text{Number of new relevant documents retrieved}}{\text{Number of documents retrieved}}$$

Measurement of database coverage requires a different evaluation procedure, one that uses specialized bibliographies; review articles are good sources of these. Suppose one wants to determine how comprehensive *Index Medicus* is in its coverage of nutrition disorders. Several review articles on specific aspects of the subject could be located in the *Bibliography of Medical Reviews*. The more review articles that are located, and the more complete they are, the better they will fulfill the evaluation purpose. Suppose three recent articles are found and that collectively they cite 120 unique papers in various sources. Each citation is checked against the author index of *Index Medicus* to determine which items are included and which are not, until the proportion of the 120 citations covered by the index is known. Examples of this procedure can be found in Martyn (1967) and Martyn and Slater (1964).

INTERPRETATION OF THE RESULTS

An evaluation can take the form of a controlled experiment or a description of the current system operation or user activity. With an experiment, statistically significant differences between the experimental group and the control group allow the researcher to conclude whether the introduction of the independent variable has had an effect—either positive or negative. Although experiments are very powerful and useful, particularly in their ability to demonstrate cause, some points about their use in information retrieval system evaluation should be noted:

1. Experimental subjects are often few in number because of the labor-intensive task of setting up and executing the experiment. The number of subjects is sometimes too small for tests to be statistically significant.

2. The researcher must ensure that the artificiality of the experiment does not affect the results and must allow for any effects that might alter the results.

3. It is often difficult to assemble two groups (experimental and control) that are truly equivalent. Thus, variations in performance can sometimes be attributed to a difference between the groups rather than to the introduction of the independent variable.

In surveys, which are often used to evaluate the performance of large retrieval systems, the researcher presents output measures and then attempts to explain system performance through failure analysis. Average recall and precision figures achieved by the system can be determined by averaging the individual performance figures of the test searches to arrive at overall performance figures. By varying search strategy within the group of test searches, one can derive a series of performance points and plot an average performance curve, which looks very much like that in Exhibit 41. This curve shows the average range of system operation at the present time.

An evaluator must realize, of course, that averages are misleading. Therefore, individual performance points should not only be plotted as a curve, but also in the form of a scatter diagram, as shown in very simplified form in Exhibit 48. Here, curve *A* represents the present average performance curve, and each X marks an individual performance point. Note that none of the individual performance figures falls exactly on the average performance curve. In fact, the individual results scatter widely. Some are very good (top right-hand corner) and some are very bad (bottom left-hand corner). Some show high

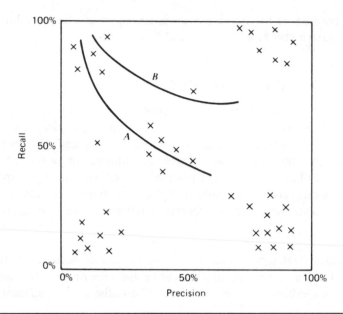

EXHIBIT 48   Scatter diagram of search results.

recall and low precision, whereas others show high precision and low recall results. And many are "middle of the road."

The most important task in an evaluation is to distinguish successes from failures. By determining what makes a search good or bad, the evaluator can identify major system problems and suggest possible solutions. If, as a result, some of the poorer searches are improved, then the average performance level of the system can be raised, that is, the average performance curve can be elevated to a higher point, closer to the ideal (although unattainable) top right-hand corner of the plot, as illustrated by curve *B* in Exhibit 48.

To determine major sources of system weaknesses, individual failures are analyzed. Performance figures are used to compare the performance of the system under varying conditions or modes of operation. (They are *not* to be used to compare the performance of one system with another that has different documents, requests, and users.) Test searches are divided in several ways so that the performance figures reveal whether there are significant differences in performance under alternative operating conditions. For example, on the average, does the system operate better in certain subject areas than in others? Does it operate better for certain user groups than for others? Although performance figures indicate that certain things are happening in the system, they do not indicate why. This requires intellectual analysis and interpretation.

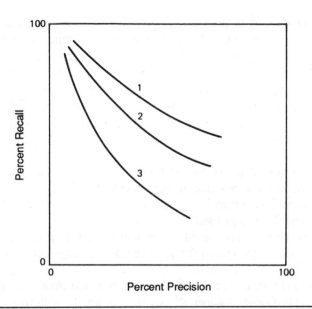

EXHIBIT 49   Recall and precision results for three groups of searches.

By dividing the evaluation results in various ways, it is possible to derive a set of performance curves, each representing the performance of the system under a particular condition of use. Such a set is illustrated in Exhibit 49. (Note that a fairly large number of searches is needed to conduct, with any level of statistical confidence, the type of comparison exemplified by this exhibit.) Group 1 has produced the best results and group 3 the worst. The curves shown in the exhibit may represent searches conducted in different subject fields, searches conducted for different types of users, and so on. An analysis of this type might indicate weaknesses in the system and ways in which performance might be improved. For example, if the group 3 curve represents searches in a particular subject area, these poor results might indicate inadequacies in the vocabulary of the system in that area. The evaluation has pinpointed a weakness and thus allows someone responsible (in this case the database producer) to take appropriate corrective action.

Recall and precision ratios have another important use. Each ratio is likely to indicate a certain number of failures, and this permits a searcher to conduct an analysis to determine why they occurred. Consider a hypothetical search in which the system retrieves 6 of the 10 known relevant items and misses 4; that is, the recall ratio is 60 percent. The requester assesses a random sample of 25 retrieved articles and judges 10 to be of value and 15 to be of no value; that is, the precision ratio is 40 percent. In this particular search, then, the analysis should be of 4 recall failures and 15 precision failures. Note that the 4 recall failures and 15 precision failures are not the only failures occurring in the search. They are just the ones that are known, and, as such, they are accepted as exemplifying the complete recall and precision failures of the search; that is, they are symptomatic of problems occurring in the search.

The hindsight analysis of a search failure is the most challenging aspect of the evaluation process. It involves, for each failure, an examination of the following:

1. The full text of the document itself
2. The index terms assigned to the document
3. The request statement
4. The search strategy used
5. The requester's completed assessment form (of particular interest in a precision failure is the reason for an article being judged of no value).

On the basis of these records, a decision is made about the prime causes of a particular failure. Almost all failures are attributable to some aspect of indexing, searching, the index language, or the area of interaction between the requester and the system. In a well-designed study, the attributing of precision failures, at least, is the joint decision of the requester and the evaluator, because the requester's statement of why a particular document is of no value is often a good guide to where the system failed. For example, suppose the requester indicates that a particular article is irrelevant because it deals with electronic noise generators when he or she wanted mechanical noise generators. Such a statement lets an evaluator know precisely why the retrieved article failed to satisfy the requester's information need. Now the necessary records must be examined to determine if the search was conducted too broadly; if the index language was not specific enough for the request; if the article was incorrectly indexed; or if the request statement was inexact (that is, it did not specify an interest in mechanical noise generators only).

Whenever possible, a single most critical cause is isolated for a given failure. In some instances, however, it is not possible to identify a single cause because two functions of the system are equally involved. For certain recall failures one might say that the article would have been retrieved if the indexer had used the additional term A_1. But equally important, the article would have been retrieved if the searcher had generalized from the adopted strategy A_1, *and* B *and* C to the reasonable approach of A *and* B *and* C. In such cases, the failure must be jointly attributed to indexing and searching, or whichever other elements of the system were jointly responsible.

In the MEDLARS evaluation (Lancaster, 1968a), more than 302 searches, 797 recall failures, and 3,038 precision failures were analyzed. Failures were

	Recall Failures	Precision Failures
Index language	81 (10.2%)	1,094 (36.0%)
Indexing	298 (37.4%)	393 (12.9%)
Searching	279 (35.0%)	983 (32.4%)
Defective user–system interaction	199 (25.0%)	503 (16.6%)
Other	11 (1.4%)	78 (2.5%)

EXHIBIT 50 Major categories of failures identified in the MEDLARS evaluation. (Totals exceed 100 percent because some failures were attributable to more than one cause.)

attributed to the principal system components, as shown in Exhibit 50. The proportions of failures, and their exact type in each category, vary from system to system. The principal types of retrieval failure, however, are common to most operating retrieval systems.

COST-EFFECTIVENESS STUDIES

Cost-effectiveness is the relationship between level of performance (effectiveness) and the costs involved in achieving it. Several methods probably could be used to obtain a particular performance level, and these can be costed. *Cost–benefit* refers to the relationship between the benefits of a particular product or service and the costs of providing it. Benefits are generally more difficult to measure than performance, except that in a commercial sense, benefits equate with return on investment. The expression cost–performance–benefits refers to the entire relationship among costs, level of effectiveness, and benefits.

The cost of an information retrieval system can be measured in terms of input of resources (funds). Both fixed costs and variable costs need to be considered. Fixed costs include equipment purchase or rental, developmental costs, and costs involved in the acquisition and indexing of the present database. Variable costs are of two kinds. One is a function of the number of transactions. For example, if the number of searches conducted is increased from 1,000 to 1,500 per year, the cost *per search* may be reduced by x dollars. The other is a function of alternative modes of operating the system. For example, one could vary the cost of retrospective searching by varying the mode of interaction with the user (personal visit, telephone), by adding or eliminating a screening operation, or by changing the professional level of the personnel conducting the searches.

One barrier to the application of cost-effectiveness or cost–benefit analysis to information systems is that the realistic costing of information products and services is not a trivial task, and cost data related to various services are rarely published. Certain savings—for example, a reduction in indexing costs by eliminating certain materials or by reducing exhaustivity of indexing—are easily determined, but how does one measure the cost-effectiveness of raising the average system performance from, say, 60 percent recall at 30 percent precision to 60 percent recall at 50 percent precision?

The problems of costing information systems have been discussed by several writers. Marron (1969) concludes that standard cost accounting procedures, as used in conventional business applications, cannot be applied to information center services. A database is not analogous to machinery or equipment, especially with regard to depreciation. Cost allocation is particularly difficult when many different products—for example, an abstracts journal, title announcement bulletin, retrospective search—are generated from the same database. It is easy to calculate direct output costs, but how does one allocate input costs over the various products and services? Marron addresses this problem but does not present an entirely satisfactory solution.

Assuming that input costs can be realistically allocated, it should be possible to get a series of unit costs for various bibliographic products and services. Typical unit costs include the cost per retrospective search, per citation retrieved, per citation printed, per page printed, or per item disseminated. These costs reflect changes in volume but not changes in performance level. Consider the cost per citation retrieved, calculated at, say, 74 cents. This unit cost fluctuates with volume of output. If search strategies are changed so that each search now retrieves an average of twice as many citations, the cost per citation retrieved might be reduced dramatically, say to 40 cents (it is unlikely to be cut in half because the larger search result will have additional costs associated with it—for example, in online connect time or printing costs). But the change in search strategies may also have caused a drastic degradation in performance; broadening the search causes additional irrelevancy, and the average search precision might drop from 50 percent to 25 percent.

Clearly, for cost-effectiveness purposes, unit costs must be sensitive to changes in the effectiveness of the system. The unit cost per relevant citation retrieved (C_r) is such a cost. Consider a system that operates at a C_r of approximately \$1.48. When changes are made in the system to raise average recall or precision performance, the C_r should be reduced. Thus, C_r is a useful unit for expressing improvements in the cost-effectiveness of an information system.

C_r may be used to compare alternative operating modes in one system or the cost-effectiveness of two or more different systems. Thus, this measure can assess the economic impact of changes in indexing procedures, vocabulary, searching strategies, or mode of interaction with the user. Raising the average indexing exhaustivity, for example, may result in a substantial improvement in recall. Even with increased indexing costs, this may mean a significant reduction in the C_r. The C_r can be used to assess the cost-effectiveness of both delegated and nondelegated searches.

Cost-effectiveness analysis is important for studying the extent to which available resources are so allocated that the maximum possible return—for example, in relevant items retrieved—is achieved for the investment made. The ultimate cost-effectiveness goal would be met when each dollar of resources yields the *best possible* return—for example, in more or better service. Usually a cost-effectiveness analysis is conducted to determine the least expensive of several alternative methods for achieving a particular level of service. The cost-effectiveness of a service can be improved by either maintaining the present level of performance but reducing the cost of achieving it or keeping costs constant but raising the level of performance. Cost-effectiveness would also improve by raising the level of performance while reducing costs. Unless one begins with an unusually bad situation, however, this type of improvement is rarely possible.

According to Hitch and McKean (1960), there are five basic steps involved in a cost-effectiveness analysis:

1. Define the objectives that must be attained.

2. Identify alternative methods for meeting the objectives.

3. Determine the costs of the various alternative methods.

4. Establish models (mathematical equations, a computer program, or merely a complete verbal description of the situation) that relate the costs of each alternative to the extent to which it helps attain the objectives.

5. Establish a criterion for ranking the alternatives in order of desirability. The criterion provides a method for weighing estimated costs against estimated effectiveness. The structure of the cost-effective analysis program is illustrated in Exhibit 51. A series of possible service alternatives, involving different combinations of results relative to the various performance criteria, are identified (some—A_2, A_8, A_3—may be considered more promising at the outset). The effect of these combinations on cost and on effectiveness is evaluated, allowing ranking of the service alternatives.

How might a cost-effectiveness analysis be applied in the comparison of alternative strategies for achieving certain desired results? A company may want to know whether it is more cost-effective to have all literature searches performed through the library or to train the company's scientists to perform

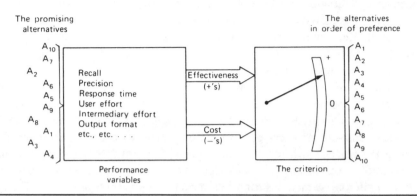

EXHIBIT 51   Structure of the cost-effectiveness analysis program. Different combinations of performance variables will have different effects on the cost and the effectiveness of the system, allowing promising service alternatives to be evaluated according to a cost-effectiveness criterion. SOURCE: Adapted from Quade (1966). Reprinted with permission of The RAND Corporation.

their own searches. The first step is to identify all the costs involved in this comparison.

Suppose that, on the average, it costs $80 per hour (excluding personnel costs) to interrogate the databases used by the company and that a librarian spends an average of 15 minutes online per search, whereas the scientist spends 20 minutes. The librarian costs the company $20 per hour, and the scientist costs $30 per hour. Taking these factors into account, then, the average cost of a scientist search is approximately $37 ([$80/hour + $30/hour] × 1/3 hour), whereas the average cost of a librarian search is $25 ([$80/hour + $20/hour] × 1/4 hour). But this comparison overlooks the costs associated with the delegation of the search by the scientist to the librarian. For a scientist to describe an information need to a librarian may take 15 minutes. Thus, for the delegated search situation, one must add a further $7.50 in scientist time ($30/hour × 1/4 hour) and $5.00 in librarian time ($20/hour × 1/4 hour), raising the cost to $37.50. Even this analysis is incomplete. If one assumes that the librarian has already been trained in online searching but the scientist has not, it will be necessary to build into the calculations the cost of training the scientist, and this cost must be amortized over some period of time.

These figures are purely hypothetical, and certain assumptions underlie the analysis (for example, that all scientists have suitable terminals in their offices). This example has been deliberately simplified to illustrate what can happen when significant costs are overlooked. A more sophisticated analysis would take into account how librarians and scientists would spend their time if they were not searching online.

One can compare online searching by librarians with searching by scientists on the basis of cost, effectiveness, and cost-effectiveness. Consider the following data:

	Librarian	*Scientist*
Cost	$37 per search	$40 per search
Effectiveness	15 pertinent items retrieved on average	20 pertinent items retrieved on average
Cost-effectiveness	$2.47 per pertinent item retrieved	$2 per pertinent item retrieved

The cost comparison favors the librarian, but the effectiveness and cost-effectiveness comparisons both favor the scientist. A more sophisticated analysis would distinguish between major value and minor value items; for example, the scientist might find more documents than the librarian, but the librarian might find the documents that the scientist judges are most valuable, perhaps because these are new to him.

Very few studies have looked at the true cost-effectiveness of end-user searching vis-á-vis librarian searching, although Nicholas, Erbach, and Harris (1987) have touched on some of the issues. A similar analysis involves comparing the cost-effectiveness of searches in an online database with that of searches on the same topics in printed indexes (or in databases in CD-ROM form). Again, in such a situation, one must be careful to take into account all costs for both options. In comparing the cost of a search in a printed tool, such as *Chemical Abstracts,* with that of a search in its online equivalent, the cost of owning the printed tool must be accounted for. A major element in the cost of an online search will be the cost of access to the database, including computer costs, telecommunications costs, and database royalties. The equivalent cost of access to the printed tool is the cost of the subscription, the cost of handling it (checking it in, claiming missing issues, and so on), and the cost of the space it occupies. Thus, if it costs $5,000 a year to own a particular database in print form and it is used 500 times a year, the cost of performing a search must include $10 for "access cost." To not do so would give a completely distorted picture in the comparison of manual versus online searching (Elchesen, 1978; Lancaster, 1981).

Huang and McHale (1990) have developed a cost-effectiveness model to help librarians decide when to discontinue a printed source and rely entirely on online access to that source. Their "online/print threshold" relates the cost of making the printed source available in the library to the average cost of an online search in that database. The average yearly cost of a printed source (annual subscription rate) is used to derive an average daily cost, which is the subscription cost divided by the number of days the library is open. If the average cost of the online search is equal to or less than this daily cost, it is assumed that the printed source should be discontinued. This approach to the analysis is original, but simplistic. It is difficult to see why average daily cost is used in place of cost per use of the printed source, other than the fact that a survey must be performed to estimate annual use, whereas average daily cost is easily derived (except that the true cost of ownership includes space occupied, handling, and other costs, as well as subscription cost). The model, in fact, is not a true cost-effectiveness model because search effectiveness is not considered (that is, it is assumed that searches in print or online databases are equally effective).

Today, librarians are concerned with print versus CD-ROM searching and online versus CD-ROM, as well as with print versus online. Welsh (1989) gives an example of the online versus CD-ROM comparison based on use of the NTIS database, estimated at 162 searches or 64 hours per year in his library. Welsh estimates the CD-ROM cost per hour to be $35.16 (annual subscription cost to the database—$2,250—divided by 64), versus per hour costs of $80 for DIALOG/DIALNET access. At the rate of 64 hours of searching per year, the annual savings from CD-ROM acquisition are estimated to be $2,870 ($5,120 minus $2,250). As Welsh recognizes, this is a simplistic cost comparison. Not considered for the online access mode are the costs of printing bibliographic records ($0.30 online, $0.45 offline), which can be a substantial component in the overall cost of a comprehensive search. On the CD-ROM side, however, some allowance must be made for the cost of the paper consumed. More important, some part of the acquisition cost of the CD-ROM equipment must be allocated to each hour of CD-ROM use. Assume that the equipment (work station and CD-ROM drive) costs $2,195, that the estimated lifetime of this equipment is five years, and that it is used for 1,600 hours of searching during the five-year period (this estimate is based on five CD-ROM databases, each used an average of 64 hours per year). Therefore, approximately $1.37 ($2,195 ÷ 1,600 hours) must be added to the cost of each hour of CD-ROM searching for equipment use, plus a little more for the paper consumed and the space that the equipment occupies in the library (which would be more or less comparable for a CD-ROM work station and an online terminal). So the actual cost of an hour of CD-ROM searching may be closer to $37 than the $35 that Welsh estimates, although this is still considerably less than the cost for online searching.

But this analysis is based only on database access costs and ignores the extremely important element of human costs. From the library's point of view, the CD-ROM database has the added advantage that most library users will perform their own searches, whereas online searches in Welsh's library (in a government agency) are performed by professional librarians. From the agency's viewpoint, however, the situation may be quite different: Users searching the CD-ROM database may be paid more, on average, than the librarians, and they probably will spend more time on a search than the librarians would (indeed, Welsh [1989] points out that users of CD-ROM tend to spend more time on a search because they know they are not paying for connect time), so the actual cost per search to the agency, taking salaries and overhead into account, could be much higher for the CD-ROM situation.

This comparison considers only the cost side of the cost-effectiveness equation or, at least, it considers cost per search as the unit of cost-effectiveness rather than cost per useful item retrieved. If the librarian can find many more useful items through the online facilities than the library users can from the CD-ROM databases, the cost per useful item retrieved (the true cost-effectiveness measure) may well be less for the online access alternative. On the other hand, the most cost-effective alternative, from the agency's point of view, might be the one where librarians perform CD-ROM searches for library users. Clearly, this comparison is quite complicated. The decision on which is the better alternative cannot be made solely on the basis of costs but must take search results (effectiveness) into account. Moreover, the decision depends largely on whether total agency costs are considered or just the library's costs.

Cost-effectiveness analysis can also be applied to input–output relationships. Mandel (1988) looks at one manifestation of the relationship between input costs and search performance. She relates various levels of detail in cataloging to (1) the probability that users will search on the access points provided and (2) the probable number of searches that will be successful given different levels of detail.

Cost-effectiveness studies are very much concerned with trade-offs and diminishing returns—determining at what level an information system can operate efficiently and economically. Examples of such considerations have been touched on elsewhere in this book. They include decisions on what to cover in a database (for example, there will exist an optimum set of journals to index so as to meet the needs of database users) and how exhaustively to index documents of different types within the database. The phenomenon of diminishing returns is closely tied to the phenomenon of bibliometric and related laws (of Bradford [1953] and Zipf [1935], in particular) and to the idea of the "90 percent library" (Bourne, 1965), which recognizes that an information service can satisfy some specified percentage of user needs (perhaps as many as 90 percent) efficiently and economically but that to go beyond this level of performance would require a completely disproportionate level of investment. The needs that can be satisfied efficiently tend to be homogeneous and predictable. Some other aspects of cost-effectiveness and cost–benefit analysis are dealt with by Lancaster (1993a) and Flowerdew and Whitehead (1974).

The broadest type of cost-effectiveness study relates to the optimum allocation of an institution's financial resources over all the services provided. Its object is to determine if a different distribution of resources will result in better service. The major problem is establishing user preferences and priorities for various services so that the budget can be allocated to correspond to user priorities. A useful technique for achieving this allocation is described by Raffel and Shishko (1969). In brief, it involves a "management game" played with samples of the user population. Users are given a list of possible services and several possible budgets, one of which is the existing budget of the institution. They are also given a list of likely outcomes (benefits and penalties) if changes are made to patterns of service and the costs associated with various options. They are asked to allocate the resources budgeted over the various service possibilities to reflect their own preferences and needs. The allocation of resources in this way gives the information center a better idea of the needs of users than simply asking the users for their preferences in a more abstract way, and different sets of priorities among different segments of the user community can be identified. It is also useful for management to know how user preferences may change when the budget is increased or decreased.

COST–BENEFIT ANALYSIS

A cost–benefit study relates the cost of providing a service to the benefits of having it available. The service is justified if the benefits will exceed the costs. Unfortunately, although the principle of cost–benefit analysis sounds simple, such studies are not easy to carry out because of the difficulties of measuring the benefits of information retrieval systems and, in particular, putting some monetary value on them. Some possible criteria for establishing a cost–benefit ratio for information retrieval systems include

1. Possible cost savings through the use of the service as compared with the costs of obtaining needed information or documents from other sources

2. Avoidance of the loss of productivity—for example, of students, faculty, or research workers—that would result if information sources were not readily available

3. Improved decision making or reduction in the level of personnel required to make decisions

4. Avoidance of duplication or waste of research and development effort on projects that either have been done before or have been proved infeasible by earlier investigators

5. Stimulation of invention or productivity by making available the literature on current developments in a particular field.

Some industrial librarians have attempted to justify the existence of their services by calculating how much it would cost the company to buy equivalent services elsewhere—another library within the organization, an external library, or a commercial information service (see, for example, Magson, 1973). In this case, the underlying assumption is that the service is worthwhile. The question being considered is whether it is better for the company to provide the service through an in-house library or in some other way.[4] The entire range of services offered by the library or just a single service can be the focus of attention. For example, it might be determined that the total cost of providing online literature searches through the library, at a level of 500 searches a year, is $35,000. To buy this level of service from a commercial agency might cost $50,000. Thus, the net benefit to the company of providing the service in-house is $15,000.

In many ways, this is a reasonable approach to justifying the existence of an information service of this type, although there are certain problems associated with it. Some services may not be suitable for delegation to an outside contractor for reasons of practicality or industrial security. There might be a convenience factor associated with the in-house facility that the outside agency could not duplicate, although it would be difficult to give this factor any real monetary value. A more practical problem is that the collection of materials owned by the library is likely to contribute to many different services— document delivery, literature searching, question answering, preparation of an information bulletin—and it is difficult to allocate the costs of the collection over the various services in any meaningful way. Nevertheless, if corporate management is satisfied with this approach to the justification of services, it has a lot to recommend it from the librarian's point of view.

A similar approach compares the cost of the librarian providing a particular service with the cost of the librarian's customers undertaking the activity for themselves (Mason, 1972; Rosenberg, 1969). To take a simple example, suppose that the average cost of a literature search provided by the librarian is $140 and that the average cost of an equivalent search undertaken by a customer is $195, because of salary differential. It could be argued, then, that the librarian saves the company $55 for every search performed. There are some underlying assumptions here: that the customer would do the search if the librarian was

---

[4] One could argue that this is more of a cost-effectiveness study—comparing alternative strategies—than a cost–benefit study.

not available and that the customer's results would be qualitatively equivalent to those of the librarian.

Rosenberg (1969) tried to expand on this method by having users weight the results of a literature search performed by the librarian, according to the following scale:

0   Useless (for example, not relevant or received too late).

1   Adequate. User would have spent the same amount of time as the librarian.

2   Good. User would have spent twice the amount of time spent by the librarian.

3   Excellent. Results could not have been achieved by the user or could not have been achieved at an acceptable cost.

These weights may be built into a "savings" equation

$$(A \times B \times C) - A$$

where A is the cost of the librarian's time, B is a multiplication factor to account for the difference in salary between the librarian and the customer, and C is the assigned weighting factor. Thus, if a literature search costs $75 in librarian time, the salary differential is 1.5, and the weight given by the user is 2, then the savings could be calculated as ($75 \times 1.5 \times 2$) − 75, or $150.

Clearly, this is very subjective, for one can have little confidence that a user could arrive at any realistic estimate of how much time it would take to perform some information retrieval task. Several other investigators have tried to justify an information service by estimating potential cost savings attributable to having these services available. It is assumed that, were the library not available, engineers or scientists would spend more of their own time in information seeking and that this would be costly to the organization. Analyses of this type are only as good as the validity of the estimates of time saved.

Nightingale (1973) attempted to do a cost–benefit analysis for a company abstracts bulletin. He calculated that it cost £2,500 per year to produce the bulletin. He used a survey to determine how many journals were regularly scanned by the recipients of the bulletin and had readers estimate how many additional journals they would scan if the bulletin was discontinued. A median value of six additional journals per year was obtained. Nightingale calculated that it would take a user an average of 10 minutes to scan a journal to identify items of interest. The cost of this activity was estimated at 18.5 hours per user per year (6 journals × 10 minutes × number of issues), which worked out to £74. With 400 users, the cost of the extra scanning would be £74 × 400, or

£29,600. The bottom line of the cost–benefit analysis, then, is an annual savings of £27,100 (£29,600 minus the £2,500 to produce the bulletin).

Nightingale's analysis is reasonably conservative. Much less conservative are the data reported by Kramer (1971), based on a study performed at Boeing Aerospace. Kramer estimated the savings to the company of having the library perform literature searches and answer factual questions rather than having the engineers do this work themselves. On the basis of questionnaires returned by 153 engineers for whom literature searches had been performed, it was estimated that 9,479 hours of engineering time would have been consumed had the engineers conducted the searches themselves. The librarian time to perform these searches was calculated to be 1,071 worker hours (approximately seven worker hours per search). Clearly, even if the librarian was paid the same hourly rate as the engineers, the savings would be considerable. Some 8,000 hours of engineer time at 1992 rates (and including all overhead) might cost more than $300,000.

Kramer (1971) also used follow-up telephone interviews with 215 engineers for whom the library had answered factual questions. Whereas the librarians averaged 12 minutes per question, the engineers estimated that it would have taken them an average of 5.42 hours per question to find the answer! For 215 questions, this represents another 1,166 hours of engineer time saved.

Estabrook (1986) also asked engineers to estimate the time savings associated with the use of a search/document delivery service and to put a dollar value on the information retrieved. She concluded that by the most conservative estimates, the company saved $2 for every $1 expended on the service. In best-case terms, however, the company might save almost $50 for each $1 invested in the information center. This latter conclusion was arrived at by including two extreme cases in which the recipients of information estimated potential savings of $1 million and $2.5 million.

A number of other studies have also attempted to get users to place a dollar value on the results received from an information service. For instance, Collette and Price (1977) present an example of justifying the cost of literature-searching activities in terms of engineer time saved and other elements of the monetary value of search results. On the basis of results from a user survey, they arrive at what they consider "ultraconservative" benefit estimates. Benefits per online search were calculated to be $315 on the average, whereas per search costs were estimated to be $112. They also make a point that is frequently overlooked: Even a library search that produces no relevant items may have value to the company, since it would probably be much more expensive for the engineers to undertake these searches themselves.

One of the better studies of the benefits of online searches is reported by Jensen, Asbury, and King (1980). Telephone interviews were conducted with a sample of users of the NASA Industrial Application Center at the University of Southern California. Users were asked to estimate the benefits of an online search performed for them in terms of hours saved (compared with having to perform the search themselves or obtaining needed information elsewhere) and the potential value of the information when applied to an existing product, process, or service or to a projected new product, process, or service. Of the 159 users surveyed, 53 percent were able to identify dollar benefits. They reported current benefits of $364,605 and five-year follow-on benefits of $873,500.

These kinds of data would provide a very impressive endorsement of an information service if they were fully credible. Unfortunately, it is difficult to believe that anyone could come up with a realistic estimate of how long it would take to perform a particular information retrieval activity, and the results achieved by Kramer (1971)—almost 30 times longer for an engineer to answer a question than for the librarian—strain the bounds of credibility. It seems even less likely that the user of an information service could put a dollar value on information received with any degree of accuracy, although Estabrook (1986) claims that such estimates may be better than are commonly supposed.

Even if an exact dollar value cannot be placed on a piece of information, there may be occasions when an industrial information service can prove its worth to the corporation in a dramatic way. For a research organization, the greatest benefit that the library can provide might be discovering information that prevents the company from performing research already done elsewhere. It is difficult to document events of this type (and even more difficult to prove that the company would not have found the information without the library), but a single case, if documented, might justify the cost of the library for several years. A large study of the unintentional duplication of research, and the cost of this duplication, was performed in the United Kingdom by Martyn (1964), who presents impressive evidence to support the claim that large amounts of money could be saved by performing more complete literature searches before research projects get under way. Cooper (1968) presents figures on the saving of research time attributable to the informal research communications distributed experimentally by the information exchange groups established by the National Institutes of Health.

Another possible measure of benefit is the loss of productivity that might occur if the library were not available in a company and the scientists or engineers were forced to wait a long time for needed information. Mueller (1959), for example, discovered that the work of some engineers was actually brought to a halt while they waited for information to complete a critical task. The assumption here, of course, is that having information saves time. Solomin (1974), however, has argued that under certain circumstances, having information increases company costs because of the time it takes to process and assimilate it.

Mondschein (1990) looked at the benefits derived from the use of selective dissemination of information (SDI) facilities in a corporate research environment; costs were not discussed. The measure of benefit adopted was improved productivity as measured by publications produced. Mondschein discovered that regular users of SDI services are more productive than nonusers or researchers who use the services infrequently.

Finally, a librarian might point to other positive effects on the company that can be traced to information provided by librarians. These include the development of a new product, the identification of ways to reduce the costs of existing products (perhaps by using materials that are cheaper but equally effective), or the award of an important contract. It is not easy to prove that the library has been directly responsible for events of this kind, but a single documented example might be enough to justify the library's existence for some time to come.

Investigators at King Research, Inc. (King et al., 1982), have carried cost–benefit analysis even further in trying to determine the value of the Energy Data Base of the U.S. Department of Energy (DOE). Through the use of questionnaires, it was estimated that the reading of articles and reports by DOE-funded scientists and engineers resulted in the location of information yielding annual savings of $13 billion (by avoiding duplication of work, by saving time, and in other ways). This contrasts with an annual expenditure by DOE for research and development of $5.3 billion and an expenditure of $500 million on information processing and use.

Although quite a few cost–benefit studies have been mentioned in this chapter, they are definitely the exception, not the rule. In most organizations, little or no attempt is made to determine the outcomes of literature-searching activities, although more work of this kind has been done in the health care field than in other professions. For example, Scura and Davidoff (1981), Greenberg et al. (1978), and Schnall and Wilson (1976)—all dealing with services provided by clinical medical librarians—asked the clinician users of the services to what extent the information provided had directly influenced patient care. Operating in a hospital library setting, King (1987) asked users of the information supplied to judge its clinical value, cognitive value (contribution to user's health care knowledge), quality, currency, relevance to the clinical situation that had prompted the request, and impact on clinical decision making. Ideally, of course, one would like to go even beyond this—attempt to determine to what extent a clinical information service might contribute to reducing morbidity and mortality, the length of time a patient stays in the hospital, or the costs of the medical care.

Wilson, Starr-Schneidkraut, and Cooper (1989) present the results of a study in which the critical incident technique was used to evaluate the benefits of searches performed in the MEDLINE database. More than 500 health professionals known to be MEDLINE users were interviewed by telephone. The subjects of the study were asked to focus on a recent MEDLINE search. Besides attempting to determine the impact on medical decision making, the investigators tried to identify longer term outcomes. They report that "information obtained via MEDLINE has had important beneficial, even lifesaving consequences" and were able to document eight lifesaving cases.

Cost–benefit analyses are difficult to perform in the information service environment, and perhaps no study of this kind has ever been fully credible. Nevertheless, one way or another, information centers must justify their existence, so the benefits of their services, even if nebulous, cannot be ignored in evaluative studies.

10

Factors Affecting Performance in Information Retrieval

Factors affecting the performance of information retrieval systems have been mentioned or briefly discussed throughout this book. This chapter pulls all this material together to present a more detailed picture of what makes a retrieval system perform well or perform badly.

Exhibit 16 (in Chapter 3) depicts a sequence of events that take place from the time that a user, needing information on some subject, comes to an information center to the time that a set of search results is delivered to him or her.[1] The user's information need must first be translated into an expressed need (stated request). The information specialist must then select the most appropriate database (or databases) in which to conduct the search and construct an appropriate strategy. The search is conducted by matching the strategy against the database, and the results may be screened by the searcher to eliminate irrelevant items before they are submitted to the user.

Each of the steps depicted in Exhibit 16 introduces potential sources of noise or information loss. Moreover, the effect is cumulative. There may be some loss of information because the request does not accurately reflect the user's true information need, more loss because the database selected is not the one most appropriate for the search, further loss due to an inadequate search strategy, and so on. In analyzing the results of an evaluation program, particularly recall and precision failures, the investigator attempts to determine

---

[1] A delegated search is assumed here. A different situation exists when users do their own searching, because the potential information loss that is inherent in an intermediary's understanding and translation of the user's information need and request into a search strategy or in the delegation of the screening operation is eliminated. Users, however, might inaccurately translate their own requests into a search strategy. Furthermore, most would be unfamiliar with system protocols, indexing policies, and search logic.

System Factors	Human Factors
Database	Indexing
Coverage	Consistency
Time lag and frequency of update	Subject expertise
Indexing and vocabulary policies	Indexing experience
Index language	Searching
Specificity	Consistency
Level of coordination	Subject expertise
Amount of explicit structure	Searching experience
	Cognitive style
Indexing	
Exhaustivity	Screening
Specificity of term assignment	Consistency
Accuracy	Subject expertise
	Screening experience
Search strategy	
Exhaustivity	
Specificity	

EXHIBIT 52   Factors studied in the evaluation of information retrieval systems.

where in the information service operation most of the problems or failures occur.

Within this framework, many important factors influence the performance of information retrieval systems (Exhibit 52). They affect the performance (effectiveness) of a search, as well as costs, in terms of money and time, incurred by the organization or the user (the notions of cost-effectiveness and cost–benefit).

Historically, it was the system factors—or as Sparck Jones (1981) states, "the character of the indexing data and search mechanisms available" (p. 216)— that were studied by information retrieval researchers. Recently, however, human factors have come under broader and more frequent scrutiny; they include the characteristics of indexers and searchers (for example, experience in indexing or searching, subject knowledge), all of which may have an effect on retrieval performance. Similarly, views on the appropriate evaluation measures for a given study have evolved. Traditionally, attention has focused on outcome measures such as recall, precision, novelty, and cost (in both time and money). Today, evaluators look increasingly toward the search process rather than the search outcome. In cases where the process is being studied, other evaluation measures have been used, such as Borgman's (1984) "negative model" and "positive model" features, where the searcher's ability to form an appropriate mental model of a search system is evaluated. These measures will be dealt with in more detail later in the chapter.

SYSTEM FACTORS IN INFORMATION RETRIEVAL

The Database

The selection (by an end user or intermediary) or the acquisition (by a database vendor) of a database is strongly influenced by the following criteria :

- Subject matter
- Cost factors
- Qualitative considerations

    - Coverage
    - Time factors
    - Indexing and vocabulary factors

For the user of databases, important cost factors include unit cost per record retrieved and unit cost per relevant record retrieved. For the organizations that develop and market the databases, the most salient cost factors are the

- Cost of developing the database
- Cost of acquiring the database
- Cost of implementing the database (start-up and running costs)
- Unit cost per record and cost in relation to the number of access points provided
- Cost in relation to volume of demand for service (unit cost per search)
- Cost in relation to qualitative characteristics (such as coverage, exhaustivity of indexing)

The qualitative criteria are important because they influence both the quality and completeness of search results. The three major types of qualitative criteria are coverage, time, and indexing and vocabulary factors (Exhibit 53).

COVERAGE

The coverage criteria, introduced in Chapter 7, include the completeness of the database, the relative completeness of two or more databases, and the extent to which two or more databases overlap or complement each other. Completeness may be considered in terms of the absolute number of items

Coverage Factors	Time Factors	Indexing and Vocabulary Factors
Number of sources	Time lag	Degree of vocabulary control
Type of sources	Frequency of update	Specificity of the vocabulary
Number of items		Searching aids provided
Time span		Semantic and syntactic ambiguity
Completeness in relation to user needs		Exhaustivity (number and variety of access points)
Uniqueness and overlap		Accuracy and consistency (observed error)

EXHIBIT 53   Some major qualitative aspects of databases.

indexed or abstracted per year, the number of sources (for example, journals) covered, the type of sources (for instance, technical reports and patents), and the time span covered. This last consideration relates only to the value of the database for retrospective searching. A database is of very limited value for retrospective searching unless it covers at least three years of the literature. It might begin to approach a high level of value when it reaches, say, five years of coverage. A longer span of coverage is likely to be more important in the social sciences and the humanities than it is in science and technology because the rate of obsolescence is usually higher in scientific and technical areas.

Unfortunately, it is impossible to measure the absolute coverage of a database in some specialized area just by counting the number of items or the number of sources covered. An estimate of the degree of coverage requires a controlled evaluation, which was dealt with in Chapter 7. The two techniques identified were (1) the "bibliography" method, where one assembles a random sample of relevant articles—review articles are particularly valuable for this purpose—and uses the references included in these papers as a "citation pool" for testing the coverage of a particular database, and (2) the "profile" method, where coverage is assessed by searching subject queries in multiple databases.

Davison and Matthews (1969), using a bibliography of 183 references on the subject of computers in mass spectrometry, discovered that among 12 databases not one covered more than 40 percent of this literature and that the coverage of *Chemical Abstracts* was only 24 percent. Bourne (1969a) estimated that the *Bibliography of Agriculture* covered only 50–60 percent of the literature relevant to agricultural research. More recently, Yonker et al. (1990) used a pool of citations selected from forensic medicine journals to determine the coverage and overlap of MEDLINE, EXCERPTA MEDICA, SCISEARCH, and CRIMINAL JUSTICE PERIODICAL INDEX. They found that EXCERPTA MEDICA had the best coverage (91 percent) and CRIMINAL JUSTICE PERIODICAL INDEX the worst (24 percent). All citations were found in at least one of the databases.

Tenopir (1982) used a very general "profile" that was intended as a truly comprehensive search on the broad topic of emergency management. Alternatively, both Sharma (1982) and Nixon (1989) used a different method, selecting a set of specific queries in the areas of community development and human nutrition, respectively. All three investigators found that more than one database had to be used to ensure that the search would be comprehensive. Furthermore, Tenopir compared her general profile method with the bibliography method and found them to be about the same in terms of coverage estimates.

Coverage studies are very useful because they show that no single source is completely comprehensive in its coverage of a particular area of the literature. The work of Bradford (1953), as well as later bibliometric analyses, confirm that many primary sources are likely to contribute to the literature of any particular subject field, although a very high percentage of this literature may come from just a few sources.

Some further aspects of coverage are worth mentioning. It is important to have an idea of how reliable an information service is in its coverage of the literature. Clearly, it must consistently scan all issues of the journals that it claims to cover. And it should distinguish between the journals it covers completely and those it covers selectively. Where a selection is made from various sources, it is also important to assess how consistent and reliable the *selection process* is. Again, this type of evaluation cannot be achieved by observation alone, but only through testing.

Another consideration in the selection of databases relates to the local availability of the sources covered. The list of sources covered by a particular database should be compared with the sources that are available locally. Buchanan, Berwind, and Carlin (1989) compared optical disk sources by determining not only how many retrieved items were held by the library but also how many could be successfully identified and found by library users. The use of current awareness or retrospective search services in a particular community creates a demand for a document delivery system, and it is necessary to assess the impact of these services on other services—for example, interlibrary loan— provided by the organization.

TIME

Certainly it is of prime importance to many users of a database that it be up-to-date. Time lag between publication of an item and its appearance in the file affects the value of the database for current awareness purposes. A good SDI service should operate at a high novelty ratio; that is, the majority of items delivered to users not only should be relevant to their interests but should also be items they have not seen before. The novelty ratio (number of pertinent items retrieved that are new to the user/number of pertinent items retrieved) obviously is greatly influenced by how quickly items are processed into the database.

In general, databases in which human intellectual processing is minimized—for example, those of the Institute for Scientific Information—are more current than those requiring more intellectual processing, such as the writing of abstracts. Ashmole, Smith, and Stern (1973), in evaluating databases for their value to the pharmaceutical industry, found that the ASCA database (Institute for Scientific Information) included items an average of 0 to 3 weeks after publication, whereas most other services averaged between 2 and 6 months and *Biological Abstracts* took between 4 and 12 months.

Related to currency is the frequency with which the database is updated. If tied to a publication cycle, frequency of update is likely to correspond to the frequency of publication—biweekly, monthly, and so on. For some services, the leasing costs vary, depending on how often the customer needs to have the file updated.

INDEXING AND VOCABULARY

Some of the indexing and vocabulary factors listed in Exhibit 53 require explanation. *Specificity* is influenced by whether the vocabulary used is controlled or natural language. A controlled vocabulary has the desirable effect of gathering documents about the same concept under the same term and also can provide aids to the searcher through its explicit semantic structure. On the other hand, it is not as specific or current as natural language. *Exhaustivity* is simply the degree to which all concepts covered in the document are represented with an index term. And *accuracy* refers to the quality of the indexing applied to the database.

Many studies have been conducted on the effects of index language and indexing policies on retrieval performance. Barber et al. (1988) studied the indexing in pharmacology databases, and Starr (1982) investigated the indexing in marine science databases. They concluded that once the indexing policy is known, it is possible to predict the suitability of each database for particular types of searches, since there is considerable variability in how a concept is treated in various databases. Konings (1985) concentrated on the individual words in computer science records, finding that very dissimilar words were used in different databases to express the same concept.

COST-EFFECTIVENESS ASPECTS OF THE DATABASE

A database vendor needs to determine the optimum literature to collect and make available in a given subject area. Bradford's law of scattering, as discussed earlier, relates to the distribution of periodical articles over the journals in which they are published (Bradford, 1953). A comprehensive literature search conducted on some subject for a specified period will reveal that the literature is scattered over a very large number of journals. These journals can be arranged in order of productivity, with the journal yielding the most articles at the top of the list. The list can then be divided into zones, such that each zone contains approximately the same number of articles. Although the number of articles in each zone is nearly the same, the number of sources yielding these articles varies considerably. The first zone, or "nucleus," contains a few highly productive journals. The last zone contains many journals, each one yielding a very small number of papers for the specified subject and period. The zones thus identified form an approximately geometric series:

$$1: \quad a: \quad a^2: \ldots a^n$$

where 1 represents the number of journals in the nucleus and a is a multiplier.

For example, a literature search might reveal that in a particular year 375 articles were published on a subject and were dispersed over 155 journals. If the journals are divided into three zones, each contributing 125 articles, the first zone (nucleus) might be found to contain 5 journals, the second zone 25, (that is, 5×5), and the third 125 (that is, 5×5^2). In the third zone, each journal contributes only a single paper to the subject.

When the results of a scatter analysis of this type are presented graphically as the cumulative percentage of articles plotted against the cumulative percentage of journals yielding them, a curve of the type shown in Exhibit 54 results. This type of distribution has been shown to apply to a number of phenomena of interest to managers of information centers, including the distribution of use of a document collection and the distribution of sources requested through interlibrary loan procedures. In applying it to the use of library materials, Trueswell (1969) called it the "80/20 rule"—roughly 20 percent of a collection is used to handle approximately 80 percent of the requests.

A Bradford type of analysis has great value in indicating how the financial resources of an information center can be allocated most efficiently in the acquisition of materials. The plot in Exhibit 54 suggests two possible acquisition strategies. Suppose one were building an information center in the field of superconductivity. Given that there is a budget of X dollars available for the acquisition of journals, the soundest strategy is to purchase journals in the order of their expected yield of relevant articles until the budget is exhausted. In the example in Exhibit 54, 30 journals can be expected to yield two-thirds of the

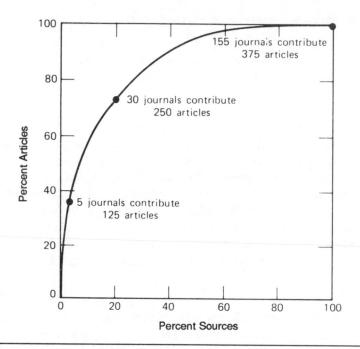

EXHIBIT 54   Bradford distribution of 375 articles published in 155 journals.

relevant literature, whereas well over 100 additional journals would be needed to yield 100 percent coverage. Furthermore, the group of high-yield journals will be relatively stable, at least over a short period of time, but the list of lower yielding journals may be very unstable. The list of journals contributing only a single paper each on superconductors in 1992 might be quite different from the list of those contributing one paper each in 1993.

For most information centers, 100 percent coverage of the literature is essentially unattainable. Even if it were attainable, it would be an unreasonable goal from a cost-effectiveness point of view. To push the coverage from, say, 85 percent to close to 100 percent would require a completely disproportionate level of expenditure, since the last 15 percent of coverage might easily cost as much as, or more than, the first 85 percent. The alternative purchasing strategy, then, is to establish some realistic goal in coverage, perhaps 85 or 90 percent, and then use the Bradford distribution, which represents a law of diminishing returns, to select those journals that have the highest probability of meeting the goal.

A number of studies have investigated the use of the 80/20 rule in decisions on acquisitions. These include studies of circulation data to select monographs

(Britten, 1990) and to examine in-library use of journal titles to make decisions about journal subscriptions and cancellations (Alligood, Russo-Martin, and Peterson, 1983).

Coupled with the "law of obsolescence," the Bradford distribution also has value in determining the optimum allocation of available storage space so that the documents that are likely to be used the most are the most accessible. The problem is clearly one of deciding which materials are likely to be in most demand and which in least demand.

The law of obsolescence states that the probability of demand for bibliographic materials declines with their age, especially in science and technology. Fussler and Simon (1969), working at the University of Chicago, found that books could be safely retired to storage areas on the bases of language and publication date only. The rate of obsolescence or aging of bibliographic materials is frequently expressed in terms of their "median use." The median use age of a particular body of literature is the number of years that are retrospectively needed to satisfy half of all the requests for literature on the subject or to attract half of all the citations made to it in the current year (median citation age). Thus, if half of all the citations appearing in the 1993 literature on superconductors are to literature published during the past 42 months, the median citation age of this literature is 3 1/2 years. Similarly, if in a particular physics library 50 percent of the requests for superconductor literature are for literature published during the last 42 months, the median use age of this literature is 3 1/2 years. It has frequently been assumed that these two methods of measuring obsolescence give roughly equivalent results; in other words, that citation patterns can be used to predict patterns of demand for bibliographic materials in libraries (Bourne, 1965; Fussler and Simon, 1969), although some researchers have cast doubt on that assertion (Sandison, 1971; Line and Sandison, 1974).

Returning to the problem of space allocation, suppose that a particular information center has enough room on its open-access shelves to store 3,000 bound volumes of periodicals. This space should be allocated so that the volumes thus stored would be those most likely needed by users. Studies of aging factors could be combined with studies of expected distribution of demand for particular titles to determine how this prime space should best be allocated. Journal X, for example, might be retained on open shelves for 10 years back, and journal Y for only three years. Such practical cost-effectiveness analyses should indicate that those volumes retained in the most accessible area can be expected to satisfy a specified percentage of user demands. Database producers can use studies of this kind to determine the optimum set of documents to collect and index, as well as how far back to maintain the database in its most accessible form—for example, how far back to keep a database online.

Such studies should be conducted at the design stage, before the system is implemented. In other words, cost-effectiveness needs to be predicted for various types of materials. This task is more difficult than evaluating usage factors in an actual operating system. There are a number of techniques, however, that make this type of prediction feasible, including citation counting, analysis of library usage or interlibrary loan traffic, and analysis of subject requests collected from sample user populations. All of these analyses can predict payoff for various materials.

The Index Language

General characteristics of the language used in retrieval were discussed in Chapter 6. They include

1. The specificity of the vocabulary—whether the language used in indexing and searching tends to be general or specific.

2. The level of coordination of the vocabulary—the degree to which individual words are precombined into more complex constructions by using phrases, subheadings, or explicit linguistic devices such as links or roles.

3. The amount of structure that is explicitly provided for the indexer or searcher in the form of semantic relationships among terms (for example, broader/narrower, related). Structure aids in term selection for queries or documents.

SPECIFICITY

The specificity of the vocabulary is the single most important factor influencing the precision with which a search can be conducted. Suppose that a user is looking for information on ultramicrofiche. If the system includes the specific term ULTRAMICROFICHE, a search of high precision can presumably be conducted. Most, if not all, of the documents retrieved should deal with the precise subject of the inquiry. But the system might have only the more generic term MICROFICHE. A search under this term, when the requirement is specifically for ultramicrofiche, inevitably results in low precision; most of the items retrieved are likely to be unrelated to the specific subject of the search. The situation is even worse if the most specific term available is MICROFORMS.

Consider three separate retrieval systems, A, B, and C, using controlled vocabularies of 2,000, 1,000, and 500 index terms, respectively. Suppose that the same collection of documents on aerodynamics has been indexed for each of the three systems. Some of these documents deal with the subject of slender delta wings.

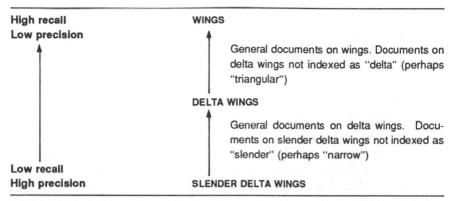

EXHIBIT 55   Effect of specificity of vocabulary on the performance of a retrieval system.

When such documents are indexed into system A, having 2,000 index terms, it may be possible to define their subject matter uniquely by means of the class label SLENDER DELTA WINGS. When the same documents are indexed into system B, with only 1,000 index terms, their content may not be so precisely defined. Perhaps they must be subsumed under the more general class label DELTA WINGS. In system C, WINGS may be the most specific term available for indexing this class of documents. The effect that this variation in specificity has on retrieval is illustrated in Exhibit 55.

When a request is input into system A on the subject of slender delta wings, the subject can be expressed as precisely in the search strategy as in the indexing, and the subset of documents retrieved can be expected to have a high precision ratio. But the recall ratio will probably be low, because the system could well be holding back a number of documents that contain useful information on the subject of slender delta wings. By asking precisely for the class of documents dealing with slender delta wings, the searcher will fail to retrieve (1) documents dealing with delta wings in general but containing substantial information on slender delta wings (these will have been indexed under delta wings) and (2) documents dealing with slender delta wings but indexed under some semantically related term or term combination, perhaps narrow delta wings.

When the same request is input into system B, recall will tend to improve. Some of the additional relevant documents missed by the search in system A will be retrieved; however, some potentially useful documents—for example, those on wings in general, that contain information on slender delta wings, and those on delta wings that have been indexed under some semantically related term or term combination, perhaps triangular wings—might still be missed. These additional useful documents would be retrieved by a search in system C, in which lack of specificity in the index language forces the requester to search under the generic class WINGS.

As the searcher goes from system A to system B to system C, the number of distinct class labels is reduced and the size of the document classes is increased. Therefore, more documents are pulled in during each search and recall performance is improved. At the same time, precision performance tends to deteriorate. In response to a request for documents on slender delta wings, the class precisely labeled SLENDER DELTA WINGS should contain a higher proportion of useful documents than the class labeled DELTA WINGS, which, in turn, should contain a higher proportion of useful documents than the class labeled WINGS.

The greater the specificity of the index language, the more precisely the subject matter can be defined and smaller document classes thus will be created; consequently, the greater the precision that can be achieved in searching the system. Recall, however, will be lower because the document classes defined by the system are so small in size.

The problem of lack of specificity is peculiar to controlled vocabulary systems because the controlled vocabulary, by definition, implies lack of complete specificity—such a vocabulary is not the complete set of terms available in a subject field but only a limited subset of them. The *Medical Subject Headings (MeSH)* used by the National Library of Medicine, for example, contains many thousands of terms, but is still considerably smaller than the vocabulary of any standard medical dictionary. In contrast, the subject matter of a document in an exclusively natural-language system is represented as specifically as the words in the document itself. For this reason, searching natural language tends to promote precision, as borne out in a number of studies in various subject areas, including chemistry (Rowlett, 1977) and law (Carrow and Nugent, 1977).

An important problem faced by managers of any information retrieval system is deciding just how specific the vocabulary needs to be. It must be sufficiently specific to allow the majority of searches to be conducted at an acceptable level of precision. This statement implies that the level of specificity varies over the vocabulary, some subject areas being developed in more detail than others. A vocabulary developed by the National Library of Medicine would need only a few general terms in mathematics, and one developed by the American Mathematical Society would need only a few general terms of a medical nature. It also implies that the vocabulary must be constantly adjusted to make it more specific, as more specific literature is published or more specific demands are made on the system. This, in turn, has a hidden implication. The managers of the system must have some user feedback to enable them to recognize vocabulary inadequacies. Thus, some continuous evaluation or quality control activity is needed, which is not a routine part of many information services.

Adjusting the specificity of an existing vocabulary is easier than arriving at an appropriate level of specificity in the initial development of a thesaurus. As early as 1911, Hulme introduced an important principle known as "literary warrant" or "bibliographic warrant." The principle, which Hulme (1911a,b, c) applied to book classification, simply states that a term is warranted if literature on the subject is known to exist. The principle can be extended to the creation of a thesaurus by saying that a term is warranted if enough literature on the topic is known to exist and that if the term was not introduced into the vocabulary, the literature would be hidden away in a much larger class and thus would not be easily retrieved.

An important corollary principle, one that is frequently overlooked, can be referred to as "user warrant": A term is justified if requests for information at this level of specificity are likely to be made fairly frequently by users of the system. User warrant is even more important than bibliographic warrant in the development of efficient controlled vocabularies for information retrieval. One could probably develop a list of several hundred species of dogs, all of which would be warranted bibliographically, but if the users of a particular system never need anything more specific than DOGS, there is no valid reason for developing this part of the vocabulary in such great detail. The implication of this is clear. The designer of a controlled vocabulary must have considerable information about the potential users of the system and about the types of requests they are likely to make, a point that is strongly emphasized by Soergel (1974) and Lancaster (1972).

Lack of specificity in the index language can cause either recall or precision failures. If a particular class of documents is not uniquely defined but some entry term is used to indicate how the class has been subsumed, precision failures will result because of lack of specificity in the vocabulary. If the notion is omitted even from the entry vocabulary, both recall and precision failures will result. Consider the topic of perceptual completion phenomena. Suppose that this concept cannot be uniquely defined but rather is indexed under the term combination VISION *and* ILLUSIONS. This decision must be recorded in the entry vocabulary as

PERCEPTUAL COMPLETION PHENOMENA *use* VISION *and* ILLUSIONS

Imagine now that there is a request for articles on this subject. The topic appears in the entry vocabulary so it is known which term combination to search on. Precision failures result because the product of the class labeled VISION and that labeled ILLUSIONS, namely, the class VISUAL ILLUSIONS, is wider than the precise class PERCEPTUAL COMPLETION PHENOMENA. Nevertheless, recall failures should not occur, because the entry vocabulary allows indexers to be consistent in their treatment of the topic, and it tells the searcher how the topic has been indexed.

Suppose, however, that there is no precise term for perceptual completion phenomena and that the notion is not included in the entry vocabulary, although articles dealing with the topic have been input to the system. The following will result:

1. Indexer omissions occur. Faced with an article that discusses perceptual completion phenomena, but not as the core topic, the indexer is more likely to omit the topic if no specific term is available in either the controlled vocabulary or the entry vocabulary.

2. Indexing inconsistencies occur. Some indexers may use VISION and ILLUSIONS, and others may use different term combinations.

3. Recall failures occur. Some are due to indexer omissions; others are due to inconsistencies (the searcher does not know how the required topic has been subsumed and fails to cover all the term combinations necessary to achieve high recall).

4. Additional precision failures occur. Because the searcher does not know how the subject has been treated, he or she is forced to try a large number of alternative term combinations, some of which may cause much irrelevancy.

A recall failure due to the lack of a specific term implies that the search topic, or some aspect of it, is not covered in the system's entry vocabulary. A precision failure due to the lack of a specific term implies that the topic is not uniquely defined by the controlled terms. Therefore, to correct precision failures due to the lack of specificity, terms or term combinations that uniquely define the notion that is not covered specifically must be introduced into the vocabulary. A unique designation is not needed to correct recall failures, but the concept must be included in the entry vocabulary.

The precision and recall failures in retrieval efforts using a controlled vocabulary, combined with the cost in both time and money involved in producing and maintaining thesauri, have prompted some to advocate the use of only natural language in databases and queries (Cleverdon, 1984). This viewpoint was adopted because of the results of retrieval experiments, most notably the ones carried out in Cranfield, England (Cleverdon, Mills, and Keen, 1966), which suggested that a minimally controlled language (where only synonyms and word endings are normalized) performs as well as or better than any type of more rigidly controlled vocabulary.

Although later studies have tended to confirm that natural language is very useful in retrieval, the results of several projects have indicated that natural language and controlled vocabulary are complementary, that is, they each contribute relevant documents that are not supplied by the other approach. These findings have been seen in different subject areas (Calkins, 1980; Katzer et al., 1982) and in databases with differing amounts of free text, including full texts of articles (Tenopir, 1985; McKinin et al., 1991).

COORDINATION

Another vocabulary characteristic that affects retrieval performance is the level of coordination of the terminology. Consider a search for information on book catalogs. If the user enters the strategy BOOKS *and* CATALOGS, two distinct types of documents could be retrieved: (1) documents on catalogs that provide access to books and (2) documents on catalogs that are in book form. But only the second is relevant to the request. Problems such as this, due to ambiguous and spurious relationships between words, were particularly prevalent in the Uniterm (single word) systems of the 1950s (Lancaster, 1972) and, in fact, led to the development of thesauri containing some phrases (Holm and Rasmussen, 1961) that enhanced the precision of the vocabulary.

Precision devices other than phrases also are found in retrieval languages. One is the coordination of main headings and subheadings at the time of indexing (for example, LIBRARIES—AUTOMATION—UNITED STATES). This device is found in vocabularies such as the *Library of Congress Subject Headings* and *Medical Subject Headings*. Another, more complicated category of coordination devices includes links and roles. These were discussed in Chapter 6. Thus, for the complex concept of "design of aircraft," one could have the following three representations:

AIRCRAFT—DESIGN	(main heading/subheading)
DESIGN(A)	(link between two terms)
AIRCRAFT(A)	
DESIGN	(semantic relationship [role]
AIRCRAFT(4)	between two terms)

In the case of subheadings and links, the two concepts, represented by the terms AIRCRAFT and DESIGN, are connected at the time of indexing. Roles go even further to specify the exact semantic relationship between the two terms, in this case indicating that the object of the design process is aircraft.

The need to incorporate linguistic devices, most notably links and roles, has been questioned in light of the Cranfield study findings (Cleverdon, Mills, and Keen, 1966), which found them to be unnecessary. Moreover, as Lancaster

(1972) has pointed out, the cost of incorporating syntactic and semantic devices—in terms of not being able to retrieve what is wanted, as well as the cost in dollars incurred in assigning them—may far outweigh the advantage of avoiding some irrelevancy in output.

The need for phrases in search strategies, however, particularly in natural-language searching of full texts, has been advocated (Tenopir and Ro, 1990). The combining of single words by means of the *and* operator may get better recall than the use of explicit phrases, but this may also bring an unacceptable level of precision.

STRUCTURE

The third retrieval language feature that affects system performance is whether there is any explicit structure in the vocabulary. Controlled vocabulary imposes a structure and natural language does not.

The controlled vocabulary helps the searcher by drawing attention to all the terms that would be needed to conduct a comprehensive search in some subject area. An engineer might need to conduct a search on the failure of a particular type of metal structure. When he consults the thesaurus, or other type of vocabulary, under the term FAILURE, the structure of the tool must lead him to more specific terms that indicate specific types of failure—for example, FRACTURE and RUPTURE—and from these to terms that are still more specific— for example, BRITTLE FRACTURE and STRESS RUPTURE. It might also lead him to possibly useful terms from other hierarchies, such as terms representing conditions that could cause or contribute to failure in metal structures— CORROSION, FATIGUE, STRESS, STABILITY, HYDROGEN EMBRITTLEMENT, and so on. Otherwise, the vocabulary does not give the searcher maximum assistance, and there is a danger that he or she may overlook some of the terms that would be needed to conduct a truly comprehensive search.

Natural language tends to promote precision because it can match any query terms, including very specific ones that would not be found in a controlled vocabulary. Its lack of explicit structure, however, makes it responsible for many recall failures, because the user must supply all the synonyms, spelling variants, and other related terms he or she can think of. Attempts to enhance the recall performance of natural-language searches include a "postcontrolled vocabulary" (Lancaster, 1986) and "hedges"—actual stored lists of words and phrases on commonly searched topics—in commercial information retrieval systems (Sievert and Boyce, 1983).

COST-EFFECTIVENESS ASPECTS OF THE INDEX LANGUAGE

Cost-effectiveness analysis is applicable to the design and implementation of index languages, but it is difficult to apply in this area and the results are hard to express in tangible terms. The more sophisticated the vocabulary, the more expensive it is likely to be to develop and maintain. An important economic consideration is vocabulary size. The more index terms in the vocabulary, the greater the vocabulary's specificity and the greater the precision capabilities of the system. A large, highly specific controlled vocabulary, however, tends to be costly to develop, apply, and update. Thus, a careful analysis of representative requests must be done when the system is being designed. In considering vocabulary specificity, allowances must be made for growth of the database and its effect on the average number of citations retrieved per search. A precision of 20 percent may be tolerable when the average search output is 12 citations, but it may be completely intolerable when the average output is 125 citations.

A closely related consideration is the need for additional precision devices such as links, role indicators, subheadings, and term weighting. These devices are intended to improve system precision by reducing the number of unwanted items retrieved in a search, resulting from false coordinations, incorrect term relationships, or highly exhaustive indexing. They are usually costly to apply. Role indicators, in particular, are likely to add substantially to indexing and search-formulating costs, and they may add to actual search-processing costs. Because they increase vocabulary specificity, they almost invariably reduce indexer consistency and frequently have a devastating effect on recall. Subheadings, which may function simultaneously as links and roles, also add to indexing costs and reduce indexer consistency; however, they tend to have a less drastic effect than role indicators. In the searching of databases, these devices serve to reduce the number of irrelevant citations that one must examine to find those that are relevant. They can be justified economically only if they prove to be cheaper than alternative methods for achieving the same results for the end user. Role indicators, for example, reduce or possibly eliminate one particular type of unwanted retrieval, namely, the incorrect term relationship— the situation in which the terms causing retrieval are related but not in the way that the requester wants them related. A cost-effectiveness analysis may well reveal that it is more economical not to use role indicators, thereby saving indexing and searching time and, instead, to allow some incorrect term relations to occur, eliminating the irrelevant citations thus retrieved through a postsearch screening operation conducted by the information staff.

A very important but usually neglected component of an index language is the entry vocabulary, a vocabulary of natural-language expressions occurring in documents or requests that map onto the controlled vocabulary of the system. Usually, the entry vocabulary comprises terms that, for indexing and retrieval purposes, either are considered synonymous with controlled vocabulary terms or are more specific than controlled vocabulary terms—for example, HELIARC WELDING *use* SHIELDED ARC WELDING. Although an extensive entry vocabulary may be expensive to construct and update, it can significantly improve performance by reducing recall failures, particularly in large retrieval systems. It can also make the system more cost-effective over time by reducing the intellectual burden on both indexers and searchers. An entry vocabulary is really a collection of records of intellectual decisions made primarily by indexers. Unless an intellectual decision made by an indexer—topic X index under term Y—is recorded, the decision will have to be made again—not necessarily with the same mapping results (hence, inconsistency)—by other indexers or the same indexer at a later date. Moreover, the system searchers also will have to make intellectual decisions—which may not agree with those of the indexers—when they come to search for literature on topic X. The larger the entry vocabulary, the fewer the intellectual decisions that need to be made by indexers and searchers, thus reducing indexing and search time; the greater the consistency in indexing; the better the recall of the system; and, possibly, the lower the professional level of the staff that is needed in the indexing operation.

Indexing

As described in Chapter 5, document indexing can be performed in a variety of ways, including human indexing by assignment or extraction, or simply by adopting natural-language words and phrases from textual fields (including title, abstract, full-document text, and index terms). Human indexing implies a selection process. Certain words or phrases are extracted to represent the subject dealt with, or the subject is represented by a set of terms that are chosen from a controlled vocabulary. In some automatic procedures, the process may involve selecting *all* words that are not on a preestablished "stop list."

Thus several decisions are made about the indexing of documents that affect retrieval performance. They include

1. Policy decisions
   a. The exhaustivity of indexing—that is, the extent to which all the distinct subjects discussed in a document are recognized and represented by the indexer.
   b. The specificity of term assignment—that is, the representation of identified concepts with language as specific as those concepts.

2. Indexer decisions (accuracy)
   a. Representation of all and only the concepts that should be represented.
   b. Appropriate term choice.

EXHAUSTIVITY

The most important policy decision related to indexing regards exhaustivity. Suppose one has a document that deals with six topics (A, B, C, D, E, F). If all six topics are recognized in the conceptual analysis stage of indexing and are expressed by appropriate combinations of index terms, then the indexer has been completely exhaustive in indexing this item. If all six topics are indexed, the document can be retrieved regardless of which of these topics or combination of topics is requested. Thus, a high level of exhaustivity of indexing tends to ensure high recall. As the exhaustivity level is reduced, the recall capabilities are diminished. If concept F is not recognized in the indexing of the document, it will never be retrieved in response to a request for literature on F, unless the terms used to describe F happen to be related, hierarchically or in some other way, to the terms used to describe A, B, C, D, and E. As the exhaustivity level is progressively reduced by successively omitting further topics, recall capabilities diminish accordingly. The phenomenon applies equally to all documents indexed. If each document is indexed at maximum exhaustivity, maximum recall capability is achieved.

Although a high level of exhaustivity of indexing tends to ensure high recall, it also tends to reduce precision. If, for every document input, all or at least a substantial proportion of the indexable topics are recognized, many topics that are indexed are treated in only minor ways. Consequently, documents will be retrieved in response to requests for which they contain little information.

Say that the six-topic (A, B, C, D, E, F) document describes certain aerodynamic phenomena and that a particular mathematical technique—say, the Pohlhausen technique—is mentioned as being applicable in a calculation applied to one of these phenomena. Also suppose that this mathematical technique has been recognized in the conceptual analysis stage of indexing and translated into appropriate index terms—in fact, this technique is topic F. For the probably rare request in which a researcher wants to retrieve every piece of literature indicating applications of the Pohlhausen technique, this document is relevant and should be retrieved. The high level of exhaustivity of indexing will prove useful for this high-recall requirement. But now consider another, probably more common, request in which the requester wants documents describing the Pohlhausen technique and how it can be applied. He or she wants only substantive articles on the technique; articles that merely mention the method in passing are nonrelevant to the requirement. A search of an aerodynamics collection, indexed at a high level of exhaustivity, however, may tend to retrieve many documents that do little more than mention the technique. In this case, the high level of exhaustivity causes many unwanted items to be retrieved.

Thus, recall failures tend to occur when exhaustivity is low. Precision failures occur as exhaustivity goes up for searches where only documents treating the concept in a substantive way are desired. Furthermore, high exhaustivity tends to reduce precision because the more topics that are recognized in indexing and the more index terms that are used to express them, the greater the potential for false coordinations in searching. Thus, in the six-topic document A, B, C, D, E, F, in which, say, A and B are related, C and D are related, and E and F are related, there is the possibility that the document will be falsely retrieved in response to any of 12 two-topic requests—A in relation to C, A in relation to D, B in relation to C, and so on. If each of the six topics is expressed by a number of distinct unlinked index terms, the possibilities for false coordinations at the index term level are highly magnified.

Now consider a situation in which indexes are prepared at the minimum level of exhaustivity. Each document is indexed under a single topic only: the central topic treated in each case. The recall potential of the index is extremely low: a document will not be retrieved in response to a request for a topic that is anything less than the core topic of discussion. But every time a document is retrieved in a search of the database, it tends to be a wanted document because it deals substantively with the subject of the request. Moreover, by indexing at minimum exhaustivity, the possibility of false coordinations at the topic level is completely eliminated and the possibility of false coordinations at the term level is substantially reduced.

The level of exhaustivity applied in indexing is a policy decision established by the managers of the retrieval system. It is not dependent on the properties of the index language, since it must be assumed that the index language used is appropriate for the subject fields treated in input documents and that any topic discussed can be translated into the language of the system, albeit at a more generic level. Nor is it within the control of the indexer. In establishing this policy decision, system managers must try to determine an optimum level of exhaustivity, one that will satisfy the majority of the requests processed by the information service. It is possible that the exhaustivity level will be related to the type of document—internal technical reports being indexed more exhaustively than other types, some journal titles being indexed more exhaustively than others, and so on. Alternatively, the policy on exhaustivity can vary with the specific subject areas dealt with in the collection. In general, the exhaustivity of the indexing is the single most important factor governing the recall that can be achieved in a particular system, and the specificity of the vocabulary is the single most important factor governing its precision (Lancaster and Mills, 1964). A number of investigators, most recently Boyce and McLain (1989), Shaw (1990a,b) and Burgin (1991), have studied the effect of exhaustivity on retrieval performance.

There are wide variations in exhaustivity among the databases that are accessible online. Reich and Biever (1991) compare AGRICOLA with CAB ABSTRACTS in this respect. Interestingly, although the mean number of terms assigned was similar (based on a sample of articles), there were many differences between the two databases when individual articles were considered.

The machine indexing of natural-language fields tends to result in document representations that are more exhaustive. Thus, it is not surprising that some studies have found that searching the databases that are indexed this way enhances recall (Markey, Atherton, and Newton, 1980). By the same token, natural-language facilitates precision (Carrow and Nugent, 1977). Svenonius (1986) states that this is a complicated situation which is still not fully understood:

A signal that research is needed is when research studies produce contradictory findings. The finding in the Markey, Atherton, and Newton [1980] study that free-text retrieval produced higher recall and lower precision than retrieval using a controlled vocabulary not only conflicts with results of earlier studies, it runs counter to "conventional wisdom" as well. Conventional wisdom holds that free-text terms contribute to precision by virtue of being more specific and more current than controlled vocabulary terms. (p. 334)

SPECIFICITY

Another indexing policy that affects recall and precision is whether assigned terms for each concept should be equal in specificity or whether an additional term at a higher level of specificity also should be assigned. For example, suppose in service X, an indexer assigns the descriptor PUBLIC LIBRARIES, which is equal in specificity to the identified concept; furthermore, by the policy of specificity of term assignment, this is the only term that should be assigned for this concept. In service Y, however, an additional descriptor at the next higher level is also assigned for this concept; in this case, the indexer might assign the additional term LIBRARIES. Suppose that in each of these services, there are 50 documents specifically about public libraries and 50 about libraries in general. In service X, 50 documents would be indexed under the term PUBLIC LIBRARIES and 50 would be indexed under the term LIBRARIES. In service Y, for those same 100 documents, 50 would be indexed under the term PUBLIC LIBRARIES, and all 100 documents would be assigned the term LIBRARIES. This situation is depicted in Exhibit 56.

Assignment of only one term that is as specific as the indexable concept facilitates precision since, in any search, only documents at that precise level will be retrieved. There may, of course, be some loss of recall: Documents that are indexed at a more general level may contain information that the user would judge relevant. Moreover, because indexing is never perfect, some items

Information service	Terms used in indexing 50 items dealing specifically with public libraries	Terms used in indexing 50 items dealing with libraries in general	Number of items retrieved in a search on public libraries	Number of items retrieved in a search on libraries in general
X	PUBLIC LIBRARIES	LIBRARIES	50	50
Y	PUBLIC LIBRARIES LIBRARIES	LIBRARIES	50	100

EXHIBIT 56   Hypothetical index term assignments for services that do (X) and do not (Y) index by the rule of exclusively specific entry.

may be indexed under the more general term that should have been indexed under the more specific term.

Where indexers assign terms at both the specific and the general level, recall tends to be enhanced, since a search at a general level (for example, everything on libraries) will automatically retrieve items at more specific levels (for example, on public libraries). The disadvantage, of course, is that it becomes much more difficult to distinguish items that deal generally with a subject from items that deal with more specific aspects.

Most information services follow the "rule of exclusively specific entry" (Wilson, 1979). A notable exception is the Library of Congress, which, for certain categories of materials, assigns two headings, one specific and the other general. Thus, a biography of a contemporary American author would be assigned not only to the person's name, but also to the class of people to which this individual belongs (for example, AUTHORS, AMERICAN—20TH CENTURY—BIOGRAPHY).

ACCURACY

Although policies on exhaustivity and specificity of term assignment are beyond the control of the indexer, the quality and accuracy of the indexing are very much within his or her control. There are two types of indexer errors: (1) the omission of terms that are necessary to describe an important topic discussed in an article, and (2) the use of terms that appear inappropriate to the subject matter of the article. Omissions normally lead to recall failures, and incorrect or nonspecific terms can cause either a precision failure (the searcher uses the term in a strategy and retrieves an irrelevant item) or a recall failure (the searcher uses the correct terms, and a wanted document is missed because it is labeled incorrectly).

Recall failures due to indexer omission must be distinguished from those due to lack of exhaustivity of indexing. Omission errors occur when a topic that appears central to the document is not covered in the indexing, although it is so important that it should be covered even in nonexhaustive indexing. When the level of exhaustivity of indexing is low as a matter of policy, an item of subject matter that is treated peripherally in an article is not covered in the indexing. The topic is not crucial to the article and presumably is excluded in favor of other topics because of general policy regarding the average number of terms to be assigned.

Unfortunately, if an important term is omitted during indexing, the document is likely to remain unretrieved in searches for which it may be highly relevant. Moreover, this type of error, although it may come to light in an evaluation program, is likely to remain undetected in the normal operation of the system. Of course, a certain number of indexing omissions are to be expected under the pressures of tight production schedules. They are more likely contributors to system failures than are inappropriate terms. If the work of one indexer is scanned (revised) by a second, incorrect terms tend to stand out clearly and are thus easily corrected in the revision process. Omissions, however, are not so readily detected because this would require a more careful examination of the document by the reviser.

COST-EFFECTIVENESS ASPECTS OF INDEXING

The elimination of human indexing can be justified through savings on input costs and timeliness of information dissemination to the user. Retention of an assignment indexing component, however, also can be justified because of the organization it imposes on the collection, thus making it easier and less time-consuming to construct effective searches. It also can be justified because natural language and controlled vocabulary have been shown to be complementary retrieval devices.

Given the justification of an assignment indexing component, there are a number of economic considerations worth investigating in relation to indexing policies and procedures:

1. The amount of time expended, on the average, in the indexing of a document.
2. The level of exhaustivity adopted in indexing, that is, the number of index terms assigned, on the average, per item.
3. The professional level of personnel used in indexing.
4. The need for an indexing revision procedure.

Probably the indexing policy that is most difficult to establish involves the most appropriate level of exhaustivity to adopt. The more exhaustive the indexing, the higher the recall of the system is likely to be, but the lower the precision. In a unique environment of documents, index language, and requests, an optimum level of exhaustivity of indexing will exist. A cost-effectiveness analysis allows one to find this optimum level—the point after which the addition of further terms is largely unproductive. Suppose a particular collection of documents is indexed at an average level of 15 terms per item and the retrieval performance of the system is tested using a representative sample of 50 requests. With optimum searching strategies, it may be found that for this particular group of requests at the indexing level adopted, the system is operating at 73 percent recall. Through additional indexing experiments, in which the requests, search strategies, and index language are held constant, it may be found that an increase in exhaustivity to an average of 20 terms raises the recall performance to 90 percent but that the average exhaustivity level needs to be raised to 35 terms per article to reach a 95 percent recall level. Under these conditions, an average of 20 terms per item might be established as an optimum level to use in this particular environment of documents, requests, and index language. After the 20-term level, there is evidence of diminishing returns, because to achieve a 5 percent improvement in overall recall, the exhaustivity level must be raised to 35 terms, which could greatly increase indexing costs. From the results of this study, a performance curve of exhaustivity level versus recall ratio can be plotted (Exhibit 57).

From a plot of this kind, a break-even point can be established for indexing exhaustivity, that is, a point beyond which the addition of further index terms, although adding appreciably to input costs, makes no appreciable difference to the recall potential of the system. If a sample of subject requests representing actual typical information requirements of potential users is collected, and if certain documents can be identified as relevant to the requests, this type of cost-effectiveness analysis can and should be done at the system design stage.

The same problem can be approached differently by studying the effect of varying time expenditures on the indexing operation. The more time that is expended in indexing, the more terms that will be assigned on the average; however, there is likely to be a very definite leveling off in the number of terms assigned after a comparatively short expenditure of time—for example, 20 terms in the first 10 minutes, 5 additional terms in the next 10 minutes, and 2 more terms in the next 10 minutes. If 90 percent of the useful terms are assigned in the first 10 minutes of indexing, but an additional 30 minutes are needed to find the extra 10 percent judged to be useful, one may reasonably conclude that 10 minutes per document is an optimum average indexing time, and indexing quotas can be established on that basis.

It is possible to conduct a cost-effectiveness analysis of the time expended on indexing by experimentation similar to that described for the establishment of optimum exhaustivity levels. Indeed, because more terms generally will be assigned as indexing time is increased, essentially the same thing is measured.

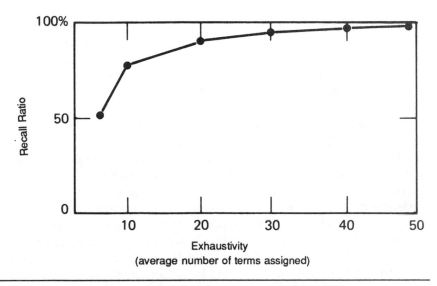

EXHIBIT 57 **Hypothetical performance curve of exhaustivity level versus recall ratio.**

It is harder to predict the effect of varying exhaustivity or indexing time on the precision of an information retrieval system, even though this is a necessary part of a realistic cost-effectiveness analysis. To do so requires a broad experiment in which, besides indexing a set of documents, each of which is known to be relevant to one or more recorded requests, the evaluator indexes a random sample of additional documents in the same general subject area. When the search strategies for the test requests are compared to the index terms assigned to both relevant and nonrelevant documents, recall and precision can be measured for the test collection and the precision extrapolated to the entire system database. This technique has been used successfully in the evaluation of experimental retrieval systems.

Variations in indexing time are likely to affect not only the average exhaustivity of the indexing but also the indexing accuracy. Therefore, cost-effectiveness analysis relating to indexing time expenditure must take into account the effect of time allowance on accuracy as well as on exhaustivity. The greater the production pressures, the more indexing errors that are likely to occur. Indexing errors can have a multiplicative effect on recall in post-coordinate retrieval systems. This can be shown by a simple example. Suppose that in the indexing of a particular document collection, index term A has been assigned to 90 percent of the documents to which, by consensus, it should have been assigned; term B has been assigned to 85 percent of the documents to which it should have been assigned; and term C has been assigned to 75 percent of the appropriate documents. Searching on term A alone retrieves 90 percent of the documents that should be retrieved; that is, there is 90 percent recall of the A documents. In a search on A *and* B, however, recall for this set may drop to 76.5 percent (90 percent × 85 percent), whereas a search on A *and* B *and* C may result in a recall of only 57.4 percent (90 percent × 85 percent × 75 percent) of the documents that properly belong to the A, B, C set. Thus, from a cost-effectiveness viewpoint, to determine the influence of indexing time on indexing accuracy, an evaluator needs to consider this multiplicative effect on retrieval performance. The evaluator must be able to estimate the average accuracy of term assignment throughout the vocabulary of the system and relate this to the average coordination level used in searches. The effect of various types of indexing errors on the effectiveness of postcoordinate searching using several search strategies has been discussed in detail by Bryant, King, and Terragno (1963). King (1965, 1967) has described an application of these techniques and has also developed a useful model for converting data for indexer consistency into data for indexer accuracy, and vice versa.

A closely related question is whether an indexing revision process is needed, that is, whether the work of one indexer should be checked by a second, usually more experienced, person. Whether or not the revision process is justified on cost-effectiveness grounds depends on

1. The amount of error occurring in unrevised indexing
2. The amount of error that is corrected by the revision process
3. The estimated effect of indexing error, revised and unrevised, on retrieval performance
4. The cost of revision.

Simple and inexpensive experiments, in which a revision process is conducted and timed on a set of indexed documents, some of which contain known errors, provide the expected correction rate for the revision operation and its costs. Revisers should be varied so that average reviser performance can be determined and the performance of various types of personnel studied. Percentage error reduction can then be related to the estimated effect on retrieval performance. As a result of this analysis, an information service should be able to say that a revision operation costing X dollars per year is likely to correct Y percent of the indexing errors that occur and that this is likely to have a specified effect on the average recall and precision performance of the system.

One further aspect of the indexing process that may be subjected to cost-effectiveness analysis is the level of personnel required to undertake the indexing. Indexing costs can be reduced substantially if not as highly educated and thus lower paid indexers can successfully be used. At least one large agency has moved from a system in which indexing was done by highly skilled analysts, all with college degrees, to one in which most of the indexing is conducted by personnel without college degrees. Another assumption that is sometimes made is that a good indexer needs to have a formal education in the subject matter of the documents handled. This has never been proved conclusively, and, in fact, most studies in this area have revealed the opposite. A number of factors determine how senior the indexing staff needs to be, including

1. *Complexity of the subject matter handled.*

2. *Type of index language used.* Free keyword indexing may require less-skilled personnel than would the use of a large controlled vocabulary.

3. *Exhaustivity and specificity of the indexing.* The greater the technical detail indexed, the greater the need for subject expertise.

4. *Stage of system development.* In the early stages of indexing a collection with a controlled vocabulary, virtually every indexing decision made is intellectual. At a later stage, providing the intellectual decisions have been recorded in an authority file or entry vocabulary, the indexing operation probably can be delegated to not as highly educated personnel who can do much of the work by following decisions made in the past.

5. *Quality of the tools provided* to aid the indexing process.

6. *Quality of the indexing training program.*

Certainly a cost-effectiveness analysis of the indexing subsystem would be incomplete without a study of required personnel levels. To do this, various document sets should be indexed by different levels of personnel and the resulting indexing compared with a standard of indexing for the test documents, as established by consensus. Time factors should be considered. The measured effectiveness of the indexing achieved by these various groups can then be compared with the indexing costs.

Search Strategy

As described in Chapter 8, a search strategy is a statement of the class membership requirements of a document expressed in terms of logical sums, products, and complements. The techniques of class intersection, summation, and complementation are used to vary the exhaustivity and specificity of the search formulation. Consider the search request in Exhibit 58, which is broken down into four concepts, or facets. The terms found within each concept group

Search request: Therapies used with female prisoners having a history of drug abuse

Search strategy

A		B		C		D
SELF CONCEPT		TREATMENT		PRISONERS		DRUG USAGE
or		or		or	and	or
SELF ESTEEM	and	THERAPIES	and	FEMALE PRISONERS		DRUG ABUSE
or		or				
SELF IMAGE		PSYCHOTHERAPY				

EXHIBIT 58 Search request and strategy (building block approach).
SOURCE: **Adapted from *Search Strategy Seminar* (1983). Reprinted with permission of Dialog Information Services, Inc.**

would be linked by a Boolean *or*. Concept groups would be linked by a Boolean *and*.

There are various ways of changing the recall and precision of this search; these are summarized in Exhibit 59. They include techniques that use the characteristics of natural language and controlled vocabulary, as well as searching devices such as Boolean operators, field restrictions, phrase constructions (proximity operators), synonyms, spelling variations, and truncation symbols.

Use of the Boolean *and* will increase the exhaustivity of the search, thereby increasing its precision. In fact, the search in Exhibit 58 is probably too exhaustive and may well retrieve no documents. Exhaustivity can be decreased by omitting facets, perhaps by searching without either concept A (self-concept) or concept B (therapies). The overall effect will probably enhance recall.

Another way to modify this search is to use additional terms in each concept group connected with the *or* operator. These can be terms that are related in meaning (broader/narrower, related—PRISONER/FEMALE PRISONER) to the assigned term; true synonyms or quasi synonyms (SELF CONCEPT/SELF IMAGE); spelling variants or acronyms; or truncated terms, which search all forms of a word having a specific root (THERAPY, THERAPIES, THERAPEUTIC). Overall, use of these devices to match on increasing numbers of terms will enhance recall, and a reduction in their use will increase precision.

Note that the strategy described thus far incorporates terminology that is intended to match both the natural-language and controlled vocabulary in the document. This approach, now quite common in online searching, should be compared with the case where only controlled-vocabulary descriptors are used. In general, the differences between the two are:

1. Many of the recall devices described (incorporation of synonyms, spelling variants, truncation) are normalized at input in the controlled vocabulary and

To Increase Recall	To Increase Precision	Searching Devices
Terms from Natural Language and/or Controlled Vocabulary		
Exclude concept groups from strategy (fewer facets connected by *and* operator)	Include additional concept groups	Boolean operators
Include additional terms in concept group (connected by *or* operator)	Exclude terms from concept group (connected by *or* operator)	
Terms from Natural Language		
Use additional terms that are spelling variations, abbreviations, acronyms	Use only common spellings, abbreviations, and acronyms	Spelling, truncation, and synonyms
Truncate to shorter word stem	Use specific terms without truncation	
Use synonyms	Reduce number of synonyms	
Terms from Natural Language		
Use single words, shorter phrases	Use longer phrases	Proximity operators

EXHIBIT 59   Ways to increase recall (may decrease precision) and precision (may decrease recall) in a given search. SOURCE: Adapted from *Search Strategy Seminar* (1983). Reprinted with permission of Dialog Information Services, Inc.

therefore do not have to be input by the searcher performing a strictly controlled-vocabulary search.

2. Words (which enhance recall) or more complex phrases (which enhance precision) can be used in natural-language searching, but simple or complex forms at this level are rigidly prescribed in thesauri. The analogous process in controlled vocabularies is the combination of main headings and subheadings into legal precoordinated combinations.

3. Searches can be made to include a variety of documents related in different ways by including in a concept group terms that bear different semantic relationships to each other. The structure of the controlled vocabulary will suggest such terms to the searcher. Using natural language, the searcher must think of all these relationships and supply the necessary terms.

Thus, recall failures with natural language may occur when the searcher fails to think of all the possible synonyms, word variants, and other related terms for a particular concept group. Precision failures may occur when the searcher does not identify all the facets in the search, or when the words used in various logical combinations produce false coordinations.

It is clear from the preceding discussion that there are many factors that must be considered when formulating a search to maximize precision or recall, or both. In the past, it was assumed that experienced intermediaries, already familiar with these devices and their use, would conduct searches for requesters. Recently, however, products and services specifically targeted to the end user have been introduced. In general, these have been the same products that were previously searched by intermediaries, although they are often packaged with a software interface to help the novice formulate the search strategy.

Thus, how much and what type of online aid is available to the searcher may affect retrieval performance. Two common types of information retrieval system interfaces are command-driven and menu-driven, and both kinds of software can be used to search online catalogs and databases of periodical articles. In an experimental study comparing the performance of two online catalogs—one menu-driven and one command-driven—Geller and Lesk (1983) found that users preferred the command system. People used keyword searches from the command line more frequently and found more relevant items. Sullivan, Borgman, and Wippern (1990) studied menu and command systems in searching two databases on DIALOG and found that the use of the menu interface did not affect the quality of retrieval or user satisfaction, although persons instructed to use native commands required less training time and interacted more with the databases than persons trained on the menu system.

Reports of end-user searching performance indicate that although many novices are quite enthusiastic about performing their own searches, these searches are not very effective, particularly when users have had no training in the use of the system or when they use it only infrequently (for example, Lancaster et al., 1992). Detailed analyses of transaction logs (electronic records of all searches performed on a system during a specified period) indicate that end users tend to use fewer search terms, resulting in both precision failures (due to lack of an exhaustive strategy) and recall failures (due to the low number of synonymous and related terms included in concept groups). Furthermore, experienced intermediaries retrieve more relevant citations in a given amount of time than do inexperienced searchers (Penhale and Taylor, 1986).

Searching in online catalogs is particularly problematic. The low exhaustivity of indexing using *Library of Congress Subject Headings,* combined with the very specific precoordinations of main headings and subheadings, make such catalogs difficult to search. To get acceptable recall, very broad searches must be performed, frequently resulting in the retrieval of hundreds of irrelevant documents and, consequently, very low precision (Lancaster et al., 1991). When searches are made more specific, recall becomes very low, and the terms input by the user often do not match any subject heading at all (Vizine-Goetz and Drabenstott, 1991).

One further operation may be conducted by the person who constructs the search strategy that may have some effect on the recall and precision of the search results, namely, the screening of the output. In some information services, the searcher carefully examines the output of the system before submitting the results to the user, attempting thereby to discard items that seem clearly irrelevant and thus to improve the precision ratio of the final product delivered to the user. The success of this screening operation is directly related to the quality of the request statement, since it is on this basis that the relevance predictions are made. If the request statement is an imperfect representation of the user's information need, the search analyst may be as likely to discard items that the user would judge relevant as to discard items he or she would judge irrelevant.

Other factors affect the screening operation, including the amount of time spent in the process and the type of document representation delivered by the system. The more complete the representation, the easier it is for the searcher to make accurate relevance predictions: Titles plus index terms may be more informative than titles alone, and titles plus abstracts may be more informative than titles plus index terms. The utility of a document record in the prediction of the document's relevance to some request statement is, in fact, likely to be directly related to the record length.

COST-EFFECTIVENESS ASPECTS OF SEARCHING

There is a possible trade-off between effort spent in the creation of a search strategy and that spent in the screening of search output. If a great deal of time is invested in the creation of a carefully constructed, tight search strategy, a high-precision search output will likely be achieved that requires little or no editing. If a broader search is conducted, more effort will be invested in removing obvious irrelevancy during the screening process. If the searcher can examine the output and make relevance predictions that match reasonably well the actual relevance decisions that would be made by the end user, the latter approach may be more effective in terms of achieving high recall at a tolerable precision. It also may be more cost-effective.

The amount of interaction that occurs between the search analyst and the requester also has implications for cost-effectiveness. Some interaction is necessary if the request statement is to accurately reflect the information requirements of the requester. The more interaction that takes place, the better the recall or precision is likely to be. Once again, however, there are possible trade-offs—for example, between the amount of effort spent interacting with the requester before the search and that expended in output screening. Moreover, there are various stages at which the interaction can take place: at the request stage; the search formulation stage—presenting the proposed strategy to the requester for approval or modification; and the output stage—an iterative search procedure in which preliminary search results are evaluated by the requester and a new strategy is constructed, manually or automatically, on the basis of the relevance assessments of retrieved items. The later the interaction takes place in the retrieval process, the better it is likely to be. Lesk and Salton (1969) discovered, in their evaluation of searches in the SMART system, that postsearch interaction is usually better than presearch interaction. There generally is an optimum set of interaction procedures in a particular environment, and some modes of interaction may actually degrade rather than improve search performance. For example, in the MEDLARS evaluation (Lancaster, 1968a), it was found that face-to-face interviews between requesters and search analysts or requesters and medical librarians did not necessarily improve the quality of requests and in some cases actually caused request distortion. Apparently it is more effective to have the requester first write out the request, in his or her own natural-language terms, and then to interact to clarify the request statement, rather than have the requester discuss his or her need with an information specialist, who then prepares a request statement.

For cost-effectiveness, the user–system interaction process may be the single most critical component of an information system. If a user makes a poor request that does not accurately reflect the information need, the search is almost certainly doomed to failure—however efficient the indexing, vocabulary, and search strategies are—and subsequent search effort is wasted. To avoid senseless waste in the construction of search strategies, the processing of the search, and the screening of output, techniques to improve the quality of requests are usually easy to justify economically. A considerable improvement may result, for example, from a well-structured form designed to help the user put the best possible request to the system. The completion of the form may require more effort on the user's part initially but may improve the search product and save time in the long run, especially the screening time of the user or search analyst.

It has been shown conclusively (for example, by Fitzgerald, 1981) that interaction between requester and information specialist while the search is in progress—that is, sitting together at a terminal—will give the best results, although it obviously is very expensive since the time of both individuals is involved.

TRADE-OFFS IN INFORMATION RETRIEVAL

There are many possible trade-offs between the various information retrieval processes. For instance, the preceding section considered indexing and vocabulary effort versus searching effort and search strategy effort versus screening effort. A cost-effectiveness analysis of a complete system compares possible trade-offs and determines the most efficient combination of procedures for obtaining a particular level of performance relative to cost.

The major trade-off to be considered is the very general one between input and output costs. Almost invariably, economies in input procedures result in an increased burden on output processes and thus increase output costs. Conversely, greater care in input processing, which usually implies increased input costs, can be expected to improve efficiency and reduce output costs. Some possible trade-offs are enumerated in the following list:

1. *A carefully controlled and structured index language versus free use of uncontrolled keywords.* The controlled vocabulary takes effort to construct and maintain and is more expensive to apply in indexing. It takes longer, on the whole, to select terms from a controlled vocabulary, which may involve a lookup operation, than it does to assign keywords freely. Moreover, keyword indexing may require less-qualified personnel than the use of a more sophisticated controlled vocabulary. The controlled vocabulary, however, saves time and effort at the output stage. Natural-language or keyword searching, without the benefit of a controlled vocabulary, puts increased burden on the searcher, who is virtually forced into constructing a segment of a controlled vocabulary each time he or she prepares a search strategy—for example, by having to think of all possible ways in which "petrochemicals" or "textile industry" could be expressed by keywords or in natural-language text. Likewise, the uncontrolled use of keywords may lead to reduced average search precision and thus require additional effort and cost in output screening.

2. *Rigid quality control of indexing—for example, by a revision operation— versus indexing with no review procedure.* The review increases the indexing costs but presumably saves output costs by reducing the screening time necessary to weed out obvious irrelevancy. Whether the input review is justified economically can be determined only by an evaluation of the number of indexing errors that are occurring and the number of these that could be corrected by quality control procedures.

3. *A highly specific controlled vocabulary versus a broader controlled vocabulary.* The former is generally more expensive to create, maintain, and apply. The more specific the vocabulary, the more difficult it becomes to achieve indexing consistency and the higher the level of the personnel that may be needed to use it. Nevertheless, a highly specific vocabulary may allow

high search precision and thus save on output screening time. A particular form of specificity is achieved by role or relational indicators, and these comments also apply to the use of such devices.

These are merely three examples of possible trade-offs between input and output effort. Many other possibilities exist. Exhibit 60 presents a trade-off comparison of two hypothetical information systems. In system A, great care and expense are put into the input operation, with a resulting economy in output effort and costs. In system B, input costs are economized and output effort and costs are increased. Neither system is necessarily more efficient than the other. The approach taken in system B may be more cost-effective than that taken in system A if it achieves an acceptable level of performance for the end user, with overall costs lower than those associated with system A.

Many different factors enter into the decision about whether to emphasize the input or output processes of an information system. The most important considerations are probably the following:

1. *The volume of documents indexed and the volume of requests processed annually.* In the extreme situation, where many documents are indexed but few requests are handled, it would be rational, all other things being equal, to economize on input costs and put an additional load on the output function. In the reverse situation—few documents are input but many requests are handled—the opposite would be true.

2. *Required input speed.* In certain situations, it is imperative to put documents into the system as rapidly as possible. This is especially true when the information system serves a dissemination (current awareness) function. Under these circumstances, it is likely that required speed of input would outweigh other considerations and that indexing economies would be adopted to get items into the database as quickly as possible.

3. *Required output speed.* In another situation, rapid and accurate response may be vital—for example, in a poison information center—and no economies at input are justified if they result in delayed response or reduced accuracy of output.

4. *By-products.* It may sometimes be possible to obtain a searchable database very inexpensively—for example, a machine-readable database, perhaps in natural-language form, that is a by-product of some other operation, perhaps publishing or report preparation, or that has been made available by another information center. Even though the input format and quality may not be ideal, if the database is available at nominal cost, it might be desirable, from a cost-effectiveness viewpoint, to make use of it, possibly with some slight modifications, and to expend more effort on the searching operation.

System A	System B
Input characteristics	
A large, carefully controlled vocabulary	A small controlled vocabulary supplemented by the free use of keywords
Indexing of medium exhaustivity (an average of 10 terms per document)	Low exhaustivity of indexing (5 terms per document)
Highly trained indexers at a high salary level	Less highly trained indexers without college degrees
An indexing revision process	No indexing revision
Average indexer productivity of 40 items per day	Average indexer productivity of 100–125 items per day
High input costs	Low input costs
Relatively long delay between publication and actual input to system	Fast throughput
Output characteristics	
Reduced burden on the searcher in the preparation of strategies	Greater burden on the searcher in the preparation of strategies
High precision of raw output	Low precision of raw output
Tolerable recall	Tolerable recall
No screening needed	Screening of raw output needed to raise precision to tolerable level for end user
Fast response time	Delayed response
Relatively low search costs	Relatively high search costs

EXHIBIT 60   Trade-off comparison of two hypothetical information systems.

Earlier, some cost-effectiveness factors relative to the various subsystems of a complete information system were discussed: indexing, index language, searching, and user–system interaction. In the analysis of cost-effectiveness, just as in the evaluation of effectiveness, it is unrealistic and dangerous to consider any one of the subsystems in isolation. All these components are very closely related, and a significant change in one will almost certainly cause repercussions throughout the entire system. Evaluators must be aware of this and, in any cost-effectiveness analysis, must consider the long-term, indirect effects of system changes as well as the immediate, direct effects. For example, suppose a decision is made to move away from a carefully controlled, sophisticated index language to something much simpler. The immediate effects will be a reduction in vocabulary control and maintenance costs, a reduction in indexing time, and improved throughput time. There will also be some long-term, less direct effects: The time required to prepare search strategies may increase, resulting in a rise in searching costs; search precision may be reduced, and an output screening operation may be needed; and, if output screening is needed, the quality of the document surrogates in the system may need to be improved. Perhaps abstracts will need to be included although they were previously unnecessary.

A similar phenomenon may occur if the average exhaustivity of indexing is increased. There would be an immediate increase in indexing time and costs, an increase in the average number of documents retrieved per search, an improvement in recall, and a drop in average precision. In the long run, an output screening operation and improved document surrogates may be needed to ensure that the precision remains at a tolerable level. Clearly, an information system is a complex organism, and changes to it have far-reaching effects.

HUMAN FACTORS IN INDEXING AND SEARCHING

Exhibit 16 depicts the steps in the retrieval process that are subject to system variability. Thus, the contents of the database, the indexing policies, the retrieval language, and the searching operations can all be changed in various ways with the resulting effects on performance that have already been described. There are other factors, however, that are very much involved in the creation and use of a database that affect the retrieval system in systematic ways. These include various relevant characteristics of human indexers and searchers, most notably their knowledge of a given subject domain and experience with the retrieval system itself.

The research in this area looks at individual differences in indexers and searchers, the importance and relevance of which are clearly stated by Saracevic (1991):

The research on individual differences in IR is significant for a number of reasons. Here are three of them. First, such research provides for an increase in our understanding of differences in human performance in IR tasks; such differences play a major role (if not THE major role) in the overall performance of any and all IR systems. Second, such research is essential for eventually predicting performance differences by people with differing characteristics; these may be used to design into IR systems and interfaces capabilities to respond and adjust to users (be they intermediary or end-users) with differing characteristics, rather than as is the case today, treating all the users the same. That is, such research could be used for systems to start incorporating some understanding of people. Finally, the contemporary technological advances in both hardware and software have increased the capabilities for flexibility, thus there are more possibilities to accommodate differences among users. Consequently, the research results are increasingly relevant for technological development. (p. 82)

Furthermore, there are two basic types of question that research into individual differences can help answer:

1. [*Questions about consistency.*] To what extent do people with some characteristic in common (e.g., professional indexers or searchers) produce similar results when doing the same IR task (e.g., indexing the same set of documents or searching the same question)? Or to put it the opposite way: how large are the differences?

2. [*Questions about performance.*] That is, to what extent do variations in given characteristic(s) (e.g., degree of expertise in a task such as indexing or searching) affect performance and results? (Saracevic, 1991, p. 82)

Consistency Studies

A consistency study measures the extent to which two or more individuals agree with each other or one individual agrees with himself or herself in some judgment or task. Such studies have been carried out in index term assignments, query term decisions, and relevance judgments.

A number of possible measures of consistency have been tried or proposed. One common measure is the "consistency pair" (CP). The CP of two indexers, A and B, is defined as

$$\frac{\text{Number of terms assigned by both A and B}}{\text{Number of terms assigned by A or B, or both}}$$

Thus, if indexer A assigns the terms A,B,C,D,E,F to a document, and B assigns the terms A,B,C,G,H to the same document, the measure of consistency is:

$$\frac{\text{A,B,C}}{\text{A,B,C,D,E,F,G,H}} \text{ or } \frac{3}{8} \text{ or } 37.5$$

This same measure can be used to express consistency between different indexers (interindexer consistency) or between decisions made by the same indexer at different times (intraindexer consistency).

Indexing consistency was investigated most seriously during the 1960s and 1970s and has been extensively covered by Oliver et al. (1966), Cooper (1969), Leonard (1975), and Markey (1984a); it has also been taken up again recently by Sievert and Andrews (1991). A common finding has been that overall consistency figures tend to be very low. Zunde and Dexter's (1969) finding that consistency for pairs of professional indexers ranges from means as low as 24 percent to as high as 41 percent is typical. A number of studies have demonstrated that indexing consistency is influenced by several factors, including

1. *The exhaustivity of the indexing.* The more exhaustive the indexing, the greater the inconsistency.

2. *The type of vocabulary used,* including its size and specificity. The larger and more complex the vocabulary, the greater the inconsistency.

3. *The types of indexing aid provided.* The less aid provided, the greater the inconsistency.

Indexing consistency is also influenced by human factors, the two major ones being the experience and training of the indexers and their knowledge of the subject domain of the database. Saracevic (1991) summarized findings from the literature:

> Mean consistency of 10% when chemical patents were indexed by experienced and inexperienced indexers.
>
> Values of 35% to 45% for experienced indexers using aids, such as controlled vocabulary, and 16% for experienced and 13% for inexperienced indexers when no aids were used.
>
> Consistency of 36% to 59% when nonpsychologists and psychologists indexed psychological abstracts. (p. 83)

The consistency of relevance judgments was also investigated in the 1960s and 1970s, and this work has been reviewed by Saracevic (1975) and Schamber, Eisenberg, and Nilan (1990). The findings are typified by the major field experiment carried out at Case Western Reserve University (Rees and Schultz, 1967) in the area of medicine, involving 184 subjects with varying amounts of search experience and medical background. Among other things, the investigators found that relevance judgments were more consistent among searchers with more subject knowledge and that relevance judgments were consistent among medical experts and among medical librarians about half of the time but that medical librarians tended to be more lenient in their relevance scale ratings than were the medical experts.

Bates (1977), Saracevic and Kantor (1988a,b), and Saracevic et al. (1988) have investigated the consistency of query term choices among searchers. Bates found a relatively low consistency in the selection of *Library of Congress Subject Headings* among online catalog searchers in the subject areas of psychology, economics, and library science. Her findings were consistent with those of Saracevic and Kantor and Saracevic et al., who had 40 requests searched in a large operational retrieval system (DIALOG). A group of professional searchers all received the same question, and consistency pair calculations were performed for a'l possible pairs of searchers. The mean overlap in selection of search terms for the same questions was 27 percent.

A number of conclusions can be drawn from consistency studies. First, the overall findings from studies in all three areas—indexing, relevance judgments, and query term decisions—indicate that consistency is low.[1] But, although these studies indicate inconsistency, it is possible for inconsistency to be good as well as bad. For example, a study may show that in a group of six indexers, two individuals are more consistent with each other than any other pair of indexers in the group. One indexer in the group is the most individualistic of all; she is the least consistent on the average when her indexing is compared with the other members of the group. The indexing of the two individuals who are most consistent with each other is not necessarily the best indexing. In fact, the individualist indexer may be the most effective because her terms best match the requests made to the system; that is, her indexing allows retrieval of more documents that are judged relevant by requesters and prevents retrieval of more documents that are judged not relevant.

Performance Studies

Although consistency studies have some value, it is only by studying the relationships of factors to measures of effectiveness that one can draw conclusions about performance. Much of this chapter has been devoted to aspects of the system and how they affect performance as measured by recall and precision. It is also possible to investigate how human factors affect these measures.

Research on individual differences in information retrieval has concentrated on characteristics of searchers—especially search experience, knowledge of subject domain, and cognitive style—and how these characteristics affect the various output measures. Studies on the topic have been extensively reviewed by Borgman (1986).

Several researchers have reported on the effect of search experience on retrieval effectiveness, measured in terms of recall, precision, and time expended. In an early experiment on this topic, Fenichel (1981) defined experience as either (1) experience with the mechanics of online searching in general or (2) experience with the ERIC database, which was the focus of her study. An analysis of search transcripts showed that differences among the groups studied were not large. Fenichel found that beginning searchers performed surprisingly well as compared with experienced searchers and that searchers having the most experience with both the retrieval system protocols and with ERIC achieved the highest level of recall and precision but also had the highest level of what were called "search effort" variables (for example, number

---

[1] As Saracevic and Kantor (1988b) point out, however, "the notion of 'low' here may not be appropriate. We do not know what is 'high' and the observed ranges may be all that is to be expected, i.e., they may be 'normal'." (p. 207)

of commands and descriptors, connect time), suggesting, not surprisingly, a relationship between search effort and recall.

Other studies similar to Fenichel's have been conducted by Howard (1982) and Geraldene Walker (1988). Howard investigated overall search experience and ERIC experience and found that experienced ERIC searchers conduct the most cost-effective searches and have the highest precision. Walker found that untrained end-users perform surprisingly well, although in her study they took twice as much time on a given search as experienced intermediaries did. Walker's findings were not supported in a more recent study by Lancaster et al. (1992), who found that faculty and graduate students searching the ERIC database on CD-ROM could find only about a third of the items of potential interest.

In an investigation of the impact of various other searcher characteristics, Bellardo (1985) pretested her subjects for online searching proficiency (by their performance on two searches); creativity level (using two self-report inventories); intelligence level (by their performance on Graduate Record Examination verbal and quantitative tests); and personality traits (using the Interpersonal Disposition Inventory). Her findings suggest that differences in searching performance are attributable only to a small degree to verbal and quantitative aptitude, artistic creativity, and an inclination toward critical and analytical thinking.

From the performance of searchers on various output measures, such as recall and precision, it is logical to begin an evaluation of searcher performance by various process variables. The first attempts in this area consisted of frequency counts of various command components, such as Boolean operators or commands to display records; Fenichel (1981) referred to these as "search effort" variables. Although it is interesting to note the use of particular command sequences or components by searchers, it becomes even more useful if these commands are viewed within a model of how a search is or should be conducted. This notion was put forth by Bates (1979a), whose "idea tactics" consisted of 17 search moves, which investigators have since attempted to validate by direct field observation (Hsieh-Yee, 1990; Wildemuth et al., 1991).

Another line of research into process variables was undertaken by Borgman (1984). She hypothesized that users who are trained with a conceptual model of how a retrieval system works will perform better than those who are simply trained to use prescribed sequences of commands. After training, she analyzed test searches for features that would indicate either a "positive model" (such as the use of Boolean logic or index browsing) or a "negative model" (such as the use of phrases rather than words) of the retrieval system. She found that, on the whole, conceptually trained individuals performed better on complex retrieval tasks, but that a surprising number of searchers, no matter how they were trained, used the "brute force" method of trial and error.

11

Automatic Methods of Information Retrieval

In conventional computerized systems most, if not all, of the intellectual processing is conducted by humans, and the computer merely acts as a giant matching device. But it is possible that fully automatic retrieval systems can be developed, in which human intellectual processing is minimized or even eliminated. Computers can be used to index documents; prepare abstracts, or at least extracts, of documents; automatically elaborate on a searching strategy; and develop links among semantically related terms, thereby creating a form of searching aid (a kind of machine-constructed thesaurus). In a fully automatic system, indexing is done by computer, an internally generated thesaurus is prepared, and search strategies are developed automatically from a natural-language statement of information need.

Experimentation with automatic methods began in the 1950s and is still being conducted. Researchers have used statistical, linguistic, and artificial intelligence techniques to automate procedures and test their effects on retrieval system performance as measured by recall and precision. This chapter reviews representative studies that describe the procedures used in both fully automatic and machine-aided systems performing automatic thesaurus construction, automatic and machine-aided indexing, automatic query formulation, and automatic abstracting. It also explores how these systems have been evaluated and how well they have performed.

GENERAL APPROACHES IN AUTOMATIC METHODS OF INFORMATION RETRIEVAL

Before describing the techniques used in automating retrieval processes, a general perspective on the concepts and methods that have been applied will

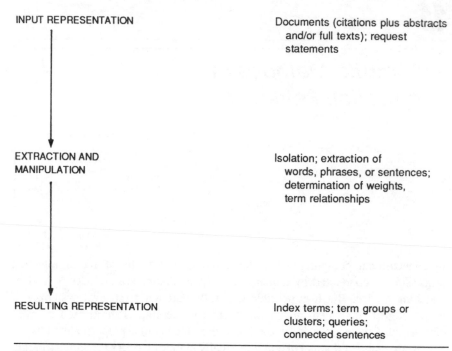

INPUT REPRESENTATION

Documents (citations plus abstracts
   and/or full texts); request
   statements

EXTRACTION AND
MANIPULATION

Isolation; extraction of
   words, phrases, or sentences;
   determination of weights,
   term relationships

RESULTING REPRESENTATION

Index terms; term groups or
   clusters; queries;
   connected sentences

EXHIBIT 61   General view of automatic methods of information retrieval.

be provided. Note that these techniques have been used almost exclusively in the experimental domain, on small collections. This has important implications for the evaluation of results, which is dealt with in the final section of this chapter, "Evaluation of Automatic Methods."

As depicted in Exhibit 61, a body of text is input (either a collection of bibliographic citations or full texts); textual elements are extracted and manipulated in some automatic process; and an encapsulated representation is generated (lists of index terms or lines of connected text). What is output is determined by the nature of what is input and the realities of efficient computation, which emphasize approaches with an acceptable level of processing overhead. Thus, most studies to date have applied computer algorithms to extract and manipulate only the existing strings in the document representation. Far fewer studies have attempted more extensive automatic analyses, although these have become more frequent in recent years.

As an example, consider the documents and requests found in Exhibit 62. The first request is for materials about using machine-readable data (for example, MARC records) as a resource in the cataloging of documents. The second request is for articles that discuss matters relevant to the cataloging of

REQUESTS

First request: "Machine-readable cataloging data"

Second request: "Cataloging machine-readable data"

PROCESSING COMPONENTS

1. Keywords extracted from these two requests:

    cataloging
    machine
    readable
    data

> (Using these four words, none of the records [a–f] would be retrieved because the matching algorithm does not take into account):

2. Spelling and/or word variants (morphology)

    cataloging
    cataloguing

> (By substituting both spelling variants, all records [a–f] would be retrieved; however, this does not distinguish between document b, relevant to the second request, and document d, relevant to the first. To make this distinction, additional linguistic information is needed):

3. Structural/grammatical variants (syntax)

    machine-readable cataloging data
    cataloging machine-readable data

> (By constructing different phrases, the distinction between these two expressions is maintained; however, it is still necessary to account for other, synonymous terms that might occur, as with document e. To do this, the meanings of expressions must be accounted for):

4. Meaning information (semantics)

    machine-readable cataloging
        synonym – MARC

> (By including synonymous expressions, documents containing completely different words that mean the same thing can be retrieved; however, there are other, contextual clues, which can also point to relevant documents):

5. Contextual information (pragmatics)

    . . .libraries seeking a machine-readable cataloging data source. They include on-line systems, CD-ROM systems. . .

> ("They," in document d, refers to "machine-readable cataloging sources," which are the topic of the discussion in document f).

EXHIBIT 62   Sample requests, processing components, and matching documents.

EXHIBIT 62   *(Continued)*

DOCUMENTS (from the ERIC database)

a.

Title: Linking approval plans and automated library acquisitions systems
Author(s): Smith, Scott A.
Journal: Library Acquisitions: Practice and Theory
Source: 11 (3) 1987, 215-216
Languages: English
Abstract: Contribution to a special section devoted to the Midwinter Meeting of the American Library Association (ALA), Chicago, Jan 87. Paper presented to the RTSD RS Automated Acquisitions/ In-Process Control Systems Discussion Group. Describes the process whereby an approval vendor provides machine-readable records corresponding to books sent to a library automatically and on approval, for loading into the library's automated acquisitions system. At present vendors are offering 2 alternatives, either an LCMARC cataloguing record, or an abbreviated MARC format bibliographic record created by the vendor. Often LC records are CIP (Cataloguing in Publication Data) level, since that is usually all that is available when the vendor ships a book. The supply of records as a feature of an approval programme introduces a new aspect of customer service.

b.

Title: Cataloguing machine-readable data files: an introduction
Author(s): Chang, Roy
Journal: Journal of Educational Media Science
Source: 19(1) Autumn 81, 17-30. illus. 11 refs
Languages: English
Abstract: Due to lack of bibliographic control and unfamiliarity, machine-readable data files (MRDFs) remain phantom material to both librarians and library users--even though more and more research materials are being produced in machine-readable form. Reviews the current status of MRDFs; discusses basic conditions for cataloguing and reviews Chapter 9 of the Anglo-American Cataloguing Rules (2nd edition) which is devoted to descriptive cataloguing rules for MRDFs, focusing on troublesome areas.

c.

Title: Is CD-ROM a threat to bibliographic networks?
Author(s): Fokker, Dirk W.
Editors: Edited by Ching-chih Chen and David I. Raitt, MicroUse Information and FID, 1989
Journal: In: Proceedings of the 2nd Pacific Conference on New Information Technology for Library & Information Professionals, Educational Media Specialists & Technologists. Singapore, 29-31 May 1989
Source: 93-101. 17 refs.
Languages: English
Abstract: Bibliographic networks concentrate on cooperative and shared cataloguing from a large central data base. The provision of machine-readable cataloguing records and other cataloguing products is one of their main functions. However, libraries may experience the participation in networks as a loss of autonomy. CD-ROM offers an alternative today. With data bases available on CD-ROM containing cataloguing information for library items, libraries can buy or subscribe to these discs which will give them a high retrieval rate. CD-ROM fits easily into traditional library practices and does away with many of the problems experienced with networks. The records can be manipulated, adapted and downloaded into local systems. The consequences of using CD-ROM as a source of cataloguing data are that the basis for cooperation can affect the viability of bibliographic networks.

EXHIBIT 62 *(Continued)*

d.

Title: CD-ROM as a cataloguing tool
Author(s): Saunders, Laverna M.
Journal: Technical Services Quarterly
Source: 6 (1) 1988, 45-59. illus. bibliog.
Languages: English
Abstract: A CD-ROM bibliographic system can be a valuable asset to larger libraries planning retro-spective conversion and to smaller libraries seeking a machine readable cataloguing data source. **They** include on-line systems, **CD-ROM systems,** or combinations of the two. The selection of a CD-ROM system should be integrated into a library's overall automation plan. Numerous questions regarding the vendor, the data base and the system's features need to be asked during the investigation process. A case study for approaching these issues is the experience of Nevada academic and public libraries with General Research Corporation's LaserQuest.

e.

Title: Thoughts on the **MARC** system at BLHSS
Author(s): Bruce, Alastair
Journal: MARC Users' Group Newsletter
Source: 87 (2) Aug 87, 4-6
Languages: English
Abstract: A fairly recent recruit to the British Library Humanities and Social Sciences cataloguing section describes his experiences of using **MARC** cataloguing records in an environment of ambiguity and change. N.L.M.

f.

Title: Comparison of three **CD-ROM cataloguing tools: BiblioFile, LaserCat, LaserQuest**
Author(s): Giesbrecht, Walter
Journal: School Libraries in Canada
Source: 9 (1) Fall 88, 23-27. table. 5 refs
Languages: English
Abstract: BiblioFile, LaserCat and LaserQuest are sources of catalogue records, they are not catalogues in themselves. All 3 products contain MARC records in the US MARC format, the number and type of record varying however. Illustrates and compares the features of the 3 products covering searching, displaying and printing of records, original cataloguing, costs and hardware requirements. The fact that LaserCat contains the holdings of many small public libraries and some regional school libraries makes it a good source of records for many of the items which school libraries are likely to have. BiblioFile and LaserQuest, on the other hand, would seem to be best suited to libraries undergoing large retrospective conversion projects. P.B.

machine-readable data files. These are two distinct requests. Presumably, a user interested in documents relevant to the first request would not want documents relevant to the second, and vice versa. Turning now to the documents, the first (a) is not relevant to either request; the second (b) is about the cataloging of machine-readable data files and is relevant to the second request; and the remaining documents (c, d, e, and f) are about using machine-readable data as a cataloging source and are relevant to the first request.

In the simplest of automatic methods, the user can enter a string of keywords that will be used to search the inverted indexes of document keywords, retrieving items that match all user-supplied elements. This approach is typical of several interfaces both to online indexes to periodical articles and online library catalogs. But all that has been automatically supplied is the logical *and* between keywords; otherwise, the machine is still acting only as a matching device. An automatic method that is this simple often results in serious retrieval errors. These are not errors in the algorithm—in fact, the machine is accurately performing its designated task. Rather, the problem arises for two reasons: (1) The algorithm is relying solely on the presence or absence of exact single word forms as the logical representation of the user's search request and (2) the document representation at this point consists of all its content words; that is, there is no selection among them of those that are more indicative of the document's content. Automatic methods have been introduced that attempt to solve these types of problems. To do this, they (1) use mechanisms that modify or supplement the individual key strings and (2) identify and select elements that are indicative of document or query content. These methods take into account the statistical and linguistic properties of text.

LINGUISTIC APPROACHES TO INFORMATION RETRIEVAL

The examples in Exhibit 62 illustrate some of the techniques and issues inherent in linguistic approaches to automatic analysis. The exhibit shows two requests and samples of items that are relevant to them, and exemplifies four components—morphological, syntactic, semantic, and pragmatic—that might be part of automatic linguistic analysis in information retrieval. Exhibit 63 (on p. 250) uses these four levels (plus a fifth—lexical—level) to compare the basic components in most commercial IR systems with the parallel components in the mostly experimental linguistic and knowledge-based approaches. This section concentrates on the typical components of commercial systems compared to those using true linguistic or knowledge-based processing. Statistical methods are covered in the next section.

In Exhibit 62, one of the keywords taken from the search requests is "cataloging." The database in the illustration, however, uses a spelling variation, "cataloguing." This is a problem that users resolve by inputting spelling variations and using truncation. In an automatic system, the program can often truncate and supply alternative spellings.

In a true morphological analysis, roots and affixes are analyzed to determine the part of speech (noun, verb, adjective, and so on) of words. Information about individual words and their parts of speech is stored in a lexicon, which is used to correctly process each item. These data then serve as input to a parser, a computer program that either partially or completely analyzes the linguistic structure of the sentences. Thus, in this situation, word affixes are retained to provide the information that is necessary for the linguistic analysis. For example, the analyzer in this stage might tag the following words as indicated:

comput-e	V	(verb)
comput-er	N	(noun)
comput-ed	PPart	(past participle)
comput-ational	Adj	(adjective)

This type of analysis is required if the input text is to be parsed into complex units such as compound noun phrases, as described below.

Once the word variation problem is resolved, other problems must be addressed. The two search requests, when reduced to keywords, are identical. The initial requests, which were in fact phrases, were distinct in meaning but are now ambiguous because of their reduction to a common list of keywords. Thus, documents b and d are retrieved for both queries, when each is only relevant in a single case. This failure in the precision of the request is now a problem because the structural variation of the phrases has been eliminated. Users resolve this problem by combining words into complete phrases, using the necessary search protocols. In an automatic system, complete phrases are parsed from free text and manipulated by using some form of syntactic analysis.

Even with the phrase problem resolved, only modifications to the original keywords are being considered. Thus, retrieval remains a matching operation, with some additional sophistication in the form of automatic truncation (stemming) and phrase analysis. But document e still will not be retrieved in response to the first search request; because that document appears relevant, there is recall failure. To retrieve document e, the user must supply other synonymous or quasi-synonymous terms that can be used in the matching operation. These are not word or phrase variations of the same forms; they are *new* words and phrases that are intended to be the same as or similar in meaning to the original term. To do this automatically, the computer must have access to a resource in which to store and efficiently access information about terms and their semantic relationships.

Finally, even with some of the semantic information provided, it is possible that relevant documents might be missed. If a user believes this to be true, he or she will often use contextual information from one relevant document to expand the search for additional, similar documents. In an automatic system, additional discourse elements in the abstract are used to refer to other relevant documents. In the case of document d, the pronoun "they" refers to "machine-

Linguistic Level	Commercial Information Retrieval	Statistical Information Retrieval	Linguistic/ Knowledge-Based Information Retrieval
Lexical	Stop word list	Stop word list	Lexicon
Morphological	Truncation symbol	Stemming	Morphological analysis
Syntactic	Proximity operators	Statistical phrases	Grammatical phrases
Semantic	Thesaurus	Clusters of co-occurring words	Network of words/phrases with semantic relationships
Pragmatic	Hedges	Relevance feedback	Expert interface with search heuristics

EXHIBIT 63   Comparison of levels of processing in commercial, statistical, and linguistic methods of information retrieval.

readable cataloguing data," followed by specific types, among them CD-ROM systems. The inference that CD-ROM systems are "machine-readable cataloging data" provides a link to document f, which is also relevant to the first request.

In linguistics, the five types of information that can be isolated and manipulated in an automated system are divided into categories, or levels, that correspond to increasing levels of complexity for the automatic system. They are the lexicon, morphology (word structure), syntax (phrase and sentence structure), semantics (meaning), and pragmatics (language in context). Note that there are parallels between what is automated and what is usually supplied manually by searchers when using commercial systems. This equivalence is discussed and illustrated by both Doszkocs (1986) and Warner (1992) and is shown in Exhibit 63.

The preceding examples have been restricted to the language of search requests and documents, where the automated system has access to a computer program that manipulates the queries and documents at various levels. There is additional knowledge that an individual brings to a search, which includes a wide variety of search heuristics—rules of thumb used to modify the search in various ways (Fidel, 1984, 1991). Search heuristics include recall devices (for example, additional terms in an *or* relationship; use of single keywords) and precision devices (for example, combinations of terms in an *and* relationship; use of complete phrases). Essentially, then, two kinds of knowledge need to be exploited: (1) The regular linguistic structures need to be identified and (2)

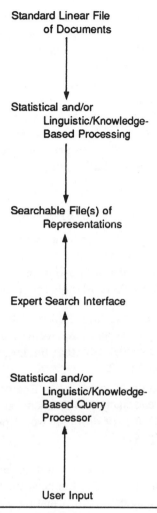

Standard Linear File
of Documents

Statistical and/or
Linguistic/Knowledge-
Based Processing

Searchable File(s) of
Representations

Expert Search Interface

Statistical and/or
Linguistic/Knowledge-
Based Query
Processor

User Input

EXHIBIT 64 Simplified architecture of an intelligent information retrieval system.

the use of these structures to achieve a given retrieval objective needs to be encoded. The general architecture of such a system is illustrated in Exhibit 64, which shows the different modules for analyzing the language of documents and queries as just described, as well as the additional expert knowledge of the search process that such a system would have to contain. A system of this type would be a true expert system for searching, making it an artificial intelligence application. Attempts to build such systems have been described in the information retrieval literature by Pollitt (1987) and Vickery (1988).

If it were possible to isolate and use all this knowledge at the level of sophistication and the flexibility and success of an experienced searcher, then automated systems could eliminate the need for the human intermediary. Linguistic applications and expert systems to date, however, have been computationally expensive; complex programs must be written for the five linguistic levels and for the exploitation of search heuristics. Furthermore, the most sophisticated systems must contain complex knowledge bases of semantic and pragmatic information, which are difficult and time-consuming to construct. Finally, these approaches have yielded surprisingly modest improvements in system performance, despite their intuitive appeal.

STATISTICAL APPROACHES TO INFORMATION RETRIEVAL

A much larger and more long-standing body of work in automatic information retrieval methods relies on certain statistical characteristics of the textual elements found in documents (see third column in Exhibit 63). This work is based on investigations by Zipf (1935), who observed, among other things, that

1. Shorter words are more frequently used in English than longer words: "However large the stock of short and long words may be, the evidence of language seems to indicate unequivocally that the larger a word is in length, the less likely it is to be used." (p. 22)

2. The frequency distribution of word use in English is skewed; there are a few very frequent words, and many less frequent ones: "As the number of occurrences increases, the number of different words possessing that number of occurrences decreases." (p. 41)

The fact that the frequency distribution of word tokens is not uniform across all word types is a basic phenomenon that has been the foundation of many of the statistical methods used in automatic information retrieval, beginning with the work of Hans Peter Luhn (1957, 1958) in the late 1950s. He suggested that after ranking by frequency of occurrence all the words contained in a collection or a sample of a collection, it would be possible to establish two cutoffs: one at the upper region, where words are so common that they are useless in distinguishing document sets, and one at the lower region, where words are so uncommon that they do not serve to cluster documents in a useful way. He referred to this characteristic of words as their "resolving power" or their "degree of discrimination" (Luhn, 1958, p. 160). Exhibit 65, from Luhn's work (1958, p. 161), shows this situation, where line C is the high-frequency boundary and line D is the low-frequency boundary, and where the words whose frequencies fall in the middle range, E, are considered to have acceptable resolving power.

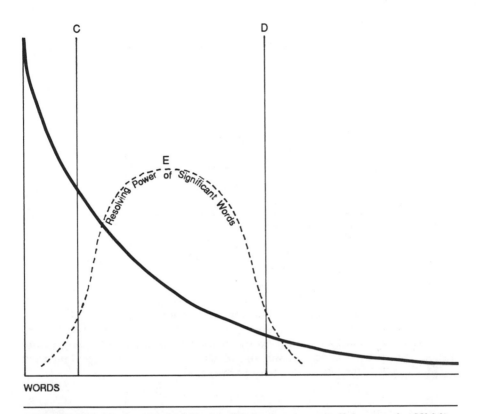

WORDS

EXHIBIT 65 Upper (C) and lower (D) frequency cutoff for words. Middle-frequency words (E) have appropriate resolving power. SOURCE: Luhn (1958). Copyright 1958 by International Business Machines Corporation; reprinted with permission.

The most common application of these frequency principles, found in both automatic statistical systems and commercial systems not based on statistical techniques, is the use of a stop list to exclude high-frequency function words from document and query representations, leaving only content words for consideration. In most statistical systems, content words are processed by using a program called a "stemmer," which is analogous to a morphological analyzer, although somewhat less sophisticated. Here, affixes are completely removed from words, leaving an underlying "key stem" or "root" so that, for example, comput[er], comput[ational] and comput[ed] can all be reduced to a single form. These forms will then be submitted to a statistical analysis.

Stemmers can work in several ways, summarized by Salton (1989) as follows:

(a)

```
"People in need of information require effective
              retrieval services."
```

(b)

```
"PEOPLE    INFORM    EFFECT    RETRIEV    SERVICE"
```

(c)

```
PEOPLE   INFORM              EFFECT    RETRIEV
INFORM   EFFECT              EFFECT    SERVICE
INFORM   RETRIEV             RETRIEV   SERVICE
INFORM   SERVICE
```

EXHIBIT 66   Example of statistical phrase generation: (a) Original sentence; (b) Word stems generated from original sentence; (c) Word pairs (phrases) generated assuming no more than three intervening words between word pairs. SOURCE: **Salton and McGill (1983, p. 134). Copyright 1983 by McGraw-Hill, Inc. Reprinted with permission.**

1. They can remove particular word suffixes and prefixes.
2. They can remove a fixed number of terminal characters from the word.
3. They can reduce each word to a stem of a fixed size.

Usually, automatic methods that incorporate statistics use only keywords for their analyses. There are a few, however, that operate on phrases; usually in these systems, a phrase is defined statistically rather than linguistically. Their purpose is to take words that are too high in frequency and combine them with other words, thus creating a phrase with a medium-frequency level. Salton and McGill (1983) describe this procedure in the SMART system:

1. Use a stop list to eliminate common function words.
2. Use a stemmer to generate word stems.
3. Take pairs of the remaining word stems, and let each pair define a phrase provided that the distance in the text between components does not exceed a desired threshold, and that at least one of the components of each phrase is a high-frequency term. (p. 133)

Word pairs that are considered phrases in this system are produced from input sentences, an example of which is shown in Exhibit 66. This method should be compared with a linguistic method for analyzing and identifying phrases, as shown in Exhibit 67.

The single or stem phrases that emerge from this process are selected or organized according to their statistical behavior, with two general methods being used: (1) "absolute frequency," where key stems or phrases that occur X times or more are selected or grouped and (2) "relative frequency," where key stems or phrases are selected or grouped when they occur more often in given documents than expected, given their frequency in the entire collection.

In one of the most well-known and long-standing automatic systems, SMART (Salton, 1968), individual content words in the request statements and the documents are extracted, stemmed, and assigned weights according to their frequency within the requests and documents. The resulting sets of weighted stems from the requests and documents are then compared and a similarity coefficient is computed, with 1 being exactly the same and 0 being completely different. An example of this, taken from Salton's work, is provided in Exhibit 68.

Finally, in the SMART system, it is also possible to make this process iterative in a procedure known as "relevance feedback," described by Salton (1968) as follows:

The user is shown some preliminary output and identifies some of the documents as either useful to him or not useful. The system then automatically adjusts the search request by increasing the weight of the request terms that were also contained in the designated set of relevant documents; at the same time, the weight of request terms also contained in the nonrelevant document set is decreased. (p. 17)

The statistical approach to automatic methods has components that are analogous to those described for the linguistic approaches and their parallel capabilities in commercial information retrieval systems, as illustrated in Exhibit 63.

Although fairly simple examples have been provided to illustrate linguistic and statistical methods in automatic information retrieval, it should not be assumed that there is an agreed-upon way to pursue either approach. In fact, given the different levels of analysis that are possible, it is not uncommon for some techniques to be linguistically based and others statistically based. For example, sometimes a parser (that is, linguistic analysis) will be used to extract grammatical noun phrases from documents that are then analyzed statistically. Indeed, automatic information retrieval systems contain many parameters that can be adjusted in various ways, but always with the hope that any adjustment will improve retrieval performance.

Sample sentence from abstract: "With the exception of the development of a negative dictionary, all system operations are completely automatic."

Yields the following grammatical analysis:

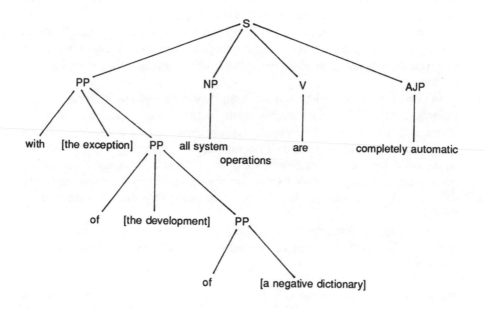

which yields the following phrases:

> Development exception
> Dictionary development
> Negative dictionary
> System operations

S = sentence
PP = prepositional phrase
NP = noun phrase
V = verb
AJP = adjectival phrase

EXHIBIT 67 Sample index phrase output from grammatical analysis. SOURCE: **Adapted from Salton (1988). Reprinted with permission of the Association for Computational Linguistics; copies of the publication from which this material is derived can be obtained from Dr. Donald E. Walker (ACL), Bellcore, MRE 2A 379, 445 South Street, Box 1910, Morristown, NJ 07960–1910.**

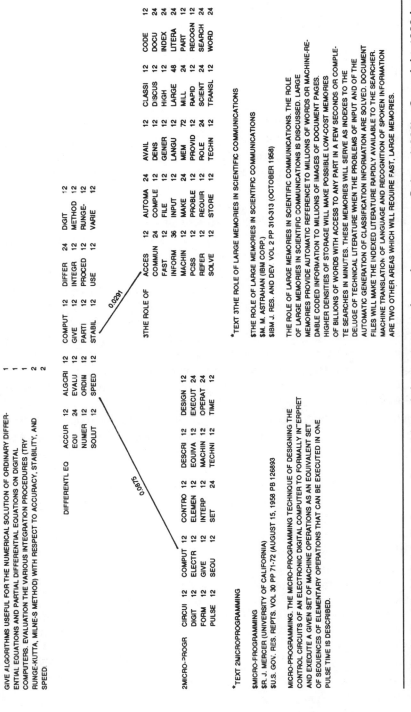

EXHIBIT 68 Statistical indexing and matching of documents and queries. SOURCE: Salton (1968). Copyright 1968 by McGraw-Hill, Inc.; reprinted with permission.

CATEGORIES OF AUTOMATIC METHODS
OF INFORMATION RETRIEVAL

There are four distinct types of automatic methods in experimental information retrieval: automatic thesaurus construction, automatic indexing, automatic query formulation, and automatic abstracting. Although separate, all are part of an information retrieval system, and much of what happens with one method has ramifications for the others. Automating these processes is not easy, because what is actually being attempted is the automation of subject analysis, a very subjective, intellectual task. This statement might prompt some to ask why these efforts are undertaken; it seems that there are both practical and research-related answers to this question.

On the practical side, it is time-consuming and expensive to manually create thesauri, abstracts, and indexes. Furthermore, although it was perhaps feasible to do all subject analysis manually in the early days of information retrieval, there is far more textual information in electronic form today, and much of it must be left without *any* subject description. Keyword searching of full texts is now a common scenario in online retrieval, and searching those files that lack any manually or automatically assigned index terms is problematic at best. In addition, whereas trained search intermediaries almost always did online searches on behalf of clients in the past, end users are now doing their own searches, and, for them, searching needs to be a straightforward, transparent process. Thus, search interfaces should incorporate flexible processing of natural-language user input, instead of always requiring rigid protocols, as they once did.

On the research side, investigators are attempting to use automatic methods to understand how information retrieval systems behave and to predict how their performance will change under various conditions. This work is valuable because it is trying to show that automatic methods can produce document and query representations that perform as well as or better than current operational systems based on Boolean searching of natural-language keywords and descriptor words and phrases. Moreover, automated approaches to information retrieval have varied widely over the years, ranging from simple to more sophisticated statistical procedures and incorporating more complex analyses of the linguistic structures and the general heuristics involved in indexing, abstracting, thesaurus construction, and query formulation. This variation is a result of the experience and understanding that researchers have gained as they have worked with these systems and of the advances in hardware and software that have made it possible to implement more computationally complex algorithms.

In the following sections, the automatic methods are compared with their manual counterparts within the framework of Smith and Warner (1984), which addresses both what is being represented and its form of representation. Examples of the results of the different procedures are also discussed to give a sense of the diversity and complexity of the approaches.

Finally, note that there are really two distinct views of what is important to accomplish in information retrieval research and experimentation. The two views basically show a difference in emphasis between researchers who study the retrieval system and those who focus on the user. The systems view emphasizes the study of the retrieval system itself, by making modifications to its various components and then determining the effect of those modifications on retrieval performance. Thus, for example, a researcher might use a number of automatic indexing algorithms and then compare them in terms of recall and precision. The users view concentrates on how to make interfaces that can be used more easily and effectively, often with retrieval systems consisting of the traditional keywords and phrases—processed from free-text fields—and assigned descriptors. Often these interfaces consist of a rich store of complex search aids and help facilities, all intended to make searching easier and more transparent.

Automatic Thesaurus Construction

Exhibit 69 compares manual and automatic approaches to thesaurus construction. In both cases, what is being represented is an organized subject terminology. As indicated in Chapter 6, vocabulary control is useful because it reduces the variability introduced by synonymy in language; in addition, it imposes greater predictability on language use in information retrieval by explicitly representing many of the important semantic relationships among words and phrases. This feature is intended to enhance search recall by ensuring that all documents on a particular topic are indexed by a single linguistic form. Thesauri, however, also contribute to search precision by the specificity of their terminology—the more specific the terms found in the thesaurus, the more that precision is enhanced (although often at the expense of recall).

In the manual approach, words and phrases are identified by a committee of experts, by extraction from the subject literature, or by a combination of the two. They are then organized into facets, and term relationships are determined. The automatic methods generate organizations of terms, which are most often extracted from the literature. Various combinations of statistical and linguistic methods are applied at different stages.

Selection procedures most commonly include the statistical notions previously outlined, which eliminate stop words and then select content words (usually stemmed) having good "resolving power" (Luhn, 1957) or "discrimination value" (Salton, 1968). Less frequently, the grammatical class (subject, object) is used to select terms (Hirschman, Grishman, and Sager, 1975). More specific

| | What to Represent: Organized Subject Terminology | | |
| | Manual | Automatic | |
		Statistics	Linguistics
Selection Procedures	Identification of terms by committee Extraction of terms from literature	Keyword selection by frequency (as good discriminators)	Selection of keywords/phrases by linguistic analysis (grammatical or part of speech)
Organization Procedures	Identification of semantic relationships	Grouping by frequency of co-occurrence, relative frequency of co-occurrence	Extraction of semantic relationships from text
Form of Representation	Lists of terms and semantic relationships	Keyword or key phrase clusters	Semantic network of terms plus relationships

EXHIBIT 69   A comparison of manual and automatic methods for thesaurus representation and construction.

A   Strings: aspect delta rectangular
    Stars: asymptotic criterion cycles problem
    Cliques: criterion cycles estimate lyapunov
    Clumps: ablating capacity shield teflon

B

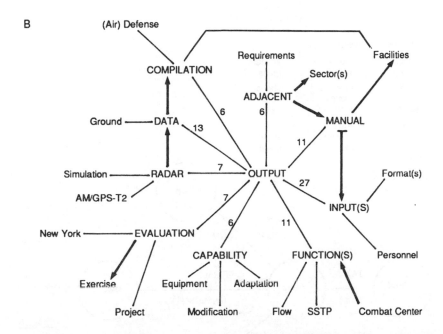

EXHIBIT 70   Results of statistical grouping of words. SOURCE: A: Sparck Jones (1971); reprinted with permission of Butterworth. B: Doyle (1961); reprinted with permission of the Association for Computing Machinery.

and complex phrases also are extracted by some type of linguistic analysis, which is necessary to ensure that the resulting word sequence is grammatical (Dillon and McDonald, 1983; Salton, 1988). Clustering procedures using grammatical phrases have also been investigated by Lewis and Croft (1990).

Organization procedures most often group words or phrases statistically, according to their frequency of co-occurrence (Sparck Jones, 1971) or their relative frequency of co-occurrence (Stiles, 1961; Doyle, 1961). Results of statistical clustering techniques are shown in Exhibit 70. There can be groups of terms (words or phrases) that are considered to be semantically related (Section A in Exhibit 70; Sparck Jones, 1971; Van Rijsbergen, 1979) or a map of terms and the strengths of their associations (Section B in Exhibit 70;

Dictionary Definitions

sheep n (pl unchanged)	grass-eating animal kept for its flesh as food (mutton) and its wool.
wool n [U] 1	soft hair of sheep, goats, and some other animals . . .
ram n 1	uncastrated male sheep.
ewe n	female sheep.
lamb n 1 [C]	young of the sheep . . .

Extracted Lexical Relations:

sheep	TAX	animal
sheep	TFOOD	grass
wool	PART	sheep
wool	PART	goat
wool	TAX	hair
ram	MALE	sheep
ewe	FEMALE	sheep
lamb	CHILD	sheep

Semantic Network:

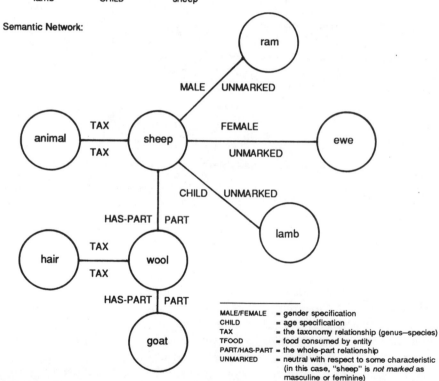

MALE/FEMALE	= gender specification
CHILD	= age specification
TAX	= the taxonomy relationship (genus—species)
TFOOD	= food consumed by entity
PART/HAS-PART	= the whole-part relationship
UNMARKED	= neutral with respect to some characteristic (in this case, "sheep" is *not marked* as masculine or feminine)

EXHIBIT 71   Results of a linguistic grouping of words and phrases. SOURCE: Fox et al. (1988). Reprinted with permission of the Association for Computational Linguistics; copies of the publication from which this material is derived can be obtained from Dr. Donald E. Walker (ACL), Bellcore, MRE 2A379, 445 South Street, Box 1910, Morristown, NJ 07960-1910.

Doyle, 1961; Stiles, 1961). What does not appear in these approaches, however, is any representation of the specific semantic relationships among the terms. In fact, Sparck Jones (1965) considers clusters generated in this way to be "semantically unobvious." Furthermore, since the text in a given document collection is used to generate these clusters, there can be questions about the representativeness of the clusters. Because they are based on the statistical properties of the collection from which they were generated, they may not be useful with other collections, perhaps not even with a collection in the same subject area.

These concerns have been addressed to some extent by Fox et al. (1988), who are attempting to produce a thesaurus (in the form of a semantic network) from a machine-readable dictionary. Exhibit 71 shows a simplified example from Fox's work. A controlled vocabulary generated in this way presumably would not be linked to a particular collection and would therefore represent general vocabulary content, applicable in many different environments.

Thesauri constructed from general lexical resources such as dictionaries are potentially very useful, because sets of words and phrases that are related in semantically specific ways (for example, genus–species, part–whole, cause–effect) can be generated. A high computational overhead, however, is needed to construct such a network, and it still is not clear how useful thesauri constructed from these machine-readable dictionaries are in actual retrieval operations, since they tend to be generated from standard English dictionaries and therefore lack much of the specialized terminology that is needed for many subject-specific search requests.

Another concern with statistical organization is that, as stated previously, the clusters which are generated usually do not contain terms that are linguistically related (Lesk, 1969). Other researchers have developed methods that do organize on linguistic principles, including the use of relationships taken from machine-readable dictionaries (Fox et al., 1988) and the automatic identification of term relationships from the free text of documents (Warner, 1990; Ruge, 1992). As with other automatic retrieval operations, it may be that statistical and linguistic procedures are useful in different situations. In fact, a few researchers have found that the use of linguistically based term groups to expand queries does in some cases improve retrieval performance (Wang, Vandendorpe, and Evens, 1985).

Automatic Indexing

Exhibit 72 compares the methods used in manual and automatic approaches to indexing. Indexing is useful because the small list of extracted or assigned key terms or descriptors is considered to be highly representative of the document's content. As stated in Chapter 10, a search of just the index terms often results in

What to Represent: Document Content

| | Manual | | Automatic | | | |
| | Extraction | Assignment | Extraction | | Assignment | |
			Statistics	Linguistics	Statistics	Linguistics
Selection Procedures	Select words or phrases	Translate to controlled vocabulary descriptors	Keywords/ word pairs	Grammatical noun phrases	From automatic word clusters	From thesaurus with semantic relations
Indication of Relationships of Relative Importance	Links, roles, weights of words/phrases either specified or unspecified	Links, roles, weights of descriptors either specified or unspecified	Weights of words/phrases	Links, roles between words/phrases	Weights of assigned terms	Links, roles between assigned terms
Form of Representation	List of words/ phrases with or without weights, links, roles	List of descriptors with or without weights, links, roles	Weighted/ unweighted words/phrases	Links, roles between words/phrases	Weighted/ unweighted assigned terms	Links, roles between assigned terms

EXHIBIT 72   A comparison of manual and automatic methods for indexing procedures and representations.

higher precision than is possible using natural language. Indexing should also facilitate recall, since the use of specified terms assigned from a controlled vocabulary helps to ensure that documents on particular concepts will be gathered under a single linguistic form.

In manual systems, index terms are commonly weighted according to how central or strongly emphasized each concept is in the document. Furthermore, systems that incorporated assigned links and roles were used during the 1960s and early 1970s. Links were assumed to help reduce the number of false coordinations in a retrieval system by tying together terms that are related in the document and separating terms that are not related. Roles, a more sophisticated device, went further to explicate the actual semantic relationship between the index terms. (Links and roles were described in more detail in Chapter 6.)

The resulting forms of representation are lists of words or phrases that have either been extracted from the document or assigned from a controlled vocabulary. Terms may be simple lists with no further distinctions made, or they may be assigned weights, links, or roles.

There are analogous processes in the automatic methods described in the literature. Elements may be individual content words (usually stemmed) extracted from documents (Salton, 1968). Furthermore, when individual words are considered to be poor discriminators, they are sometimes paired with a co-occurring word in an attempt to make more specific word pairs with an acceptable frequency of occurrence (Salton, 1968).

In the approach just described, no attempt is made to ensure that the word pairs are true grammatical phrases. There are other approaches, however, that use only grammatical phrases as index terms; these must be taken from the text through some type of linguistic analysis that can range from simple systems that tag parts of speech and then identify legitimate sequences as noun phrases (Dillon and Gray, 1983) to more complex full parses of the input (Fagan, 1988).

Automatic indexing by assignment is much less frequent than automatic indexing by extraction and is more difficult. In one approach, terms are extracted statistically as just described. They are then matched with terms in stored clusters (such as those produced by methods described by Sparck Jones, 1971) or with terms in electronic versions of manual thesauri (Field, 1975), and additional assignments are made from the matched groups. An even more elaborate method performs a linguistic analysis on the input sentences, which are reduced to a standard structural form for consistent and successful mapping to a similarly stored thesaurus (Evans et al., 1991).

Emphasis of concepts in the document is specified statistically by weighting the terms (Salton, 1968), and the semantic relationships among terms are expressed linguistically by links or roles (Courrier, 1980). Exhibit 73 shows the variety of results that are possible with automatic indexing, ranging from

A.

* TEXT 2MICRO-PROGRAMMING .

$MICRO-PROGRAMMING
$R. J. MERCER   (UNIVERSITY OF CALIFORNIA)
$U.S. GOV. RES. REPTS. VOL 30 PP 71-72(A) (AUGUST 15,1958) PB 126893

MICRO-PROGRAMMING . THE MICRO-PROGRAMMING TECHNIQUE OF DESIGNING THE
CONTROL CIRCUITS OF AN ELECTRONIC DIGITAL COMPUTER TO FORMALLY INTERPRET
AND EXECUTE A GIVEN SET OF MACHINE OPERATIONS AS AN EQUIVALENT SET
OF SEQUENCES OF ELEMENTARY OPERATIONS THAT CAN BE EXECUTED IN ONE
PULSE TIME IS DESCRIBED .

2MICRO-PROGR	CIRCUI	12	COMPUT	12	CONTRO	12	DESCRI	12	DESIGN	12
	DIGIT	12	ELECTR	12	ELEMEN	12	EQUIVA	12	EXECUT	24
	FORM	12	GIVE	12	INTERP	12	MACHIN	12	OPERAT	24
	PULSE	12	SEQU	12	SET	24	TECHNI	12	TIME	12

B.

Title: "A data/knowledge base management testbed and experimental results on data/knowledge base
query and update processing."

Presents experience in designing and implementing a data/knowledge base management testbed. The
testbed consists of two layers, the knowledge manager and the database management system, with the
former at the top. The testbed is based on the logic programming paradigm, wherein data, knowledge,
and queries are all expressed as Horn clauses. The knowledge manager compiles pure, function-free
Horn clause queries into embedded-SQL programs, which are executed by the database management
system to produce the query results. The database management system is a commercial relational
database system and provides storage for both rules and facts. First, the testbed architecture and major
data structures and algorithms are described. Then, several preliminary tests conducted using the current
version of the testbed and the conclusions from the test results are presented. The principle contributions
of this work have been to unify various concepts, both previously published and new ones developed,
into a real system and to present several insights into data/knowledge base management system design
gleaned from the test results and the design and implementation experience.

• Exact Matches to Certified Terms in the Thesaurus:

    – HORN-CLAUSE
    – ALGORITHM
    – DATABASE MANAGEMENT SYSTEM

**EXHIBIT 73   Automatic indexing results. SOURCES: A: Salton (1968). Copy-
right 1968 by McGraw-Hill, Inc.; reproduced with permission. B: Evans et al.
(1991); reprinted with permission of Elsevier Science Publishers B.V. and
author. C: Courrier (1980); reprinted with permission of Marcel Dekker, Inc.**

EXHIBIT 73 *(Continued)*

- Matches to More General Terms in the Thesaurus:

    - DATA/KNOWLEDGE ←Data/Knowledge Base Management Testbed
    - DATABASE ←Database Management System
    - RELATIONAL-DATABASE ←Commercial Relational Database System
    - DATA-STRUCTURE ←Major Data Structures and Algorithms
    - DATABASE MANAGEMENT ←Database Management System
    - LOGIC PROGRAMMING ←Logic Programming Paradigm
    - ARCHITECTURE ←Testbed Architecture
    - LOGIC ←Logic Programming Paradigm

- Novel Terms (in the Text) that Utilize Concepts Represented in the above Sets of Terms (hence are Specified Matches) or have 'high' Compositional or Scored Matches:

    - FUNCTION-FREE HORN-CLAUSE QUERY
    - DATA/KNOWLEDGE BASE QUERY
    - DATA/KNOWLEDGE BASE MANAGEMENT TESTBED
    - TEST ARCHITECTURE
    - QUERY RESULT
    - MAJOR DATA-STRUCTURE
    - DATA/KNOWLEDGE BASE MANAGEMENT SYSTEM DESIGN
    - EMBEDDED-SQL PROGRAM
    - COMMERCIAL RELATIONAL-DATABASE SYSTEM
    - LOGIC PROGRAMMING PARADIGM

C.

Abstract in natural language:

Experimental observations on the prevention of seizures by intravenous procaine injection. Ten monkeys were stimulated by a direct cortical electrochoc. An intravenous injection of procaine has protected them from epilepsy for 30 min.

SYNTOL representation:

```
[PROCAINE]————————————R₂————————————→[CRISIS]
[PROCAINE]————————————R₂————————————→[EPILEPSY]
[PROCAINE]————————————R₂————————————→[PROTECTION]
[PROTECTION]——————————R₄————————————→[EPILEPSY]
[DIRECT] —————————————R₄————————————→[CORTEX]
[ELECTROCHOC] ————————R₄————————————→[CORTEX]
[ELECTROCHOC] ————————R₄————————————→[STIMULATION]
[STIMULATION]—————————R₄————————————→[BEING]
```

R_2: Associative relation
R_4: Coordinative relation (the coordinated relation is not oriented)

Abstract

Evaluation problems in interactive information retrieval—G. Salton: Department of Computer Science, Cornell University, Ithaca, New York 14850

```
    1       2    6     1     1    1     1  1  1      1       1      1    6
```
Summary—Interactive retrieval procedures are normally based on rapidly accessible files. Special storage

```
    6      4  1   6     6     1    1  4  1     6    6 1  1  1  1  1    1    1
```
organizations and file search techniques are used, and the system user is made to fulfill an important role

```
   1   1   6     1
```
during the retrieval process.

```
 1  1   1     1    1    2      6        6   1  1     1      1   1     6    1
```
In the present study, the interactive retrieval environment is briefly examined. The special problems which

```
   1  1  1    1    8  2     6    1  1      1     4    1   1     1     1    1
```
arise in the evaluation of interactive retrieval are then discussed, and methods are described for evaluating

```
   2   1   1   4  6    6       6       1     1      1    1  1    3    6
```
partial file searches and user feedback techniques. Evaluation results obtained with the SMART system

```
   1    1
```
are presented. (*Inform. Stor. Retr.* 1970, 6, 29—44.)

Candidate index terms

INTERACTIVE RETRIEVAL	(2,6--adj.,noun)
STORAGE ORGANIZATIONS	(6,6--noun,noun)
SEARCH TECHNIQUES	(6,6--noun,noun)
SYSTEM USER	(6,6--noun,noun)
INTERACTIVE RETRIEVAL ENVIRONMENT	(2,6,6--adj.,noun,noun)
INTERACTIVE RETRIEVAL	(2,6--adj.,noun)
USER FEEDBACK TECHNIQUES	(6,6,6--noun,noun,noun)
SMART SYSTEM	(3,6--proper noun,noun)

EXHIBIT 74   Example of results from a machine-aided indexing operation. SOURCE: **Klingbiel (1973). Reprinted with permission of Pergamon Press, Inc.**

lists of weighted keywords or phrases (A: Salton, 1968), to complex phrases assigned from a thesaurus (B: Evans et al., 1991), to the more sophisticated SYNTOL system, with its sets of semantic relations (C: Courrier, 1980).

The vast majority of efforts in automatic indexing make use of statistical techniques, with the assumption that if a word is a good discriminator, then it should be used as an index term because it is useful in building relevant sets of documents. A human indexer, however, does not consciously make this type of distinction when deciding what a document is about and either extracting or assigning appropriate terms. The hope is that the statistical technique can end up with plausible sets of index terms even though the terms are arrived at quite differently in the automated method.

Clearly, one of the reasons statistics are used in automatic indexing (justifiably) is that it is difficult to automate the rules that the human indexer follows.

Indexer prompted for the following slot values:

disease: cysts
body-part: **value:** Popliteal Artery
procedure: **value:** Angiography + Tomography X-Ray Computed
+ Ultrasonic Diagnosis

symptom: **value:** Intermittent Claudication

Program substitutes legal *Medical Subject Headings* [words in bold face indicate substituted descriptors]

```
(setq frame:
    '(cyst_85140959 (is-a (value cyst))
        (body-part (value popliteal_artery))
        (procedure
            (value angiography
            x-ray_computed_tomography
            ultrasonography))
        (symptom (value intermittent_claudication))
        (contained-in (value document_85140959)))))
```

EXHIBIT 75 Example of results from a machine-aided indexing system at the National Library of Medicine. SOURCE: Humphrey and Miller (1987). Reprinted with permission of John Wiley & Sons, Inc.

Another approach is to abandon the goal of fully automatic indexing and to use some machine-aided technique to automate the easier parts of the indexing process and to accept indexer input at various stages as necessary.

One effort by Klingbiel (1973) uses dictionaries of words and allowable sequences of words to tag and extract candidate index terms from free text, which are then evaluated and accepted or rejected by a human indexer. Exhibit 74 shows a sample tagged excerpt from this system, along with the candidate index terms it identified.

Another more recent and ambitious project at the National Library of Medicine uses a knowledge base composed of frames to prompt indexers for specified categories of index terms and to automatically supply input based on information that has been derived from applying inferences using explicitly encoded relationships found in the frames (Humphrey and Miller, 1987). A simplified example from this system is found in Exhibit 75.

Automatic Query Formulation

Given that documents and queries must match at some level for retrieval to be successful, it is not surprising that there are many parallels between their representations in manual and automated systems. As Exhibit 76 shows,

	What to Represent: Query Content					
	Manual		Automatic			
	Extraction	Assignment	Extraction		Assignment	
			Statistics	Linguistics	Statistics	Linguistics
Selection Procedures	Select words/phrases from query	Translate to controlled vocabulary descriptors	Keywords/word pairs	Grammatical noun phrases	Expansion with word/phrase clusters	From thesaurus with semantic relationships
Indications of Relationships of Relative Importance	Boolean operators; links; roles; weights specified	Boolean operators; links; roles; weights specified	Weights of words/pairs	Boolean operators, links, roles, between words/phrases	Weights of assigned words/phrases	Boolean operators, links, roles, between words/phrases
Form of Representation	Weights; Boolean operators; links, roles for extracted words/phrases	Weights; Boolean operators; links; roles for assigned descriptors	Weighted/ unweighted words/pairs	Boolean operators, links, roles, between words/phrases	Weighted/unweighted assigned terms	Boolean operators, links, roles between words/phrases

EXHIBIT 76   A comparison of manual and automatic approaches to query analysis and representation.

queries can consist of natural-language words and phrases from the searcher's own vocabulary or can be extracted from the user's search request. Or the searcher can use descriptors assigned from a controlled vocabulary instead of, or in combination with, natural-language search terms. In many systems, the terms must be connected with Boolean operators, as described in Chapter 8. Terms may also be weighted according to their importance in the request, and, less frequently, links and roles may connect them. Weighting and links and roles, of course, can only be used in queries if they have been used in the document representations. The result is that the user's search request, usually stated in natural language, is manually converted to a string of index terms, often interconnected with Boolean operators and occasionally weighted or semantically linked.

Fully automatic methods start with request statements in natural language, which are then processed to extract the necessary terms as well as the logical operators, weights, and links and roles. In all cases, the goal is to produce a query form with the same elements as the documents in the system. Representative automatic query formulations are found in Exhibits 68 and 77.

In statistical approaches, key stems and stem pairs are directly extracted from the user's statement (ignoring stop words and other nonsubstantive expressions), weighted, and then compared with weighted-document representations, as in Exhibit 68 (Salton, 1968). Furthermore, documents retrieved in this way by the system can be presented to the user for relevance assessment and the query may be modified and resubmitted to the system in a continuous, iterative approach known as "relevance feedback" (Salton, 1968). The elements from the search statement may also be linked by Boolean operators, either through a linguistic processing of the request to determine how the elements should be logically connected (Das Gupta, 1987) or statistically (the number of retrieved documents is computed for each Boolean connection and a formulation is arrived at on the basis of a given specified number of retrieved documents) (Salton, Buckley, and Fox, 1983).

Alternatively, the input may be partly or fully parsed to find grammatical noun phrases (Dillon and Gray, 1983; Croft, Turtle, and Lewis, 1991). Less frequently, terms are assigned from a thesaurus that is produced either with term clusters from the statistical techniques described in the section "Automatic Thesaurus Construction" (Sparck Jones, 1971) or manually, so that terms in specific semantic relationships can be added to the strategy. Semantic or syntactic roles or links can be identified, usually by further processing of the input to find lexical clues that signal various semantic relationships such as cause–effect or part–whole (Courrier, 1980).

In contrast to the approach where document and query processing are designed as part of an entire experimental system, there are other approaches that are intended to function as "interfaces" or "front ends" to existing

A. Automatic Boolean query formulation (compared with manual):

Manual Form (Boolean Statement)	Automatic Form
1. (catalogue *or* catalog) *and* (mechanization *or* automatic *or* computerization)	[(<catalogue,6.36>*or* (2) <catalog,5.36>), 5.86] *and* 1.5) [<mechanization,4.04>] *and* (1.5) [<automation,2.66>*and* (1.5)] [<computerization,1.60>), 2.13].
2. (information *and* science) *and* (education *or* training)	[<information,0.90>] *and* (1.5) [<science,2.19>] *and* (1.5) [(<education,4.36>*or* (1.5) <training,3.78>), 4.06]

B. Search statement: Automatic manufacture of mesh screens for widgets

[semantic processor]

Two groups of searchable paraphrases:

AUTOMATIC MANUFACTURE   SCREENS FOR WIDGETS
AUTOMATED MANUFACTURE   SCREENS OF MESH FOR WIDGETS
AUTOMATIC MANUFACTURING   MESH SCREENING FOR WIDGETS
MANUFACTURE BY AUTOMATION   MESH SCREENING FOR A WIDGET

C. Search statement: Side effects of aspirin on the liver

[yields]

[ASPIRIN] ———————————— R_2 ———————————— [LIVER]

agent   consecutive   patient
                     relation

EXHIBIT 77   Automatic query formulations. SOURCES: A – Salton, Buckley, and Fox (1983); reprinted with permission of John Wiley & Sons, Inc. B – Tait and Sparck Jones (1983); reprinted with permission of The British Library. C – Courrier (1980); reprinted with permission of Marcel Dekker, Inc.

systems, where documents have already been represented and processed for an operational, commercially available system. The purpose of these systems is to make the complexities of searching an already developed system transparent to the end user. The emphasis in the development of these searching tools is therefore on determining what functions should be included to help the user fully articulate the search by supplying or suggesting appropriate search term variants and logical or linguistic connectors. The usual way to interact with the user in these systems is to develop a program that can act as a machine-aided search advisory system, or what is often called an "expert intermediary system." A number of such systems now exist, including CANSEARCH (Pollitt, 1987), an expert system for searching the cancer therapy literature, and PLEXUS (Vickery and Brooks, 1987), an expert system for searching a referral database on gardening. Vickery (1992) describes currently available intelligent interfaces in Europe, and Parrott (1992) surveys some that have been developed in the United States. Most of these retrieve bibliographic citations; more recent efforts have developed interfaces to full-text systems (Gauch and Smith, 1993).

Brooks (1987) describes the general capabilities that define an expert system. The system must be able to obtain the same level of performance that a human expert achieves at the same task. The problem the system is designed to tackle should be complex enough that it requires the intelligence of a human expert to solve it. The expert system should be able to take a problem stated in some arbitrary initial form and translate it into an internal representation that can be processed using the system's expert rules and knowledge bases. Finally, the system should be able to reason about its own processes and to explain its decisions to the user.

To carry out these functions, an expert search intermediary would need the following components:

1. *Knowledge.* The knowledge that such a system needs to have is extensive, including knowledge of the task (rules of search strategy, negotiation, and formulation), of the relationships between documents and their descriptions, of the database protocols (that is, search strategy formulation rules), about the user and specifically of the information need, and of the subject domain and its terminology.

2. *Reasoning.* The reasoning mechanisms should contain procedures that infer appropriate search strategies using facts from the stores of knowledge just described.

3. *User Interface.* In developing the strategy, the system should act as an adviser and interact with the user in a cooperative and flexible way that makes the underlying system transparent to the user. It should also be able to explain to the user how it arrived at its conclusions.

Expert systems development is an ongoing effort that began in the mid-1980s (Smith, 1987). The reports of such systems in the literature are really descriptions of thoughtfully engineered prototypes rather than operational systems. There are significant limitations to these systems, in their subject domain, in the range of terminology they can handle, in the variety of input they will accept from the user, and in the degree to which they will flexibly respond to user error. Nevertheless, they have proved successful in restricted subject areas and have certainly shed light on what researchers need to know about the search process and its context to build more successful systems.

Automatic Abstracting

As shown in Exhibit 78, manual approaches to abstracting can use not only true paraphrases and summaries of documents, but may also make use of sentences that are extracted directly from the original document, although this practice is uncommon. In human abstracting, text is often provided about the original author's objectives, methods, results, and conclusions, but beyond that, abstracts may be stylistically very different.

With automatic methods, extraction is more common than abstracting. As in indexing, the added step of converting extracted texts to a new form is difficult, and it is not clear whether the results are much better than the simpler extraction method.

Sentences can be automatically extracted by either statistical or linguistic techniques. As with indexing, some of the first work done in this area was by Luhn (1958), who computed an overall score for sentences after deleting common function words and those that occur below a certain frequency. Other statistical approaches use variations on this basic technique and include assigning higher scores to sentences that include phrases (Luhn, 1958), sentences in which content words match words that are found in titles or subheadings (Edmundson, 1969), or sentences that occur at the beginning or end of a paragraph (Edmundson, 1969).

Other techniques compute a numeric score for sentences but use linguistic criteria in the process. A list of words and expressions that are particularly indicative or nonindicative of document content is used to give the sentence either a positive or negative score. Words such as "purpose" and "present research" are given positive weights, whereas words such as "unimportant" or "impossible" are given negative values (Rush, Salvador, and Zamora, 1971). In some cases, more complex expressions such as "The main aim of the present paper is to describe. . ." or "The purpose of this article is to review. . ." can be processed (Paice, 1990).

An even more sophisticated addition to automatic abstracting involves taking into account certain aspects of text structure, particularly the fact

| | What to Represent: Document Content | | | |
| | Manual | | Automatic | |
	Extraction	Paraphrasing	Extraction	Paraphrasing
Selection Procedures	Select key sentences	Paraphrase key concepts/sentences	Select sentences by highest numeric score	Modify sentences by linguistic analysis
Organization Procedures	Organize into coherent paragraph	Organize into coherent paragraph	Organize sentences by rank statistical order or by sequence in which they occur	Organize sentences by structural analysis
Form of Representation	Extract	Abstract	Extract	Abstract

EXHIBIT 78   A comparison of manual and automatic methods for abstracting procedures and representations.

A. Keyword approach

Document

Source: The Scientific American, Vol. 196, No. 2, 86-94, February, 1957

Title: Messengers of the Nervous System

Author: Amodeo S. Marrazzi

Auto-Abstract

It seems reasonable to credit the single-celled organisms with a system of chemical communication by diffusion of stimulating substances through the cell, and these correspond to the chemical messengers (e.g., hormones) that carry stimuli from cell to cell in the more complex organisms (7.0)

Finally, in the vertebrate animals there are special glands (e.g., the adrenals) for producing chemical messengers, and the nervous and chemical communication systems are intertwined: for instance, release of adrenalin by the adrenal gland is subject to control both by nerve impulses and by chemicals brought to the gland by the blood (6.4)

The experiments clearly demonstrated that acetylcholine (and related substances) and adrenalin (and its relatives) exert opposing actions which maintain a balanced regulation of the transmission of nerve impulses (6.3)

It is reasonable to suppose that the tranquilizing drugs counteract the inhibitory effect of excessive adrenalin or serotonin or some related inhibitor in the human nervous system (7.3)

[Sentences were selected by statistical analysis when they had a degree of significance of 6 and over.]

B. Cue method plus grammatical modification

Document

Source: Journal of the American Society for Information Science; March-April, 1973; 101-110.

Title: Improvement of Automatic Abstracts by the Use of Structural Analysis

Author: Mathis, Betty A.; Rush, James E.; Young, Carol E.
        [auto-abstract of their article describing their method]

Abstract

We have undertaken to extend the capabilities of the abstracting system described by Rush, Salvador and Zamora by adding to the system a modification procedure that could be employed to make the abstracts produced by the system more acceptable to the reader. Results of this study are reported in this paper. Our purpose is to present a rationale for the modification phase of an abstracting system and to describe several modification rules whose implementation is an initial step toward the automated production of abstracts that contain sentences written especially for the abstract. We have described several methods for improving the readability of abstracts produced by computer program. The research described in this paper was performed as a part of a larger project whose aim is the development of an operational automatic abstracting system.

[Cue words: undertaken, purpose, methods, aim]
[Modification of text: We have **therefore** undertaken to extend the capabilities of the abstracting system described by Rush, Salvador and Zamora--deleted **therefore**]

EXHIBIT 79   Results from two automatic abstracting procedures. SOURCES: A – Luhn (1958); copyright 1958 by International Business Machines Corporation; reprinted with permission. B – Mathis, Rush, and Young (1973); reprinted with permission of John Wiley & Sons, Inc.

that many concepts are referred to several times using different synonyms and "referring expressions" such as pronouns. Black (1990) describes how statistical approaches to automatic abstracting can identify and count *concepts* by extracting and counting all the *words* that refer to a concept. For example, there are two mentions of the concept underlying the boldface expression in the following sentence: "As the **ISO standards** become more stable, **they** will replace the Coloured Book protocols."

In contrast to extraction procedures, there are few true automatic abstracting systems where the text is changed from the original. Mathis, Rush, and Young (1973) described an addition to an automatic extracting system whereby sentences can be modified especially for the abstract. This task consisted mostly of combining individual sentences into more complex and terse expressions. Thus, the two sentences

> Individual manufacturers offer ALGOL, BASIC, and FOCAL compilers.

and

> Most manufacturers offer programming support on an individually negotiated contract basis.

can be combined as follows:

> Individual and most manufacturers offer ALGOL, BASIC, and FOCAL compilers, and programming support on an individually negotiated basis, respectively.

In addition to the need to identify and extract sentences, there is the need to organize them in some way. One method places the sentences in the final abstract in order of decreasing statistical weight. More recent approaches have also added the feature of keeping together all sentences that refer to the same concept, resulting in abstracts that are considered somewhat more coherent in that they contain few or no unknown references (Paice, 1990).

Results from two automatic abstracting procedures are shown in Exhibit 79. Exhibit A is generated by a simple word-frequency approach, while Exhibit B is derived by more sophisticated procedures that look for the occurrence of words that are likely to introduce sentences that will be good indicators of content (for example, "purpose" and "aim").

Automatic Methods Applied to Online Catalogs

Some experiments also have been performed to apply automatic or semi-automatic procedures to library online catalogs, although the research in this area has not been as extensive or long-standing as on other online bibliographic files. One reason is that online catalogs did not come into widespread use until the early 1980s. Another reason is the early assumption that the lack of subject searching in paper catalogs reflected true user needs in electronic catalogs as well, an assumption that was soon dispelled by studies of online catalog use. This finding was borne out on a large scale by the nationwide Council on Library Resources study (Matthews, Lawrence, and Ferguson, 1983), which showed a high volume of subject searching by users of operational catalogs and found that users desire more extensive and flexible subject-searching capabilities. It is not surprising, then, that the experimental studies involving online catalogs have included tests of many subject search features.

The OKAPI Project (Walker, 1987, 1988) is an ongoing experimental online catalog at the Polytechnic of Central London. This system allows users to input words or phrases that are then stemmed and looked up in all source fields with subject content, including titles and subtitles, subject headings, and content notes. If two or more words occur in the index, they are automatically combined with a Boolean *and*. If no records match using this strategy, the words are assigned weights inversely proportional to their frequency in the file. Thus, OKAPI works with both logical operators and statistical weights.

The statistical approach was used even more extensively in CITE, an experimental online catalog developed at the National Library of Medicine (Doszkocs, 1983). CITE was able to accept free-form language, including sentences or paragraphs as well as words and phrases. The words were stemmed, and the resulting elements were assigned weights based on their inverse frequency in the document collection. A special feature of the system was its ability to search *Medical Subject Headings,* to retrieve and suggest possible index terms that could then be used in the search (Doszkocs, 1978).

An even more recent experimental online catalog—CHESHIRE—is described by Larson (1992). This project uses a modified version of Salton's SMART system to test the effectiveness of several well-known automatic retrieval devices on a test collection of approximately 30,000 MARC records. The methods include different retrieval models (vector and probabilistic); expansion of queries with term clusters; and various stemming algorithms. This work is important because it tests and compares the effectiveness of a wide variety of system parameters in an experimental online catalog.

EVALUATION OF AUTOMATIC METHODS

In considering the evaluation of automatic methods, it is important to look at three areas: how automatic systems have been evaluated; what the results have been; and what impact these systems have had on the retrieval industry.

The range of system evaluation criteria is wide, but general categories of evaluations can be identified. It is logical that the first studies in automatic methods were really feasibility studies, carried out to determine if reasonably good output could be generated by a given approach. Usually the finding was reported by the actual investigator and included impressions of the output and the computational and intellectual difficulties in deriving it. This was true of the first automatic indexing and abstracting studies, which concentrated on statistical techniques. It is also true of studies of both linguistic and artificial intelligence techniques in automatic indexing, abstracting, and query formulation, which tend to be reports of methods being worked out and the researcher's experience with them. A statement made by Marchetti and Belkin (1991) is typical:

In this paper, we have attempted to demonstrate how a particular theoretical stance to the issue of information retrieval (that is, interaction as central to the IR process, a hypertext model of the IR database) has led to specific research results which in turn have led to practical operational system implementations that promise to help end-user searching substantially. (p. 242)

Another way to evaluate experimental automatic systems is to compare their output with some standard, usually a manually produced tool that is considered to be of high quality. In fact, this is the primary evaluation method for automatic abstracting. Thus, Edmundson (1969) compares his automatically produced abstracts to "target abstracts"—extracts where subjects have manually selected sentences for inclusion based on written instructions. There are also cases where comparison to a manually produced standard is applied to the results of automatic indexing and automatic thesaurus construction. Evans et al. (1991) compared their automatic indexing program to the output of indexers who manually assigned terms to the same documents, and Borko and Bernick (1963) compared human and machine assignment of documents to the terms of a small controlled vocabulary.

The general consensus of these types of evaluations is that manually produced output is significantly different from that produced by a machine. On the one hand, this can be considered a discouraging result, if the goal of automatic methods is to produce the same results as a manual process. On the other hand, it may be that automatic methods can be considered complementary to manual ones. In general, the automatic methods, based as they are on literary warrant, may in fact reflect another aspect of the complementary nature of natural-language and controlled vocabulary.

The most common way to evaluate automatic indexing, thesaurus construction, and query formulation is to determine performance in terms of recall and precision. This task is usually done by using a test collection consisting of a sample of documents from a retrieval system along with queries and relevance judgments. The availability and sharing of these test collections enables researchers to perform experiments where comparative recall and precision values may be derived for automatic systems operating with and without the mechanism being studied. One of the largest and most long-standing projects of this type is the SMART system, in which various parameters, such as term-weighting mechanisms and vocabulary-control devices such as thesauri, are compared and contrasted to measure their effects on retrieval performance (Salton, 1968).

Sparck Jones (1981) summarizes much of the work on experimental information retrieval and concludes that the use of natural-language stemmed words is about as good as other more elaborate linguistic devices such as links and roles. Furthermore, she concludes that the automatic methods have not been much more effective than manual ones. One should interpret these findings with some caution, however, for the following reasons:

1. Many retrieval experiments are performed on small collections (a few hundred to a few thousand items). There is evidence that the size variable may have a significant impact on performance measures (Blair and Maron, 1985).

2. Similarly, many experiments have been performed with few queries, sometimes 10 or fewer. Again, it is difficult to determine whether findings produced under these circumstances can predict performance for operational systems that handle many more and varied search requests.

3. There is a large range in the results. In some cases recall and precision figures can be quite different both between researchers working with the same collection and for the same researcher using a particular experimental method in a variety of collections.

Sparck Jones (1981) concludes her survey of 20 years of information retrieval experiments by stating that it is still not possible to accurately predict performance because of the complexity of retrieval systems. This fact, along with the generalization that most of the methods attempted have not improved that much over manual methods in terms of recall and precision, probably explains why very little of what has happened in experimental information retrieval has made its way into the operational environment.

In more recent discussions of evaluation in information retrieval, many of the problems just described—including collection size (Salton, 1992) and difficulties involved in scaling experimental procedures to large operational systems (Ledwith, 1992)—are addressed. Current experimental and operational work shows that these issues are being tackled in a serious way:

1. The TREC and TIPSTER initiatives are investigating a wide variety of experimental methods using a very large database (3 gigabytes) (Harmon, 1992).

2. One experimental method—ranked retrieval output arrived at by statistical weighting procedures—has found its way into a few commercial products (Visschedijk and Gibb, 1993).

12

Trends and Possible
Future Developments

Some important trends that affect information retrieval systems can be found in Exhibit 80, which illustrates a dichotomy between technology (the devices, or media, for storing, organizing, and transmitting information) and the environment in which the technology is applied (the intellectual content of information sources and the organizations and individuals that use them). A general summary of the points made in the exhibit will set the stage for the in-depth discussion that follows.

There has been a steady growth in the products and formats of information technology, including computers, databases, software, and storage media (previously only print-on-paper and microform but now including machine-readable formats such as magnetic and optical disks). There also has been a clear trend toward networking, with many organizations and individuals gaining access to a wider variety of remote sources through telecommunications networks such as Bitnet and Internet.

As with most important inventions, the electronic devices and formats have been introduced to address concerns and solve problems. Due to their impact on the organizations and individuals that use them, however, they are often applied in ways that were never intended. For example, Shurkin (1984) traced the development of the computer and notes that it was developed both to demonstrate its feasibility as a device and to speed the vast number of calculations that engineers needed to make during World War II. It has since become an integral part of virtually all types of businesses and other organizations (including libraries) and is used today in efforts as diverse as business inventory management, searching and retrieving legal statutes, organizing hospital records, and personal financial management (Stallings, Hutchinson, and Sawyer, 1988). Indeed, individuals with all types of backgrounds and abilities are accessing a vast array of computer-readable sources

Information Technology	Information Environment
Migration from paper to electronic document forms	Preservation and copyright issues
Proliferation of hardware and software—databases, programs, systems, publications media	Information marketplace
Networking, distributed computing, and telefacsimile	Access issues and the virtual library

EXHIBIT 80   Information technology resources and environment: Trends and issues.

in many different places. This phenomenon introduces a broad range of issues that need to be resolved, including the ethics of using computers in certain tasks (for example, to monitor employee performance or to create credit histories) (Marx and Sherizen, 1989) and significant questions of who does and who does not have access to the information infrastructure. All these issues have made the objective of information retrieval—to locate and extract the information needed from the appropriate sources—an increasingly challenging enterprise.

PROLIFERATION OF INFORMATION SOURCES AND INFORMATION TECHNOLOGY

Information technology can be defined very broadly to include the following:

1. The hardware (or medium) for storing information, including print-on-paper, microform, and various electronic devices such as magnetic and optical disks.

2. The hardware for processing and transmitting information, including photocopiers, telefacsimile machines, computers, and modems.

3. The intellectual and physical entities in which information is provided. These include primary publications containing full texts, such as journals, books, and reports, as well as secondary and tertiary sources such as encyclo-pedias, subject indexes, and library catalogs that point to items in the primary literature. Paper publications are often rendered as books, whereas electronic materials are contained in files known as databases.

4. The mechanisms for retrieving and displaying elements from the primary and secondary sources. In the case of print on paper, bound volumes or card

catalogs may be used in manual searching. In the case of the computer, there is interface software consisting of commands and instructions that are invoked by a user to retrieve and display information.

In the last 40 years, there has been a great proliferation of information sources and information technologies:

1. Growth in the number of publications, especially of scholarly journals and the articles they contain.

2. Growth in the number of secondary sources (for example, indexes and catalogs) in various media (such as print on paper and optical disk) and in the number of entries that are found in these sources.

3. Growth in the number of computers that are used by an ever more diverse set of organizations and individual users.

4. Growth in the number and variety of software products that are available in the public domain and as commercial products and systems.

These phenomena are all characterized by exponential growth. According to Meadows et al. (1972), "A quantity exhibits exponential growth when it increases by a constant percentage of the whole in a constant time period" (p. 27). What this means is that growth is affected greatly by the size of the base number—when it is small, the quantity added will be small, but as the base rises to larger and larger numbers, the amount added is increasingly large.

One of the most famous accounts of exponential growth is given by Derek de Solla Price, whose works *Science Since Babylon* (1961) and *Little Science, Big Science* (1963) documented the pattern of exponential growth in science, particularly in the form first of scientific journal titles and articles and later in the indexing and abstracting sources that were introduced to keep scientists aware of the work being done in a given field. Price pointed out that the growth in the scientific literature was not only exponential, it was amazingly rapid. In fact, he claimed that for most areas of scientific inquiry, the quantity of literature doubles in 10 years (Price, 1963, p. 6).

Not only is the number of primary and secondary publications rising exponentially, but so too is the number of systems one must know how to use to access all these publications. Nearly as astounding is the growth in online vendors, gateways, and databases, although there are signs that it may not be as rapid as it was in the early 1980s (Williams, 1990).

The general categories of computer hardware and software have also undergone exponential growth. This is true not only of the number of computers purchased, but also of various important computer software and hardware characteristics. In other words, the speed, complexity, and storage capacity

	Batch	Time-sharing	Desktop	Network
Decade	1960s	1970s	1980s	1990s
Location	Computer room	Terminal room	Desktop	Mobile
Users	Experts	Specialists	Individuals	Groups
User Status	Subservience	Dependence	Independence	Freedom
Data	Alpha-numeric	Text, vector	Fonts, graphs	Script, voice
Objective	Calculate	Access	Present	Communicate
User Activity	Punch and try (submit)	Remember and type (interact)	See and point (drive)	Ask and tell (delegate)
Interconnect	Peripherals	Terminals	Desktops	Palmtops
Applications	Custom	Standard	Generic	Components

EXHIBIT 81   The four paradigms of computing.   SOURCE: Adapted from Tesler (1991). Reprinted with permission of Scientific American, Inc.

of computers have increased exponentially. But although these numbers are continually rising, others are falling at an equally rapid pace, including the cost of a given piece of hardware and the size of individual units. Thus, for a given amount of money, one can purchase a personal computer that is much more powerful than those of just a few years ago, not only in terms of how fast it executes instructions but also the complexity of the programs it can run and the quantity of data it can store.

In this book, a model of computing has been assumed that consists of either a time-sharing environment, in which users are connected to and communicate with databases on a large mainframe computer, or an environment consisting of desktop microcomputers or other powerful workstations, in which users access and manipulate data locally—for example, on CD-ROM. Exhibit 81 shows these paradigms of computing and provides a framework to describe where computing has been and where it is headed. The scenarios underlying each decade's efforts are described by Tesler (1991) as follows:

The original computer paradigm was invented in the late 1940s, when the programmable calculator was designed as an engineering tool; it became commercially practical in the 1950s. The first shift came in the 1960s, when the computer was adopted as a data-processing engine by corporations. The second came in the 1970s, when the computer's services were shared among many subscribers. The third shift, in the 1980s, transformed the computer into a desktop productivity tool for individuals. The fourth is now under way. Its harbingers are the increasingly networked laptop devices and electronic pocket calendars—mobile machines I call pericomputers. Pericomputers are valuable both for the limited functions they can perform in isolation and for the access they afford to an electronically embodied world of information. (pp. 87–88)

Such a world of information can be accessed through an increasingly powerful and ubiquitous web of telecommunications networks. This networked environment is very important for two reasons: (1) It provides access to a wider variety of resources for individual users, and (2) it allows groups of users to communicate with each other (Quarterman, 1990).

Access to resources is achieved through telecommunications networks such as Bitnet and Internet. Bitnet is a cooperative network that, in 1988, served more than 2,300 hosts in 32 countries. Internet, which is actually a network of networks, serves a wide geographic area including the United States, Canada, Europe, and Asia. Internet usage has grown rapidly over time, from 213 hosts in 1981 to 727,000 hosts at the beginning of 1992 (Lottor, 1992).

The resources that are accessible though these networks include not only databases and the software that is needed to exploit them, but also hardware resources such as storage space and printers. Thus, the computing environment of the 1990s is highly decentralized but still interconnected, in contrast to the centralization of the 1960s and 1970s and the relative autonomy provided by the increasingly powerful desktop computers of the 1980s. In the 1990s, the user increasingly can access his or her own resources and supplement them with a wide array of hardware and software resources that can be accessed over the network.

The other significant factor in the interconnected environment of the 1990s is the ability of individuals to communicate electronically with one another. A variety of services exist for this purpose, including electronic mail and computer conferencing systems that facilitate discussion among many participants. Related to this capacity is the increasing possibility for groups to collaborate electronically on a project. At the center of this concept is the "shared document," to which each individual can make additions, changes, and deletions (Schrage, 1990). In some cases, this document can be thought of as a compound document, consisting of a variety of media such as text, images, structured drawings, spreadsheets, and audio and video signals (Heller, 1991). Compound documents highlight yet another important aspect of the computing environment of the 1990s and beyond: Whereas databases of the 1960s and 1970s were primarily textual and numeric, recent ones are "interactive" and contain images, sounds, and other media (Lucky, 1989; Cawkell, 1992).

INFORMATION RETRIEVAL AND THE PARADIGMS OF COMPUTING

It is not surprising that the history of information retrieval has followed the paradigms of computing outlined and described in the previous section (as well as in Chapter 2). A number of batch processing systems were in place by the 1960s, including the MEDLARS search service at the National Library of Medicine and the Online Computer Library Center's (OCLC) system for providing catalog cards to libraries from its store of machine-readable cataloging records in the MARC format. The advances in storage and access technology and telecommunications that were commonplace by the 1970s resulted in the evolution of these services and in the introduction of new systems based on online interactive retrieval. Hence, MEDLARS became MEDLINE (MEDLARS online) and OCLC's batch service became accessible in a time-sharing mode so that catalogers could input, edit, and produce records interactively. In addition, many other retrieval systems were introduced, and online catalogs began appearing in large academic libraries that could afford to implement and maintain them on large mainframes.

During the 1970s, access to large databases through a number of bibliographic retrieval services continued to be a mainstay in information retrieval. With decreases in the size and cost of computers, however, many libraries, even small ones, could afford to build and maintain an online catalog using commercially available turnkey systems—packages of hardware and software designed and marketed for various library operations, such as circulation, interlibrary loan, and catalog searching. The further miniaturization of computer components resulted in the introduction of the microcomputer, which made computing power affordable by an even larger part of the library community. It is now common for libraries to develop and maintain a variety of in-house databases, composed of records downloaded from other sources or created from scratch, that provide access to part or all of the library's collection (Tenopir and Lundeen, 1988). Furthermore, the introduction of commercial databases on CD-ROM has made large collections—including those previously accessed online on a mainframe computer—available to libraries. As with other databases and media, the growth in the number of CD-ROMs sold to and in use by libraries continues to rise. In 1990, Nicholls and Van Den Elshout (1990) found that there were approximately 500 CD-ROM products for libraries; in 1993, there were more than 1,300.

It is interesting to note how technology has changed the relationship of libraries to their environment. Libraries have participated in cooperative efforts mostly because of the effects of automation. Before the introduction of computers, libraries functioned as relatively autonomous units, although there were a few examples of large cooperative efforts, such as the *National Union*

Catalog, created and maintained for the purpose of resource sharing. With the advent of computing and online retrieval, libraries became increasingly tied to remote centralized resources like those provided by the bibliographic retrieval services and the bibliographic utilities. Due to decreases in the cost of computers and the accompanying increases in their processing power and storage capacity, it became feasible for more and more libraries to provide relatively autonomous service from databases that were built and maintained locally or leased from a vendor. The most recent development, however, has taken place as many libraries and information centers have become part of the decentralized, interconnected, and distributed computing environment of the 1990s. For example, *The Barron's Guide* (Barron, 1992) lists more than 300 online catalogs that are available through Internet and can be accessed and searched by anyone with a network account. Furthermore, an increasingly large number of heterogeneous information sources are accessible over the network through services such as WAIS (Wide Area Information Server), GOPHER, and WWW (World Wide Web) (Krol, 1992).

THE MIGRATION FROM PRINT ON PAPER TO THE ELECTRONIC DOCUMENT

Well over a decade ago, Lancaster (1978) presented a vision of a paperless society and further projected what its impact would be on libraries (Lancaster, 1982). He predicted that certain events would take place within a number of facets that he summarized as follows (Lancaster, 1985, p. 554):

Facet 1: Type of publication

Various types are influenced by electronics in a logical sequence, reflecting relative needs and perceived benefits

Facet 2: Application of computers to publishing (in evolutionary order)

a. To print on paper
b. To make available the electronic equivalent of a printed publication
c. To generate new publications having no printed equivalent
d. To introduce publication forms with completely new capabilities
e. To cause the replacement of existing printed forms

Facet 3: Amount stored

a. Citations only
b. Abstracts
c. Complete text

Facet 4: Type of information service affected

a. Literature searching
b. Question answering
c. Document delivery

Facet 5:   Subject matter

      a.   Science and technology
      b.   Social sciences
      c.   Humanities and popular literature

Facet 6:   Type of audience affected

      a.   Institutional users
      b.   Individuals

or, in library terms:

      a.   Special libraries
      b.   Academic libraries
      c.   Public libraries

Much of what is outlined here has already happened or is evolving, and there are many indicators that the predicted trends will continue. It is useful, therefore, to take stock of where the field is and where it is likely to be in the future and to envision the impact of these trends on information retrieval and dissemination.

Chapter 2 presented the evolution of online retrieval systems as stemming from a by-product of the publishing process—computer typesetting, which replaced more expensive and time-consuming technologies—and the result of that operation—a computer-readable format of the database that was used in batch and then online information retrieval. Publications have now appeared that exist only in machine-readable form. In some cases the database might be too specialized to earn a profit in the print market. In other cases, the material may be very ephemeral (for example, some full-text newsletter databases), might change too frequently (for example, some numeric databases such as those of daily stock quotations), or might reflect late-breaking developments that must reach users quickly (such as *The Online Journal of Current Clinical Trials* published by OCLC and the American Association for the Advancement of Science) (Rogers, 1991). Furthermore, publications containing citations only, citations plus abstracts, and full texts may exist in print only, in both print and online formats, and in online form exclusively. Moreover, they span the range of disciplines, from science and technology to popular literature (Williams, 1985).

Publication forms with completely new capabilities were proposed early in the history of information retrieval and have since made a significant contribution to information retrieval research and applications. Vannevar Bush was probably the first to recognize that new devices were necessary for the effective organization of and access to information. In an article in *The Atlantic Monthly,* he envisioned a device that he called the "memex," in which a user could store a private file of documents (Bush, 1945). The memex would have powerful and flexible retrieval capabilities that would allow the user to build a trail of associations between items of interest and to insert his or her own comments.

On the basis of this article, Bush has been credited both with the beginnings of modern information retrieval and the origin of the idea for hypertext, later expanded and developed by Nelson (1967). Hypertext differs from conventional documents, both in paper and machine-readable form, in several important ways. Conventional text is linear and static. Words are built into documents in a sequential manner. Once they are written and published, they remain the same. Finally, although it is possible to access them in a variety of ways, including searching on individual words or parts of words, and to retrieve all or a portion of their texts in response to a query, each author-produced text is really fixed in time and stands alone. It is either retrieved or not retrieved, along with other documents containing terms that match the query.

With hypertext, textual elements are actually linked with each other in a variety of ways. Thus, there are not only individual texts in the system but also links between them that the user can traverse however he or she wishes. Nielsen (1990) refers to hypertext as "nonsequential writing" and further describes it as:

> . . . a directed graph, where each node contains some amount of text or other information. The nodes are connected by directed links. In most hypertext systems, a node may have several out-going links, each of which is then associated with some smaller part of the node called an anchor. When users activate an anchor, they follow the associated link to its destination node, thus navigating the hypertext network. Users backtrack by following the links they have used in navigation in the reverse direction. Landmarks are nodes which are especially prominent in the network, for example, by being directly accessible from any (or all) nodes. (p. 298)

Exhibit 82 shows the conceptual structure of elements as they relate to each other in linear paper and hypertext systems. For the purposes of this example, it does not matter whether the individual units in each case are entire documents, portions of documents, citations, images, or sounds. What is important is that in the linear arrangement, the elements follow each other in a sequence. In such systems, it may be possible for the user to vary the order of presentation. For example, if the elements were texts accompanied by publication date, their order could be either alphabetic or chronological, but they would be presented sequentially nonetheless.

In a hypertext application, individual elements (nodes) are connected in many ways by links. The result is a "hyperdocument," which is in fact partly constructed by the system designer who created and placed the links and partly by the reader, who traverses those links in the way desired when the system is used. Because the paths taken in each case determine the structure of the

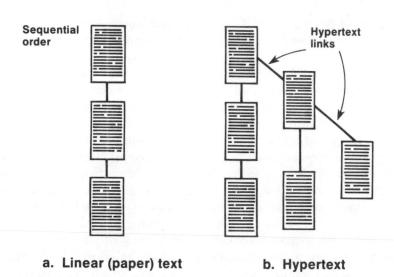

a. Linear (paper) text   **b. Hypertext**

EXHIBIT 82   Comparison between traditional and hypertext documents. SOURCE: **Adapted from Littleford (1991). Reprinted with permission of Mc-Graw-Hill, Inc.**

hyperdocument, it is not possible to obtain a hard copy of the hyperdocument—it varies every time the system is used.

Hypertext and hypermedia systems (that is, systems that incorporate sounds and images as well as text) hold much promise. They have been the subject of many research projects and applications reported on in the information retrieval literature. Applications have included *Hypertext on Hypertext,* a series of hypertext-structured documents on the subject of hypertext. (Fox, Rous, and Marchionini, 1991); the Perseus Project, a hypermedia journey through ancient Greece (Bannon, 1991; Mylonas, 1992); and PathMAC, a hypermedia tool to help students study introductory pathology (Diaz, 1991).

Despite their many advantages, these systems do have their drawbacks (Berk and Devlin, 1991). Due to their nonlinear nature, it is easy for the user to lose his or her way in the maze of links. To remedy this, some designers have provided users with graphic images of the path they have taken, which can be used as a point of reference. Furthermore, because the actual links are usually created at the time the system is implemented, any logical connections between nodes that the designers did not anticipate at the outset are not available for the user to traverse at a later time. The suggested solutions to this problem are either to allow the readers to create links at the time of use or to endow the system with enough intelligence to program its own links.

The last stage in the migration from print on paper to the electronic format involves the total elimination of paper documents. The most obvious example of this is the fact that after the introduction of the electronic catalog, many libraries completely removed their card catalog. Taken to its logical conclusion, this migration means a totally paperless world, with users interacting only with electronic information systems of both primary and secondary documents. Although it is possible that this situation may exist at some point, there are many barriers to its occurrence. These are not technological, but intellectual and political.

THE LIBRARY AND INFORMATION CENTER ENVIRONMENT

To determine where today's libraries and information centers are likely to be headed, it is necessary to describe the current situation. Change occurs on a continuum and at different paces for different organizations, depending on a variety of factors. The following are a number of generalizations that attempt to sketch where information centers fall on several continua. These are depicted in Exhibit 83, and correspond to the categories of storage, processing, and transmission.

The exclusively paper-based approach took place before the advent of computer technology. Information centers built and maintained large collections of primary documents that were stored mainly as print on paper, although some documents, particularly those of mainly archival interest, were maintained in microform. Searches for primary documents in the collection were done in the information center's paper catalog or in many printed indexing and abstracting

	Paper	Hybrid	Electronic
Storage	Paper collection of primary and secondary sources	Primary sources in paper; secondary sources in paper or electronic form	Totally electronic
Processing	Search of paper secondary sources; retrieval from primary paper collection	Online search of secondary sources; retrieval from primary paper collection	Online search and retrieval of electronic documents
Transmission	Conventional mailing of paper documents	Digital transmission of original paper documents	Digital transmission over distributed computing network

EXHIBIT 83 Storage, transmission, and processing by libraries and information centers.

sources purchased from commercial publishers. Searches in the catalog retrieved only those documents that were owned by the information center. But searches in any of the other tools often uncovered documents that were not owned locally and had to be requested from some remote source, usually another information center. As information center budgets shrank and the number and cost of primary and secondary sources grew, any given information center could own a smaller and smaller percentage of the published literature, making document delivery through interlibrary loan increasingly important. Significant delays in document delivery in this exclusively paper-based system, however, were common, because many of the documents were either photocopied or microfilmed and then mailed.

Generally, when an information center uses both print-on-paper and electronic sources (the hybrid approach in Exhibit 83), its collection of primary documents is still maintained in paper form, whereas the secondary sources are accessed in electronic form. In many cases, the same sources can be consulted in either electronic or paper format. Thus, many information centers have both paper and online catalogs, as well as paper indexes, and access to these same tools in electronic form through large retrieval services such as DIALOG—accessed by trained information specialists—and locally owned CD-ROM products, typically accessed by end users. Access to the actual documents these sources refer to, however, still must be through a paper collection. Document delivery from remote information centers can be through the mail or, in more and more cases, by digital telefacsimile (FAX) (Brown, 1989).

The third approach—electronic—is not yet fully in place. It involves electronic access to primary documents and secondary sources. Documents would be created and stored in electronic form and could be accessed and transmitted over long distances via high-speed telecommunications networks. The image presented in the literature is one of a "virtual library" (Mitchell and Saunders, 1991) or, if one prefers a term without institutional bias, the "universal workstation environment" (Dougherty and Hughes, 1991). In discussions of these concepts, it often is not clear how much actual primary literature should be online; however, there is agreement that the goal is to provide

. . . an integrated library/computer facility, transparent to the user; comprehensive access to national databases in all formats; information "virtually" accessible in one place; workstations for everyone for all of the information needed; a universal terminal that can handle multimedia in all formats; workstation access to all media—in many locations; universal access to databases, regardless of user and resource location. (Dougherty and Hughes, 1991, p. 11)

This scenario has several profound implications. An information environment such as the one described would change the roles of both the information professional and the information center as an institution:

1. The library as a building housing a collection of primarily paper documents would no longer be of central importance and, in fact, might no longer exist.

2. The "collection" would really be all the sources located in a variety of locations, both locally and remotely accessible.

3. The information professional would no longer act primarily as an interface between the user and the collection of paper documents, but would instead help in the design and use of powerful search and retrieval systems for increasingly autonomous end users.

Evidence already exists to support all of the points made in the scenario just described:

1. Some libraries are making available online the full-text versions of journal articles for search and downloading by users.

2. It is now possible, and increasingly prevalent, for users and information professionals to access catalogs and databases in remote locations through networks, such as Internet.

3. The role of the end user is becoming more important, particularly in the use of online catalogs and other databases in CD-ROM format.

It is now feasible to store large quantities of information compactly (CD-ROM offers approximately 500 million characters of storage on one small disk) and to transmit large quantities of information over high-speed networks in fractions of a second. Thus, the hardware is in place to store vast quantities of the world's literature, both the full texts and the accompanying graphs, charts, and pictures. Furthermore, it is projected that by the mid-1990s, computers will be 1,000 times faster than those of the late 1980s and that the National Research and Education Network (NREN) will transmit billions of characters per second over an increasingly interconnected distributed computing environment.

But even though the computer hardware can support storage and transmission of larger quantities of information, there are a number of significant barriers to the effective provision and use of all this information. One of these obstacles involves the enforcement of copyright. As stated by Weber (1990):

Although copyright is an important protection for authors and publishers, by the end of this century it will be largely dead in cases where information is created, distributed and exchanged electronically. This situation will make authors and publishers reluctant to abandon traditional publishing on paper. (p. 80)

Although publishers will undoubtedly use technical means to monitor access to documents and to collect royalties, this task appears complicated, particularly considering the difficulty in tracking a document as it moves from one person to another. Thus, although electronic publishing is a developing industry, the legal ramifications of copyright have slowed its adoption.

Another barrier to a completely electronic information system is directly related to much of the material presented in this book and involves issues of access. One access problem is caused by the increased connectivity over the networks, which is quickly leading to information overload on a giant scale. The selection of relevant and useful information, the central problem of information retrieval, has become more difficult in a networked environment that consists of growing amounts of both formal and informal communication, much of which is not yet organized in any systematic way.[1]

The same comments about the lack of effective organization apply to full-text document access. Keyword searching of the increasing volume of these documents retrieves sets of mostly irrelevant information that are too large to be browsed effectively. Some systems have improved this situation by developing software that ranks documents by probable relevance, but the basic problem is one of subject analysis and representation—full-text documents are not as dense in content as are other representations, such as abstracts and index terms. Furthermore, the online mechanisms that are necessary for describing, organizing, and accessing images, sounds, and other nonalphanumeric information are just beginning to be explored.

Thus, the major challenges to information retrieval include the following:

1. *Access:* Users can currently gain access to larger numbers of online files than ever before, including highly varied modes of presentation such as text, images, and sound. How can effective tools be provided to monitor the network on an ongoing basis for relevant information given the interest profile of a user? Furthermore, how can powerful, intelligent interfaces be designed that will help the user to navigate, search, and screen information that is available in a variety of locations and is presented as texts, numbers, images, and sounds?

2. *Document delivery:* Users can currently obtain large numbers of references online, but delivery of primary documents remains mostly paper-based. How can the copyright issues be surmounted so that all information can be accessible electronically?

---

[1] There are several ongoing attempts to organize the resources that are available over Internet, including research being carried out by OCLC to develop a system for cataloging them. OCLC's research includes an investigation of the degree to which cataloging could be carried out automatically (OCLC, 1991).

OTHER VIEWS ON THE FUTURE

At the time this book was being written, one of the authors was also editing a book of essays on the future of the library (Lancaster, 1993b). The volume consists of contributions from several eminent librarians, information scientists, and other scholars from the United States and elsewhere. Almost without exception, the authors point out that technological innovations, and other changes in the world around us, can be viewed either as a threat to the library or as a rare opportunity for the library profession to make itself more valuable to society than it has ever been before. The contributors represent a wide variety of libraries and related institutions on four continents. With such diversity of background, one would expect that the visionary statements would differ widely. But, in fact, there is often considerable agreement.

Penniman (1993) stresses that libraries must be active, not passive, and emphasize the delivery of information rather than its storage. He further asserts that libraries should be evaluated on the basis of services delivered, not assets controlled. Writing as the president of the Council on Library Resources, he claims that information retrieval specialists must focus their energies on research partnerships that ensure that libraries become the information delivery systems needed in the future and that the profession has the leadership skills necessary to make libraries essential delivery systems. At present, he suggests, libraries are in jeopardy because they lack true leadership.

Writing on the academic library environment, Molholt (1993), emphasizes technological developments. She argues that the increasing power and sophistication of information technologies, which threaten the existence of the "traditional" library, could, in the future, make the institution and the profession of greater value than ever before. She agrees with Penniman that changes need to occur in the profession:

The technologies of networking and distributed information resources, of non-linear programs accommodating rich linking among information resources, and the movement toward cinematic and interactive systems will change what libraries are and what librarians do. We need to plan for a change in emphasis from being the keepers of the book to being guides through the universe of knowledge. . . . The ability of librarians to be imaginative, to move outside of the library and into broader information roles will be a measure of the future librarian.

Dowlin (1993) and Young (1993), representing public and academic libraries, respectively, agree with Penniman and Molholt in that they, too, stress the need for change in the profession. The metaphors used by these various authors may differ, but the message is much the same. Dowlin views the present library as a fortress when, in fact, it should be a pipeline. Like Penniman, he sees a danger that the profession is not producing the leaders it needs to transform the library from fortress to pipeline. Library schools are producing graduates at the level of skilled craftsmen or general contractors, but they are not producing architects of vision.

Dowlin constructs his vision of the future of the public library from plans for the development of his own library, the San Francisco Public Library. This library will in no sense be the "library without walls" predicted by some writers (Lancaster, 1982). Indeed, it will be an "intelligent" structure that includes video and audio studios capable of exporting library services into the home. Dowlin expects that by the year 2000, every home in San Francisco will be connected to the library by cable television or telephone lines and that the building will be the "hub of a community network." He believes that electronic technology can provide users with a library that has the "ambience and sense of the community of a small town" and that, at the same time, allows for instantaneous global connections.

Young (1993) emphasizes that libraries will have to provide information in whatever format is most appropriate to the user—print, electronic, optical, or some format yet to be devised. (It is worth noting that most contributors to this volume do not see the new formats as replacing the old but, rather, as existing side by side with them.) Young believes that the ultimate goal of the profession is the creation of a "virtual library," consisting of "the sum total of accessible information available anywhere." In this scenario, the library building becomes merely a "retrieval node."

Raitt (1993) reviews the information technologies that are available today or that are likely to be available in the near future. He claims that an important role of the librarian must be the evaluation of appropriate technology and the education of others on the capabilities of this technology. At present, technology is not being developed by the disseminators of information but by a "parallel information industry" (mostly the computer and entertainment industries). Raitt implies that librarians need to be more active in determining how the technologies will be used.

Presenting a British perspective, Line (1993) agrees with Penniman that libraries must be evaluated in terms of the services they provide, not the collections they own. He claims that technology will make the library "less of a place to which people come and more of a resource that can be used remotely." Indeed, most of the authors agree that libraries as institutions, and even library buildings, will continue to exist, but that their roles will change.

The less developed countries are represented by Neelameghan (1993) and Kremer (1993). Neelameghan believes that technology will have great beneficial impact on Third World nations. Libraries there will be able to "provide access to a wider range of information through networks at the national, regional and international levels and by using databases in electro-optic media, e.g., CD-ROM." Focusing on the situation in Brazil, Kremer, while not discrediting the potential role of technology, emphasizes that libraries and information services will develop in that country to the extent that they can demonstrate their value in meeting the nation's social, technological, and cultural demands. Put somewhat differently, technology may well help Third World libraries to achieve their goals, but the implementation of new technologies should not become a goal in and of itself.

Kilgour's (1993) view of the library of the future is less conventional than that of many of the other contributors. He visualizes an electronic library system consisting of a centralized database of the full text of books, articles, and other items, with remote library access databases that provide various indexes to this full text.

It is perhaps ironic that the most radical departure from the present type of library is predicted by a scholarly user of libraries (Lauren Seiler) rather than by a librarian, although he is aided and abetted by a professor of library and information science (Tom Surprenant). Seiler and Surprenant (1993) claim confidently that the end of the print library is in sight and that print on paper is becoming extinct. They describe a library world in which all sources of information, inspiration, and entertainment are electronic, and suggest that the "virtual information center" that Young (1993) refers to may be the ultimate goal of the library profession. In the virtual information center, shelves of books are replaced by images of shelves of books, and each user can browse electronically through essentially the world's store of recorded knowledge without leaving home.

Let us now turn to another set of forecasts: *Information UK 2000*, edited by Martyn, Vickers, and Feeney (1990). This volume presents the results of a study initiated by The British Library to predict how information is likely to be generated, stored, and handled during the next decade or so. The study considered more than a technological perspective, also taking in social, economic, and related issues. Planning for the project began early in 1989, and most of the data were gathered in late 1989 and early 1990. The study is based on inputs solicited from approximately 60 "subject experts," organized into a series of 11 task forces. Each member of a task force prepared a separate forecast; these were then combined to form a consolidated forecast for each area. Contributions also were obtained from individuals who were not on the task forces.

Eleven of the 15 chapters of the book consist of the task force reports covering the following areas: social trends; technology; archives, libraries, and information services (the shortest of the task force reports, which might suggest that libraries and traditional information services were not considered too important in the big picture); recording and reproducing; communications infrastructure; publishing, new products, distribution, and marketing; individual and domestic uses of information; organizations and their use of information;

manpower, education, and training; issues for information users; and issues of policy from the policymakers' viewpoint.

Information UK 2000 contains too many projections, especially in the areas of technology, to summarize it effectively. Because the topic of *Information Retrieval Today* is information retrieval systems, this discussion concentrates on the forecasts that relate to libraries and the future of the library and information science profession. It is predicted that budgetary constraints will cause a shift from the purchase of materials to the purchase of access, that a "super league" of very large libraries will emerge as the basis of the holdings that other libraries will access, and that local libraries will primarily become switching centers. There is nothing too startling in these predictions. In fact, forecasts of this type can be traced back approximately 20 years. A more controversial prediction is that academic libraries in general will decline. According to the editors, academic departments will provide their own access to electronic resources and the academic library will become little more than a study hall.

Turning to education and training, it is predicted that opportunities for employment in "traditional" settings (presumably libraries) will decline but that new types of positions will emerge. These include

Research and information analysis in support of decision-making and policy formulation, and information design, ranging from technical writing to a responsibility for the management and design of an organization's overall information production activity. . . . There will be an increase in the numbers of consultants and intermediaries. (p. 29)

It is further predicted that a shift away from formal training in library and information science will occur and that future curricula will deal more with information technology and management and less with "social aspects."

The editors see the library and information profession, as it now exists, as threatened:

More widespread use of technology, more automation, more computer literacy among the population at large, greater commercial pressures to sell information products of various kinds to the public—all these factors will tend to weaken the position of the traditional librarian or information scientist. (p. 262)

Of course, it is not yet known which of the various visions put forward by librarians and others will prove most "correct." That in itself is not important. What is important is that significant changes will occur in how sources of information, inspiration, and entertainment will be made available and that these changes will have a major impact on the library and the information profession.

Certainly, many changes are taking place in the environment within which libraries function, and the future of the library will, to a large extent, be governed by developments outside the library's immediate control. The most obvious factor influencing the future of the library will be what occurs in the publishing industry and in the entire system of scholarly communication. It is clear that more and more information resources will be published in electronic form and that conventional print on paper will decline in importance. What is less clear is how these electronic information resources will be made available: accessed through electronic networks or distributed as physical artifacts such as CD-ROM or other forms yet to be devised. Distributed electronic forms can be acquired by libraries in much the same way that printed sources are acquired, but resources that are accessible only through electronic networks present the library with a different set of problems and put libraries in a somewhat different role as an information provider.

The shape of the library of the future will also be determined by the shape of the institution of which it forms a part. The United States is moving rapidly toward an "electronic university," in which much of the learning and scholarly communication takes place through electronic media. David Lewis, Lehman Librarian at Columbia University, has discussed the implications of this for the academic library of the future (Lewis, 1988). He points out that the automation of old systems is not enough; the complete restructuring of institutions will be needed. Moreover, users will demand more from the library than they have in the past:

Students may expect the library to be as powerful and easy to use as electronic teaching tools. Unfortunately, libraries are rarely easy to use. If analysis with new computer tools becomes easier and more productive than library research, students can be expected to use the new tools rather than the library. If libraries do not improve their services so that they remain an essential teaching tool, they risk becoming irrelevant to the teaching process. If this is allowed to happen, it is easy to predict a decline in library funding. (p. 293)

ARTIFICIAL INTELLIGENCE AND EXPERT SYSTEMS

One manifestation of technology is often seen as the solution to all library and information service problems: artificial intelligence (AI) or expert systems. Any discussion of applications of artificial intelligence is hampered by the fact that there is no universally accepted definition of the term. Indeed, several of the books written on AI make no real attempt to define it.[2] Even worse, the term is

---

[2] The objective of artificial intelligence is at least well illustrated by Kurzweil (1991), quoting Elaine Rich, as "how to make computers do things at which, at the moment, people are better." (p. 69)

used carelessly, often to refer to operations in which no machine intelligence is involved (for example, human selection from a computer-displayed menu). Indeed, it is ironic that work on automatic indexing or abstracting of the type performed by such pioneers as Luhn (1958) and Baxendale (1958), where words were extracted from text on the basis of frequency criteria, then considered an application of computational linguistics, should now be considered an AI application!

Perhaps Fenly (1992) has offered the clearest, most concise statement on what AI is, or should be:

[C]omputer programs have been developed which exhibit human-like reasoning, which may be able to learn from their mistakes, and which quickly and cleverly perform tasks normally done by scarce and expensive human experts. (p. 52)

In other words, AI attempts to develop systems that perform some of the tasks normally performed by experts in a particular area; perhaps the most obvious example is medical diagnosis. For this reason, such systems are frequently referred to as "expert systems." The terms "knowledge-based systems" and "rule-based systems" are now used more or less interchangeably with "expert systems." The reason is that systems of this type must be given a body of knowledge (for example, symptoms and signs associated with a particular disease state) to work on, and some of these knowledge bases consist of rules, such as rules for descriptive cataloging.

In fact, because descriptive cataloging is rule-based, it is a prime candidate for an expert systems application, and some work has been done in this area (for example, Weibel, 1992; Borko and Ercegovac, 1989; Jeng, 1986; and Schwarz, 1986). Fenly (1992), however, claims that the results have so far been unconvincing. He believes that a cataloging system with genuine expertise is much more difficult to implement than a system that merely casts cataloging rules in an automated format. As he points out, "genuine expert systems, with the depth and power to solve substantial and meaningful problems, are time-consuming and costly to develop" (p. 54). He does suggest, however, that certain descriptive cataloging problems may exist that require an unusual amount of intellectual effort and that problems of this type might justify the expense of a full expert systems approach. One such application is the cataloging of series.

Weibel (1992) has done research at OCLC on the feasibility of automatic descriptive cataloging from images of title pages, but he sees a "thread of unreality" in much of the research performed in this area. He claims that "large obstacles to implementation of production systems" exist and that expert systems techniques are "unlikely to change technical processing in the library in the next five years" (p. 72). Like Fenly, however, he believes that certain specialized tasks in cataloging might benefit from an expert systems treatment. In his view, it is more important that automated approaches to cataloging be "intelligently implemented" than that they be "intelligent."

The assignment of terms to documents to represent the subjects dealt with is another activity that might benefit from the application of AI. Although subject indexing cannot be as rule-based as descriptive cataloging, certain rules must be followed. In very large systems, such as those operated by the National Library of Medicine, these rules are extensive. For example, one set of rules prescribes which subheadings can be used with which categories of main headings.

An interactive program, MedIndEx, is being developed at the National Library of Medicine with expert systems principles to help indexers use *Medical Subject Headings* to represent the subject matter of biomedical articles (Humphrey, 1992). In essence, the program can perform two major tasks: (1) It can prompt the indexer to assign a particular term or type of term, and (2) it can correct the indexer when he or she uses a term inappropriately.

Other approaches to automatic indexing or computer-aided indexing described in the literature also claim to use AI or expert systems techniques; however, it is difficult to understand how systems that assign terms to documents on the basis of similarity between words that occur in document text (for example, titles and abstracts) and in word "profiles" associated with the terms can be regarded as involving AI. On the other hand, AI could be involved if the indexing system learned from its mistakes and was thus able to improve its own performance.

A lot of work has been done on the development of "intelligent front-ends" or "intelligent interfaces" to aid the exploitation of databases through online networks. For example, Hu (1987) has evaluated one such interface that was designed to help an individual select the database that appears most appropriate for a particular information need. Hu's study indicates that this particular interface operates almost entirely through the use of menus, from which the user makes a selection, and shows no evidence of any real "intelligence" in database selection.

Other interfaces are designed to help a user construct a search strategy that appropriately reflects an information need. Several such interfaces have been reviewed by Vickery (1992) and by Alberico and Micco (1990). Some of these operate through menus, some prompt the user by asking questions designed to usefully limit the scope of the search, and some accept input from the user in the form of a narrative statement of information need. Although many of these interfaces are ingenious and useful tools, it is not clear whether they actually involve the use of AI.

The universal question-answering device envisioned by Dana (1916) has not yet been achieved, but some progress has certainly been made toward the development of systems that will at least tell a library user which reference source to consult to answer a particular question. A good example of such a system is Answerman (Waters, 1986), conceptualized at the National Agricultural Library. In this conceptualization, menus are intended to narrow the scope of the user's question and to lead the user to the type of tool (directory, gazetteer, specialized dictionary, and so on) needed to answer the question. Waters (1992) considers question answering to be an obvious application of expert systems approaches because similar questions are asked repeatedly and because some libraries record questions received and answers supplied, thus creating an appropriate "knowledge base." Parrott (1992) has prepared a comprehensive review and typology of expert systems that were designed to assist the reference process in libraries.

Many years ago, when Luhn (1959) first described an approach to SDI using computers, he envisioned a system that would learn from its mistakes. The profiles of interest of participants in the SDI program would automatically be modified in response to their evaluations of the items received. Terms appearing in the profiles would be upweighted or downweighted, depending on whether they were associated with items judged by the recipient to be useful or not useful. A term would automatically be deleted from a profile if the SDI recipient repeatedly rejected as irrelevant the items retrieved by this term. Luhn's automatic approach to profile updating was difficult to implement and was never fully adopted in an operating system. In principle, though, there is no reason why it should not work. If it did, it could be said to exhibit intelligence because it learns from its mistakes.

Very few of the systems referred to as "expert" or as incorporating AI, in the library context, have any true learning features. A notable exception is an application described by Pontigo et al. (1992). The system described is designed to help the librarian decide from which source a particular book or other item should be ordered. The knowledge base used ties document identifiers (for example, ISBN's and technical report numbers) to probable sources of supply. The system is said to be "dynamic and adaptive": Data on success rates in acquiring particular types of materials from particular suppliers can be fed back to update the knowledge base and thus to improve the probability that a particular item will be available from the supplier selected.

Fenly (1992) has summarized the potential benefits of expert systems identified in the literature. Expert systems:

1. Make scarce expertise more widely available, thereby helping nonexperts achieve expertlike results
2. Free some of the time of human experts for other activities
3. Promote standardization and consistency in relatively unstructured tasks
4. Provide incentives for creating a database of knowledge in a permanent form (for example, not dependent on the availability of particular individuals)

5. Perform at a consistently high level (for example, not influenced by fatigue or lack of concentration).

These benefits are very real, and there is little doubt that carefully designed knowledge-based systems could be valuable to the library profession when applied to highly specialized activities that are now accomplished only through the expenditure of significant amounts of time by expensive human experts. Expert systems could also be of value in tasks that can obviously benefit from learning capabilities, such as the document-ordering activities dealt with by Pontigo et al. (1992). There is, however, little to support the belief that equipment with "intelligence" will soon be able to take over many of the intellectual tasks now performed by a well-trained and experienced librarian, and many writers on this subject seem much too optimistic on this point. For example, Metzler (1992) has said:

The library of the future may be able to provide a far richer access to, and utilization of, the knowledge contained (often implicitly) in its collection. The most immediately feasible development along this line would be content-based information retrieval. This, of course, would require a far more general and robust brand of artificial intelligence and natural language understanding than what we have available now. The step beyond that would involve not only understanding text well enough to determine whether it is relevant to a general information need expressed by a user, but to understand it well enough to actually extract information that can be used by a program. (pp. 8–9)

The enthusiasm for AI that exists in some segments of the library profession today is reminiscent of the enthusiasm for machine-aided diagnosis that existed in some segments of the medical profession approximately 20 years ago. Machine-aided diagnosis has not been widely accepted by the medical community, and it is now realized that the problems are much greater than they once appeared to be. Human experts operate through a combination of knowledge, experience, and intuition. Capturing the knowledge in some electronic form is possible, if not easy, but recording human experience is a more difficult problem, and human intuition is unlikely to be replaced for a very long time.

Most of the activities performed by librarians require less knowledge, experience, and intuition than does medical diagnosis. Nevertheless, the problems involved in automating even the simplest of intellectual tasks are frequently underestimated. As Davies (1986) has rightly pointed out: "The expertise in cataloging is not explicit in the rules; rather, it is implicit in the heuristics employed by the experts who do the work" (p. 58). Similarly, Weibel (1992), referring to work performed by Borko and Ercegovac (1989) on the cataloging of maps, points to their conclusions that necessary expertise in such procedures "extends beyond that which is articulated in formal rule sets" (p. 71) and that the complexity of the activity militates against the application of an expert systems approach.

The fact is, of course, that the true intellectual tasks associated with the library profession, and dealt with in detail in this book—subject analysis, interpretation of information needs, search strategy, and the like—are not easily delegated to machines. Whatever may happen to the library as an institution—that is, as a collection of physical artifacts—it is unlikely that the expertise of the skilled librarian will be replaced by artificial intelligence or any other technology in the foreseeable future. As Horton (1982) has stated so eloquently: "Creativity, talent, and brainpower. . . are the real 'capital assets' of the Information Economy, not information handling machines" (p. 39).

Bibliography

Alberico, Ralph, and Mary Micco. *Expert Systems for Reference and Information Retrieval.* Wesport, Conn., Meckler, 1990.

Albright, John B. "Some Limits to Subject Retrieval from a Large Published Index." Doctoral dissertation. Urbana, Ill., University of Illinois, Graduate School of Library Science, 1979.

Al-Hawamdeh, S., et al. "Best Match Document Retrieval: Development and Use of INSTRUCT." In: *Online Information 88. 12th International Online Information Meeting, London, 6–8 December 1988. Proceedings.* Vol. 2. Oxford, Eng., Learned Information, 1988, pp. 761–777.

Allen, Bryce L. "Bibliographic and Text-Linguistic Schemata in the User-Intermediary Interaction." Doctoral dissertation. London, Ont., Can., University of Western Ontario, School of Library and Information Science, 1988.

Allen, Thomas J., and P. G. Gerstberger. *Criteria for Selection of an Information Source.* Cambridge, Mass., Massachusetts Institute of Technology, Sloan School of Management, 1966. Another version appears in *Journal of Applied Psychology,* 52(4):272–279, 1968.

Alligood, Elaine C.; Elaine Russo-Martin; and Richard Peterson. "Use Study of Excerpta Medica Abstract Journals: To Drop or Not to Drop?" *Bulletin of the Medical Library Association,* 71(3):251–258, July 1983.

Anderson, Charles R. "Online Ready Reference in the Public Library." In: *Questions and Answers: Strategies for Using the Electronic Reference Collection. Proceedings of the 1987 Clinic on Library Applications of Data Processing.* Edited by Linda C. Smith. Urbana, Ill., University of Illinois, Graduate School of Library and Information Science, 1989, pp. 71–84.

Anderson, James D. "Essential Decisions in Indexing Systems Design." In: *Indexing Specialized Formats and Subjects.* Edited by Hilda Feinberg. Metuchen, N.J., Scarecrow Press, 1983, pp. 1–21.

Ashmole, R. F.; D. E. Smith; and B. T. Stern. "Cost Effectiveness of Current Awareness Sources in the Pharmaceutical Industry." *Journal of the American Society for Information Science,* 24(1):29–39, January/February 1973.

307

Atkinson, Stephen D., and Michael Knee. *Subject Index to Databases Available from Computer Search Service*. Albany, N.Y., State University of New York, University Libraries, 1986. ED 267 825

Austin, Derek. *PRECIS: A Manual of Concept Analysis and Subject Indexing*. 2nd ed. London, Eng., The British Library, 1984.

Bannon, Cynthia. "The Perseus Project." In: *Hypertext/Hypermedia Handbook*. Edited by Emily Berk and Joseph Devlin. New York, McGraw-Hill, 1991, pp. 480–487.

Bar, Jacob. "The Multifile Multidisciplinary (Horizontal) Search Approach—Justification and Principles." *Online Review*, *12*(1):47–58, February 1988.

Barber, John, et al. "Case Studies of the Indexing and Retrieval of Pharmacology Papers." *Information Processing and Management*, *24*(2):141–150, 1988.

Barron, Billy. *The Barron's Guide to Internet Accessible Library Catalogs*. Denton, Tex., University of North Texas, 1992 (available via anonymous FTP on the node FTP.unt.edu).

Bates, Marcia J. "How to Use Information Search Tactics Online." *Online*, *11*(3):47–54, May 1987.

————. "Subject Access in Online Catalogs: a Design Model." *Journal of the American Society for Information Science*, *37*(6):357–376, November 1986.

————. "Idea Tactics." *Journal of the American Society for Information Science*, *30*(5):280–289, September 1979a.

————. "Information Search Tactics." *Journal of the American Society for Information Science*, *30*(4):205–214, July 1979b.

————. "System Meets User: Problems in Matching Subject Search Terms." *Information Processing and Management*, *13*(6):367–375, 1977.

Baxendale, Phyllis B. "Machine-Made Index for Technical Literature—An Experiment." *IBM Journal of Research and Development*, *2*(4):354–361, October 1958.

Belkin, Nicholas J. "Anomalous States of Knowledge as a Basis for Information Retrieval." *Canadian Journal of Information Science*, *5*:133–143, May 1980.

Belkin, Nicholas J., et al. "ASK for Information Retrieval: Part I. Background and Theory." *Journal of Documentation*, *38*(2):61–71, June 1982a.

————. "ASK for Information Retrieval: Part II. Results of a Design Study." *Journal of Documentation*, *38*(3):145–164, September 1982b.

Bellardo, Trudi. "An Investigation of Online Searcher Traits and Their Relationships to Search Outcome." *Journal of the American Society for Information Science*, *36*(4):241–250, July 1985.

Belzer, Jack. "Information Theory as a Measure of Information Content." *Journal of the American Society for Information Science*, *24*(4):300–304, July–August 1973.

Berger, Mary C., and Judith Wanger. "Retrieval, Analysis and Display of Numeric Data." *Drexel Library Quarterly*, *18*(3/4):11–26, Summer/Fall 1982.

Berk, Emily, and Joseph Devlin. "What is Hypertext? In: *Hypertext/Hypermedia Handbook*. Edited by Emily Berk and Joseph Devlin. New York, McGraw Hill, 1991, pp. 3–7.

Bernier, Charles L. "Correlative Indexes. 1. Alphabetical Correlative Indexes." *American Documentation*, *7*(4):283–288, October 1956.

Black, William J. "Knowledge-Based Abstracting." *Online Review*, *14*(5):327–340, October 1990.

Blackshaw, Lyn, and Baruch Fischhoff. "Decision Making in Online Searching." *Journal of the American Society for Information Science, 39*(6):369–389, November 1988.

Blair, David C. *Language and Representation in Information Retrieval.* Amsterdam, Neth., Elsevier Science, 1990.

————. "Full Text Retrieval: Evaluation and Implications." *International Classification, 13*(1):18–23, 1986.

Blair, David C., and M. E. Maron. "An Evaluation of Retrieval Effectiveness for a Full-Text Document System." *Communications of the Association for Computing Machinery, 28*(3):289–299, March 1985.

Borgman, Christine L. "Why Are Online Catalogs Hard to Use? Lessons Learned from Information-Retrieval Studies." *Journal of the American Society for Information Science, 37*(6):387–400, November 1986.

————. "The User's Mental Model of an Information Retrieval System: Effects on Performance." Doctoral dissertation. Palo Alto, Calif., Stanford University, 1984.

Borgman, Christine L.; D. Moghdam; and P. K. Corbett. *Effective Online Searching: A Basic Text.* New York, Marcel Dekker, 1984.

Borko, Harold, and M. Bernick. "Automatic Document Classification." *Journal of the Association for Computing Machinery, 10*:151–162, 1963.

Borko, Harold, and Zorana Ercegovac. "Knowledge-Based Descriptive Cataloging of Cartographic Publications." In: *Annual Review of OCLC Research, July 1988–June 1989.* Dublin, Ohio, OCLC, 1989, pp. 49–50.

Bourne, Charles P. *Characteristics of Coverage by the Bibliography of Agriculture of the Literature Relating to Agricultural Research and Development.* Palo Alto, Calif., Information General Corporation, 1969a. PB 185425

————. *Overlapping Coverage of the Bibliography of Agriculture by Fifteen Other Secondary Sources.* Palo Alto, Calif., Information General Corporation, 1969b. PB 185069

————. "Some User Requirements Stated Quantitatively in Terms of the 90 Percent Library." In: *Electronic Information Handling.* Edited by Allen Kent and Orrin E. Taulbee. Washington, D.C., Spartan Books, 1965, pp. 93–110.

Boyce, Bert R., and John P. McLain. "Entry Point Depth and Online Search Using a Controlled Vocabulary." *Journal of the American Society for Information Science, 40*(4):273–276, July 1989.

Bradford, S. C. *Documentation.* 2nd ed. London, Eng., Crosby Lockwood, 1953.

British Standards Institution. *British Standard Guide to Establishment and Development of Monolingual Thesauri.* London, Eng., British Standards Institution, 1987. BS 5723

————. *Guidelines for the Establishment and Development of Monolingual Thesauri.* London, Eng., British Standards Institution, 1979.

Brittain, J. Michael, and S. A. Roberts. "Rationalization of Secondary Services: Measurement of Coverage of Primary Journals and Overlap Between Services." *Journal of the American Society for Information Science, 31*(3):131–142, May 1980.

Britten, William A. "A Use Statistic for Collection Management: The 80/20 Rule Revisited." *Library Acquisitions: Practice and Theory, 14*(2):183–189, 1990.

Brooks, H. M. "Expert Systems and Intelligent Information Retrieval." *Information Processing and Management, 23*(4):367–382, 1987.

Brown, Steven Allan. "Telefacsimile in Libraries: New Deal in the 1980's." *Library Trends, 37*(3):343–356, Winter 1989.

Bryant, Edward C.; Donald W. King; and P. James Terragno. *Some Technical Notes on Coding Errors*. Bethesda, Md., Westat Research, Inc., 1963. PB 166487

BSO Referral Index: a Subject Index to 36 Data-bases in the DIALOG System. The Hague, Neth., Fédération Internationale de Documentation, 1985.

Buchanan, Lori E.; Anne May Berwind; and Don Carlin. "Optical Disk-Based Periodical Indexes for Undergraduates." *College and Research Libraries News*, 50(1):10–14, January 1989.

Burgin, Robert. "The Effect of Indexing Exhaustivity on Retrieval Performance." *Information Processing and Management*, 27(6):623–628, 1991.

Bush, Vannevar. "As We May Think." *The Atlantic Monthly*, 176(1):101–108, July 1945.

Busha, Charles H., and Stephen P. Harter. *Research Methods in Librarianship: Techniques and Interpretation*. New York, Academic Press, 1980.

Byler, Anne Meyer, and Mary Ravenhall. "Using Dialindex for the Identification of Online Databases Relevant to Urban and Regional Planning." *Online Review*, 12(2):119–133, April 1988.

Calkins, Mary L. "Free Text or Controlled Vocabulary? A Case History Step-by-Step Analysis. . .Plus Other Aspects of Search Strategy." *Database*, 3(2):53–67, June 1980.

Campbell, Donald T., and Julian C. Stanley. *Experimental and Quasi-Experimental Design for Research*. Chicago, Ill., Rand-McNally, 1963.

Carrow, Deborah, and Joan Nugent. "Comparison of Free-Text and Index Search Abilities in an Operating Information System." In: *Proceedings of the American Society for Information Science, 40th Annual Meeting, Chicago, Ill., September 26–October 1, 1977*. Vol. 14. White Plains, N.Y., Knowledge Industry Publications, 1977. (On microfiche card 2 of 10, E8-F3.)

Cawkell, A. E. "Selected Aspects of Image Processing and Management: Review and Future Prospects." *Journal of Information Science*, 18(3):179–192, 1992.

Chamis, Alice Y. "Selection of Online Databases Using Switching Vocabularies." *Journal of the American Society for Information Science*, 39(3):217–218, May 1988.

Cleverdon, Cyril W. "Optimizing Convenient Online Access to Bibliographic Databases." *Information Services and Use*, 4(1–2):37–47, April 1984.

————. *Report on the Testing and Analysis of an Investigation into the Comparative Efficiency of Indexing Systems*. Cranfield, Eng., College of Aeronautics, 1962.

Cleverdon, Cyril W.; Jack Mills; and E. Michael Keen. *Factors Determining the Performance of Indexing Systems*. 3 vols. Cranfield, Eng., College of Aeronautics, 1966.

Cochrane, Pauline A. *Improving LCSH for Use in Online Catalogs*. Littleton, Colo., Libraries Unlimited, 1986.

Collette, A. D., and J. A. Price. "A Cost/Benefit Evaluation of Online Interactive Bibliographic Searching in a Research and Engineering Organization." In: *The Value of Information: Collection of Papers Presented at the Sixth Mid-Year Meeting, American Society for Information Science, Syracuse University, Syracuse, N.Y., May 19–21, 1977*. Washington, D.C., American Society for Information Science, 1977, pp. 24–34.

Cooper, Marianne. "Current Information Dissemination: Ideas and Practices." *Journal of Chemical Documentation*, 8(4):207–218, November 1968.

Cooper, William S. "On Selecting a Measure of Retrieval Effectiveness." *Journal of the American Society for Information Science, 24*(2):87–100, March–April 1973.

─────── . "A Definition of Relevance for Information Retrieval." *Information Storage and Retrieval, 7*(1):19–37, June 1971.

─────── . "Is Interindexer Consistency a Hobgoblin?" *American Documentation, 20*(3): 268–278, July 1969.

Courrier, Yves. "SYNTOL." In: *Encyclopedia of Library and Information Science.* Vol. 29. Edited by Allen Kent et al. New York, Marcel Dekker, 1980, pp. 357–381.

Croft, W. Bruce; Howard R. Turtle; and David D. Lewis. "The Use of Phrases and Structured Queries in Information Retrieval." In: *Proceedings of the Fourteenth Annual International ACM/SIGIR Conference on Research and Development in Information Retrieval, 13–16 October, 1991, Chicago, Illinois.* Edited by A. Bookstein, Y. Chiaramella, G. Salton, and V. V. Raghavan. New York, Association for Computing Machinery, 1991, pp. 32–45.

Crum, Norman J. "The Librarian-Customer Relationship: Dynamics of Filling Requests for Information." *Special Libraries, 60*(5):269–277, May–June 1969.

Cuadra Associates. *Directory of Online Databases.* Vol. 13, No. 2. Edited by K. Y. Marcaccio. Detroit, Mich., Cuadra/Gale, 1992.

Cuadra, Carlos A., and Robert V. Katter. "Opening the Black Box of 'Relevance.'" *Journal of Documentation, 23*(4):291–303, December 1967a.

─────── . "The Relevance of Relevance Assessment." In: *Proceedings of the American Documentation Institute.* Vol. 4. Washington, D.C., Thompson Book Company, 1967b, pp. 95–99.

Cuadra, Carlos A.; Robert V. Katter; Emory H. Holmes; and Everett M. Wallace. *Experimental Studies of Relevance Judgments: Final Report.* 3 vols. Santa Monica, Calif., System Development Corporation, 1967.

Cutter, Charles A. *Rules for a Dictionary Catalog.* Washington, D.C., U.S. Government Printing Office, 1876.

Dana, John Cotton. *Libraries: Addresses and Essays.* White Plains, N.Y., H. W. Wilson Co., 1916.

Das Gupta, Padmini. "Boolean Interpretations of Conjunctions for Document Retrieval." *Journal of the American Society for Information Science, 38*(4):245–254, July 1987.

Davies, Roy. "Expert Systems and Cataloguing: New Wine in Old Bottles?" In *Expert Systems in Libraries.* Edited by Forbes Gibb. London, Eng., Taylor Graham, 1986, pp. 67–82.

Davison, P. S., and D. A. R. Matthews. "Assessment of Information Services." *Aslib Proceedings, 21*(7):280–283, July 1969.

Dialog Information Services, Inc. *Search Strategy Seminar.* Palo Alto, Calif., Dialog Information Services, Inc., 1983.

Diaz, Lily. "PathMAC: An Alternative Approach to Medical Education." In: *Hypertext/Hypermedia Handbook.* Edited by Emily Berk and Joseph Devlin. New York, McGraw Hill, 1991, pp. 488–492.

Dillon, Martin, and Ann S. Gray. "FASIT: A Fully Automatic Syntactically Based Indexing System." *Journal of the American Society for Information Science, 34*(2):99–108, March 1983.

Dillon, Martin, and Laura McDonald. "Fully Automatic Book Indexing." *Journal of Documentation, 39*(3):135–154, September 1983.

Doszkocs, Tamas E. "Natural Language Processing in Information Retrieval." *Journal of the American Society for Information Science, 37*(4):191–196, July 1986.

————. "CITE NLM: Natural-Language Searching in an Online Catalog." *Information Technology and Libraries, 2*(4):364–380, December 1983.

————. "AID, an Associative Interactive Dictionary for Online Searching." *Online Review, 2*(2):163–173, June 1978.

Dougherty, Richard M., and Carol Hughes. *Preferred Futures for Libraries: A Summary of Six Workshops with University Provosts and Library Directors.* Mountain View, Calif., Research Libraries Group, 1991.

Dowlin, Kenneth E. "The Neographic Library." In: *Libraries and the Future: Essays on the Library in the Twenty-first Century.* Edited by F. W. Lancaster. Binghampton, N.Y., Haworth Press, forthcoming 1993.

Doyle, Lauren B. "Semantic Road Maps for Literature Searchers." *Journal of the Association for Computing Machinery, 8*(4):553–578, October 1961.

Dykstra, Mary. "Can Subject Headings Be Saved?" *Library Journal, 113*(15):55–58, September 15, 1988a.

————. "LC Subject Headings Disguised as a Thesaurus." *Library Journal, 113*(4): 42–46, March 1, 1988b.

Dym, Eleanor D. "Relevance Predictability: I. Investigation Background and Procedures." In: *Electronic Handling of Information: Testing and Evaluation.* Edited by Allen Kent et al. Washington, D.C., Thompson Book Co., 1967, pp. 175–185.

Edmundson, H. P. "New Methods in Automatic Extracting." *Journal of the Association for Computing Machinery, 16*(2):264–285, April 1969.

Eisenberg, Michael, and Carol Berry. "Order Effects: a Study of the Possible Influence of Presentation Order on User Judgments of Document Relevance." *Journal of the American Society for Information Science, 39*(5):293–300, September 1988.

Elchesen, Dennis R. "Cost-Effectiveness Comparison of Manual and On-Line Retrospective Bibliographic Searching." *Journal of the American Society for Information Science, 29*(2):56–66, March 1978.

El-Shooky, E., et al. *Selecting the Most Appropriate Databases to Answer Industrial Information Requests.* The Hague, Neth., International Federation for Information and Documentation, 1988.

Estabrook, Leigh Stewart. "Valuing a Document Delivery System." *RQ, 26*(1):58–62, Fall 1986.

Evans, David A., et al. "Automatic Indexing Using Selective NLP and First-Order Thesauri." In: *Proceedings of RIAO 1991—Intelligent Text and Image Handling, 2–5 April 1991, Barcelona, Spain.* Edited by A. Lichnerowicz. Amsterdam, Neth., Elsevier, 1991, pp. 624–643.

Fagan, Joel L. *Experiments in Automatic Phrase Indexing for Document Retrieval: A Comparison of Syntactic and Non-Syntactic Methods.* Ithaca, N.Y., Cornell University, 1988.

Fairthorne, R. A. Unpublished notes. 1965.

Fenichel, Carol Hansen. "Online Searching: Measures that Discriminate Among Users with Different Types of Experiences." *Journal of the American Society for Information Science, 32*(1):23–32, January 1981.

————. "An Examination of the Relationship Between Searching Behavior and Searcher Background." *Online Review, 4*(4):341–347, December 1980a.

———. "The Process of Searching Online Bibliographic Databases: a Review of Research." *Library Research,* 2(2):107–127, Summer 1980b.

Fenly, Charles. "Technical Services Processes as Models for Assessing Expert System Suitability and Benefits." In: *Artificial Intelligence and Expert Systems: Will They Change the Library? Proceedings of the 27th Annual Clinic on Library Applications of Data Processing.* Edited by F. W. Lancaster and Linda C. Smith. Urbana, Ill., University of Illinois, Graduate School of Library and Information Science, 1992, pp. 50–66.

Fidel, Raya. "Who Needs Controlled Vocabulary?" *Special Libraries, 83*(1):1–9, Winter 1992.

———. "Searchers' Selection of Search Keys." *Journal of the American Society for Information Science, 42*(7):490–527, August 1991.

———. "Writing Abstracts for Free-Text Searching." *Journal of Documentation, 42*(1):11–21, March 1986.

———. "Individual Variability in Online Search Behavior." In: *Proceedings of the 48th American Society for Information Science Annual Meeting, Las Vegas, Nevada, October 20–24, 1985.* Vol. 22. Edited by Carol A. Parkhurst. White Plains, N.Y., Knowledge Industry Publications, 1985, pp. 69–72.

———. "Online Searching Styles: a Case-Study-Based Model of Searching Behavior." *Journal of the American Society for Information Science, 35*(4):211–221, July 1984.

Field, B. J. "Towards Automatic Indexing: Automatic Assignment of Controlled-Language Indexing and Classification from Free Indexing." *Journal of Documentation, 31*(4):246–265, December 1975.

Fitzgerald, Evelyn L. C. "The Value of the Search Request Form in the Negotiation Process Between Requester and Librarian." Doctoral dissertation. Urbana, Ill., University of Illinois, Graduate School of Library and Information Science, 1981.

Flowerdew, A. D. J., and C. M. E. Whitehead. *Cost-Effectiveness and Cost Benefit Analysis in Information Science.* London, Eng., London School of Economics and Political Science, 1974. OSTI Report No. 5206

Foskett, D. J. "A Note on the Concept of 'Relevance.'" *Information Storage and Retrieval, 8*(2):77–78, April 1972.

———. "Classification and Indexing in the Social Sciences." *Aslib Proceedings, 22*(3):90–101, March 1970.

Fox, Edward A.; Bernard Rous; and Gary Marchionini. "ACM's Hypertext and Hypermedia Publishing Projects." In: *Hypertext/Hypermedia Handbook.* Edited by Emily Berk and Joseph Devlin. New York, McGraw Hill, 1991, pp. 460–464.

Fox, Edward A., et al. "Building a Large Thesaurus for Information Retrieval." In: *Proceedings of the Second Conference on Applied Natural Language Processing, Austin, Texas, February 9–12, 1988.* Morristown, N.J., Association for Computational Linguistics, 1988, pp. 101–108.

Fussler, Herman H., and Julian L. Simon. *Patterns in the Use of Books in Large Research Libraries.* 2nd ed. Chicago, Ill., University of Chicago Press, 1969.

Gardin, Jean Claude. *SYNTOL.* New Brunswick, N.J., Rutgers, the State University, 1965.

Gauch, Susan, and John B. Smith. "An Expert System for Automatic Query Reformation." *Journal of the American Society for Information Science, 44*(3):124–136, 1993.

Geller, Valerie, and Michael E. Lesk. "An On-Line Library Catalog Offering Menu and Keyword User Interfaces." In: *Proceedings of the Fourth National Online Meeting,*

New York, April 12–14, 1983. Medford, N.J., Learned Information, 1983, pp. 159–165.

Goffman, William. "On Relevance as a Measure." *Information Storage and Retrieval,* 2(3):201–203, December 1964.

Goffman, William, and V. A. Newill. *Methodology for Test and Evaluation of Information Retrieval Systems*. Cleveland, Ohio, Case Western Reserve University, Center for Documentation and Communication Research, 1964.

Goldhor, Herbert. *An Introduction to Scientific Research in Librarianship*. Urbana, Ill., University of Illinois, Graduate School of Library Science, 1972. Graduate School of Library Science Monograph No. 12

Graham, Deborah L. "Simultaneous Remote Search." *Bulletin of the Medical Library Association, 68*(4):370–371, October 1980.

Greenberg, Bette, et al. "Evaluation of a Clinical Medical Librarian Program at the Yale Medical Library." *Bulletin of the Medical Library Association, 66*(3):319–326, July 1978.

Hansen, Kathleen A. "The Effect of Presearch Experience on the Success of Naive (End-User) Searches." *Journal of the American Society for Information Science, 37*(5):315–318, September 1986.

Harmon, Donna. "The DARPA TIPSTER Project." *SIGIR Forum, 26*(2):26–28, 1992.

Harter, Stephen P. "Detrimental Effects of Searching with Precoordinated Terms." *Online Review, 12*(4):205–210, August 1988.

————. *Online Information Retrieval: Concepts, Principles and Techniques*. Orlando, Fla., Academic Press, 1986.

————. "Online Searching Styles: an Exploratory Study." *College and Research Libraries, 45*(4):249–258, July 1984.

Havener, W. Michael. "Answering Ready Reference Questions: Print Versus Online." *Online, 14*(1):22–28, January 1990.

Hawkins, Donald T. "Applications of Artificial Intelligence (AI) and Expert Systems for Online Searching." *Online, 12*(1):31–43, January 1988.

Heaps, Doreen M., and Paul Sorenson. "An On-Line Personal Documentation System." In: *Proceedings of the American Society for Information Science, 31st Annual Meeting, Columbus, Ohio, October 20–24, 1968*. Vol. 5. New York, Greenwood Publishing, 1968, pp. 201–207.

Heller, Martin. "Future Documents." *Byte, 16*(5):126–129, 132, 134–135, May 1991.

Hirschman, Lynette; Ralph Grishman; and Naomi Sager. "Grammatically-Based Automatic Word Class Formation." *Information Processing and Management, 11*(1/2):39–57, June 1975.

Hitch, Charles J., and Roland McKean. *The Economics of Defense for the Nuclear Age*. Cambridge, Mass., Harvard University, 1960.

Holm, B. E., and L. E. Rasmussen. "Development of a Technical Thesaurus." *American Documentation, 12*(3):184–190, July 1961.

Horton, Forest W., Jr. "Human Capital Investment: Key to the Information Age." *Information and Records Management, 16*(7):38–39, July 1982.

Howard, Helen. "Measures that Discriminate Among Online Searchers with Different Training and Experience." *Online Review, 6*(4):315–327, August 1982.

Hsieh-Yee, Ingrid. "The Search Tactics of Novice and Experienced Searchers." Doctoral dissertation. Madison, Wis., University of Wisconsin, Madison, 1990.

Hu, Chengren. "An Evaluation of a Gateway System for Automated Online Database Selection." In: *Proceedings of the Ninth National Online Meeting, New York, N.Y., May 10–12, 1988*. Medford, N.J., Learned Information, 1988, pp. 107–114.

————. "An Evaluation of Online Database Selection by a Gateway System with Artificial Intelligence Techniques." Doctoral dissertation. Urbana, Ill., University of Illinois, Graduate School of Library and Information Science, 1987.

Huang, Samuel T., and Terrence J. McHale. "A Cost-Effectiveness Comparison Between Print and Online Versions of the Same Frequently-Used Sources of Business and Financial Information." In: *Proceedings of the Eleventh National Online Meeting, New York, N.Y., May 1–3, 1990*. Edited by Martha E. Williams. Medford, N.J., Learned Information, 1990, pp. 161–168.

Hulme, E. Wyndham. "Principles of Book Classification: An Introduction." *Library Association Record, 13*:354–356, 1911a.

————. "Principles of Book Classification: Chapter II. Principles in Book Classification." *Library Association Record, 13*:389–394, 1911b.

————. "Principles of Book Classification: Chapter III. On the Definition of Class Headings, and the Natural Limit to the Extension of Book Classification." *Library Association Record, 13*:444–449, 1911c.

Humphrey, Susanne M. "Interactive Knowledge-Based Systems for Improved Subject Analysis and Retrieval." In: *Artificial Intelligence and Expert Systems: Will They Change the Library? Proceedings of the 27th Annual Clinic on Library Applications of Data Processing*. Edited by F. W. Lancaster and Linda C. Smith. Urbana, Ill., University of Illinois, Graduate School of Library and Information Science, 1992, pp. 81–117.

Humphrey, Susanne M., and Nancy E. Miller. "Knowledge-Based Indexing of the Medical Literature: The Indexing Aid Project." *Journal of the American Society for Information Science, 38*(3):184–196, May 1987.

Hutchins, W. J. "The Concept of 'Aboutness' in Subject Indexing." *Aslib Proceedings, 30*(5):172–181, May 1978.

Ide, E., and Gerard Salton. "Interactive Search Strategies and Dynamic File Organization." In: *The SMART Retrieval System—Experiments in Automatic Document Processing*. Edited by Gerard Salton. Englewood Cliffs, N.J., Prentice Hall, 1971, pp. 373–393.

Ingwersen, Peter. "Search Procedures in the Library—Analysed from the Cognitive Point of View." *Journal of Documentation, 38*(3):165–191, September 1982.

International Organization for Standardization. *Guidelines for the Establishment and Development of Monolingual Thesauri*. Geneva, Switzerland, ISO, 1986. ISO 2788

Janes, Joseph W. "Relevance Judgments and the Incremental Presentation of Document Representations." *Information Processing and Management, 27*(6):629–646, 1991.

Jeng, Ling-Hwey. "An Expert System for Determining Title Proper in Descriptive Cataloging: A Conceptual Model." *Cataloging and Classification Quarterly, 7*(2):55–70, Winter 1986.

Jensen, Rebecca J.; Herbert O. Asbury; and Radford G. King. "Costs and Benefits to Industry of Online Literature Searches." *Special Libraries, 71*(7):291–299, July 1980.

Jones, Kevin P. "Problems Associated with the Use of Compound Words in Thesauri with Special Reference to BS 5723:1979." *Journal of Documentation, 37*(2):53–68, June 1981.

————. "Compound Words: A Problem in Post Coordinate Retrieval Systems." *Journal of the American Society for Information Science,* 22(4):242–250, July/August 1971.

Katz, William. "The Reference Interview and Levels of Service." In: *Introduction to Reference Work.* Vol. 2. New York, McGraw Hill, 1987, pp. 39–58.

Katzer, Jeffrey, et al. "A Study of the Overlap Among Document Representations." *Information Technology: Research and Development,* 1(4):261–274, October 1982.

Keen, E. Michael. "Evaluation Parameters." In: *The SMART Retrieval System: Experiments in Automatic Document Processing.* Edited by Gerard Salton. Englewood Cliffs, N.J., Prentice Hall, 1971, pp. 74-111.

————. *Measures and Averaging Methods Used in Performance Testing of Indexing Systems.* Cranfield, Eng., Aslib Cranfield Research Project, 1966.

Kemp, D. A. "Relevance, Pertinence and Information System Development." *Information Storage and Retrieval,* 10(2):37–49, February 1974.

Kent, Allen, et al. "Relevance Predictability in Information Retrieval Systems." *Methods of Information in Medicine,* 6(2):45–51, April 1967.

————. "Machine Literature Searching. VIII. Operational Criteria for Designing Information Retrieval Systems." *American Documentation,* 6(2):93–101, April 1955.

Kilgour, Frederick G. "The Metamorphosis of Libraries During the Foreseeable Future." In: *Libraries and the Future: Essays on the Library in the Twenty-first Century.* Edited by F. W. Lancaster. Binghampton, N.Y., Haworth Press, forthcoming 1993.

King, David N. "The Contribution of Hospital Library Information Services to Clinical Care: a Study in Eight Hospitals." *Bulletin of the Medical Library Association,* 75(4):291–301, October 1987.

King, Donald W. *Comments on the Meaning and Interpretation of Consistency Measures for Evaluating Indexing Processes.* Bethesda, Md., Westat Research, Inc., 1967.

————. "Evaluation of Coordinate Index Systems During File Development." *Journal of Chemical Documentation,* 5(2):96–99, May 1965.

King, Donald W., and Edward C. Bryant. *The Evaluation of Information Services and Products.* Arlington, Va., Information Resources Press, 1971.

King, Donald W., et al. *The Value of the Energy Data Base.* Rockville, Md., King Research, Inc., 1982. DOE/OR/11232-1-(DE82014250)

King, Geraldine B. "The Reference Interview." *RQ,* 12(2):157–160, Winter 1972.

Klingbiel, Paul H. "A Technique for Machine-Aided Indexing." *Information Storage and Retrieval,* 9(9):477–494, September 1973.

Knapp, Sara D. "The Reference Interview in the Computer-Based Setting." *RQ,* 17(4): 320–324, Summer 1978.

Kochen, M. "Organizing Knowledge for Coping with Needs." In: *Ordering Systems for Global Information Networks: Proceedings of the Third International Study Conference on Classification Research, Bombay, India, 6–11 January 1975.* Edited by A. Neelameghan. Bangalore, India, FID/CR and Sarada Ranganathan Endowment for Library Science, 1979, pp. 142–149.

Konings, C. A. G. "Comparison and Evaluation of Nine Bibliographies/Bibliographic Databases in the Field of Computer Science." *Online Review,* 9(2):121–133, April 1985.

Kramer, Joseph. "How to Survive in Industry: Cost Justifying Library Services." *Special Libraries,* 62(11):487–489, November 1971.

Kremer, Jeannette M. "Perspectives for Information Services and Professionals in Brazil." In: *Libraries and the Future: Essays on the Library in the Twenty-first Century*. Edited by F. W. Lancaster. Binghampton, N.Y., Haworth Press, forthcoming 1993.

Krol, E. *The Whole Internet: User's Guide and Catalog*. Sebastopol, Calif., O'Reilly and Associates, 1992.

Kurzweil, Raymond. "Machine Intelligence: The First 80 years." *Library Journal, 116*(13):69–71, August 1991.

Lancaster, F. W. *If You Want to Evaluate Your Library. . .* 2nd ed. Urbana, Ill., University of Illinois, Graduate School of Library and Information Science, 1993a.

————, ed. *Libraries and the Future: Essays on the Library in the Twenty-first Century*. Binghampton, N.Y., Haworth Press, forthcoming 1993b.

————. *Indexing and Abstracting in Theory and Practice*. Urbana, Ill., University of Illinois, Graduate School of Library and Information Science, 1991.

————. *Vocabulary Control for Information Retrieval*. 2nd ed. Arlington, Va., Information Resources Press, 1986.

————. "The Paperless Society Revisited." *American Libraries, 16*(8):553–555, September 1985.

————. *Libraries and Librarians in an Age of Electronics*. Arlington, Va., Information Resources Press, 1982.

————. "Some Considerations Relating to the Cost-Effectiveness of Online Services in Libraries." *Aslib Proceedings, 33*(1):10–14, January 1981.

————. *Toward Paperless Information Systems*. New York, Academic Press, 1978.

————. "The Information Services Librarian." *Australian Special Libraries News, 7*(6):139–149, November 1974a.

————. "A Study of Current Awareness Publications in the Neurosciences." *Journal of Documentation, 30*(3):255–272, September 1974b.

————. *Vocabulary Control for Information Retrieval*. Arlington, Va., Information Resources Press, 1972.

————. "Aftermath of an Evaluation." *Journal of Documentation, 27*(1):1–10, March 1971.

————. *Evaluation of the MEDLARS Demand Search Service*. Bethesda, Md., National Library of Medicine, 1968a.

————. Letter to the Editor. *American Documentation, 19*(2):206, April 1968b.

Lancaster, F. W., and Ja-Lih Lee. "Bibliometric Techniques Applied to Issues Management: A Case Study." *Journal of the American Society for Information Science, 36*(6):389–397, November 1985.

Lancaster, F. W., and Jack Mills. "Testing Indexes and Index Language Devices: The Aslib Cranfield Project." *American Documentation, 15*(1):4–13, January 1964.

Lancaster, F. W., et al. "Searching Databases on CD-ROM: Comparison of the Results of End User Searching with Results from Two Modes of Searching by Skilled Intermediaries." Submitted for publication in *RQ*, 1993.

————. *Searching Databases on CD-ROM: Comparison of the Results of End User Searching with Results from Two Modes of Searching by Skilled Intermediaries*. A report to the Council on Library Resources. Urbana, Ill., University of Illinois, Graduate School of Library and Information Science, 1992.

————. "Identifying Barriers to Effective Subject Access in Library Catalogs." *Library Resources and Technical Services, 35*(4):377–391, October 1991.

Landau, Herbert B. "International Ownership in the U.S. Information Marketplace: Myths, Paradoxes, and Ironies." *Information Services and Use*, 8(2/3/4):63–71, 1988.

Larson, Ray R. "Evaluation of Advanced Retrieval Techniques in an Experimental Online Catalog." *Journal of the American Society for Information Science*, 43(1):34–53, 1992.

Ledwith, Robert. "On the Difficulties of Applying the Results of Information Retrieval to Aid in the Searching of Large Scientific Databases." *Information Processing and Management*, 28(4):451–455, July–August 1992.

Lefever, Maureen; Barbara Freedman; and Louise Schultz. "Managing an Uncontrolled Vocabulary Ex Post Facto." *Journal of the American Society for Information Science*, 23(6):339–342, November/December 1972.

Leonard, Lawrence E. "Inter-Indexer Consistency and Retrieval Effectiveness: Measurement of Relationships." Doctoral dissertation. Urbana, Ill., University of Illinois, Graduate School of Library Science, 1975.

Lesk, Michael E. "Word-Word Associations in Document Retrieval Systems." *American Documentation*, 20(1):27–38, 1969.

Lesk, Michael E., and Gerard Salton. "Interactive Search and Retrieval Methods Using Automatic Information Displays." In: *AFIPS Conference Proceedings, 1969 Spring Joint Computer Conference, Boston, Mass., May 14–16, 1969*. Montvale, N.J., AFIPS Press, 1969, pp. 435–446.

––––––––. "Relevance Assessments and Retrieval System Evaluation." *Information Storage and Retrieval*, 4(4):343–359, December 1968.

Lewis, D. D., and W. B. Croft. "Term Clustering of Syntactic Phrases." In: *Proceedings of the 13th International Conference on Research and Development in Information Retrieval, 5–7 September 1990, Brussels, Belgium*. Edited by Jean-Luc Vidick. New York, Association for Computing Machinery, 1990, pp. 385–404.

Lewis, David W. "Inventing the Electronic University." *College and Research Libraries*, 49(4):291–304, July 1988.

Lilley, Oliver L. "Evaluation of the Subject Catalog." *American Documentation*, 5(2):41–60, April 1954.

Line, Maurice B. "Libraries and Information Services in 25 Years' Time: A British Perspective." In: *Libraries and the Future: Essays on the Library in the Twenty-first Century*. Edited by F. W. Lancaster. Binghampton, N.Y., Haworth Press, forthcoming 1993.

––––––––. "The Ability of a University Library to Provide Books Wanted by Researchers." *Journal of Librarianship*, 5(1):37–51, January 1973.

Line, Maurice B., and A. Sandison. "'Obsolescence' and Changes in the Use of Literature with Time." *Journal of Documentation*, 30(3):283–350, September 1974.

Littleford, Alan. "Artificial Intelligence and Hypermedia." In: *Hypertext/Hypermedia Handbook*. Edited by Emily Berk and Joseph Devlin. New York, McGraw Hill, 1991, pp. 357–378.

Logan, Elisabeth L. "Cognitive Styles and Online Behavior of Novice Searchers." *Information Processing and Management*, 26(4):503–510, 1990.

Lottor, M. *Internet Growth (1981–1991)*. Palo Alto, Calif., Network Information Systems Center, SRI International, 1992.

Lucky, Robert W. *Silicon Dreams: Information, Man, and Machine*. New York, St. Martin's Press, 1989.

Luhn, Hans Peter. *Selective Dissemination of New Scientific Information with the Aid of Electronic Processing Equipment*. Yorktown Heights, N.Y., IBM Advanced Systems Development Division, 1959.

————. "The Automatic Creation of Literature Abstracts." *IBM Journal of Research and Development*, 2(2):159–165, April 1958.

————. "A Statistical Approach to Mechanized Encoding and Searching of Literary Information." *IBM Journal of Research and Development*, 1(4):309–317, October 1957.

Lynch, Mary Jo. "Reference Interviews in Public Libraries." *Library Quarterly, 48*(2): 119–142, April 1978.

Magson, M. S. "Techniques for the Measurement of Cost–Benefit in Information Centers." *Aslib Proceedings, 25*(5):164–185, May 1973.

Mandel, Carol A. "Trade-offs: Quantifying Quality in Library Technical Services." *Journal of Academic Librarianship, 14*(4):214–220, September 1988.

Mandersloot, Wim G. B.; Eleanor M. B. Douglas; and Neville Spicer. "Thesaurus Control—the Selection, Grouping and Cross-Referencing of Terms for Inclusion in a Coordinate Index Word List." *Journal of the American Society for Information Science, 21*(1):49–57, January/February 1970.

Marcaccio, Kathleen Young; Juli Adams; and Martha E. Williams, eds. *Computer-Readable Databases: A Directory and Data Sourcebook*. 6th ed. Detroit, Mich., Gale Research, 1990.

Marchetti, Pier Giorgio, and Nicholas J. Belkin. "Interactive Online Search Formulation Support." In: *Proceedings of the Twelfth National Online Meeting, New York, N.Y., May 7–9, 1991*. Edited by Martha E. Williams. Medford, N.Y., Learned Information, 1991, pp. 237–243.

Marcus, Richard S., and Fred J. Reintjes. *Computer Interface for User Access to Heterogeneous Information Retrieval Systems*. Cambridge, Mass., MIT Electronic Systems Laboratory, 1977. (ESL-R-739)

Marcus, Richard S.; Alan R. Benenfeld; and Peter Kugel. "The User Interface for the Intrex Retrieval System." In: *Interactive Bibliographic Search: The User/Computer Interface*. Edited by Donald E. Walker. Montvale, N.J., AFIPS Press, 1971, pp. 159–201.

Markey, Karen. "Interindexer Consistency Tests: A Literature Review and Report of a Test of Consistency in Indexing Visual Materials." *Library and Information Science Research, 6*(2):155–177, April/June 1984a.

————. *Subject Searching in Library Catalogs: Before and After the Introduction of Online Catalogs*. Dublin, Ohio, OCLC, Inc., 1984b.

————. "Levels of Question Formulation in Negotiation of Information Need During the Online Presearch Interview: a Proposed Model." *Information Processing and Management, 17*(5):215–225, 1981.

Markey, Karen, and Pauline Cochrane. *ONTAP: Online Training and Practice Manual for ERIC Data Base Searchers*. 2nd ed. Syracuse, N.Y., Syracuse University, ERIC Clearinghouse on Information Resources, 1981.

Markey, Karen; Pauline Atherton; and Claudia Newton. "An Analysis of Controlled Vocabulary and Free Text Search Statements in Online Searches." *Online Review, 4*(3):225–236, September 1980.

Maron, M. E. "On Indexing, Retrieval and the Meaning of About." *Journal of the American Society for Information Science,* 28(1):38–43, January 1977.

Marron, Harvey. "On Costing Information Services." In: *Proceedings of the American Society for Information Science, 32nd Annual Meeting, San Francisco, Calif., October 1–4, 1969.* Vol. 6. Edited by Jeanne B. North. Westport, Conn., Greenwood Publishing, 1969, pp. 515–520.

Martyn, John. "Tests on Abstracts Journals: Coverage, Overlap, and Indexing." *Journal of Documentation,* 23(1):45–70, March 1967.

———. "Unintentional Duplication of Research." *New Scientist,* 21(377):338, February 6, 1964.

Martyn, John, and F. W. Lancaster. *Investigative Methods in Library and Information Science.* Arlington, Va., Information Resources Press, 1981.

Martyn, John, and Margaret Slater. "Tests on Abstracts Journals." *Journal of Documentation,* 20(4):212–235, December 1964.

Martyn, John; Peter Vickers; and Mary Feeney, eds. *Information UK 2000.* London, Eng., Bowker-Saur, 1990.

Marx, Gary T., and Sanford Sherizen. "Ethical Issues: Monitoring on the Job." In: *Computers in the Human Context.* Edited by Tom Forester. Cambridge, Mass., MIT Press, 1989, pp. 397–406.

Mason, Donald. "PPBS: Application to an Industrial Information and Library Service." *Journal of Librarianship,* 4(2):91–105, April 1972.

Mathis, Betty A.; James E. Rush; and Carol E. Young. "Improvement of Automatic Abstracts by the Use of Structural Analysis." *Journal of the American Society for Information Science,* 24(2):101–109, March/April 1973.

Matthews, Joseph R.; Gary S. Lawrence; and Douglas K. Ferguson. *Using Online Catalogs: A Nationwide Survey.* New York, Neal-Schuman, 1983.

McCarthy, Martin V. "InfoMaster: a Powerful Information Retrieval Service for Business." *Online,* 10(6):53–58, November 1986.

McCue, Janice H. *Online Searching in Public Libraries: a Comparative Study of Performance.* Metuchen, N.J., Scarecrow Press, 1988.

McKinin, Emma Jean, et al. "The Medline/Full-Text Research Project." *Journal of the American Society for Information Science,* 42(4):297–307, May 1991.

Meadows, Donella H., et al. *The Limits to Growth.* New York, Universal Books, 1972.

Metzler, Douglas P. "Artificial Intelligence: What Will They Think of Next?" In: *Artificial Intelligence and Expert Systems: Will They Change the Library? Proceedings of the 27th Annual Clinic on Library Applications of Data Processing.* Edited by F. W. Lancaster and Linda C. Smith. Urbana, Ill., University of Illinois, Graduate School of Library and Information Science, 1992, pp. 2–49.

Meyer, Daniel E., and Den Ruiz. "End-User Selection of Databases – Part I: Science/Technology/Medicine." *Database,* 13(3):21–29, June 1990a.

———. "End-User Selection of Databases – Part II: Business/Law." *Database,* 13(4):35–42, August 1990b.

———. "End-User Selection of Databases – Part III: Social Science/Arts & Humanities." *Database,* 13(5):59–64, October 1990c.

Milstead, Jessica. *Subject Access Systems: Alternatives in Design.* Orlando, Fla., Academic Press, 1984.

Mitchell, Maurice, and Laverne M. Saunders. "The Virtual Library: An Agenda for the 1990s." *Computers in Libraries, 11*(4):8, 10–11, April 1991.

Molholt, Patricia. "Libraries as Bridges: Librarians as Builders." In: *Libraries and the Future: Essays on the Library in the Twenty-first Century.* Edited by F. W. Lancaster. Binghampton, N.Y., Haworth Press, forthcoming 1993.

Mondschein, Lawrence G. "SDI Use and Productivity in the Corporate Research Environment." *Special Libraries, 81*(4):265–279, Fall 1990.

Morris, A.; G. Tseng; and G. Newham. "The Selection of Online Databases and Hosts— an Expert System Approach." In: *Online Information 88: 12th International Online Information Meeting, London, 6–8 December 1988. Proceedings.* Vol. 1. Oxford, Eng., Learned Information, 1988, pp. 139–148.

Morrison, Margaret. "The NISO Common Command Language." *Online, 13*(4):46–52, July 1989.

Mueller, M. W. "Time, Cost and Value Factors in Information Retrieval." Paper presented at the IBM Information Systems Conference, Poughkeepsie, N.Y., September 21–23, 1959.

Mylonas, Elli. "An Interface to Classical Greek Civilization." *Journal of the American Society for Information Science, 43*(2):192–201, 1992.

Neelameghan, A. "Libraries and Information Services in Third World Countries." In: *Libraries and the Future: Essays on the Library in the Twenty-first Century.* Edited by F. W. Lancaster. Binghampton, N.Y., Haworth Press, forthcoming 1993.

Nelson, Theodor H. "Getting It Out of Our System." In: *Information Retrieval: A Critical View.* Edited by George Schecter. Washington, D.C., Thompson Book Co., 1967, pp. 191–210.

Nicholas, David; Gertrud Erbach; and Kevin Harris. "Online: Views on Costs and Cost-Effectiveness." *Journal of Information Science, 13*(2):109–115, 1987.

Nicholls, Paul, and Ria Van Den Elshout. "Survey of Databases Available on CD-ROM: Types, Availability, and Content." *Database, 13*(1):18–23, February 1990.

Niehoff, Robert, and Greg Mack. "The Vocabulary Switching System. Description of Evaluation Studies." *International Classification, 12*(1):2–6, 1985.

Nielsen, Jakob. "The Art of Navigating Through Hypertext." *Communications of the Association for Computing Machinery, 33*(3):296–310, March 1990.

Nightingale, R. A. "A Cost–Benefit Study of a Manually-Produced Current Awareness Bulletin." *Aslib Proceedings, 25*(4):153–157, April 1973.

Nixon, Judith M. "Online Searching of Human Nutrition: An Evaluation of Databases." *Medical Reference Services Quarterly, 8*(3):27–35, Fall 1989.

O'Brien, Ann. "Relevance as an Aid to Evaluation in OPACs." *Journal of Information Science, 16*(4):265–271, 1990.

OCLC, Inc. *Assessing Information on the Internet: Toward Providing Library Services for Computer-Mediated Communication.* Proposal to the U.S. Department of Education. May 1991–January 1992.

————. *OCLC Annual Report: 1990–1991.* Dublin, Ohio, OCLC Online Computer Library Center, 1991.

O'Connor, John. "Some Independent Agreements and Resolved Disagreements About Answer-Providing Documents." *American Documentation, 20*(4):311–319, October 1969.

————. "Some Questions Concerning 'Information Need.'" *American Documentation, 19*(2):200–203, April 1968a.

————. Letter to the Editor. *American Documentation, 19*(4):416–417, October 1968b.

————. "Relevance Disagreements and Unclear Request Forms." *American Documentation, 18*(3):165–177, July 1967.

O'Leary, Mick. "Easynet Revisited: Pushing the Online Frontier." *Online, 12*(5):22–30, September 1988.

————. "DIALOG Business Connection: DIALOG for the End-User." *Online, 10*(5): 15–24, September 1986.

Oliver, Lawrence H., et al. *An Investigation of the Basic Processes Involved in the Manual Indexing of Scientific Documents.* Bethesda, Md., General Electric Co., Information Systems Operation, 1966. PB 169415

Paice, Chris D. "Constructing Literature Abstracts by Computer: Techniques and Prospects." *Information Processing and Management, 26*(1):171–186, 1990.

Pao, Miranda L. *Concepts of Information Retrieval.* Englewood, Colo., Libraries Unlimited, 1989.

Parker, Lorraine M. P., and Robert E. Johnson. "Does Order of Presentation Affect Users' Judgment of Documents?" *Journal of the American Society for Information Science, 41*(7):493–494, October 1990.

Parrott, James R. "Reference Expert Systems: Foundations in Reference Theory." In: *Artificial Intelligence and Expert Systems: Will They Change the Library? Proceedings of the 27th Annual Clinic on Library Applications of Data Processing.* Edited by F. W. Lancaster and Linda C. Smith. Urbana, Ill., University of Illinois, Graduate School of Library and Information Science, 1992, pp. 118–160.

Penhale, Sara J., and Nancy Taylor. "Integrating End-User Searching into a Bibliographic Instruction Program." *RQ, 26*(2):212–220, Winter 1986.

Penniman, W. David. "Shaping the Future for Libraries through Leadership and Research." In: *Libraries and the Future: Essays on the Library in the Twenty-first Century.* Edited by F. W. Lancaster. Binghampton, N.Y., Haworth Press, forthcoming 1993.

Pollitt, Steven. "CANSEARCH: An Expert System Approach to Document Retrieval." *Information Processing and Management, 23*(2):119–138, 1987.

Pontigo, Jaime, et al. "Expert Systems in Document Delivery: The Feasibility of Learning Capabilities." In: *Artificial Intelligence and Expert Systems: Will They Change the Library? Proceedings of the 27th Annual Clinic on Library Applications of Data Processing.* Edited by F. W. Lancaster and Linda C. Smith. Urbana, Ill., University of Illinois, Graduate School of Library and Information Science, 1992, pp. 254–266.

Potter, William Gray. "Expanding the Online Catalog." *Information Technology and Libraries, 8*(2):99–104, June 1989.

Powell, Ronald R. *Basic Research Methods for Librarians.* Norwood, N.J., Ablex, 1985.

Price, Derek J. de Solla. *Little Science, Big Science.* New York, Columbia University Press, 1963.

————. *Science Since Babylon.* New Haven, Conn., Yale University Press, 1961.

Quade, E. S. *Systems Analysis Techniques for Planning-Programming-Budgeting.* Santa Monica, Calif, The Rand Corporation, 1966. P-3322

Quarterman, John S. *The Matrix: Computer Networks and Conferencing Systems World-wide.* Bedford, Mass., Digital Press, 1990.

Rada, Roy; Hafedh Mill; Gary Letourneau; and Doug Johnston. "Creating and Evaluating Entry Terms." *Journal of Documentation,* 44(1):19–41, March 1988.

Raffel, Jeffrey S., and Robert Shishko. *Systematic Analysis of University Libraries.* Cambridge, Mass., MIT Press, 1969.

Raitt, David. "The Library of the Future." In: *Libraries and the Future: Essays on the Library in the Twenty-first Century.* Edited by F. W. Lancaster. Binghampton, N.Y., Haworth Press, forthcoming 1993.

Rath, G. J., et al. "Comparison of Four Types of Lexical Indicators of Content." *American Documentation,* 12(2):126–130, April 1961.

Rees, Alan M. "The Relevance of Relevance to the Testing and Evaluation of Document Retrieval Systems." *Aslib Proceedings,* 18(11):316–324, November 1966.

Rees, Alan M., and Tefko Saracevic. "The Measurability of Relevance." *Proceedings of the American Documentation Institute. Annual Meeting, Santa Monica, Calif, October 3–7, 1966.* Vol. 3. Woodland Hills, Calif, Adrianne Press, 1966, pp. 225–234.

Rees, Alan M., and Douglas G. Schultz. *A Field Experimental Approach to the Study of Relevance Assessments in Relation to Document Searching: Final Report.* 2 vols. Cleveland, Ohio, Case Western Reserve University, 1967.

Reich, Phyllis, and Erik J. Biever. "Indexing Consistency: The Input/Output Function of Thesauri." *College and Research Libraries,* 52(4):336–342, July 1991.

Resnick, A. "Relative Effectiveness of Document Titles and Abstracts for Determining Relevance of Documents." *Science,* 134(3484):1004–1006, October 6, 1961.

Robertson, S. E. "The Parametric Description of Retrieval Tests." *Journal of Documentation,* 25(2):93–107, June 1969.

Rogers, Michael. "First Electronic Medical Journal to Debut in 1992." *Library Journal,* 116(18):32, 34, November 1, 1991.

Roloff, Michael E. "Communication at the User-System Interface: a Review of Research." *Library Research,* 1(1):1–18, Spring 1979.

Rosenberg, Kenyon C. "Evaluation of an Industrial Library: A Simple-Minded Technique." *Special Libraries,* 60(10):635–638, December 1969.

Rosenberg, Victor. "The Application of Psychometric Techniques to Determine the Attitudes of Individuals Toward Information Seeking." Bethlehem, Pa., Lehigh University, Center for Information Sciences, 1966. Another version appears in *Information Storage and Retrieval,* 3(3):119–127, July 1967.

Rowlett, Russell J., Jr. "Keywords vs. Index Terms." *Journal of Chemical Information and Computer Sciences,* 17(3):192–193, August 1977.

Ruge, Gerda. "Experiments on Linguistically-Based Term Associations." *Information Processing and Management,* 28(3):317–332, 1992.

Ruiz, Den, and Daniel E. Meyer. "End-User Selection of Databases – Part IV: People/News/General Reference." *Database,* 13(5):65–67, October 1990.

Rush, James E.; R. Salvador; and A. Zamora. "Automatic Abstracting and Indexing. II. Production of Indicative Abstracts by Application of Contextual Inference and Syntactic Coherence Criteria." *Journal of the American Society for Information Science,* 22(4):260–274, July/August 1971.

Salton, Gerard. "The State of Retrieval System Evaluation." *Information Processing and Management,* 28(4):441–449, 1992.

————. *Automatic Text Processing: The Transformation, Analysis and Retrieval of Information by Computer.* Reading, Mass., Addison-Wesley, 1989.

————. "Syntactic Approaches to Automatic Book Indexing." In: *Proceedings of the 2nd Applied Natural Language Processing Conference, 9–12 February 1988, Austin, Texas.* Morristown, N.J., Association for Computational Linguistics, 1988, pp. 204–210.

————, ed. *The SMART Retrieval System: Experiments in Automatic Document Processing.* Englewood Cliffs, N.J., Prentice-Hall, 1971.

————. *Automatic Information Organization and Retrieval.* New York, McGraw-Hill, 1968.

Salton, Gerard, and Michael J. McGill. *Introduction to Modern Information Retrieval.* New York, McGraw Hill, 1983.

Salton, Gerard; C. Buckley; and E. A. Fox. "Automatic Query Formulations in Information Retrieval." *Journal of the American Society for Information Science, 34*(4):262–280, July 1983.

Sandison, A. "The Use of Older Literature and Its Obsolescence." *Journal of Documentation, 27*(3):184–199, September 1971.

Saracevic, Tefko. "Individual Differences in Organizing, Searching and Retrieving Information." In: *Proceedings of the American Society for Information Science, 54th Annual Meeting, Washington, D.C., October 27–31, 1991.* Vol. 28. Edited by José-Marie Griffiths. Medford, N.J., Learned Information, 1991, pp. 82–86.

————. "Relevance: A Review of and a Framework for the Thinking on the Notion in Information Science." *Journal of the American Society for Information Science, 26*(6):321–343, November/December 1975.

————. "On the Concept of Relevance in Information Science." Doctoral dissertation. Cleveland, Ohio, Case Western Reserve University, 1970a.

————. "Ten Years of Relevance Experimentation—A Summary and Synthesis of Conclusions." In: *Proceedings of the American Society for Information Science, 33rd Annual Meeting, Philadelphia, Pa., October 11–15, 1970.* Vol. 7. Edited by Jeanne B. North. Washington, D.C., American Society for Information Science, 1970b, pp. 33–36.

————. "Comparative Effects of Titles, Abstracts and Full Texts on Relevance Judgments." In: *Proceedings of the American Society for Information Science, 32nd Annual Meeting, San Francisco, Calif., October 1–4, 1969.* Vol. 6. Edited by Jeanne B. North. Westport, Conn., Greenwood Publishing, 1969, pp. 293–299.

Saracevic, Tefko, and Paul Kantor. "A Study of Information Seeking and Retrieving: II. Users, Questions, and Effectiveness." *Journal of the American Society for Information Science, 39*(3):177–196, May 1988a.

————. "A Study of Information Seeking and Retrieving: III. Searchers, Searches, and Overlap." *Journal of the American Society for Information Science, 39*(3):197–216, May 1988b.

Saracevic, Tefko, et al. "A Study of Information Seeking and Retrieving: I. Background and Methodology." *Journal of the American Society for Information Science, 39*(3):161–176, May 1988.

Schamber, Linda; Michael B. Eisenberg; and Michael S. Nilan. "A Re-Examination of Relevance: Toward a Dynamic, Situational Definition." *Information Processing and Management, 26*(6):755–776, 1990.

Schnall, Janet G., and Joan W. Wilson. "Evaluation of a Clinical Medical Librarianship Program at a University Health Sciences Library." *Bulletin of the Medical Library Association, 64*(3):278–283, July 1976.

Schrage, Michael. *Shared Minds: The New Technologies of Collaboration.* New York, Random House, 1990.

Schwarz, Helga. "Expert Systems and the Future of Cataloguing: a Possible Approach." *LIBER Bulletin, 26*:23–50, 1986.

Scura, Georgia, and Frank Davidoff. "Case-Related Use of the Medical Literature: Clinical Librarian Services for Improving Patient Care." *Journal of the American Medical Association, 245*(1):50–52, January 2, 1981.

Seiler, Lauren H., and Thomas T. Surprenant. "The Virtual Information Center: Scholars and Information in the 21st Century." In: *Libraries and the Future: Essays on the Library in the Twenty-first Century.* Edited by F. W. Lancaster. Binghampton, N.Y., Haworth Press, forthcoming 1993.

Self, Phyllis C.; Thomas W. Filardo; and F. W. Lancaster. "Acquired Immunodeficiency Syndrome (AIDS) and the Epidemic Growth of Its Literature." *Scientometrics, 17*(1/2):49–60, July 1989.

Sharma, V. S. "A Comparative Evaluation of Online Databases in Relation to Welfare and Corrective Services, and Community Development." *Online Review, 6*(4):297–313, August 1982.

Shaw, W. M., Jr. "Subject Indexing and Citation Indexing. Part I: Clustering Structure in the Cystic Fibrosis Document Collection." *Information Processing and Management, 26*(6):693–703, 1990a.

————. "Subject Indexing and Citation Indexing. Part II: An Evaluation and Comparison." *Information Processing and Management, 26*(6):705–718, 1990b.

Shirey, Donald L., and Marvin Kurfeerst. "Relevance Predictability: II. Data Reduction." In: *Electronic Handling of Information: Testing and Evaluation.* Edited by Allen Kent et al. Washington, D.C., Thompson Book Company, 1967, pp. 187–198.

Shurkin, Joel. *Engines of the Mind: A History of the Computer.* New York, W. W. Norton and Company, Inc., 1984.

Sievert, MaryEllen, and Mark J. Andrews. "Indexing Consistency in *Information Science Abstracts.*" *Journal of the American Society for Information Science, 42*(1):1–6, January 1991.

Sievert, MaryEllen, and Bert R. Boyce. "Hedge Trimming and the Resurrection of the Controlled Vocabulary in Online Searching." *Online Review, 7*(6):489–494, December 1983.

Smith, Linda C. "Artificial Intelligence in Information Retrieval." In: *Annual Review of Information Science and Technology.* Edited by Martha E. Williams. Vol. 22. Amsterdam, Neth., Elsevier, 1987, pp. 41–77.

————. "Knowledge-Based Systems, Artificial Intelligence and Human Factors." In: *Information Technology and Information Use: Towards a Unified View of Information and Information Technology, May 8–10, 1985, Copenhagen, Denmark.* Edited by P. Ingwersen, L. Kajberg, and A. M. Pejtersen. London, Eng., Taylor Graham, 1986, pp. 98–110.

Smith, Linda C., and Amy J. Warner. "A Taxonomy of Representations in Information Retrieval System Design." *Journal of Information Science, 8*(3):113–121, April 1984.

Smith, Sallye Wry. "Venn Diagramming for On-Line Searching." *Special Libraries*, 67(11):510–517, November 1976.

Snow, Bonnie. "Database Selection in the Life Sciences." *Database*, 8(3):15–44, August 1985.

Soergel, Dagobert. *Indexing Languages and Thesauri: Construction and Maintenance*. Los Angeles, Calif., Melville Publishing Co., 1974.

Solomin, V. M. "Efficiency Indexes for the Performance of Information Agencies." English translation appears in *Scientific and Technical Information Processing*, 2:16–23, 1974.

Somerville, Arleen N. "The Place of the Reference Interview in Computer Searching: the Academic Setting." *Online*, 1(4):14–23, October 1977.

Sommar, Helen G., and Don E. Dennis. "A New Method of Weighted Term Searching with a Highly Structured Thesaurus." In: *Proceedings of the American Society for Information Science, 32nd Annual Meeting, San Francisco, Calif., October 1–4, 1969*. Vol. 6. Edited by Jeanne B. North. Westport, Conn., Greenwood Publishing, 1969, pp. 193–198.

Sparck Jones, Karen, ed. *Information Retrieval Experiment*. London, Eng., Butterworth, 1981.

————. *Automatic Keyword Classification for Information Retrieval*. London, Eng., Butterworth, 1971.

————. "Experiments in Semantic Classification." *MT: Mechanical Translation*, 8(3/4):97–112, June/October 1965.

Stallings, Warren D; Sarah E. Hutchinson; and Stacey C. Sawyer. *Computers: The User Perspective*. St. Louis, Mo., Times Mirror/Mosby, 1988.

Starr, Susan S. "Databases in the Marine Sciences." *Online Review*, 6(2):109–126, April 1982.

Stiles, H. Edmund. "The Association Factor in Information Retrieval." *Journal of the Association for Computing Machinery*, 8(2):271–279, April 1961.

Sullivan, Michael V.; Christine L. Borgman; and Dorothy Wippern. "End-Users, Mediated Searches, and Front-End Assistance Programs on Dialog: A Comparision of Learning, Performance, and Satisfaction." *Journal of the American Society for Information Science*, 41(1):27–42, January 1990.

Svenonius, Elaine. "Unanswered Questions in the Design of Controlled Vocabularies." *Journal of the American Society for Information Science*, 37(5):331–340, September 1986.

Swanson, Don R. "Subjective Versus Objective Relevance in Bibliographic Retrieval Systems." *Library Quarterly*, 56(4):389–398, October 1986.

————. "Information Retrieval as a Trial-and-Error Process." *Library Quarterly*, 47(2):128–148, April 1977.

Swets, John A. "Information Retrieval Systems." *Science*, 141(3577):245–250, July 19, 1963.

Swift, D. F.; V. Winn; and D. Bramer. " 'Aboutness' as a Strategy for Retrieval in the Social Sciences." *Aslib Proceedings*, 30(5):182–187, May 1978.

Tait, J. I., and Karen Sparck Jones. *Automatic Search Term Variant Generation for Document Retrieval*. Cambridge, Eng., University of Cambridge, Computer Laboratory, 1983. British Library R&D Report 5793

Taylor, Robert S. *Question Negotiation and Information-Seeking in Libraries*. Bethlehem,

Pa., Lehigh University, Center for the Information Sciences, 1967. Also in *College and Research Libraries, 29*(3):178–194, May 1968.

Tenopir, Carol. "Four Options for End User Searching." *Library Journal, 111*(12):56–57, July 1986.

————. "Full Text Database Retrieval Performance." *Online Review, 9*(2):149–164, April 1985.

————. "Retrieval Performance in a Full Text Journal Article Database." Doctoral dissertation. Urbana, Ill., University of Illinois, Graduate School of Library and Information Science, 1984.

————. "Evaluation of Database Coverage: A Comparison of Two Methodologies." *Online Review, 6*(5):423–441, October 1982.

Tenopir, Carol, and Gerald W. Lundeen. "Software Choices for In-House Databases." *Database, 11*(3):34–42, June 1988.

Tenopir, Carol, and Jung Soon Ro. *Full Text Databases.* New York, Greenwood Press, 1990.

Tesler, Lawrence G. "Networked Computing in the 1990s." *Scientific American, 265*(3): 86–93, September 1991.

Thompson, N. J. "DIALOGLINK and TRADEMARKSCAN—FEDERAL Pioneers in Online Images." *Online, 13*(3):15–26, May 1989.

Thorpe, Peter. "An Evaluation of *Index Medicus* in Rheumatology: Coverage, Currency, and Efficiency." *Methods of Information in Medicine, 13*(1):44–47, January 1974.

Trautman, Rodes, and Sara von Flittner. "An Expert System for Microcomputers to Aid Selection of Online Databases." *Reference Librarian, 23*:207–238, August 1989.

Trueswell, Richard L. "Some Behavioral Patterns of Library Users: The 80/20 Rule." *Wilson Library Bulletin, 43*(5):458–461, January 1969.

Ullmann, Stephen. *The Principles of Semantics.* 2nd ed. Oxford, Eng., Blackwell, 1963.

Unesco. *Unesco Guidelines for the Establishment and Development of Monolingual Thesauri.* 2nd ed. (Prepared by Derek Austin and Peter Dale). Paris, 1981.

van Brakel, P. A. "EasyNet: Intelligent Gateway to Online Searching." *South African Journal of Library and Information Science, 56*(3):191–197, September 1988a.

————. "Evaluating an Intelligent Gateway: a Methodology." *South African Journal of Library and Information Science, 56*(4):277–290, December 1988b.

Van Rijsbergen, C. J. *Information Retrieval.* 2nd ed. London, Eng., Butterworth, 1979.

Vickery, Alina. "The Experience of Building Expert Search Systems." In: *Online Information 88: 12th International Online Information Meeting, London, 6–8 December 1988. Proceedings.* Vol. 1. Oxford, Eng., Learned Information, 1988, pp. 301–313.

Vickery, Alina, and H. M. Brooks. "PLEXUS —The Expert System for Referral." *Information Processing and Management, 23*(2):99–117, 1987.

Vickery, Brian C. "Intelligent Interfaces to Online Databases." In: *Artificial Intelligence and Expert Systems: Will They Change the Library? Proceedings of the 27th Annual Clinic on Library Applications of Data Processing.* Edited by F. W. Lancaster and Linda C. Smith. Urbana, Ill., University of Illinois, Graduate School of Library and Information Science, 1992, pp. 239–253.

Visschedijk, Ankie, and Forbes Gibb. "Unconventional Text Retrieval Systems." *Online & CD-ROM Review, 17*(1):11–23, 1993.

Vizine-Goetz, Diane, and Karen Markey Drabenstott. "Computer and Manual Analysis of Subject Terms Entered by Online Catalog Users." In: *Proceedings of the American Society for Information Science, 54th Annual Meeting, Washington, D.C., October 27–31, 1991.* Vol. 28. Edited by José-Marie Griffiths. Medford, N.J., Learned Information, 1991, pp. 156–161.

Walker, Geraldene. "The Search Performance of End-Users." In: *Proceedings of the Ninth National Online Meeting, New York, N.Y., May 10–12, 1988.* Medford, N.J., Learned Information, 1988, pp. 403–410.

Walker, J., and S. D. Atkinson. "Online Searching in the Humanities: Implications for End-Users and Intermediaries." In: *Online Information 1988, 12th International Online Information Meeting, London, 6–8 December 1988. Proceedings.* Vol. 1. Oxford, Eng., Learned Information, 1988, pp. 401–412.

Walker, Stephen. "Improving Subject Access Painlessly: Recent Work on the OKAPI Online Catalogue Projects." *Program,* 22(1):21–31, January 1988.

————. "OKAPI: Evaluating and Enhancing an Experimental Online Catalog." *Library Trends,* 35(4):631–645, Spring 1987.

Wang, Yih-Chen; James Vandendorpe; and Martha Evens. "Relational Thesauri in Information Retrieval." *Journal of the American Society for Information Science,* 36(1):15–27, January 1985.

Wanger, Judith. "Multiple Database Use: the Challenge of the Database Selection Process." *Online,* 1(4):35–41, October 1977.

Wanger, Judith; Dennis McDonald; and Mary C. Berger. *Evaluation of the On-Line Search Process.* Bethesda, Md., National Library of Medicine, 1980.

Warner, Amy J. "Natural Language Processing: Current Status for Libraries." In: *Artificial Intelligence and Expert Systems: Will They Change the Library? Proceedings of the 27th Annual Clinic on Library Applications of Data Processing.* Edited by F. W. Lancaster and Linda C. Smith. Urbana, Ill., University of Illinois, Graduate School of Library and Information Science, 1992, pp. 194–214.

————. "A Linguistic Approach to Automatic Hierarchical Organization of Phrases." In: *Information in the Year 2000: From Research to Application, Proceedings of the 53rd Annual Meeting of the American Society for Information Science, 4–8 November, 1990, Toronto, Canada.* Edited by Diane Henderson. Medford, N.J., Learned Information, 1990, pp. 220–227.

Waters, Samuel T. "Expert Systems at the National Agricultural Library: Past, Present, and Future." In: *Artificial Intelligence and Expert Systems: Will They Change the Library? Proceedings of the 27th Annual Clinic on Library Applications of Data Processing.* Edited by F. W. Lancaster and Linda C. Smith. Urbana, Ill., University of Illinois, Graduate School of Library and Information Science, 1992, pp. 161–177.

————. "Answerman, the Expert Information Specialist: An Expert System for Retrieval of Information from Library Reference Books." *Information Technology and Libraries,* 5(3):204–212, September 1986.

Weber, Robert. "The Clouded Future of Electronic Publishing." *Publishers Weekly,* 237(26):76–80, June 29, 1990.

Weibel, Stuart. "Automated Cataloging: Implications for Libraries and Patrons." In: *Artificial Intelligence and Expert Systems: Will They Change the Library? Proceedings of the 27th Annual Clinic on Library Applications of Data Processing.* Edited by F. W. Lancaster and Linda C. Smith. Urbana, Ill., University of Illinois, Graduate School of Library and Information Science, 1992, pp. 67–80.

Welsh, John J. "Evaluation of CD-ROM Use in a Government Research Library." *Laserdisk Professional,* 2(6):55–61, November 1989.

Whitcomb, Laurie. "OCLC's EPIC System Offers a New Way to Search the OCLC Database." *Online, 14*(1):45–50, January 1990.

White, Marilyn Domas. "Evaluation of the Reference Interview." *RQ, 25*(1):76–84, Fall 1985.

————. "The Reference Encounter Model." *Drexel Library Quarterly, 19*(2):38–55, Spring 1983.

————. "The Dimensions of the Reference Interview." *RQ, 20*(4):373–381, Summer 1981.

Wildemuth, Barbara M., et al. "A Detailed Analysis of End-User Search Behaviors." In: *Proceedings of the American Society for Information Science, 54th Annual Meeting, Washington, D.C., October 27–31, 1991.* Vol. 28. Edited by José-Marie Griffiths. Medford, N.J., Learned Information, 1991, pp. 302–312.

Williams, Martha E. "The State of Databases Today: 1992." In: *Computer-Readable Databases: A Directory and Data Sourcebook.* 8th ed. Edited by Kathleen Young Marcaccio, Kevin Hillstrom, and Gwen E. Turecki. Detroit, Mich., Gale Research, 1992, pp. xi–xxi.

————. "Highlights of the Online Database Industry and the Quality of Information and Data." In: *Proceedings of the Eleventh National Online Meeting, New York, N.Y., May 1–3, 1990.* Edited by Martha E. Williams. Medford, N.J., Learned Information, 1990, pp. 1–4.

————. "Highlights of the Online Database Field: New Technologies for Online." In: *Proceedings of the Ninth National Online Meeting, New York, N.Y., May 10–12, 1988.* Edited by Martha E. Williams. Medford, N.J., Learned Information, 1988, pp. 1–4.

————. "Transparent Information Systems Through Gateways, Front Ends, Intermediaries and Interfaces." *Journal of the American Society for Information Science, 37*(4):204–214, July 1986.

————. "Electronic Databases." *Science, 228*(4698):445–456, April 26, 1985.

————. "Database and Online Statistics for 1979." *Bulletin of the American Society for Information Science, 7*(2):27–29, December 1980a.

————. "Future Directions for Machine-Readable Data Bases and Their Use." In: *Proceedings of the 1979 Clinic on Library Applications of Data Processing.* Edited by F. W. Lancaster. Urbana, Ill., University of Illinois, Graduate School of Library Science, 1980b, pp. 82–93.

————. *An Integrated Man/Machine Interface (Transparent System) to Facilitate Network Resource Utilization—a Feasibility Study.* Urbana, Ill., University of Illinois, Coordinated Science Laboratory, 1977.

Wilson, Patrick. "The End of Specificity." *Library Resources and Technical Services, 23*(2):116–122, Spring 1979.

————. "Situational Relevance." *Information Storage and Retrieval, 9*(8):457–471, August 1973.

Wilson, Sandra R.; Norma Starr-Schneidkraut; and Michael D. Cooper. *Use of the Critical Incident Technique to Evaluate the Impact of MEDLINE. Final Report.* Palo Alto, Calif., American Institute for Research, 1989. PB 90-142522

Yonker, Valeria A., et al. "Coverage and Overlaps in Bibliographic Databases Relevant to

Forensic Medicine: A Comparative Analysis of MEDLINE." *Bulletin of the Medical Library Association,* 78(1):49–56, January 1990.

Young, Philip H. "Visions of Academic Libraries in a Brave, New Future." In: *Libraries and the Future: Essays on the Library in the Twenty-first Century.* Edited by F. W. Lancaster. Binghampton, N.Y., Haworth Press, forthcoming 1993.

Zipf, George Kingsley. *The Psycho-Biology of Language.* Boston, Mass., Houghton-Mifflin, 1935.

Zunde, Pranas, and Margaret E. Dexter. "Indexing Consistency and Quality." *American Documentation,* 20(3):259–267, July 1969.

Index

Aboutness, 81, 84
Abstracting automatically, 274–277
Abstracts, 87–88
Academic American Encyclopedia, 35
Accessibility
  of information services, 159–160
  of materials, 4–5
Accuracy
  of data, 173
  of indexing, 208, 220, 224–225
Adams, J., 27, 319
Aids to database selection, 112–115
Alberico, R., 303, 307
Albright, J. B., 123, 307
Al-Hawamdeh, S., 153, 307
Allen, B. L., 72–73, 307
Allen, T. J., 159, 307
Alligood, E. C., 211, 307
Allocation
  of resources, 196
  of space, 211
Ambiguous and spurious relationships,
  97–98
America: History and Life, 30–31
American Association for the
  Advancement of Science, 290
American Library Directory, 35
American Men and Women of Science,
  30–31
AmericanProfile, 35

American Psychological Association, 38
American Society for Metals, 21
Anderson, C. R., 109–110, 307
Anderson, J. D., 87, 307
Andrews, M. J., 239, 325
Anomalous state of knowledge, 14, 72
Answerman, 304
Armed Services Technical Information
  Agency *see* Defense Technical
  Information Center
Artificial intelligence, 113–115, 127,
  251–252, 301–306
  in cataloging, 302–303
  in database selection, 113–115
  in question-answering, 303–304
  in searching, 251–252
Asbury, H. O., 199–200, 315
Ashmole, R. F., 208, 307
Assignment indexing, 79–84
Assimilation of information, 3, 11–12
Atherton, P., 223, 319
Atkinson, S. D., 110, 121, 308, 328
Austin, D., 96, 308
Automatic aids to database selection,
  112–115
Automatic methods, 243–281, 303
  applied to online catalogs, 277–278
  evaluation of, 278–281
  in abstracting, 274–277
  in indexing, 263–269, 303

in query formulation, 269–274
in thesaurus construction, 259–263
linguistic approaches, 248–252
statistical approaches, 252–257

Bannon, C., 292, 308
Bar, J., 127, 308
Barber, J., 208, 308
Barron, B., 289, 308
Batch processing, 22–23
Bates, M., 14, 140, 155, 240, 242, 308
Baxendale, P. B., 302, 308
Belkin, N. J., 14, 72, 279, 308, 319
Bellardo, T., 155, 242, 308
Belzer, J., 59–60, 308
Benefit analysis, 161–162, 196–202
Benenfeld, A. R., 60, 319
Berger, M. C., 33, 154, 308, 328
Berk, E., 292, 308
Bernick, M., 279, 309
Bernier, C. L., 96, 308
Berry, C., 54, 312
Berwind, A. M., 207, 310
Best match retrieval, 153
Bibliographic Retrieval Services see BRS
    Information Technologies
Bibliographic utilities, 25–27, 41–42
Bibliographic warrant, 93, 215
Bibliometric phenomena, 119–121, 195,
    207, 209–211
Biever, E. J., 223, 323
Bitnet, 287
Black, W. J., 277, 308
Blackshaw, L., 155, 309
Blair, D. C., 88, 181, 183–184, 280, 309
Boolean logic, 129–133
Borgman, C. L., 30, 204–205, 232,
    241–242, 309, 326
Borko, H., 279, 302, 305–306, 309
Bourne, C. P., 121, 195, 206, 211, 309
Boyce, B. R., 106, 218, 222, 309, 325
Bradford, S. C., 119–121, 195, 207,
    209–211, 309
Bradford's law, 119–121, 195, 207,
    209–211
Bramer, D., 84, 326
British Library, 42, 299

British Standards Institution, 98, 309
Brittain, J. M., 119, 309
Britten, W. A., 211, 309
Brooks, H. M., 273, 309, 327
Brown, S. A., 294, 309
BRS/Afterdark, 40
BRS Information Technologies, 35, 40,
    111
Bryant, E. C., 171, 228, 310, 316
BSO Referral Index, 110, 310
Buchanan, L. E., 207, 310
Buckley, C., 271, 272, 324
Burgin, R., 222, 310
Bush, V., 290–291, 310
Busha, C. H., 173, 175, 310
Byler, A. M., 112, 310

Calkins, M. L., 217, 310
Campbell, D. T., 174–175, 310
CANSEARCH, 273
Carlin, D., 207, 310
Carrow, D., 214, 223, 310
Case Western Reserve University, 21,
    60–61, 240
Cataloging, 18–20
    expert systems in, 302–303
    rules for, 25–26
    subject, defined, 18–20, 25–26,
        302–303
Cawkell, A. E., 287, 310
CD-ROM, 16–17, 35, 41–42, 194–195,
    288, 295
    versus print, 194–195
Chamis, A. Y., 115, 310
Characteristics of searchers, 154–156
CHESHIRE, 278
CITE, 278
Classification
    as form of controlled vocabulary,
        18–20, 103–104
    of databases, 30–35
Cleverdon, C. W., 105, 153, 169,
    216–218, 310
Cliques, 261
Clumps, 261
Clustering methods, 261–263

Cochrane, P. A., 104, 107, 138–139, 310, 319
Collette, A. D., 199, 310
Command-driven versus menu-driven systems, 232
Common command language, 40
Comparative recall, 181–182
Components of information retrieval systems, 15–16
Comprehensive search, 92
CompuServe Information Service, 38
Conceptual analysis, 7–9, 18–20
Consistency
  in indexing, 239–240
  in relevance judgements, 240–241
  in search strategy, 240–241
Controlled vocabularies *see* Index languages
Co-occurrence statistics, 261
Cooper, M., 200, 310
Cooper, M. D., 201–202, 329
Cooper, W. S., 58, 239, 311
Coordination level
  in an index language, 217–218
  in searching, 153
Copyright issues, 295–296
Corbett, P. K., 30, 309
Cost
  of information services, 189–190
  per relevant citation, 167, 190–191
Cost–benefit analysis, 161–162, 196–202
Cost criteria, 159–161
Cost-effectiveness, 161–162, 189–196, 209–212, 218–220, 225–229, 233–238
  applied to databases, 209–212
  of index languages, 218–220
  of indexing, 225–229
  of search procedures, 233–234
Courrier, Y., 265–268, 271–272, 311
Coverage, 116–121, 170, 184–185, 205–207, 209–212
Cranfield Project, 169, 216
Croft, W. B., 261, 271, 311, 318
Crum, N. J., 73, 311
Cuadra Associates, 27, 110, 311
Cuadra, C. A., 60, 311

Current awareness
  needs, 6
  services, 10
  see also Selective dissemination of information
Current Index to Journals in Education, 82–83, 86
Cutter, C. A., 104, 311

Dana, J. C., 303, 311
Das Gupta, P., 271, 311
Database classification, 30–35
Database evaluation, 115–125, 205–212
  cost-effectiveness aspects, 209–212
Database indexes, 111–112
Database industry, 21–42
Database producers, 16
Database quality, 115–125
Database selection, 109–115
Database-use chain, 27–28
Database vendors, 35–41
Data-Star, 38
Davidoff, F., 201, 325
Davies, R., 305, 311
Davison, P. S., 206, 311
Defense Documentation Center *see* Defense Technical Information Center
Defense Technical Information Center, 21
Delegated search, 65–77
Demands on information services, 5–7, 65–77
  versus information needs, 65–69
Dennis, D. E., 153, 326
Depth of indexing, 83
Derivation of performance figures, 177–185
Derivative indexing, 84
Descriptors, 83
Devlin, J., 292, 308
Dexter, M. E., 239, 330
DIALINDEX, 111–112, 115, 126
Dialog Information Services, 38, 40–41, 85, 113–115, 230–231, 311
Diaz, L., 292, 311
Dillon, M., 261, 265, 271, 311
Diminishing returns, 195, 225–229

Directories of databases, 110
Discrimination value, 253, 259
Document delivery, 10
Doszkocs, T. E., 250, 278, 312
Dougherty, R. M., 249, 312
Douglas, E. M. B., 91, 319
Dow Jones News/Retrieval, 38
Dowlin, K. E., 297–298, 312
Doyle, L. B., 261, 263, 312
Drabenstott, K. M., 233, 327–328
Dykstra, M., 103–104, 312
Dym, E. D., 60, 312

Ease of use, 159–160
EASYNET, 40, 113–115, 127
Edmundson, H. P., 274, 279, 312
Educational Resources Information
    Center (ERIC), 35, 42, 82–86
Effectiveness evaluation, 159–189
Effort, 164, 166–168
Eighty/twenty rule, 209–210
Eisenberg, M. B., 54, 62–63, 240, 312,
    324
Elchesen, D. R., 193, 312
Electronic publishing, 289–296
El-Shooky, E., 115, 127, 312
EMBASE, 37–39
End user searching, 232, 242
End user systems, 40
Entry vocabulary, 106, 215–216,
    219–220
Enumerative versus synthetic
    vocabularies, 94–95
EPIC, 41
Erbach, G., 193, 321
Ercegovac, Z., 302, 305–306, 309
ERIC, 35, 42, 82–86
Errors in indexing, 208, 220, 224–225
Estabrook, L. S., 199, 200, 312
Evaluation
    criteria, 43–63, 159–170
    methods, 171–189
    of automatic processing methods,
        278–281
    of databases, 115–125
    see also Cost–benefit analysis;
    Cost-effectiveness

Evans, D. A., 265–268, 279, 312
Evens, M., 104, 263, 328
Excerpta Medica, 38
Exclusively specific entry, 223–224
Exhaustivity
    of indexing, 81–83, 208, 221–223,
        225–227
    of search strategies, 136–140, 230–231
Experimental design, 173–176
Expert systems, 113–115, 127, 251–252,
    269, 272–274, 302–304
    in cataloging, 302–303
    in database searching, 251–252,
        272–274
    in database selection, 113–115, 127
    in indexing, 269, 303
    in question-answering, 303–304
Explode capability, 138
Exponential growth, 285–286
Extracting automatically, 274–277
Extraction indexing, 84

Factors affecting performance of
    information systems, 45–47,
    203–242
Factors affecting success of a search,
    156–158
Fagan, J. L., 265, 312
Fairthorne, R. A., 168, 312
Fallout, 169
False coordinations, 97–98
Feeney, M., 299–300, 320
Fenichel, C. H., 154, 241–242, 312–313
Fenly, C., 302, 304–305, 313
Ferguson, D. K., 278, 320
Fidel, R., 88, 107, 155–156, 250, 313
Field, B. J., 265, 313
Filardo, T. W., 119, 325
First Search, 42
Fischhoff, B., 155, 309
Fitzgerald, E. L. C., 76, 234, 313
Flowerdew, A. D. J., 196, 313
Forms to record user requests, 77
Foskett, D. J., 57–58, 313
Fox, E. A., 262–263, 271–272, 292, 313,
    324
Fractional search, 153

Free text *see* Natural language
Freedman, B., 106, 318
Front-end software, 40–41, 271–274,
    303–304
Full-text databases, 32–33, 85–87
Functions of information retrieval
    systems, 7–12
Fussler, H. H., 211, 313
Future
    of information systems, 283–306
    of libraries, 293–306

Gardin, J. C., 92, 313
Gateway services, 27–28, 40, 113–115
Gauch, S., 273, 313
Geller, V., 232, 313
Generality, 169–170
Gerstberger, P. G., 159, 307
Gibb, F., 281, 327
Goffman, W., 58, 168–169, 314
Goldhor, H., 175, 314
GOPHER, 42, 289
Graham, D. L., 76–77, 314
Grammatical analysis, 248–249, 256
Gray, A. S., 265, 271, 311
Greenberg, B., 201, 314
Grishman, R., 259, 314
Grolier's Electronic Encyclopedia, 35
Growth
    of databases, 27
    of information resources, 284–287

Hansen, K. A., 156, 314
Harmon, D., 281, 314
Harris, K., 193, 321
Harter, S. P., 30, 136, 154, 173, 175,
    310, 314
Harvard Business Review, 32–33
Havener, W. M., 109, 314
Hawkins, D. T., 156, 314
Heaps, D. M., 153, 314
Hedges, 106, 218
Heller, M., 287, 314
Hirschman, L., 259, 314
Hitch, C. J., 191, 314

Holm, B. E., 217, 314
Holmes, E. H., 60, 311
Homographs, 91–92
Horton, F. W., 306, 314
Howard, H., 242, 314
Hsieh-Yee, I., 242, 314
Hu, C., 112, 113–115, 127, 303, 315
Huang, S. T., 193–194, 315
Hughes, C., 294, 312
Hulme, E. W., 215, 315
Human factors, 238–242
Humphrey, S. M., 269, 303, 315
Hutchins, W. J., 81, 84, 315
Hutchinson, S. E., 283, 326
Hypertext, 291–292

I. P. Sharp Associates, 38
Ide, E., 41, 315
Identifiers, 83–84
Incorrect term relationships, 97–98
Index languages, 83–84, 89–107,
    212–220
    construction of, 93–104
    cost-effectiveness aspects, 218–220
    functions of, 92–93
    specificity, 212–217
    see also Natural language
Indexable matter, 81
Indexing, 7–9, 18–20, 79–88, 208,
    220–229, 239–240, 263–269
    accuracy, 220, 224–225
    automatic methods, 263–269
    consistency, 239–240
    cost-effectiveness aspects, 225–229
    exhaustivity, 81–83, 208, 221–223,
        225–227
    personnel, 228–229
    policies, 208, 220, 225–226
    specificity, 83–84, 208, 223–224
Indicativity of records, 60
INFOMASTER, 113–114, 127
InfoPro Technologies, 35, 111, 113
Information centers, roles of, 2–4
Information needs, 5–7, 48–63, 65–77,
    160
    contrasted with demands, 65–69

Information retrieval
  definition, 11–12
  functions, 7–12
  problems, 12–14
Information services, role of, 1–5
Information transfer cycle, 1–4
Information UK 2000, 299–300
Ingwersen, P., 73, 315
Input versus output costs, 235–238
Institute for Scientific Information, 208
Interface role of information services,
  4–5
Interfaces to retrieval systems, 40–41,
  272–274, 303–304
International Organization for
  Standardization, 98, 104, 315
Internet, 42, 287
Interpretation of evaluation results,
  185–189
Interviewing of users, 73–77
Inverted files, 23–24
Iterative searching, 255, 271

Janes, J. W., 60, 125, 177–179, 315
Jeng, L.-H., 302, 315
Jensen, R. J., 199–200, 315
Johnson, R. E., 54–55, 322
Johnston, D., 106, 323
Jones, K. P., 98, 315–316

Kantor, P., 154, 182, 240–241, 324
Katter, R. V., 60, 311
Katz, W., 73, 316
Katzer, J., 107, 217, 316
Keen, E. M., 169, 216–218, 310, 316
Kemp, D. A., 57–58, 316
Kent, A., 60, 168–169, 316
Kilgour, F. G., 299, 316
King, D. N., 201, 316
King, D. W., 171, 201, 228, 310, 316
King, G. B., 73, 316
King, R. G., 199–200, 315
Klingbiel, P. H., 268, 269, 316
Knapp, S. D., 73, 316
Knee, M., 110, 308
Knowledge Index, 40
Known-item need, 6

Kochen, M., 66–67, 316
Konings, C. A. G., 208, 316
Kramer, J., 199–200, 316
Kremer, J. M., 298–299, 317
Krol, E., 42, 289, 317
Kugel, P., 60, 319
Kurfeerst, M., 60, 325
Kurzweil, R., 301, 317

Lack of standardization
  in databases, 38–41
Lancaster, F. W., 35, 53, 56, 59–60,
  67, 70–71, 74–77, 93–94, 96–98,
  104, 113, 119, 125, 127, 140,
  155, 179, 182, 188–189, 193, 196,
  215, 217–218, 222, 232–234, 242,
  289–290, 297–298, 317, 320, 325
Landau, H. B., 27, 318
Language in retrieval *see* Index
  languages
Larson, R. R., 278, 318
Lawrence, G. S., 278, 320
Least common factor in searching, 139,
  148–149
Ledwith, R., 280, 318
Lee, J.-L., 127, 317
Lefever, M., 106, 318
Leonard, L. E., 239, 318
Lesk, M. E., 62, 232, 234, 263, 313, 318
Less developed countries, 298–299
Letourneau, G., 106, 323
Lewis, D. D., 261, 271, 311, 318
Lewis, D. W., 301, 318
Libraries as information retrieval
  systems, 16–20
Library Literature database, 24
Library of Congress, 42
Library of Congress Subject Headings,
  100, 102–104
Lilley, O. L., 155, 318
Line, M. B., 66, 211, 298, 318
Linear files, 23–24
Linguistic approaches to information
  retrieval, 248–252
Linguistic groupings in automatic
  thesaurus construction, 262–263
Links, 97–98, 217–219, 265

Literary warrant, 93, 215
Littleford, A., 292, 318
Logan, E. L., 156, 318
Logical relevance, 58
Lottor, M., 287, 318
Lucky, R. W., 287, 318
Luhn, H. P., 252–253, 259, 274, 276, 302, 304, 319
Lundeen, G. W., 288, 327
Lynch, M. J., 73, 319

Machine-aided indexing, 268–269
Machine Readable Cataloging (MARC), 25–26, 40–42
Mack, G., 41, 321
Macroevaluation, 171
Magson, M. S., 197, 319
Major and minor descriptors, 83
Mandel, C. A., 195, 319
Mandersloot, W. G. B., 91, 319
MARC, 25–26, 40–42
Marcaccio, K. Y., 27, 319
Marchetti, P. G., 279, 319
Marchionini, G., 292, 313
Marcus, R. S., 60, 113, 319
Markey, K., 73, 107, 138–139, 223, 239, 319
Maron, M. E., 84, 280, 309, 320
Marron, H., 190, 320
Martyn, J., 116, 121, 125, 185, 200, 299–300, 320
Marx, G. T., 284, 320
Mason, D., 197, 320
Mathis, B. A., 276–277, 320
Matthews, D. A. R., 206, 311
Matthews, J. R., 278, 320
McCarthy, M. V., 113, 320
McCue, J. H., 155–156, 320
McDonald, D., 154, 328
McDonald, L., 261, 311
McGill, M. J., 254, 324
McHale, T. J., 193–194, 315
McKean, R., 191, 314
McKinin, E. J., 217, 320
McLain, J. P., 222, 309
Mead Data Central, 38
Meadows, D. H., 285, 320

Measures of retrieval performance, 43–47
Medical Literature Analysis and Retrieval System (MEDLARS), 21, 288
evaluation of, 53, 56, 70–71, 74, 76–77, 179–180, 182, 188–189, 234
Medical Subject Headings, 100–101, 103–104
MedIndEx system, 269, 303
MEDLINE, 29, 35–39, 154, 201–202
Memex, 290–291
Menu-driven versus command-driven systems, 232
Metzler, D. P., 305, 320
Meyer, D. E., 114, 320, 323
Micco, M., 303, 307
Microevaluation, 171
Migration from print on paper, 289–293
Mill, H., 106, 323
Miller, N. E., 269, 315
Mills, J., 169, 216–218, 222, 310, 317
Milstead, J., 95, 320
MIRLYN online catalog, 81–83
Mitchell, M., 294, 321
Modes of interaction, 74–77
Moghdam, D., 30, 309
Molholt, P., 297, 321
Mondschein, L. G., 200–201, 321
Morphological analysis, 248–249, 256
Morris, A., 127, 321
Morrison, M., 40, 321
Mueller, M. W., 200, 321
Multiplicative effect of indexing error, 227–228
Multipurpose information systems, 21–22
Mylonas, E., 292, 321

National Aeronautics and Space Administration, 21
National Information Standards Organization, 40
National Library of Medicine, 21, 29, 38, 269, 303
see also Medical Literature Analysis and Retrieval System; MEDLINE

National Research and Education
    Network, 295
Natural language, 32–33, 85–87,
    104–107, 148–151, 214, 216–218,
    223, 230–232
    compared with controlled vocabularies,
        148, 214, 216–218, 223, 230–232
Naval Ordnance Laboratory, 21
Near synonyms, 91
Needs *see* Information needs
Neelameghan, A., 298, 321
Nelson, T. H., 291, 321
Networked environment, 287
Newham, G., 127, 321
Newill, V. A., 168–169, 314
Newton, C., 223, 319
Nicholas, D., 193, 321
Nicholls, P., 35, 288, 321
Niehoff, R., 41, 321
Nielsen, J., 291
Nightingale, R. A., 198–199, 321
Nilan, M. S., 62–63, 240, 324
Ninety percent library, 195
Nixon, J. M., 207, 321
Novelty ratio, 170, 184
Nugent, J., 214, 223, 310
Number-oriented databases, 33

O'Brien, A., 62, 321
Obsolescence, 211
OCLC, Inc., 25–27, 38, 41–42, 288,
    290, 296, 321
O'Connor, J., 59, 321–322
Offline systems, 22–23
OKAPI, 278
O'Leary, M., 113, 115, 322
Oliver, L. H., 239, 322
Omissions in indexing, 224–225
OncoDisk, 35
Online access versus printed tools,
    193–194
Online catalogs, 18, 41–42, 232–233,
    277–278
    automatic aids, 277–278
    contrasted with commercial online
        services, 41–42

Online Computer Library Center, Inc.,
    25–27, 38, 41–42, 288, 290, 296,
    321
Online industry, 21–42
Online journals, 290
Online searching, 16–18, 129–158
Online systems, 23–42
ORBIT Search Service, 35, 111
Output versus input costs, 235–238

Packet switching networks, 23
Paice, C. D., 274, 277, 322
Pao, M. L., 79–80, 322
Paradigms of computing, 286–289
Parker, L. M. P., 54–55, 322
Parrott, J. R., 273, 304, 322
Patent and Trademark Office, 35
Penhale, S. J., 232, 322
Penniman, W. D., 297, 322
Performance measures, 43–47
Pertinence and relevance, 47–63
Peterson, R., 211, 307
Phrase searching, 218
Picture-oriented databases, 34–35
PLEXUS, 273
Pollitt, S., 251, 273, 322
Pontigo, J., 304–305, 322
Postcontrolled vocabulary, 105–106, 218
Postcoordinate versus precoordinate
    systems, 93–98
Potter, W. G., 41–42, 322
Powell, R. R., 175, 322
PRECIS, 96
Precision, 43–47, 162–168, 177–189
    measurement of, 177–181
Precoordinate versus postcoordinate
    systems, 93–98
Predicasts, 33
Predictability of relevance, 124–125
Price, D. J. de Solla, 285, 322
Price, J. A., 199, 310
Print versus CD-ROM, 194–195
Print versus online, 193–194
Probability that information exists, 69
Problem solving needs, 6–7
Problems of information retrieval, 12–14,
    43–47

Proliferation of information resources, 27, 284–287
PRO-SEARCH, 40
PsycINFO database, 36–37
PTS U.S. Time Series, 33

Quade, E. S., 192, 322
Quality
  criteria, 160–170
  of databases, 115–125
  of indexing, 220, 224–225, 239–240
  of user requests, 72–77
Quarterman, J. S., 287, 323
Quasi-synonyms, 91
Query formulation *see* Search procedures
Questel, 38
Question-answering, 12, 303–304
Quorum function search, 153

Rada, R., 106, 323
Raffel, J. S., 196, 323
Raitt, D., 298, 323
Ranked output, 169
Ranking of databases, 111–115, 126
Rasmussen, L. E., 217, 314
Rath, G. J., 60, 323
Ravenhall, M., 112, 310
Ready-reference questions, 109–110
Recall, 43–47, 121–124, 162–168, 181–189
  estimation of, 181–184
Rees, A. M., 47–48, 60–61, 240, 323
Reich, P., 223, 323
Reintjes, F. J., 113, 319
Relevance and pertinence, 47–63
Relevance assessments, 51–52, 177–181, 240
Relevance feedback, 255, 271
Requests for information, 48–63, 69–77
Resnick, A., 60, 323
Resolving power, 253, 259
Response time, 159–161, 168
Retrievability *see* Recall
Retrospective searching, 6–7
Revision of indexing, 228
Rich, E., 301
Ro, J. S., 218, 327

Roberts, S. A., 119, 309
Robertson, S. E., 169, 323
Rogers, M., 290, 323
Role indicators, 98, 217–219, 265
Roloff, M. E., 73, 323
Rootwords, 253–255
Rosenberg, K. C., 197–198, 323
Rosenberg, V., 159, 323
Rous, B., 292, 313
Rowlett, R. J., 214, 323
Ruge, G., 263, 323
Ruiz, D., 114, 320, 323
Rush, J. E., 274, 276–277, 320, 323
Russo-Martin, E., 211, 307

Sager, N., 259, 314
Salton, G., 41, 62, 169, 234, 253–257, 259, 261, 265–268, 271–272, 280, 315, 318, 323–324
Salvador, R., 274, 323
Sandison, A., 211, 318, 324
Saracevic, T., 47–48, 60–61, 154, 182, 238–241, 323–324
Saunders, L. M., 294, 321
Sawyer, S. C., 283, 326
Scatter
  of literature, 119–121, 209–211
  of search results, 185–186
  over databases, 125–127
  over index terms, 122–124
Schamber, L., 62–63, 240, 324
Schnall, J. G., 201, 325
Schrage, M. 287, 325
Schultz, D. G., 60–61, 240, 323
Schultz, L., 106, 318
Schwarz, H., 302, 325
Screening of output, 46–47, 153–154, 233
Scura, G., 201, 325
SDI *see* Selective dissemination of information
Search logic, 129–133
Search procedures, 9–10, 16–18, 129–158, 229–234, 240, 250–252, 269–274
  automatic methods, 269–274
  cost-effectiveness aspects, 233–234

heuristics, 250–252
in natural language, 148–151
Search request forms, 77, 177–178
Searcher characteristics, 154–156, 241–242
Seiler, L. H., 299, 325
Selecting databases, 109–115
Selective dissemination of information, 10, 200–201, 304
Self, P. C., 119, 325
Semantic ambiguities, 96–98
Semantic road maps, 261–263
Sharma, V. S., 207, 325
Shaw, W. M., 222, 325
Sherizen, S., 284, 320
Shirey, D. L., 60, 325
Shishko, R., 196, 323
Shurkin, J., 283, 325
Sievert, M. E., 106, 218, 239, 325
Simon, J. L., 211, 313
Simulations in studies of retrieval, 122–124
Simultaneous remote search, 76–77
Situational relevance, 58–59
Slater, M., 116, 121, 185, 320
SMART, 234, 254–257, 278, 280
Smith, D. E., 208, 307
Smith, J. B., 273, 313
Smith, L. C., 41, 258–259, 274, 325
Smith, S. W., 144, 326
Snow, B., 115, 326
Soergel, D., 93, 96, 215, 326
Solomin, V. M., 200, 326
Somerville, A. N., 73, 326
Sommar, H. G., 153, 326
Sorenson, P., 153, 314
Space allocation, 211
Sparck Jones, K., 204, 261, 263, 265, 271–272, 280, 326
Specificity
in indexing, 83–84, 208, 223–224
in searching, 136–140
in vocabularies, 212–217
of requests, 70–72, 75
Spicer, N., 91, 319
Stallings, W. D., 283, 326
Standardization in databases, 38–41

Stanley, J. C., 174–175, 310
Star clusters, 261
Starr, S. S., 208, 326
Starr-Schneidkraut, N., 201–202, 329
Statistical groupings of words, 259–261
Statistical methods in information processing, 252–257
Statistical phrases, 254–255
Stemming in automatic processing, 253–255
Stern, B. T., 208, 307
Stiles, H. E., 261, 263, 326
STN International, 38
Strings, 261
Structure of vocabulary, 218
Subheadings, 97, 217
Subject access problems, 43–47
Subject analysis, 7–9, 79–88
Subject cataloging see Cataloging
Subject headings, 100–104
Subject indexing see Indexing
Subject needs, 6–7
Sullivan, M. V., 232, 326
Summarization, 81, 84
Surprenant, T. T., 299, 325
Surrogates, effect on relevance judgements, 59–61
Svenonius, E., 223, 326
Swanson, D. R., 59, 326
Swets, J. A., 168–169, 326
Swift, D. F., 84, 326
Switching languages, 41
Synonym control, 90–91
Syntactic analysis, 248–249, 256
Synthetic versus enumerative vocabularies, 94–95
SYNTOL, 265–268, 272

Tait, J. I., 272, 326
Taylor, N., 232, 322
Taylor, R. S., 72–73, 326
Telebase Systems Inc., 113
Telenet, 23
Tenopir, C., 40, 107, 207, 217–218, 288, 327
Terragno, P. J., 228, 310
Tesler, L. G., 286–287, 327

Text indexing, 85–87
Thesauri, 99–100, 259–263
  automatic processing, 259–263
Thompson, N. J., 35, 327
Thorpe, P., 119, 327
Time criteria, 159–161
Time required for indexing, 226–227
Timeliness of databases, 125, 207–208
TRADEMARKSCAN—FEDERAL,
  34–35
Trade-offs in information systems, 195,
  235–238
Translation step of indexing, 7–9, 19–20
Transparent interfaces, 40–41
Trautman, R., 113, 127, 327
Tree structures, 101
Trueswell, R. L., 209, 327
Truncation, 147, 150–151
Tseng, G., 127, 321
Turtle, H. R., 271, 311
Tymnet, 23

Ullmann, S., 91, 327
Unesco, 98, 103–104, 327
Uniterm system, 217
Universal workstation environment, 294
Up-posting, 223–224
User effort, 164, 166–168
User–intermediary interface, 65–77
User-system interaction, 65–77, 233–234
User warrant, 93, 215
Utility of search results, 58

Value of information, 69
van Brakel, P., 113, 115, 327
Van Den Elshout, R., 35, 288, 321
Van Rijsbergen, C. J., 261, 327
Vandendorpe, J., 104, 263, 328
Venn diagrams, 130–133
Vickers, P., 299–300, 320
Vickery, A., 251, 273, 327
Vickery, B. C., 273, 303, 327
Virtual library, 294–295, 299
Visschedijk, A., 281, 327
Vizine-Goetz, D., 233, 327–328
Vocabulary control *see* Index languages
von Flittner, S., 113, 127, 327

VU/TEXT, 38

Walker, G., 242, 328
Walker, J., 121, 328
Walker, S., 278, 328
Wallace, E. M., 60, 311
Wang, Y.-C., 104, 263, 328
Wanger, J., 33, 115, 154, 308, 328
Warner, A. J., 250, 258–259, 263, 325,
  328
Waters, S. T., 304, 328
Weber, R., 295, 328
Weibel, S., 302, 305–306, 328
Weighted indexing, 83, 147
Weighted-term searching, 151–153
Welsh, J. J., 194–195, 329
Western Reserve University, 21, 60–61,
  240
Western Union Telegraph Co., 113
Whitcomb, L., 41, 329
White, M. D., 73, 329
Whitehead, C. M. E., 196, 313
Wide Area Information Server (WAIS),
  42, 289
Wildemuth, B. M., 242, 329
Williams, M. E., 27–30, 38, 113, 285,
  290, 319, 329
WILSEARCH, 40
Wilson, J. W., 201, 325
Wilson, P., 58–59, 224, 329
Wilson, S. R., 201–202, 329
Winn, V., 84, 326
Wippern, D., 232, 326
Word fragment searching, 147, 150–151
  see also Stemming
Word frequency criteria, 252–253, 274
Word roots, 253–255
World Wide Web (WWW), 42, 289
Written requests, 74–77

Yonker, V. A., 206–207, 329–330
Young, C. E., 276, 277, 320
Young, P. H., 297–299, 330

Zamora, A., 274, 323
Zipf, G. K., 195, 252, 330
Zunde, P., 239, 330